PRAISE FOR
READING DISABILITIES: BEATING THE ODDS

I love the book. Simply written with incredible depth and breadth. Parents will feel like they are getting support from a trusted friend. Professionals would do well to read it—to remind us of what we were meant to do!

— Gloria Lodato Wilson, Ph.D.
Associate Professor of Special Education
Hofstra University

This book should be in the hands of every parent who has a child with reading or learning disabilities. It is by far the best book I have read to help parents help their children. Well written and easy to understand. Bravo!

— Teresa Allissa Citro
Executive Director
Learning Disabilities Worldwide

Finally, a practical, well-organized book for parents of youngsters with reading and learning disabilities that provides a comprehensive process for developing and getting appropriate programs. Especially important are the sections on assessing risk, understanding evaluations, understanding the principles of reading instruction, and resolving conflicts with schools. Together, they arm parents with the comprehensive, practical, in-depth, realistic tools they need to help their children. This is truly the best book I have read on the subject. It is well-written and sorely overdue.

—Arthur Shapiro, Ed.D.
Professor Emeritus, Special Education & Counseling
Kean University

With this book, Margolis and Brannigan have given us insight into the complexities of reading disabilities. Their personal connections and writing style foster understanding and make information accessible. Moreover, their expertise, experience, and sheer honesty have created an aerial view of the educational maze. This readable, practical resource is a must have for parents and educators who advocate for children.

— Karen Russo, Ed.D.
Assistant Professor of Child Study
St. Joseph College, New York

Impressive. Written for concerned parents, this important book provides accessible insight into the complexities of reading disabilities. Using easily understood language, Howard Margolis and Gary Brannigan provide a wealth of information to help you craft a unique, individualized support program for your child at home. Furthermore, the information in this book will help parents advocate effectively with the schools to develop successful instructional plans. Highly recommended reading for parents and professionals.

— *Bruce Saddler, Ph.D.*
Associate Professor of Educational Psychology and Methodology
State University of New York at Albany

This is a book for parents to use, not merely read. Keep it handy. It is, by any definition, a valuable resource for all parents of children with reading and learning disabilities. It provides concrete tools for parents to assess their child's reading capabilities, offers them techniques they'll need throughout their child's development, and educates them about their child's educational rights. Margolis and Brannigan have given parents an important resource.

— *Ila Keiner, M.Ed., MSW/LCSW, JD*
Director of Outpatient Services Cape Counseling Services
Cape May Court House, NJ

Beating the Odds is an outstanding resource for parents of children with reading disabilities. As a parent and an educator, I highly recommend it to all parents of struggling readers. It's informative, balanced, and gives parents the information needed to identify their child's reading difficulties and get needed services. Howard Margolis and Gary Brannigan offer indispensable strategies for helping children beat the odds. It's a must read for all parents of struggling readers.

— *Sueanne Agger*
Parent of a struggling reader and Director of the Country School
Cape May, NJ

Every parent and every teacher who has felt the frustration of obtaining needed services and education for children with learning disabilities should read *Reading Disabilities: Beating the Odds*, not as a novel or a textbook, but as a recipe for successfully helping our kids. It's a portable support group.

— *Theresa C. Cavanaugh, LDT-C*
President, Learning Disabilities Association of New Jersey

Reading Disabilities: Beating the Odds is a wonderful, practical tool for parents of struggling readers who need to advocate for their children. Its critical questions, checklists, and guided actions will help parents and teachers focus their efforts on improving instruction. Howard Margolis and Gary Brannigan offer practical, insightful ways of problem solving and using education and civil rights laws to successfully get struggling readers the evaluations and services they need. I urge you to read this book.

— *Claire Drapkin, M.Ed.*
The Youth Group Advocates
Manalapan, NJ

Reading Disabilities: Beating the Odds should be required reading for all Child Study Teams.

Beating the Odds is hard to put down. As a guide, it will help parents of struggling readers assess and work with their children and negotiate the daunting bureaucracies of schools. Well-written, encyclopedic in its depth, clear in its recommendations, hard-nosed and compassionate in tone, fair to parents and teachers, this outstanding work should be read by everyone trying to help struggling readers.

Finally: A resource to help parents of struggling readers successfully navigate the complex world of education and advocate for their children. *Beating the Odds* provides a complete, well-organized explanation of reading disabilities, the school system's responsibilities, and the educational laws that bind the two. Howard Margolis and Gary Brannigan have combined their extensive knowledge and experience to produce a comprehensive work that parents can read in its entirety or use to answer specific questions. It's an invaluable guide for answering the question: How can I help my child beat the odds?

Reading Disabilities: Beating the Odds is a fabulous book. It's an invaluable resource for parents of struggling readers and for teachers and other school staff who strive to help these students. More than a clearly written, comprehensive guide to understanding reading disabilities, it offers practical, step-by-step advice for getting struggling readers the services they need, for resolving conflicts, and for monitoring the effectiveness of programs. It offers parents case studies that clarify important points, clear definitions of critical, but difficult to understand technical terms, checklists to guide their efforts, and quotes from experts and laws that parents can use to ensure their children get what they need. In short, *Beating the Odds* is a terrific, *must have* resource for parents, teachers, and school staff who care about struggling readers.

Finally, the book that parents and others who take care of children have been waiting for and deserve is here. Howard Margolis and Gary G. Brannigan, two highly renowned educators with a wealth of experience, offer research-based information for parents on recognizing the early signs of reading and learning problems as well as practical suggestions for negotiating the educational bureaucracy and understanding the language of educators. Written in a reader friendly style, *Reading Disabilities: Beating the Odds* is a plan of action to maximize children's academic success. It's a must read.

— Patrick P. McCabe, Ph.D.
Coordinator, Ph.D. in Literacy Program
St. John's University

A great book for parents of struggling readers. Clear and comprehensive. Parents (and professionals) will find it brimming with practical, easy to implement suggestions. I will be recommending it to many of my clients. In fact, I will keep copies in my waiting room.

— John Manni, Ed.D.
Clinical Psychologist
Former Coordinator of School Psychology, Lehigh University

A wonderful book!!! Brilliant, comprehensive, and easy to read. It attacks important questions from all sides. It prepares parents to meet their children's learning problems head on. As a parent and child advocate, I recommend that parents of struggling learners keep studying and using *Beating the Odds*. It will be invaluable throughout their children's school years. It can prevent failure and anguish.

— Ronee Groff
Former President of the Learning Disabilities Association of New Jersey
Former President of the Atlantic County Special Services School Board of New Jersey

READING DISABILITIES:
BEATING THE ODDS

HOWARD MARGOLIS & GARY G. BRANNIGAN

2008

Reading2008 & Beyond
Voorhees, New Jersey 08043

Reading2008 & Beyond
1067 Pendleton Court
Voorhees, New Jersey 08043-1809

Cover and book design by Lori Pedrick

Printed in the United States of America

ISBN: 978-0-615-27900-8

Library of Congress Control Number: 2009923025

Reading Disabilities: Beating the Odds aims to educate and inform. It does not offer
legal advice or advice about a particular child or situation. Moreover, law, science, and
best practices will change, requiring some of the information in this book to change in
future editions. Thus, for legal advice, readers should seek the counsel of an attorney.
For advice about a particular child or situation, readers should seek the advice of competent professionals. Neither the authors nor publisher accepts responsibility for decisions made on the basis of this book.

DEDICATIONS

To six people who made the world better for children:
Robert Huffine, Esther Levine, Howard Norris, Florence Wasserman,
Corinne J. Weithorn, and Joseph E. Zins.
When days get tough, their memory inspires me to work harder, to never give up.

— Howard Margolis

To my children, Marc and Michael, and my grandchildren, Liam and Sawyer,
who keep me focused on educational issues.

— Gary G. Brannigan

CONTENTS

PREFACE

In an open letter to his daughters in *Parade* magazine, two days before his inauguration, President Obama wrote: "I want all our children to go to schools worthy of their potential — schools that challenge them, inspire them, and instill in them a sense of wonder about the world around them."

This too is our wish! But when children with reading disabilities struggle daily to survive in our educational system, it's difficult for them to experience a "sense of wonder."

In *Reading Disabilities: Beating the Odds*, we share our decades of experience in helping parents become informed, active participants in the educational process that determines the course of their children's lives. In fact, we cannot overestimate the importance of the parents' role in education. It's the underlying principle that guides our work.

ACKNOWLEDGEMENTS

Many people, knowingly and unknowingly, contributed to this book. They are too numerous to name here. Instead, we wish to express gratitude to all those who have touched our lives and helped us to "beat the odds."

HM
GGB

READING DISABILITIES:
BEATING THE ODDS

CHAPTER 1
INTRODUCTION

Millions of American children struggle with reading. Many read so poorly that by ninth grade they've been held back one or more times. Politicians have called this an "educational recession." We call it a tragedy.

Parents are worried. They don't understand reading disabilities. They don't recognize its signs until it's too late. And, by third grade, it's often too late. More than 70% of third graders with reading problems continue to struggle with reading in high school.[1] In despair or anger, many give up and drop out of school.[2]

Most reading authorities assert that prolonged reading difficulties cause children great emotional and social anguish. As Jules Abrams observed:

> It is almost inevitable that a child who is experiencing severe difficulty in reading will develop intense feelings of frustration. As the reading failure continues, many symptoms of social and emotional maladjustment will appear. Children, increasingly bewildered by their inability to meet the expectations of their parents, their teachers, and their peers, develop a kind of hypersensitivity to the possibility of failure. This fear of further wounding to their pride exacerbates the problem simply because children cannot take the chance of risking any further humiliation. Instead, all too often, the child acts out aggressively, withdraws, becomes depressed, or chooses any one of a number of other maladaptive solutions. These problems certainly do not terminate with the onset of adolescence. It has become increasingly clear that many of the serious problems that are found in both adolescents and adults in our society today have had their roots in early academic failure.[3]

This does not have to happen to your child!

REASONS FOR HOPE
For many reasons, you should have hope. Here are several.

Reading Disabilities Can Often be Identified at an Early Age. Moreover, in many cases, early intervention can prevent, minimize, or eliminate reading disabilities.[4] If you suspect that your child has or is at risk for reading disabilities, get her evaluated as early as possible. The earlier her reading disabilities are identified and addressed, the better chance she has of succeeding in reading and avoiding emotional scars. Chapter 2 will help you determine if your child is at risk for reading disabilities. Chapters 3 and 4 will help you determine if your child is showing definite signs of reading disabilities. Chapters 4 and 5 will help you to get a quality reading evaluation. They will also help you to understand the nature of your child's reading disabilities.

Research Has Identified Many Ingredients of Successful Reading Instruction. By understanding these ingredients, you're more likely to get your child the right program of instruction and supports. This can prevent, minimize, or eliminate reading disabilities.

If you suspect that your child has or is at risk for reading disabilities, seek out educators who have studied the research on effective instruction and supports. They know that effective instruction provides relevant, precisely focused, intensive, and consistent coursework, based on each child's unique needs. They also know that struggling readers need daily instruction that emphasizes moderate challenge, explicit strategy instruction, frequent modeling, individual and small-group instruction, high rates of correct student responses, ample practice learning new skills, interesting activities, student generated questions, and lots of opportunities to listen to and read interesting materials.

You Can Influence Your Child's Success. Parents can do many simple things at home and in the community to help their children develop the background, abilities, and motivation needed to succeed in reading. Activities include reading books to children, listening intently when they speak, playing rhyming and sound games, visiting and talking about different places, labeling new experiences with relevant vocabulary, and helping them create elaborate sentences. Parents can also strengthen their children's motivation to read, despite children's difficulties. In chapter 6 we suggest simple but effective activities for you to help your child develop the background, abilities, and motivation needed to successfully learn to read.

Federal Laws Can Provide Extensive Opportunity and Support. Parents can often use the *Individuals with Disabilities Education Improvement Act of 2004* (IDEA-2004)[5] and *Section 504 of the Rehabilitation Act of 1973* (Section 504)[6] to get children services needed to prevent, minimize, or eliminate reading disabilities. Similarly, the *No Child Left Behind Act of 2001* (NCLB)[7] can help. Although far less personalized and far more limited than IDEA-2004 and Section 504, NCLB can often provide parents with the leverage needed to get additional reading services.

If your child qualifies for services, and you understand the essence of problem solving, conflict resolution, and Federal special education laws, you can often get whatever educational services your child needs, at no cost to you, even if your child has yet to reach kindergarten age. Chapters 7 through 13 discuss how to work effectively with school personnel, problem solve, resolve conflicts, and use special education and related laws to get your child a quality reading program.

You Can Develop an Insightful Advocacy Plan for Your Child. As you progress through *Beating the Odds*, you will quickly realize that parents *alone* have little chance of remediating serious reading disabilities. Once your child enters school, her success in reading may depend—almost entirely—on the school's resources and the skill and willingness of school personnel to provide quality programs and make logical adjustments to classwork and homework. This means that you must collaborate and advocate effectively.

Chapter 13 will help you develop an advocacy plan that puts everything together. By studying the first twelve chapters, which focus on the intricacies of reading disabilities, the complexities of schools, and the critical laws, you have a good chance of using the information in chapter 13 to develop a plan that can prevent, minimize, or eliminate reading disabilities.

READING DISABILITIES

Before studying *Beating the Odds*, you need to understand that professionals disagree about the definition of "reading disabilities." The term lacks scientific rigor. As Deborah Speece and Lesley Shekitka found:

> Children with reading disabilities vary in their response to treatment, their area of difficulty, and possible co-occurring disabilities .... [There is] uncertainty among experts on what criteria should operationalize a definition of reading disabilities.[8]

The issues of definition and identification are important for researchers and clinicians. For parents whose children struggle to read, however, it's more important to have a functional, practical definition to which teachers and other school personnel can relate. Thus, in *Beating the Odds*, we will use a broad, global definition of a child with reading disabilities that is inadequate for research purposes, but adequate for you to help your child:

> A child with reading disabilities is any child who struggles more than the average child to learn to read. Usually, such a child cannot, with typical instruction, successfully read grade-level materials or complete grade-level reading assignments; if she can, she often reads in a slow, laborious manner or has difficulty understanding the materials. The terms reading disability and struggling reader do not suggest any particular cause for the child's struggle with reading.

Although parents and teachers should find our definition useful, a more precise, more technical definition is required for special education classification. Practically speaking, this definition is developing through a Federally supported instructional and diagnostic process called Response To Intervention (RTI), which we discuss in chapter 9.

Personally, we don't like the term *reading disabilities*; we prefer *reading problems* or *reading difficulties*. The word disabilities implies a permanent inability within the child, an inability that can perhaps be compensated for but not cured. Initially, however, many reading difficulties have temporary, external causes, like poor instruction—a cause that has nothing to do with permanent inabilities within the child. So why do we use the term reading disabilities? It's part of the language, it's a major term in the professional literature, it's what people respond to, it conveys the seriousness and pervasiveness of the problem, it conveys the need for intensive, knowledgeable, skilled instruction, and it often has legal implications.

As you encounter the term reading disabilities in this book, be careful; don't fall into the trap of assuming it means a permanent, unalterable, or incomprehensible inability. Remember—it's only a label. With the right instruction and the right supports, many children labeled as having reading disabilities can make meaningful strides in reading. Many can become proficient readers.

READING AND USING THIS BOOK

Reading Disabilities: Beating the Odds aims to help you understand the complex nature of reading disabilities and maximize your child's odds of becoming a proficient reader. To achieve these aims, we discuss many important topics and issues. Some, however, may be irrelevant for your child. Each child is unique and, therefore, has different needs. One child may need intensive instruction in phonemic awareness. Another may need intensive instruction only in reading comprehension. Giving this child intensive instruction in phonemic awareness diverts instruction from her primary need—reading comprehension—wasting her time and squandering her chances of success.

Therefore, in first reading this book, we suggest that you skim the chapters to determine what's most important for your child. Then, study—underline, highlight, take notes, think about, talk to others about—sections and chapters relevant to her immediate needs.

Beating the Odds endeavors to accommodate individual needs. As such, we highlight important points, occasionally repeat them in different chapters, and discuss them in detail. Because you may want additional information, we provide extensive endnotes. Because you may need to understand and use Federal education laws and case law, we often quote relevant portions for you to reflect upon and, if necessary, share with school personnel. For similar reasons, we provide valuable quotations from distinguished scholars.

Any book explaining a complex and often contentious subject like reading disabilities has two major limitations. One is content. Serious authors who have devoted decades to a subject can always cover more topics and elaborate on more points. But this can overwhelm readers. To keep *Beating the Odds* manageable for you, and to give you options about what you want to learn more about, we developed a website—www.reading2008.com—with even more resources to help you help your child *beat the odds*. We encourage you to visit it, read and study the information relevant to your child's needs, and share this information with parents and teachers.[9]

A second limitation is expertise. No expert is all-knowing; none is infallible. You may disagree with some of our conclusions. That's okay. You might be right. But make sure to base your disagreement on good science, not ideology, not the colorful advertisements and grandiose claims of publishers or the zealous beliefs of parents, school personnel, or professors who love a particular program that lacks a critical ingredient: adequate research support.

Throughout the book, we name and discuss many struggling readers. They're composites. What's important is not their fictitious names, but their stories and the points they illustrate.

KEEP IN MIND

Although we discuss education laws, we're not attorneys. We *do not* offer legal advice. Instead, we offer the views of an educator and a psychologist who have each worked with education laws for decades. If we're not attorneys, why have we worked with and interpreted special education and related laws? Because they strongly influence schools' policies and practices and define the rights of children. They often define our roles. And Howard had to interpret and apply the laws as a State Hearing Officer who ruled on special education issues.[10]

For many years, Howard taught reading and special education to children from some of the poorest and wealthiest districts in New York and New Jersey. In addition to becoming a professor of both reading disabilities and special education, coordinating graduate programs in these areas, and editing the *Journal of Educational and Psychological Consultation* and the *Reading & Writing Quarterly: Overcoming Learning Difficulties*, he earned numerous certifications requiring him to understand Federal and State education laws and related policies and practices. In New Jersey, for example, his certifications include Reading Specialist, School Psychologist, Teacher of the Handicapped, and Learning Disabilities Teacher-Consultant. He's helped many school districts and families deal with both reading and special education issues.

Gary has practiced school psychology and clinical psychology for more than 35 years. Thus, he had to master the intricacies of special education and related laws, as well as policies and practices designed to implement them. In addition, as a professor of psychology Gary has published a great deal of research that directly affects the lives of children with reading and learning disabilities. He has published twelve books on psychology and education and was recently honored with the State University of New York Chancellor's Award for Excellence in Scholarship.

Both of us have children and grandchildren and spouses. Nothing is more important to us. Clearly, this influences our opinions about children's needs and the roles and responsibilities of parents, schools, and society.

Please keep our backgrounds in mind as you read this book. They help to explain our values and the basis for our views.

ENDNOTES

---

[1] G. Reid Lyon, former Chief of the Child Development and Behavior Branch at the National Institute of Child Health and Human Development, reported that "Longitudinal studies show that, of the youngsters who are identified in the third grade, approximately 74% remain reading disabled through the ninth grade. This appears to be true even when special education has been provided. It should be made clear, however, that interventions applied *after* a child has failed in reading for two or three years may not be effective for several reasons, including the student's declining motivation and impaired self-concept" (Lyon, G. R., 1996. Learning disabilities. *Special Education for Students with Disabilities, 6* (1), 54-74, p. 66, italics added). Thus it's critical to intervene as early as possible, before the child begins to think of herself as a hopeless failure.

[2] In 1996, Benita Blachman summarized the chronic, devastating nature of the problem: "The tragic consequences of early reading failure are well documented. From research supported by

NICHD [the National Institute of Child Health and Human Development] ... we know that 74% of the students who are unsuccessful readers in third grade are still unsuccessful readers in ninth grade. These early literacy problems lead not only to low literacy rates among adults but also to a host of devastating problems including high dropout rates in schools and unemployment" (Blachman, B. A., 1996. Preventing early reading failure. In S. C. Cramer & W. Ellis (Eds.), *Learning Disabilities: Lifelong Issues* (pp. 65-70). Baltimore, MD: Paul H. Brookes, p. 65). Today, with work requiring greater literacy abilities, and with struggling readers' scores on high stakes tests frequently preventing promotion and graduation, their situation has gotten far more difficult and stressful.

3   Abrams, J. C., 1991. Introduction to the theme, Reading disabilities: The affective component. *Journal of Reading, Writing and Learning Disabilities International, 7* (3), pp. iii-iv, p. iii.

4   For an excellent discussion, you might want to read Torgesen, J., 2004. Preventing early reading failure—and its devastating downward spiral: The evidence for early intervention. *American Educator*; retrieved 1/3/08, from http://www.aft.org/pubs-reports/american_educator/issues/ fall04/reading.htm. As a leading researcher on the topic and a Distinguished Professor of Psychology and Education at Florida State University, Torgesen's expertise on the topic is outstanding.

5   The Individuals with Disabilities Education Improvement Act of 2004, Public Law 108-446.

6   Section 504 of the Rehabilitation Act of 1973, Public Law 93-112.

7   The No Child Left Behind Act of 2001, Public Law 107–110.

8   Speece, D. L., & Shekitka, L., 2002. How should reading disabilities be operationalized? A survey of experts. *Learning Disabilities Research and Practice, 17* (2), 118-123, pp. 118, 122.

9   Local and county libraries are also good sources of information on reading and learning disabilities. Their electronic databases are vaults of valuable, downloadable information. By helping you design your database search, their librarians can often save you hours of work.

10   To be consistent with the Federal regulations for the Individuals with Disabilities Education Improvement Act of 2004, we will capitalize the words State and Federal.

CHAPTER 2
RISK FACTORS

If your child is about to enter kindergarten, is in kindergarten, or is just about to enter first grade, and has not participated in a formal reading program, you should informally compare him to the factors that predict reading difficulties. This chapter describes these factors and offers critical questions that focus on your child's risk.

If you answer "yes" to any of the critical questions below, consider your child at risk for reading disabilities. At risk does *not* mean that he will definitely have reading difficulties. It means, however, that a State certified specialist should evaluate him to assess the degree of risk and to recommend interventions.[1] It may also mean that he requires a different class, school, or set of services.

RISK FACTORS: YOUR CHILD

In the section below, we occasionally ask you to compare your child to other children his age. As you probably know, this is far more difficult than it sounds. For example, which children do you compare him to? And how do you make sure that you're "objective" or "impartial," as it's your child, the child you love? And if you're like most of us, you tend to see him in the best light, whether or not it represents his true abilities.

We suggest that, if possible, you compare him to children that most parents and teachers consider "average achieving." This will give you a rough, but by no means infallible yardstick. We also suggest that in trying to be objective, you say to yourself, "I need to focus on his behavior, the behavior I see. What did I see that suggests he has mastered this, compared to average-achieving children his age? What did I see that suggests he did not? What would a teacher or a specialist likely say?"

Also, keep this in mind: It's better to err by saying there might be a problem than by saying there's no problem. If you say there might be a problem, a specialist can check it out. If your fears are confirmed—there's a problem—you can intervene now. But if you err by saying there's no problem—when there is—early intervention is unlikely. This is unfortunate as the earlier the intervention, the higher the odds of success. You can probably guess what's next: The later the intervention, the lower the odds.

Expressive (Oral) Language Difficulties. *Critical Question – Compared to children his age, does your child have more difficulty expressing himself?*

Observe and listen to children your child's age. Then observe and listen to your child while he's playing and talking. Ask yourself: Does he have unusual difficulty finding the right words to name and describe objects or events, speaking in grammatically correct sentences, sticking to a topic, or pronouncing words clearly? Do people often ask him to explain what he means or tell him to "say it slowly and clearly"?

Expressive language difficulties require the immediate intervention of a speech and language specialist or a reading specialist (often referred to as a literacy specialist).[2] Such specialists can develop a joint in-school and in-home program to improve your child's expressive abilities, including his vocabulary. They can often teach you simple language games and strategies that children enjoy.

Receptive Language Difficulties. *Critical Question – Compared to children his age, does your child have difficulty understanding what people say or read to him?*

Observe how well children your child's age understand what they hear, especially when adults speak or read to them. Then observe your child in similar circumstances. Ask yourself: Does he understand the gist of what people say to him? Does he understand what the words mean? Can he follow simple directions (e.g., "Put the cup on the table")? Does he show interest in books read aloud to him? Can he accurately retell some of what happened in a story just read to him? Can he retell parts of a favorite story? Can he repeat, word-for-word, a sentence of five or six syllables (e.g., "The red ball is big")?

Like expressive language difficulties, receptive language difficulties require the immediate intervention of a speech and language specialist or a reading specialist. Such specialists can work with you to develop a program to improve your child's ability to understand what he hears.

Letter Recognition Difficulties. *Critical Questions – Does your child have more difficulty recognizing letters than most children his age? Is he apathetic about recognizing letters?*

If either seems true, and if other children your child's age are starting to recognize letters, or want to recognize them, you need to find out why he's having difficulty or is apathetic. This is especially true if you've tried to interest him in recognizing letters, tried to teach him their names, and encouraged him to watch Sesame Street-like television shows that stress letter recognition.

If your child is age five or so, and does not recognize letters or know their names, he may learn to recognize and name them with structured, explicit, professional instruction. If such instruction proves successful—he learns to *quickly* recognize and name all or most of the 26 letters—celebrate. But remain vigilant. Simply learning to recognize and name letters does not automatically improve his chance of becoming a skilled, motivated reader. It's possible that the underlying factors that caused his difficulty or apathy will cause further reading difficulties. Unfortunately, the underlying reasons may remain a mystery.

If he's received such instruction, and he still has above-average difficulty recognizing and naming letters, he should be evaluated by a psychologist or reading specialist to find out why he's having difficulty and what can be done to improve his learning. The reason is simple: Reading becomes a struggle for many children who have difficulty quickly recognizing and naming letters. But again, think beyond letter recognition and letter naming. Note that we recommended a learning evaluation. Why? Because difficulties recognizing and naming letters often signal more serious learning difficulties.

Phonological Awareness and Phonemic Awareness Difficulties. *Critical Question – Compared to children his age, does your child have difficulty attending to, isolating, and manipulating sounds?*

Compared to difficulties with expressive language, receptive language, and letter recognition and identification, difficulties attending to, isolating, and manipulating sounds—called phonological awareness and phonemic awareness—are almost invisible unless you know what you're looking for. Moreover, both are counterintuitive and, in many ways, are the most abstract and technical of the risk factors.

Despite their abstract nature, you need to understand both phonological awareness and phonemic awareness. The reason is simple: Difficulties isolating and manipulating sounds that by themselves have no meaning can cause severe reading disabilities. Because both are so important and so complex, this section is longer than most. But please be patient—your understanding of both can dramatically influence your child's chances of becoming a successful reader.

Your child's *general* understanding that words consist of large and small sounds that can be isolated and manipulated is called phonological awareness. Large units might be syllables, like the two in basket: /bas/ /ket/.[3] Small units are the sounds of individual letters, like the three in cat, /c/ /a/ /t/, or letter combinations that many people would consider a single unit of sound, like the digraph /ch/ in chin or the diphthong /oi/ in oil.[4] Your child's *specific* understanding that words consist of these small, single units of sound, called phonemes, is called phonemic awareness. According to the International Reading Association's Literacy Dictionary, a phoneme is "a minimal sound unit of speech that, when contrasted with another phoneme, affects the meaning of words ... as /b/ in *book* contrasts with /t/ in *took*."[5]

Many children who find it easy to attend to, isolate, and manipulate large sounds, like syllables, have difficulty doing so with the small sounds, the phonemes. Consequently, most of these children will struggle with reading.[6]

To make these abstractions clearer, here are two examples:

- Phonological awareness: "Ryan, tell me a word that rhymes with *fat, cat*, and *mat*?" Rhyming requires Ryan to search his memory for /at/, the larger unit of sound.
- Phonemic awareness: "Ryan, say the three different sounds you hear in the word bat." This requires Ryan to isolate the phonemes, the smallest sounds in the word that affect meaning.

To get a rough understanding of your child's phonological awareness abilities, listen to him play games with sounds.[7] Ask yourself: Does he have difficulty with many of these kindergarten and early first grade activities?

- Hearing the number of words in a short sentence:
  "Each time you hear me say a word, clap your hands once."
- Identifying rhyming words: "If these two words rhyme, clap your hands: *fall ... tall.*
- Producing rhyming words: "Tell me a word that ends like *fat, bat, mat*."
- Identifying a similar sound: "Tell me which word begins like *song: dog ... sun ... house*."
- Isolating and pronouncing the first sound in simple words:
  "Make the first sound you hear in the word *dog*."

- Blending sounds in short, two phoneme words: "What word am I saying?
  [Pause a second between sounds] /b/ /oy/.
- Isolating and making the different sounds in simple words:
  "Say the three sounds you hear in the word *bat*."
- Blending sounds in short, three phoneme words: "What word am I saying?
  [Pause a second between sounds] /m /a/ /t/.

Gauging children's phonological awareness requires knowledge of its developmental sequence, knowledge of the skill levels that constitute proficiency at different ages, knowledge of the phonological skills the curriculum is emphasizing, astute observational skills, and expertise in structuring assessments for young children who find testing difficult.

Thus, if you suspect that your child has difficulties attending to, isolating, and manipulating sounds, have a speech and language specialist or a reading specialist evaluate his phonological awareness abilities. If he has difficulties in these areas, specialists can give you lots of brief, game-like activities to play virtually anywhere: at home, in the park, in the supermarket. As with most of your efforts to help him become a skilled reader, the key to helping him develop his phonological abilities is a word with three phonemes: /f/ /u/ /n/.

Dialect Differences. *Critical Question – Is your child's dialect different from his teachers' and classmates'?*

Dialect differences can cause your child a great deal of confusion in phonological awareness, phonics, and other word recognition activities. They can also cause him to misunderstand what's said to him and can cause other children to ridicule him.

More than anything else, preventing or minimizing the difficulties caused by dialect differences depends on teachers' sensitivity and responsiveness to the issue. Often, preschool, kindergarten, and primary grade teachers are unaware that dialect differences can cause reading difficulties. To prevent or minimize potential difficulties, discuss the issue at a joint meeting with your child's teachers, the school's speech and language specialist, and the school's reading specialist.

At such meetings, develop a plan that unites everyone around the goal of minimizing your child's difficulties by ensuring that he understands whatever is said; that he accurately identifies the words and sounds used in phonological awareness, phonics, and other word identification lessons; and that he has many opportunities to demonstrate his competence in other areas that he and his peers value (e.g., coloring, drawing, kicking a soccer ball). If he's too young for kindergarten and he's not in preschool, consider having him evaluated by a speech and language specialist.

Intellectual Difficulties. *Critical Questions – Compared to children his age, does your child have excessive difficulty understanding the world about him, and what other people say and do? Does he repeatedly have difficulty learning and remembering new things?*

Although these difficulties can have many causes (e.g., a developmental delay, a lack of confidence, excessive sleep problems, frequent ear infections), and may be temporary, it's important to have your child evaluated by a school psychologist who specializes in the learning difficulties of preschool and elementary school-age children. Make sure that the psychologist does not limit her evaluation to testing him and interviewing you.

To ensure that the evaluation transcends what the psychologist sees in her office, give her samples of your child's work, even if it's just scribbling and coloring. Also give her a record of what you tried to teach your child and how well he learned and remembered it. You might, for example, try to teach him the word cereal while he's eating cereal: "Joshua, this is a box of *cereal*. You're eating *cereal*." By keeping a simple record of the words and activities you introduced, and whether or not he remembered the experiences and the words ("Joshua, you ate this for breakfast yesterday. What's it called?), and correctly used the words, you can give the psychologist valuable information that can help her better interpret her testing.

Also valuable to helping the psychologist understand your child's intellectual abilities are cassette or digital audio recordings of his comments and conversations, recorded when he's playing with peers, having dinner, or speaking to you. Digital recorders make this quite easy—they're small, lightweight, inexpensive, and easy to use. Many use files that you can put on a computer and send as e-mail attachments, making it easy to share information.

Even better are video recordings. If at all possible, show the psychologist a video of your child playing, speaking, and doing routine things at home and in the community. Try to get videos of his best and typical functioning. Use a software program to edit the video down to 15 minutes and put it on a tape or DVD. (Many video-editing programs are inexpensive and easy to use.) If you don't have a video camera, consider renting one or buying an inexpensive one.

The work samples, records of your teaching efforts, and recordings can demonstrate if your child has strengths or weaknesses that psychological tests ignore or measure inadequately. As such, your information can help the psychologist more accurately determine the kind of help your child might need. The importance of accurately determining his abilities and needs cannot be overstated: Inaccuracy can hurt, accuracy can help.

Behavioral and Social Difficulties. *Critical Question – Does your child have difficulty working cooperatively with classmates, making friends, or following class rules?*

In many cases, students with behavioral and social difficulties become excellent readers. In other cases, however, their difficulties in working cooperatively with classmates or following class rules lead to rejection by peers and discipline by teachers. Even in kindergarten, this can generate a dislike for school that accelerates a downward spiral of animosity, resistance to schoolwork, and reading difficulties. Because prereading and reading activities take up considerable class time and often require students to work both independently and in small groups, they often become flash points for behavioral and social difficulties.

If these difficulties describe your child, even remotely, immediately request that a specialist in applied behavior analysis (e.g., a school psychologist or special educator) conduct a functional behavioral assessment in class and at home to identify what triggers and reinforces the troublesome behaviors. Then request a joint program planning meeting with the behavioral specialist and your child's teachers. The purpose of the meeting is to develop an intervention plan that eliminates the factors triggering your child's troublesome behaviors, reinforces him for cooperative behaviors, and teaches him whatever behavioral and social skills he needs to master.

Often, the behavioral and social difficulties that cause problems in school also cause emotionally-destructive problems at home. *Do not*—again, *do not* view these difficulties as signs that your child is "bad" or that you're a "bad" parent. Instead, view them as signs that he needs to learn a better, socially acceptable set of behaviors and strategies that effectively satisfy his needs. The earlier he learns these, the greater his chances for social and academic success. And the happier everyone will be: you, your child, and his teachers.

Learning a new, acceptable set of behaviors and strategies can often be achieved through a well-designed program of applied behavior analysis, especially one that emphasizes positive supports and positive reinforcement, and includes you and your child's teachers. Working with both home and school makes sense. After all, difficulties at home affect behavior in school and vice versa. Using the same or similar behavioral strategies in both situations improves consistency, creates more opportunities for positive reinforcement, helps reduce anxiety, and increases motivation, thereby increasing the likelihood of success.

Despite volumes of research and dozens of graduate-level textbooks supporting the use of applied behavior analysis and positive behavioral supports, many teachers and school personnel revert to blaming the child. Many schools will not provide behavioral supports and programs until they or the courts find a child eligible for special education. More than just creating anguish for children, parents, and yes, even for the teachers who might blame the child, it perpetuates the problem. Later in the book, we offer suggestions for resolving disputes with schools and for getting needed services.

If your child has behavioral difficulties, you need to become as knowledgeable and proficient as possible about applied behavior analysis. Understanding its broad principles will give you a tremendous edge in helping your child at home, resolving disputes with schools, and getting services. An easy-to-find, straightforward book that can teach you what teachers should know about applied behavior analysis, increase your influence in negotiating with schools, and help you to understand the kind of behavioral program your child needs is Paul Alberto and Anne Troutman's *Applied Behavior Analysis for Teachers.*[8]

Hearing Problems. *Critical Question – Does your child have difficulty understanding what people are saying, hearing what's happening around him, correctly pronouncing words, or figuring out the location of nearby sounds?*

If you suspect a hearing problem, have an audiologist assess your child's hearing. Be sure the audiologist holds a Certificate of Clinical Competence in Audiology from the American Speech and Hearing Association (ASHA).

If your child frequently gets ear infections, have him examined by a physician who specializes in ear problems (e.g., an otologist or otolaryngologist). Keep in mind that your child may have hearing problems only when his ears are infected or filled with fluid. Such intermittent hearing problems can cause reading disabilities if his hearing problems occur when teachers focus on phonological awareness or phonics—he won't hear, won't hear accurately, or will be in too much pain to attend.

Also, keep in mind that school hearing tests often fail to identify intermittent hearing problems. Therefore, a negative finding (meaning that no problem was found) may be misleading.

So, what does all of this mean? If you have the slightest suspicion that your child has a hearing problem—even a mild one—have a specialist evaluate him. Follow that old saying: Better safe than sorry.

Visual Problems. *Critical Question – Does your child have difficulty seeing things, visually following people or objects, or distinguishing among people and objects?*

Ask yourself: Does your child frequently complain that his eyes hurt or he has a headache? Does he frequently squint, tell you that he can't see things clearly, lose sight of moving objects, confuse similar looking objects or people, hold books in atypical positions or unusually close or far away? If so, he may have a visual problem. This, however, does not mean he will have reading difficulties. Once corrected, visual problems seldom hinder progress in reading.

Many parents and teachers believe that children who invert letters (e.g., *m* for *w*) or reverse letters (e.g., *b* for *d*) or words (*was* for *saw*) have visual problems that cause reading disabilities. Usually, they're wrong. During the preschool and early primary school years, many successful readers invert letters or reverse letters and words. By mid-third grade, it usually indicates a lack of reading knowledge or inattention, rather than visual problems.

Although all children should receive a visual examination by an ophthalmologist (medical doctor) or optometrist (nonmedical vision specialist), a professional examination is especially important if you suspect visual problems. Why such an examination instead of relying on a pediatrician or a school nurse to test your child's vision with an eye chart? Because these charts, sometimes referred to as Snellen eye charts, often miss major problems. Like screening tests for hearing, a negative finding on an eye-chart screening ("His vision is fine. We didn't find anything wrong") doesn't mean "all is well." Again, follow that old saying: Better safe than sorry.

Every so often, after a visual examination from an optometrist, parents are told that their child needs visual perceptual training or visual tracking training to prevent or remediate reading difficulties. Be wary of this. It's expensive and time consuming. Moreover, a compelling body of quality research has yet to show it works. By investing time and money in such training, you might prevent your child from getting the extra *reading* instruction he needs.

RISK FACTORS: YOUR CHILD'S CLASS AND SCHOOL

Not all factors that place your child at risk for reading disabilities are his personal attributes. Some are attributes of his teacher, his curriculum, and his school. Such factors, which we'll call high-risk school factors, can devastate his reading abilities and mental health. Although school factors are every bit as important as your child's risk-creating attributes (e.g., receptive language difficulties), they're often more difficult and costly to overcome. The first step in overcoming them is recognizing them. The second step is understanding them. The third is working with schools and resolving conflicts, which we discuss in later chapters. For now, we'll focus on recognizing teacher problems, curriculum problems, and school-wide problems.

Teacher Problems. *Critical Question – Is your child's teacher incompetent or apathetic?*

To succeed in reading, kindergartners and first graders need teachers who are conscientious about helping children succeed in reading and enthusiastic about doing so. Their teachers need to be highly knowledgeable about and skilled in teaching reading, especially to children who struggle with reading. As Asha Jitendra, Professor for the Advancement of Teaching and Learning at the University of Minnesota, and her colleagues have argued, they need teachers who know how to modify instruction to meet children's needs:

> Instruction for children who are at risk of reading failure must be more explicit, more comprehensive, more supportive, and more intensive than reading instruction required by average readers.[9]

Fortunately, many teachers can meet these standards; unfortunately, many can't.

Kindergarten and first-grade teachers with little skill in teaching reading can cause reading disabilities, even in children not otherwise at risk. The actions of these teachers often erode children's strengths and magnify their limitations. In contrast, teachers highly proficient in teaching reading and enthusiastic about doing so can help at-risk children become successful readers. Through their decisions and actions, these teachers can minimize, overcome, or compensate for children's vulnerabilities; this is especially important for children with high-risk characteristics.

If you suspect that your child is having the slightest difficulty with reading (or any other subject), ask to observe his class. If you don't observe, you have no idea what's happening, even if you think you do. All you know is what others say. And that may be wrong.

When observing, ask yourself: Does the teacher have control of her class? Does she treat students with respect? Is the class well organized and well managed? Are more than two hours a day spent on language activities that children find enjoyable and moderately challenging? Does your child have easy, daily access to plenty of interesting books? Is he given lots of opportunities to read to himself each day, or to browse through books, or to listen to adults read aloud? Does the teacher demonstrate interest in reading and enthusiasm for teaching? Is reading instruction clear, focused, and well organized? Does the teacher provide your child with academic and emotional support whenever needed? Does the teacher have a positive, supportive relationship with him?

Related to your observation are these questions: Does the teacher keep relevant, well-organized, ongoing records of your child's progress? Does she frequently inform you of his progress? Are her answers to your questions direct, focused, specific, and knowledgeable?

If many of your answers are "no," and they're supported by other information, don't attack the teacher. Teaching is a hard, complex, ten-to-fifteen-hours-a-day job, especially for new teachers; moreover, it takes many years for most teachers to become skilled at teaching reading. And unfortunately, in many schools, teachers, especially new teachers, don't get the instructional guidance and support they need.[10]

Despite your understanding of the situation, and perhaps your empathy for the teacher, if your child's teacher is poor at teaching reading, things must change quickly. First, document everything: Write down what you saw. Then, ask the principal to transfer him to a different class—he has no time to lose. (Often, a principal will observe the class, or have someone else observe; the observer may or may not be qualified.) If your request is denied, ask for in-class reading support from a highly qualified teacher (not an aide), or daily, supplemental tutoring by a reading specialist, or daily tutoring from a highly-trained Reading Recovery teacher.[11] Keep in mind, however, that our last three suggestions cannot compensate fully for poor in-class instruction.

If your requests are denied, don't be afraid to meet with the superintendent or the Board of Education. By asking them for changes, you're not "attacking" the teacher; you're simply meeting your parental obligations. You're asking for what your child needs to succeed. Perhaps they have ideas that differ from ours and perhaps theirs will work. So, share your documentation, and ask for changes, changes that ensure your child will get quality reading instruction.

By identifying a problem and asking for changes, you'll learn a lot about your school. Good schools welcome well-justified suggestions and constructively work with teachers to help them improve their skills. Poor schools put up smoke screens, divert attention from problems, and create barriers to change.

Curriculum Problems. *Critical Question – Does your child get little opportunity to listen to good books and to read such books?*

Good kindergarten and first-grade reading programs have teachers and other adults frequently read aloud to children. Among other things, this teaches them listening skills, sparks conversation, builds vocabulary, teaches story structures, and generates interest in topics. Thus, if you suspect that very little reading aloud is done, diplomatically and respectfully ask your child's teacher these questions: What books did she recently read aloud to him? About how much time, each day, does she devote to reading books aloud to the class, or to his group? A few times a week you might ask your child, "What book did your teacher read to you today? What was it about?"

Good kindergarten and first-grade programs should also stress free reading, in which children browse through books, look at the pictures, and, without feeling pressured, try to read as much as they want. To get a sense of your child's reading opportunities, you might ask the teacher these questions: How often do children choose books to read by themselves or with partners? About how much time, each day, does my child read whatever he wants? What's your policy for allowing children to get books from the class or school library? About how many books at my child's independent level (the level at which he can succeed by himself) and instructional level (the level at which he can succeed, without frustration, when he gets the teacher's help) are in the class library? How are the books displayed?

School-Wide Problems. *Critical Question – Does your child's school have major, persistent problems that negatively affect instruction and achievement?*

Is your child's school characterized by poor student achievement, large class sizes, poor student discipline, unwillingness or inability to adapt to student needs, high rates of grade retention (keeping children back), social promotion without adequate remediation and supports, poor communication with parents, general disorganization, low faculty morale, high faculty turnover, piddling libraries of interesting reading materials, uninterested or passive administrators? If one of these describes his school, seriously consider transferring him to another school; if several, work hard to transfer him—quickly.

Although transferring your child is far easier said than done and can cause family upheaval and financial hardship, he does not have the time to waste in a school that can destroy his future. It's sad, but he's racing against the tyranny of time and the devastation of failure.[12]

Putting your child in another school may make you feel guilty. Don't, even if you're concerned about the other children. Yes, the other children need help. What they need is informed political action that focuses on research-supported solutions, not oversimplified bumper sticker solutions, like phonics, vouchers, and uniforms. So, if you want to help the other children, learn all you can about reading and effective change strategies, and join a political-action group, like the Children's Defense Fund.

But in the meantime, do all you can to get your child into a good school, or if he has to remain in his school—the one with all the problems—do all you can to have him placed with an exceptionally good teacher. (Even the worst schools have some excellent teachers, and the best schools some terrible teachers.) Remember, he's racing against the tyranny of time.

RISK FACTORS: YOUR FAMILY AND HOME

Identifying risk factors in your family and home is hard to do. If you're like most people, you see your family and home through a narrow, biased set of lenses. The key is to be as objective as possible, to seek the input of people who know your family and who will assess situations as objectively as possible. Of course, like much in life, it's easier said than done.

Family History of Reading Difficulties. *Critical Question – Has anyone in your child's biological family had reading difficulties?*

If any member of your child's biological family, including grandparents, has had reading and writing difficulties, he has an increased chance of suffering similar difficulties. Finding out about the problem, however, can be a sensitive issue.

Look at Howard's family. His father had a reading problem that he hid until well after Howard earned his doctorate in reading. Although Howard's father continued to hide the problem, it became obvious when he was unexpectedly forced to read and sign some legal and medical papers. Coincidentally, Howard has the same difficulties as his father; he has difficulty manipulating sounds and pronouncing words. But he doesn't have significant difficulties when he reads silently. Why? His first- and second-grade teachers probably used methods that bypassed his difficulties and the school's speech therapist taught him how to compensate.

Whether the cause is genetic, environmental, or unknown (the highest probability), the general interventions are similar. You need to read to your child daily, give him lots of interesting experiences, encourage the development of language and phonological awareness, and carefully monitor all the factors discussed in this chapter. At the first sign of difficulty, arrange for a professional evaluation. If interventions are needed, arrange for emotionally supportive interventions that fully address his difficulties.

If you suspect a family link, don't make the fatal mistake of blaming yourself or anyone else. Without accomplishing anything positive, blame creates unnecessary stress for everyone. Besides, correlation is not causation: Just because two things go together, one doesn't necessarily cause the other. In other words, because some family members have reading difficulties doesn't mean they're responsible for your child's difficulties. In reading, we rarely know the exact, underlying cause of a child's problem. Even if we did, even if we identified a specific gene as the culprit, blame doesn't change his genetics.

Little Opportunity to Read or Listen to Adults Read. *Critical Questions – Does your child get insufficient opportunity to read books? Does he get insufficient opportunity to listen to adults read fiction and nonfiction?*

Without plenty of reading materials that your child wants to listen to, thumb through, and read at home, he's unlikely to develop the deeply-felt, abiding interest in reading so critical to overcoming the minor reading difficulties typical of beginning readers.

By having your child listen to, thumb through, or read *enjoyable, moderately challenging* reading materials, you're not just encouraging interest—you're creating opportunities for him to learn many things he must learn to succeed in reading. For example, reading to children a few times a day, for a total of 20 to 30 minutes, typically motivates them to read and improves reading comprehension by teaching them the parts of books, the structure of sentences, the structure of stories, and the meaning of vocabulary. Even reading the same book to them, over and over and over—their favorite—strengthens their love of reading and desire to master it, as long as it's fun, it's interesting, it's not forced. In Howard's home, his 5-year-old grandson couldn't get enough of Dr Seuss' *Cat in the Hat*. He continually asked Howard to read it to him. Now, Howard's grandson has two new Dr Seuss favorites: *The Lorax* and *The Sneetches*. He wants to hear them again and again and again. Yes—he's memorized all three storylines, but hasn't tired of them.

Look at your child's reading opportunities at home. Ask yourself: Are there lots of books he enjoys? Is he read to more than 15 minutes a day? Is he frequently taken to the library and allowed to choose books? Is he given lots of opportunities to read or thumb through books he chooses? If your answers are "yes," great; if "no," try to improve the situation. To us, filling your home with books your child loves and reading to him daily is better than investing in Google at $1.00 a share (despite the fact that as we write this, Google closed at $474 a share).

Mental Illness. *Critical Question – Does anyone in your family suffer from mental illness?*

Mental illness—depression, manic-depression, obsessive-compulsiveness, schizophrenia, panic attacks, and the like—is far more common than most people think. According to a recent report from the Surgeon General, mental illness affects about 20% of the population.[13]

Many families are ashamed of having a member with mental illness. Consequently, they and their family member work unceasingly to hide the problem. For three reasons, this makes no sense. First, science has discovered that mental illness is often caused, in whole or part, by biological factors; mental illness can suddenly strike the kindest, most thoughtful, most intelligent of people. Second, people who quickly get professional help are much more apt to overcome or control their mental illness than people who deny it or try to run from it. Finally, getting professional help is not a sign of weakness. It's a sign of strength, courage, and intelligence—a sign that the sufferer refuses to be dominated by an illness.

Unfortunately, the urgent, pressing, nagging nature of mental illness often dominates a family's attention, exhausts its finances, creates havoc, sours relationships, and perpetuates a hyper-vigilant climate of intense despair. In describing one form of mental illness, his depression, Andrew Solomon, wrote:

> When it comes, it degrades one's self and ultimately eclipses the capacity
> to give or receive affection .... It destroys not only connection to others but
> also the ability to be peacefully alone with oneself.... You are less than
> yourself and in the clutches of something alien.[14]

If a member of your family suffers from mental illness, immediately try to get help from a highly trained, highly competent psychiatrist, psychologist, or clinical social worker. Fortunately, research has shown that carefully monitored combinations of medication, verbal therapy, and social supports can markedly improve mental illness. But improvement is uncertain. Often, it's a torturous, frightening journey, full of false starts and wrong turns. As such, mental illness can devastate everyone within the family; no one—parents, grandparents, children—is immune.[15]

Sometimes, the family member with mental illness will refuse help. Often, you can't change the situation. Although you may not be able to help the afflicted member, you can help yourself and your child by meeting with professionals or a self-help group to develop a plan for dealing with the situation. The plan might involve counseling for you and your child, or more after-school activities for him. Whatever the plan, having a plan in place, where everyone knows their role, can create a sense of certainty and purposefulness that reduces anxiety.

Whether or not the involved family member gets professional help, you must aim to provide your child with a supportive home, free from undue anxiety. This aim may never be fully realized. That's okay—think in degrees, such as more or less; shun all-or-nothing, black-or-white thinking. Try to make each day as positive, as productive, as enjoyable as possible for your child: "Wow, are your pants dirty. Looks like you and your friends had fun. Want to play with them after school tomorrow?"

To minimize the effects of mental illness in families takes thought, knowledge, effort, diligence, perseverance, and lots of luck. But by providing supports—by reading to your child, playing sound games with him, listening to him, letting him engage in enjoyable activities, arranging lots of interesting experiences, using new words he's likely to understand, putting him in situations where he'll make friends, ensuring that he has a good teacher, and, if necessary, providing counseling and other therapies—you're reducing the likelihood of emotional distress, behavioral difficulties, and reading difficulties. Like most things in life, you're dealing with probabilities, not certainties, not guarantees. But if you deal directly with the issues raised by mental illness, and work to balance difficulties at home with lots of good experiences, you're increasing his odds of success.

RISK FACTORS: HEALTH AND HEALTH-RELATED FACTORS

In addition to damaging your child's emotional and social well-being, health factors can cause or intensify reading difficulties. If any of the previously discussed high-risk factors describe your child, health factors can further increase the likelihood of reading difficulties. In some cases, a single health factor might trigger a serious reading problem.

By avoiding tobacco, drugs, or alcohol during pregnancy, women can prevent problems like fetal alcohol syndrome. By making sure their children are not exposed to environmental toxins, such as lead paint, lead dust, or lead in dishes, parents can often prevent neurological or cognitive problems.

Parents' habits or addictions can hurt children at any age. For example, parents' smoking can aggravate children's asthma, causing inattention and excessive school absences. Alcoholism can cause family chaos and emotional distress for children, which in turn, can cause or complicate reading difficulties. Similarly, parents' uninformed decisions can create children's health problems, like the decision to sand lead paint from the walls of an old home, without properly sealing the room. Such sanding creates lead dust, which toddlers ingest, perhaps causing neurological and intellectual problems.

Some health problems are chronic. In addition to causing excessive absences, they can produce fatigue, anxiety, and depression. They can also cause difficulties with attention, concentration, and information processing (such as children's ability to remember sounds in sequence). Anyone of these can cause or intensify reading difficulties.

If high-risk health factors are part of your child's life, you need to act quickly to lessen or eliminate their negative effects. In some cases, this can be difficult, costly, and stressful. To escape lead, for example, you may have to replace your water pipes or move. If anyone in your family is alcoholic, counseling, rehabilitation, and separation may be warranted. Even with professional assistance, options may be limited and difficult. But, whether or not you take action, you will make a choice—inaction is a choice. The question is this: Will your choice help or hurt your child?

In considering health factors, it's important to avoid the guilt trap. The most conscientious of pregnant women, who follow medical advice to the letter, can give birth prematurely. The most conscientious and caring of parents can unknowingly expose their children to lead dust in the soil or to lead leaching from neighborhood water pipes. And science often lacks answers to the medical problems that terrify parents long into the night. One key to improving the situation and avoiding the debilitating, immobilizing effects of guilt is to acknowledge the past while focusing on what you can do—now and in the future—to help you and your child.

If chronic health problems significantly block your child's progress in reading (or other academic areas), you need to act quickly to improve the situation. As explained in later chapters, Federal laws can compel schools to provide supplemental instruction, as well as supplemental aids (e.g., air conditioning, specialized software) and services (e.g., tutoring) to any child who qualifies for such under the *Individuals with Disabilities Education Improvement Act of 2004* (IDEA-2004) or *Section 504 of the Rehabilitation Act of 1973* (Section 504).[16]

KEEP IN MIND

If you had difficulty answering any of our questions, or you believe your child is at risk for reading difficulties, we recommend that you keep these five points in mind:

- Stay calm.
- Don't blame anything on anyone, including yourself.
- Learn all you can about reading disabilities and quality reading instruction.
- Get whatever evaluations your child needs, including medical, visual, auditory, speech and language, psychological, and reading.
- Be optimistic.

By staying calm, avoiding the emotional drain of blame, and learning about reading disabilities and quality reading instruction, you're likely to use logic to focus on what can help. Similarly, by getting your child whatever evaluations he needs, you're likely to better understand his needs and develop a sensible course of action for home and school. Fortunately, even for preschoolers, Federal law often requires schools to provide needed evaluations.

By being optimistic, you'll generate the energy you need to effectively advocate for your child. Research supports optimism:

> A large portion (*always more than 50%*) of children who are *most at risk* for reading failure can be helped to learn at roughly normal rates in early elementary school by applying the best of what we know right now about reading instruction.[17]

Upcoming chapters will provide the detailed information you need to help your child at home and in school. The more you know about the topics in these chapters—types of reading difficulties, characteristics of effective and ineffective reading instruction, helping your child at home, listening and problem solving, and Federal education laws—the more effectively you can prevent a reading disability or help to overcome one. Unfortunately, the converse is also true; the less you know, the less effective your help.

CHAPTER 2: CHECKLIST

PREDICTIVE FACTORS: IS MY CHILD AT RISK FOR READING DISABILITIES?

A variety of factors can cause reading disabilities. However, in some cases just one factor can cause reading disabilities.

Before using this list, read this chapter. It explains the factors that predict reading disabilities. Remember that our definition of reading disabilities does *not* imply a permanent, immutable inability.

This is an informal list. Use it as a *guide* to better understand the probability that your child will have difficulties. "Maybe" means that you're unsure if your child has a problem; to answer the question you should get professional help. If you check a "Yes," your child *may* be at risk for reading disabilities.

Compared to his classmates or children his age, does my child have difficulties:

- Expressing himself? Yes ☐ No ☐ Maybe ☐
- Understanding what other people say or read to him? Yes ☐ No ☐ Maybe ☐
- Remembering what other people say or read to him? Yes ☐ No ☐ Maybe ☐
- Quickly recognizing and naming letters? Yes ☐ No ☐ Maybe ☐
- Recognizing and manipulating sounds in words (e.g., rhyming words, pronouncing the first sound in simple words, blending sounds into words)? Yes ☐ No ☐ Maybe ☐
- Making and keeping friends? Yes ☐ No ☐ Maybe ☐
- Working with other children in groups? Yes ☐ No ☐ Maybe ☐
- Following directions? Yes ☐ No ☐ Maybe ☐
- Paying attention? Yes ☐ No ☐ Maybe ☐

Does my child have:

- Hearing difficulties? Yes ☐ No ☐ Maybe ☐
- Visual difficulties? Yes ☐ No ☐ Maybe ☐
- Intellectual difficulties? Yes ☐ No ☐ Maybe ☐
- Emotional difficulties? Yes ☐ No ☐ Maybe ☐
- Chronic health problems that create fatigue, anxiety, depression, inattention, concentration difficulties, or difficulties processing information? Yes ☐ No ☐ Maybe ☐
- Chronic health difficulties that cause frequent absences from school? Yes ☐ No ☐ Maybe ☐

Does my child's:

- Primary language differ from that of his classmates or teacher? Yes ☐ No ☐ Maybe ☐

continues...

○ Dialect differ from that of his classmates or teacher?	Yes ☐	No ☐	Maybe ☐
○ Family have significant mental health problems?	Yes ☐	No ☐	Maybe ☐

Do I suspect that:

○ My child's teacher is inadequate?	Yes ☐	No ☐	Maybe ☐
○ My child's school is inadequate?	Yes ☐	No ☐	Maybe ☐
○ My child is read to infrequently?	Yes ☐	No ☐	Maybe ☐

Historically:

○ Was there significant use of tobacco, alcohol, or drugs during pregnancy?	Yes ☐	No ☐	Maybe ☐
○ Were there pregnancy or delivery problems?	Yes ☐	No ☐	Maybe ☐
○ Was my child exposed to environmental toxins?	Yes ☐	No ☐	Maybe ☐
○ Was my child exposed to lead?	Yes ☐	No ☐	Maybe ☐
○ Is there a family history of reading difficulties?	Yes ☐	No ☐	Maybe ☐

ENDNOTES

---

[1] Many State departments of education offer certifications in reading and literacy. In New Jersey, for example, a teacher with a master's degree in reading is eligible for certification as a Reading Specialist. Beware, however, of non-state certifications that are offered by companies that sell particular materials, or by organizations that advocate for particular approaches to reading. Frequently, people with these certifications have little background in reading and are proponents of particular instructional approaches that lack an adequate research base. Howard's experience is that such people often have a very narrow, ideological approach to reading that ignores the more compelling research, especially research that doesn't support their views.

[2] Unfortunately, many speech and language specialists who work in the public schools do not hold a Certificate of Clinical Competence in Speech and Language Pathology (CCC-SLP) from the American Speech and Hearing Association (ASHA). The CCC verifies that the specialist has had intensely supervised, relevant experiences, has done well in coursework, and has passed a rigorous test of knowledge. The lack of a CCC, however, does not mean that you should dismiss the findings and opinions of the school's speech and language specialist. As with all professional findings and opinions, you should look for other evidence that confirms or disconfirms their findings and opinions. The better educated professionals are about their subject, the less likely they are to make mistakes—but all professionals do, including us.

[3] Caldwell and Leslie offer a technical definition of a syllable: "A phonological unit of sounds that must include a vowel sound." Gillet and her colleagues put this into perspective: "Syllables are the pulses of speech that carry its rhythm.... Children usually show awareness of syllables—by being

able to clap along with them—by the age of 4." (Caldwell, J. S., & Leslie, L., 2005. *Intervention Strategies to Follow Informal Reading Inventory Assessment.* Boston: Pearson, Allyn & Bacon, p. 33; Gillet, J. W., Temple, C., & Crawford, A. N., 2004. *Understanding Reading Problems: Assessment and Instruction* (6th ed.). Boston: Pearson, Allyn & Bacon, p. 16.)

[4] A slash before and after a letter, a series of letters, or a word means that we're referring to the sound. Thus, /b/ refers to the sound of b, not the letter name.

The Literacy Dictionary defines digraph as "two letters that represent one speech sound [such as the] ea for /e/ in bread." It defines diphthong as a vowel sound, such as the sound made by ay in bay (Harris, T. L., & Hodges, R. E. (Eds.), 1995. *The Literacy Dictionary: The Vocabulary of Reading and Writing.* Newark, DE: International Reading Association, p. 60.)

[5] Harris & Hodges, p. 183.

[6] Why do some children, even some with good oral language, have so much difficulty with phonemic awareness? Michael Graves, Connie Juel, and Bonnie Graves give a clear explanation: "Phonemic awareness is an awareness of the sounds of language; it is not a part of learning to understand or speak oral language. [It] does not come naturally. Achieving it demands that a child attend to the form, rather than the meaning, of speech. This is difficult because our natural inclination is to attend to meaning.... Phonemic awareness is not necessary for speaking or for listening, but it is vital to reading. Understanding phonemes is complicated by the fact that we rarely say them separately; instead, they run together. In speech, we actually begin forming our mouths to pronounce the upcoming phoneme as we are still saying the previous one.... It is this overlapping, called coarticulation, of phonemes that allows our rapid speech. But it is exactly this coarticulation that makes learning to read words so hard. A letter in a printed word does not map onto one clear, distinct sound" (Graves, M. F., Juel, C., & Graves, B. B., 2007. *Teaching Reading in the 21st Century* (4th ed.). Boston: Allyn & Bacon, p. 95).

[7] Phonological awareness (and its component, phonemic awareness) is purely auditory and expressive. Unlike phonics, children are not asked to identify written words by memorizing the sounds of letters and then sounding-out the written letters in a word to identify it. Phonological awareness doesn't ask children to look at the word *"book"* and identify the printed word by making the sound of the b, the oo, and the k. Nevertheless, if children have difficulty with phonological awareness, including phonemic awareness, they're likely to have difficulty sounding out and identifying printed words. This causes many reading difficulties.

[8] Alberto, P. A., & Troutman, A. C., 2008. *Applied Behavior Analysis for Teachers* (8th ed.). Upper Saddle River, NJ: Pearson Merrill Prentice Hall.

[9] Jitendra, A. K., Edwards, L. L., Starosta, K., Sacks, G., Jacobson, L. A., & Choutka, C. M., 2004. Early reading instruction for children with reading difficulties: Meeting the needs of diverse learners. *Journal of Learning Disabilities, 37* (5), 421–439, p. 422.

[10] In his first year of teaching, Howard was a terrible teacher. Despite dedicating himself to his work and his students, he was, to be kind, ineffective. He quickly learned that teaching was a difficult, strenuous, demanding job that required him to keep learning and refining his skills. He wanted to help his students, but didn't know how to. Administration offered no help, other than to admonish him to wash his chalkboards. Unfortunately, in many districts, especially poorer ones, new teachers must fend for themselves. The result? Children suffer. Teachers quit.

¹¹ Reading Recovery is a popular one-to-one tutoring program for first graders who struggle with reading. (Some experts think that groups of three students offer equal benefit.) Specially trained Reading Recovery teachers tutor these children some 30 to 40 minutes daily for 12 to 20 weeks. Although the program has many critics, in 2007 the United States Department of Education's What Works Clearinghouse recognized it as an effective program. The Reading Recovery Council of North America claims that "by intervening early, Reading Recovery helps to close the achievement gap between lowest-achieving children and their peers before the gap becomes too large to bridge." For more information on Reading Recovery, visit www.readingrecovery.org.

¹² For an excellent discussion of the tyranny of time, see Kame'enui, E. J., 1993. Diverse learners and the tyranny of time: Don't fix blame; fix the leaky roof. *The Reading Teacher, 46,* 376-383.

¹³ In 1999, the Surgeon General issued a report summarizing the state of mental health in the United States. The report noted that "about one in five Americans experiences a mental disorder in the course of a year [and that]… a range of treatments of well-documented efficacy exists for most mental disorders" (U.S. Department of Health and Human Services, 1999. *Mental Health: A Report of the Surgeon General—Executive Summary.* Rockville, MD: U.S. Department of Health and Human Services, Substance Abuse and Mental Health Services Administration, Center for Mental Health Services, National Institutes of Health, National Institute of Mental Health, p. xii). If you suspect that a member of your family is having problems with his or her mental health, we urge you to read the report's Executive Summary. It dispels many myths while providing excellent information about what to do. The full report can be downloaded for free: http://www.surgeongeneral. gov/library/mentalhealth/home.html.

¹⁴ Solomon, A., 2001. *The Noonday Demon: An Atlas of Depression.* New York: Scribner, p. 15. This book deserves its excellent reviews. The late William Styron, who suffered from depression, described it as "an amazingly rich and absorbing work… in its flow of insights and its scope." Kay Redfield Jamison, an outstanding scholar who suffers from a bi-polar disorder, wrote that it is "an eloquent, harrowing account of melancholy and dread. It informs deeply in every manner— personal, scientific, historical, and political."

¹⁵ In addition to the Surgeon General's full report (*Mental Health: A Report of the Surgeon General,* 1999), if a member of your family suffers from mental health difficulties, you may want to read Martin E. Seligman's *What You Can Change and What You Can't* (New York: Ballantine Books, 1995). Although a decade old, it contains valuable insights from one of psychology's most influential researchers and thinkers. For children, Edward Christophersen and Susan Mortweet's *Treatments That Work with Children: Empirically Supported Strategies for Managing Childhood Problems* (2001, Washington, D.C.: American Psychological Association) might help you to avoid the many pitfalls that befall parents seeking help for their children's mental health problems.

¹⁶ IDEA-2004 has more stringent conditions for eligibility than Section 504. Under Section 504, a child can qualify for many services and accommodations if he has a health problem "that substantially impairs or restricts one or more major life activities, such as hearing, speaking, breathing, [and] learning."

¹⁷ Torgesen, J., 2000. Individual differences in response to early interventions in reading: The lingering problem of treatment resisters. *Learning Disabilities Research & Practice, 15,* 55–64, p. 61, emphasis added.

CHAPTER 3
KINDERGARTEN AND FIRST GRADE DIFFICULTIES

Historically, formal reading instruction began in first grade. Usually, two hours a day of formal reading instruction worked well *if* children found the word identification activities, comprehension activities, and reading materials interesting and moderately challenging. Unfortunately, for many children the work was overwhelming. They couldn't handle it. It frustrated them. It made them think they were failures.

Today, because of the *No Child Left Behind Act* (NCLB) and other political pressures, many districts are forcing kindergarten teachers to start formal reading instruction a few weeks after school begins. Depending on the activities, some children will thrive; they come to school with many reading skills. But many don't. The activities and materials they're required to master confuse and overwhelm them. Many kindergarten teachers recognize this, but must follow a script, a timetable—they can't adjust instruction to meet the children's abilities to master the new concepts and materials.[1] As many kindergartners struggle unsuccessfully to read, they start believing they're failures.

This means that as early as kindergarten, you need to know how well your child is succeeding in reading compared to her classmates and to the district's timetable for success. By knowing this, you can decide if quick, intensive action is needed to improve your child's reading abilities.

The timetable—loosely referred to as the district's or the State's standards, or the objectives or proficiencies or core curriculum for the grade—is important because many schools feel compelled to tie instruction to the calendar rather than to what children are ready to master. If your child starts falling behind the timetable—even slightly—her teachers may require her to master concepts that she's not ready for. This is a formula for failure.

So, from the first day of school, be vigilant. Closely monitor your child's progress. Don't wait until New Year's Day to see how she's doing. If all is going well, great. If, however, she's falling behind her peers or the district's timetable—even slightly—quickly get practical answers about how to improve her reading. Practical answers mean action steps that will likely work. Why action steps? Because without action, testing and talking don't help. Because without action, children who struggle with reading in kindergarten and first grade will likely struggle for years. For some, the struggle will never end. Many will just go through the motions, apparently uncaring, until they drop out of school. Others will develop behavioral problems, in and out of school.

THE EARLY STAGE OF FORMAL READING INSTRUCTION

To fully understand if your child has a reading disability, and, if so, what her weaknesses are, you need to consider the factors discussed in chapter 2 as well as the Curriculum and Non-Curriculum Factors discussed in this chapter.[2]

Curriculum Factors refer to what children must master to succeed in reading—concepts-about-print, letter recognition and naming, phonological awareness (which includes phonemic awareness), and listening comprehension. Although indirectly, Non-Curriculum Factors, such as attentional problems and difficulties on reading readiness tests, can also influence your child's success in reading. Poor attention can cause her to miss what the teacher is saying; to ignore the visual differences between a "*b*," a "*d*," and a "*p*"; to follow the path of a spider while ignoring the lesson on how to blend the sounds /h/ and /at/ to make the word *hat*.

The influence of Non-Curriculum Factors, such as attention and motivation, is indirect because improvement does not always improve reading abilities. In contrast, considerable improvements in Curriculum Factors, such as listening comprehension, will likely improve a child's ability to identify words.

So, what does this mean to you? If your child is in kindergarten or first grade and starts having difficulties with reading—even small ones—review this entire chapter. It may help you to identify the factors responsible for her difficulties. As you read, keep this in mind: One factor seldom causes *sustained* reading disabilities; usually, it takes several.

HIGH RISK CURRICULUM FACTORS

Difficulty with Concepts-about-print. *Critical Question – Compared to other children her age, does your child have difficulty understanding how print is used?*

Concepts-about-print refers to a child's knowledge about how print is used.[3] As you'll see below, it's more basic than recognizing specific letters and words. Here are some ways to gauge your child's knowledge.

Observe her with a story book with which she's familiar. Ask her to point to specific parts of the book, such as the front cover, the title, the top of a page, the bottom of a page. Then ask her to point to a picture, a letter, two letters, three letters, and a word. Then read the book to her. Ask her to show you where on a page to begin reading, where to stop, where the story begins, and where it ends. If she has difficulty with these requests, spend ten minutes a day with her, for several days, showing and explaining the parts of a book. Follow this by reading a new book to her, several times, over several days, and again asking her these questions.

Until your child knows the different parts of a book and the general way in which print works (for example, in English, people read from left to right), asking her to read books will confuse her. Simple, direct instruction, focused on the print concepts she needs to learn, can help to eliminate such confusion and improve her chances of becoming a successful reader. You can find a "concepts-about-print" checklist on our website, www.reading2008.com.

Difficulty with Letter Recognition and Letter Naming. *Critical Question – After some-one has tried to teach your child to recognize and name letters, does she have difficulty quickly pointing to specific letters by name?*

Even before children are taught to identify words, difficulty learning to quickly recognize and name letters often distinguishes kindergartners and first graders who will struggle with reading from classmates who will excel. Before becoming concerned about difficulties with letter recognition and naming, ask two questions: Did my child's teacher spend as much time teaching her to recognize and name letters as he spent with most children? When someone else tries to teach her to recognize and name letters, does she learn this as quickly as others her age?[4]

Generally, children who have difficulties with letter recognition and naming require a daily, systematic program of small-group instruction (two or three children) that stresses mastery of both. Although mastery does not directly affect word identification ability, ongoing difficulties can negatively influence phonemic awareness and set the stage for continued reading disabilities.[5]

If, after several weeks of instruction in a small group, your child still has trouble quickly and accurately recognizing and naming letters, she will require a more intensive, systematic program of individual tutoring. At this point, we recommend that you request an evaluation from both a school psychologist and a reading specialist. The reading specialist's evaluation should include diagnostic teaching, in which the specialist teaches your child to recognize and name letters, using different strategies. By comparing the effectiveness of different strategies, the specialist can often determine which strategies to avoid, which to stress. The school psychologist's evaluation should seek to understand general difficulties that may affect your child's reading and related academic achievement. These can include the ability to focus, to cooperate, to deal with stress, to understand oral language, to remember and retrieve information.

Difficulty with Phonological Awareness. *Critical Question – Does your child have difficulty with hearing-saying (auditory-oral) activities like rhyming words, blending sounds into words, and isolating and saying the individual sounds in short words.*

Early reading success requires children to master these auditory-oral or phonological awareness skills to successfully sound out and quickly identify words. As Hugh Catts and Tiffany Hogan noted, "Phonological awareness allows children to match sounds with letters and use this knowledge to phonetically decode words.... Difficulties in phonological awareness are apparent in at-risk children even prior to beginning reading instruction, and ... these deficits lead to subsequent problems in learning to read."[6]

If your child has started a formal reading program and has difficulty with phonological awareness activities—which include phonemic awareness activities that deal with the smallest units of sound that distinguish words from one another, such as the sounds of individual letters—you might ask her teacher if he's using *visual* letters to support instruction in phonological awareness. This is important, as some teachers do not, despite the research. Here's what Linnea Ehri, Distinguished Professor at the City University of New York, found:

> Younger children acquired phonemic awareness better with letters.... Phonemic awareness instruction with letters produced a [gain] that was almost twice as large as the [gain] without letters on reading outcomes. [Perhaps this was because letters] provide concrete, lasting symbols for sounds that are short-lived and hard to grasp.[7]

At the same time, you should request that the school evaluate your child's hearing and that a speech and language specialist or a reading specialist formally evaluate her phonological awareness skills.[8] If the specialist finds that progress has been inadequate, request 10 to 15 minutes of additional, daily instruction by a specialist or a teacher who is highly trained in teaching and assessing phonological awareness.[9] The reason we stress "highly trained" is that many teachers are not, which can dramatically hinder your child's progress.[10]

You might also ask the teacher or specialist to let you know what unit of sound—words, syllables, the beginning and ending parts of syllables, phonemes—your child is ready to work with and what skills she's ready to learn.[10] Then ask him to demonstrate how he'll teach her these skills. By asking and watching, you might get ideas about how you can help your child at home, in friendly, supportive ways.

Asking might also give you insight about the teacher's or specialist's knowledge of phonological awareness. For example, some teachers and specialists don't know that it's best to start instruction with larger, easier sound units, such as words, then syllables, and progress toward smaller, more difficult units, such as syllable parts and letter sounds or phonemes.[10] Instruction often falters when it starts with units of sound that are too small and thus too difficult for the child.

Notice the difference in difficulty between segmenting words into syllables and into phonemes:

- Syllables: "There are two syllables in *hotdog*; they're /hot/ ... /dog/. What two syllables do you hear in *baseball*?"
- Syllables: "There are two syllables in *garden*; they're /gar/ ... /den/. What two syllables do you hear in *basket*?"
- Phonemes: "There are two small sounds in *hay*. They're /h/ and /ay/. What two sounds do you hear in *go*?"

Segmenting words into phonemes is far more difficult. If instruction prematurely emphasizes this, failure is likely.

Similarly, some teachers and specialists don't know that instruction can falter if many skills are emphasized. Linnea Ehri's review of the research strongly suggests that it's best to focus on blending and segmentation as "teaching these two phonological awareness skills produced greater benefits in reading than [did] a multiple-skills approach."[13] Here are examples of blending and segmenting:

> Blending: "What word am I trying to say?—/t/ ... /oy/." [The three dots indicate a one second pause between the sound of /t/ and the sound of /oy/.]
> Segmenting a compound word: "Clap each time you hear a little word. Here we go—toothbrush."

When requesting additional, daily instruction to strengthen phonological awareness, don't initially insist on one-to-one instruction. First see if small-group instruction works. This is not a concession; research shows that for phonological awareness small-group instruction is often more effective than one-to-one instruction.[14] Keep in mind, however, that some children, especially those with serious attention, impulsivity, or behavior problems may need one-to-one instruction.

To prevent your child from becoming confused and to make sure she gets enough practice and reinforcement, politely but firmly insist that the teacher or specialist providing the additional instruction meticulously coordinates it with your child's daily, in-class reading instruction. This helps ensure that all her teachers better understand her needs, her current problems, what should be re-taught or practiced, and what sound units and skills she's ready to master. In other words, coordination helps everyone to focus on the same skill, on the same unit of sound, in the same way. It provides greater practice and reinforcement.

If started early—before your child falls far behind her peers or the school's instructional timetable—additional phonological awareness instruction that's simple, focused, timely, and coordinated with in-class instruction can help to prevent, minimize, or reverse reading difficulties.[15] In many instances, problems disappear in a few months. So, if your child needs help with phonological awareness, don't wait—ask for help immediately.

Difficulty Understanding What's Read Aloud. *Critical Questions – Compared to other children in your child's class, does she have difficulty understanding stories that are read to her? Does she have difficulty telling you the basic points or the gist of these stories?*

Children who struggle to understand stories read aloud need to learn how to understand them. If they don't, they may have difficulties with reading comprehension.

Learning how to listen can be taught. Some students need to learn that first they should think about the topic of the story and what they know about it. If the topic is flying, they might think about planes, pilots, and clouds. They might think about their experiences: "When I flew with Mom, we had to buckle our seatbelts, like in a car." Some students need to learn that stories have sequential structure: an introduction, a problem, a search for solutions, a resolution. Relating what they know to the story and understanding its structure can help children predict what's likely to happen and what makes sense. Many children need to learn that listening is an active process; it involves concentrating, figuring out the meanings of words, asking questions, and seeking answers.

Fortunately, daily, systematic instruction in listening comprehension can frequently improve reading comprehension. Teachers can use many strategies to help children, including at-risk and struggling readers, improve their listening abilities. Teachers might, for example, use read-alouds in which they read interesting, slightly challenging stories to the entire class or to a small group; as part of the read-aloud, they model fluent reading, ask questions, encourage their students to ask questions, model the thought processes that help students understand the stories, and have students discuss the stories. Or they might teach their students to retell parts of stories read to them. If teachers read aloud and discuss interesting, slightly challenging stories, they can often increase children's motivation to read and their understanding of what's read.

If your child's teacher has frequently read aloud to her and has systematically used listening comprehension strategies like those we described, but your child's understanding remains below that of her peers, she may have underlying problems with hearing, language, intellect, attention, or information processing. To quickly identify the causes of her ongoing difficulties, request a hearing evaluation, a comprehensive speech and language evaluation, and a psychological evaluation. As with phonological awareness, don't wait—ask immediately.

HIGH RISK NON-CURRICULUM FACTORS

Difficulty with Attention. *Critical Question – Compared to other children her age, does your child have difficulty attending to and thinking about reading activities, organizing her time and work, and sticking to and finishing work on time?*

Loosely speaking, educators call a continued pattern of such behaviors "attention problems." Please remember the phrase we used: "a continued pattern." Attention problems are not sporadic, infrequent instances of inattention or procrastination. Daily, for brief periods, even the most accomplished children and adults exhibit attentional and organizational difficulties. Do you, for example, ever misplace your keys or dawdle instead of balancing your checkbook, a task you dislike? Do you daydream?

One of the problems with "attention problems" is its definition. Often, different teachers have different definitions. One teacher might say, "Ben has an attention deficit disorder." Another might say, "Ben's just fidgety, like most 5-year olds."

To understand what's typical in this murky, ill-defined area, look closely at the behavior of other children in your child's grade—even better, in your child's class—to identify the behavioral patterns teachers think typify attention problems. If, after this, you think your child has an attention problem, don't panic, don't assume she'll have a reading problem. Although attention problems can cause or add to reading difficulties, many children with professionally diagnosed, validated attention problems learn to read quite well. The two problems are different and often unrelated.

Whether or not your child is at risk for reading disabilities, you must quickly address any attention problems she may have, before they career out of control. By themselves, attention problems can be emotionally and socially devastating; they can cause other problems, such as bad grades, discipline problems, and alienation from family and school. Combined with reading difficulties, attention problems can make life even worse.

To improve the situation, you need to identify the factors *currently* causing the problems. This requires that a reading specialist, school psychologist, special educator, or expert in applied behavior analysis, highly skilled in dealing with attention problems, observe your child in typical school situations in which her attention is poor and in typical situations in which it's good. By assessing what precedes, accompanies, and follows periods of attention and inattention, and assessing what happens when teachers alter these factors, school staff can often pinpoint the immediate causes of your child's attention difficulties and identify possible remedies. This is called a functional behavioral assessment (FBA). Without an FBA, with just a visit to a neurologist or psychiatrist's office, diagnosis is incomplete, reducing the odds that an intervention based solely on this diagnosis—an office diagnosis that ignores environmental factors—will work.

In the era of Ritalin and other drugs designed to improve children's attention, professionals and parents often forget that attention problems may not have neurological or chemical causes. Instead, the work may be too hard (frustrating) or too easy (boring), the child may feel anxious about something (e.g., bullying at recess), the class may be poorly organized, or the lessons too long. If your child suffers from attention problems, and an FBA has been completed, ask your child's teachers and support staff to systematically alter and collect data on all environmental or instructional factors that might contribute to the problem. Changes—like shortening assignments, making work easier or more interesting, reinforcing attention, seating your child elsewhere—often lessen or eliminate attention problems.[16]

If, however, the changes don't fully solve the problem, request a psychological, pediatric, or neurological evaluation.

And don't, without studying the literature, dismiss medication out-of-hand. Yes, the debate about medication is raging. On the negative side, the long-term effects are unknown. On the positive side, many parents passionately believe medication has helped their children turn failure into success.

Difficulty with Reading Readiness Tests. *Critical Question – Did your child do poorly on a "reading readiness" test?*

Reading readiness (or emergent literacy) tests are formal or informal tests that many schools use to predict a child's readiness to benefit from beginning reading instruction.[17] They're usually administered in kindergarten or early first grade. Although such tests have earned a great deal of well-deserved criticism, many schools and teachers continue to use them as if they were flawless diagnostic tools and faultless predictors of children's reading abilities. They're not.

Sometimes a child's score on a reading readiness test accurately predicts her readiness to benefit from the school's reading program. But often, reading readiness tests miss the mark. Children can do poorly on such tests for reasons irrelevant to reading. Ask yourself: Was my child feeling well when she took the test? Did she get a good night's sleep and eat a nutritional breakfast? Ask the teacher: Did my child attend to the test and persevere throughout testing? Did she make a good effort to succeed? Was she anxious? Do the test results accurately represent her work in class?

Sometimes, reading readiness tests are unrelated to the curriculum. Ask the teacher: Does the test directly measure what was taught? Are all the areas tested critical for success in reading? What has the research shown about the test's ability to predict children's success in reading when *this school's* reading programs are used? What has research shown about remediating the weaknesses identified by the test?

Unfortunately, many teachers and other school personnel, including reading specialists and speech and language specialists, can answer only the first question: Does the test directly measure what was taught? Many make decisions about students' needs without studying the reviews of the tests that influence or trigger their decisions. This often results in poor decision making, such as ignoring abilities important to reading while remediating unimportant ones.

To begin interpreting the test results in knowledgeable ways, we urge you and your child's teachers to study expert reviews of the tests given to your child. Perhaps the best source of expert reviews, reviews that will help you judge the strengths and weaknesses of the tests and determine the degree of confidence you can have in the results, is the Mental Measurements Yearbook (commonly referred to as Buros).[18] It reviews many of the more important tests and is available in many libraries. You can also download copies of these reviews from the University of Nebraska's test-review website: http://buros.unl.edu/buros/jsp.

Poor results on reading readiness tests or other predictive measures require a follow-up evaluation by a reading specialist. The evaluation should focus on identifying the reasons for your child's poor performance. If the evaluation identifies critical weaknesses directly related to reading achievement, such as phonological awareness or oral language weaknesses, immediately request a program likely to strengthen these weaknesses. Keep in mind that reading and reading-related programs, like programs to improve listening and memory, should not be static or inflexible—they should not be set in stone. Instead, they should aim to strengthen critical weaknesses, including motivation.[19] They should quickly respond to your child's abilities and difficulties in ways that help her succeed. This is the essence of individualizing instruction. Thus, a poor performance on a readiness test or a set of weaknesses identified by a follow-up evaluation need not condemn your child to reading failure. Odds are that an inflexible program—one set in stone—will.

When discussing your child's follow-up evaluation with the reading specialist, ask for objectives to gauge the effects of instruction over the next six to eight weeks. Such short-term objectives, like the example below, should be so clear and so specific that you'll know if your child's progress is adequate or if she's struggling. If she's struggling, she may need even more instruction, or instruction in smaller groups, or in one-to-one tutorials, or a different curriculum, or easier work, or a combination of these. She and her teacher may also need additional help from the reading specialist.

A short-term objective

When orally given a word, and asked what sound remains after the first sound is omitted, Carol will pronounce the remaining sound. Example: "What sound is left when I take the /b/ off of /bat/?"). Carol will achieve this on 9 of 10 trials with different words by 10/31/09.

IDENTIFYING WORDS AND UNDERSTANDING TEXT

Once formal reading instruction begins, teachers usually emphasize the memorization of common words, strategies for sounding out unknown words, and understanding what's read. Here are the more technical terms:

- The memorization of common words: development of sight vocabulary.
- Strategies for sounding out unknown words: decoding or phonics and structural analysis.
- Understanding what's read: reading comprehension.

At this point, you need to compare your child's progress in these areas to her classmates' and to the district's reading timetable. For a very simple but dramatic reason, assessing progress in the first two months of formal reading instruction is particularly important: Children who start off poorly and don't immediately get the help they need usually fall further and further behind. Without extra help, help that's knowledgeable and skilled, they rarely catch up.[20]

Unfortunately, during the first few months of reading instruction some teachers won't tell you if your child's struggling. Some don't know; they don't understand reading. Some new teachers, especially those in alternative certification programs (where they're changing careers and have little background in education), don't know what to expect of children, don't understand their teachers' manuals, and certainly don't understand reading disabilities. Some, even some with lots of experience, who care deeply about children, erroneously think that slow starters will catch up. Thus, you must informally assess your child's reading progress and, if you suspect difficulties, request a formal reading evaluation. Again, follow the old saying: Better safe than sorry.

You can assess your child's progress by examining the high-risk factors in the next section, reviewing her written work, listening to her read books she's read in school, speaking to her teacher, and comparing her progress to the district's timetable for success. As mentioned previously, this timetable is loosely referred to as the district's or the State's standards, or the objectives or proficiencies for the grade.

When reviewing the high-risk *reading* factors in the next section, keep in mind the predictive factors summarized in chapter 2's checklist. Unlike these predictive factors, the high-risk reading factors below don't focus on the future. Instead, they focus directly on how well your child reads—*now*. They ask two basic questions: How well does she identify words—*now*? How well does she understand what she reads—*now*?

HIGH-RISK READING FACTORS

Difficulty Identifying Basic Sight Words. *Critical Question – Compared to average readers in your child's grade, does she have difficulty quickly identifying many of the common words taught in class?*

To read successfully, children must identify most words within a fraction of a second,[21] especially the 300 to 500 most common words in English, such as *an, and, is, the, that, what.* These 300 to 500 common words, which are emphasized in most programs for beginning readers,[22] make up the majority of words read. Just look at the common words in the last sentence: *these, to, which, are, in, most, for, make, up, of, the, we.* As a group, these words are so important that they have many names: core words, glue words, working words, instant words, service words, common sight words, basic sight vocabulary, high-frequency sight words, basic sight words. Because basic sight words are often abstract and difficult to define (e.g., *the, would, which*), difficult to spell or impossible to decode (*is, said, they*), and because they often look like other words (*whose* and *where, were* and *was, has* and *have*), they cause struggling readers great difficulty. Good readers, however, quickly learn to identify the words taught in their grade; and by the mid-to-end of third grade they instantly identify far more words than the 300 to 500 basic sight words.[23]

Inability to quickly identify most basic sight words and other words emphasized in class makes reading a slow, laborious, and unpleasant struggle. Some children continue to struggle, doing the best they can. Others quit. Some who quit become passive; they go through the motions, giving little thought to instruction, to the reading strategies they need to apply, to understanding their reading materials. Others disrupt class to escape reading. Both responses create a vicious cycle: Struggling readers resist—either passively or aggressively—the widespread reading essential to developing competence. By escaping, they may momentarily avoid struggle or humiliation. Ironically, by escaping, they ultimately decrease their odds of success.[24]

If you suspect that your child has difficulty with sight vocabulary, ask her to read aloud a story she *recently read* in school. Just listen: Don't correct her. If she struggles with a word for more than three seconds, tell her to skip it and continue reading.[25] Minimally, she should quickly and accurately identify 95% of the words. If the story has a hundred words, she should quickly and accurately identify 95 or more. Interestingly, if she already read and studied the material, some authorities would justifiably argue that correctly identifying only 95% is too low.

If you need more information, ask her teacher for a list of words he recently taught your child. Put them on index cards and flash them to her, one at a time. Ask her to tell you each word. If she needs more than two seconds, flash the next one and ask her to say it. As these words have already been taught to her, she should identify the vast majority in less than two seconds of seeing them.[26] Calculate the percentage of words she correctly identified in less than two seconds. If she finds the task frustrating, stop. Do something she likes.

If your child has difficulty reading aloud stories she's read in school, or identifying words flashed on index cards, discuss her progress and your concerns with her teacher. Meetings often get better results than phone calls. Ask how well your child's doing compared to the class' top and average readers. Also ask the teacher to show you the books your child typically reads and those typically read by the top and average readers. If, after this, you think her progress is inadequate, formally request an evaluation from a reading specialist. Usually, a formal request requires you to complete an official referral form. Photocopy the completed referral.

Difficulty Identifying or Decoding Unknown Words. *Critical Question – Does your child have difficulty quickly identifying or decoding unknown words?*

During reading, children inevitably run into words they know the meaning of, but can't identify or decode quickly; they need more than a second to figure out each of these words. Even though children understand these words, they're called *unknown words*—unknown because children can't identify them quickly. By looking at them, they don't know how to pronounce them.

To become successful readers, children need to quickly identify thousands of unknown words; to do so, they need to decode the phonetically regular words (e.g., back, lack, pack) by sounding out their parts and need to memorize the irregularly spelled ones, which include many basic sight words (e.g., of, the, they, laugh). Trying to quickly memorize most words during the first few years of reading instruction, however, doesn't work—there are too many words. Thus, children must learn to decode, accurately and quickly. Over the years, with lots of practice and lots of easy reading, most words they've decoded become sight words.

At first, decoding is a slow, fumbling process. Over time, successful readers gradually learn to decode quickly, almost effortlessly. They turn thousands of unknown words—words they need to decode by sounding out their parts—into sight words, words they no longer need to decode.

For the word *but*, typical mid-first graders might sound out the individual letters *b*, *u*, and *t*; for *chin*, typical mid-second graders might sound out the two larger letter-sound units, *ch* and *in*.[27] Before third grade, typical readers will turn *but* and *chin* and lots of other words into sight words, words they identify quickly, virtually effortlessly. These examples illustrate that at different stages of word identification or decoding, children use different strategies. As they advance, they focus on larger letter-sound units and turn unknown words into sight words.

Here's how Sharon Walpole and Michael McKenna describe the stages. In each stage, children do something new:

> Children move from attending to some aspect of the physical shape of words [e.g., the length], to processing some of the letters [e.g., sounding out the first letter], to processing all of the letters [e.g., sounding out the b—u—t in *but*], to recognizing most words automatically [as sight words]. At first, when children begin to read words, they focus their attention on only one salient aspect of the word (e.g., ... part of the shape of the word). They leave this stage when they have enough phonemic awareness and enough alphabet knowledge to focus on partial alphabet cues—typically, initial and final consonants [e.g., the *b* and *t* in *but*]. They leave this stage when they know and are able to use letter sounds, including the vowels in the middle, to decode words. Finally, they recognize familiar words automatically, with no need for decoding.[28]

But most struggling readers find this difficult. They struggle to identify words.[29] To help them, you need to know what stage they're in.

By keeping Sharon Walpole and Michael McKenna's sequence in mind, you and your child's teacher can determine the stage your child is in. This can help determine if she's falling behind or keeping pace with her class. It can help you spot specific problems or stop you from worrying about imaginary disabilities. It can shed light on the appropriateness of instruction.

Another way of spotting word identification or decoding difficulties is to consider some of the more common ones. Several are listed in Table 3.1. To the right of each is what successful readers might think. When reviewing these difficulties, keep three things in mind: the emphasis of your child's reading curriculum, the word identification or decoding stages that Sharon Walpole and Michael McKenna describe, and your child's grade. By mid-first grade, typically developing readers should be fairly adept at recognizing the letters in one- and two-syllable words and applying the specific letter-sound associations taught in class; by the end of first grade, they should be somewhat adept at recognizing and applying small units of meaning taught in class (e.g., knowing that the *s* at the end of *cats* means more than one).

TABLE 3.1: COMMON DIFFICULTIES IDENTIFYING UNKNOWN WORDS

COMMON DIFFICULTIES IDENTIFYING UNKNOWN WORDS	WHAT SUCCESSFUL READERS MIGHT THINK
Difficulty recognizing individual letters (e.g., the *c* in *caboose*) and letter combinations (e.g., the *ch* in *chair*) in unknown words.	"I need to look at each letter, starting with this one: *c*."
Difficulty generating the specific sounds associated with each letter or letter combination.	"The *c* probably makes the */kuh/* or */suh/* sound" [the word is still unknown].
Difficulty recognizing and applying small units of meaning (called morphemes), such as the *un* in *unhappy*.	"The un before happy means he's sad, not *happy*."
Difficulty using the meaning of nearby words to identify unknown words.	"The first sentence said it's the last car in the train and the c can make a */kuh/* sound. It's probably caboose."
Difficulty using the meaning of nearby words to check if the newly decoded word makes sense.	"Yeah. It's probably *caboose*. It says the crew eats in it. That's where crews eat— in the *caboose*. *Caboose* makes sense."

Note that we added the meaning of nearby words, called context clues. Although context clues alone are not nearly as effective in identifying unknown words as sounding out their parts, they can make the process more efficient. Consider this sentence: "Because it was hot and Ray's mouth was dry, he asked Mrs. Piccolo for a *drink*." To identify the unknown word drink, typical mid-second graders might first sound out *dr* and then consider the context. Together, the sound of *dr* and the context might quickly suggest that *d-r-i-n-k* spells *drink*. The unknown word's been decoded.

In sum, to quickly and accurately identify unknown words, children need to skillfully isolate and manipulate non-meaningful sounds within words, apply letter-sound associations, apply knowledge of root words, prefixes, and suffixes[30], and apply knowledge of vocabulary, sentence structure, and paragraphs. The aim is to move beyond decoding, to transform decoded words into sight words—words identified effortlessly, in a fraction of a second. When children identify the vast majority of words on sight, they can more readily focus on understanding the text.

Terms used to discuss how children identify unknown words include alphabetic principle, decoding, phonics, word identification, word attack, word analysis, word perception, and word recognition. Because school personnel and reading textbooks frequently use these terms in general, fuzzy ways, when they're used, ask for definitions. Here are some general ones:

- *Alphabetic principle* refers to children's understanding that "spoken sounds can be represented by written letters,"[31] that each letter or commonly occurring set of letters, such as *bl* in *blank*, is usually associated with particular speech sounds. Despite its apparent simplicity, some children struggle with this. Edward J. Daly III and his colleagues assert that many children have difficulty understanding the relationship between letters and sounds because "the significance of a letter is often modified by its surrounding letters. That is, each letter does not correspond neatly with only one sound, but can change in the context of various combinations. For example, the letter *c* makes a different sound in *cat, city,* and *chat.*"[32]

- *Decoding,* as defined by John Savage, Professor Emeritus at Boston College, refers to children "attaching the appropriate sound or sound sequence to the corresponding letter or letter sequence" to identify unknown words.[33] Some authorities would add using the meaning of surrounding words to identify the unknown word. It's figuring out—naming—the unknown word. Often, inadequate instruction in phonological awareness creates difficulty learning and applying letter-sound associations (phonics), which causes decoding problems.

- *Phonics* is part of decoding. When children, especially beginning readers, use their knowledge of letter sounds to name written words they don't recognize, they're using phonics. Programs that fail to remediate phonological awareness difficulties can cause children to struggle with phonics. Programs that overemphasize phonics at the expense of other components of reading, such as reading to understand and enjoy stories, can make reading boring and comprehension difficult.

- *Word identification* is frequently referred to as *word attack, word analysis,* and *word perception.* It refers to children's abilities to use their knowledge of letter sounds, word parts, word meanings, surrounding words, and sentence structure to identify unknown words. Instruction in quickly identifying unknown words is critical, but insufficient for children to become proficient readers. They also need instruction in many other areas, like fluency, vocabulary, and reading comprehension, as well as lots of experiences that make them want to read, read, and read.

- *Word recognition* refers to the quick, almost instantaneous naming of words. Unlike word identification, which requires a child to consciously use different strategies to figure out and name an unknown word, word recognition does not require the conscious use of such strategies. Sandra McCormick, Professor Emeritus from Ohio State University, said it well: "Word recognition refers to the instant recall of words in which the reader resorts to no obvious mechanisms to recognize the word.... When the reader recognizes a word in this way—and can say the word with no hesitation—it is said that he or she has developed automaticity."[34]

If you suspect that your child has difficulty identifying unknown words, ask her teacher for a list of words that average readers in her class should be able to sound out. Write these on index cards, one word per card. Ask your child to pronounce each word. If she takes more than two seconds to pronounce a word correctly, consider it unknown and show her the next one. Don't give her clues about the correctness of her responses. If you sense frustration, stop. Switch to something she enjoys.

If your child had difficulty sounding out these words, or you have other reasons to suspect decoding problems, discuss your concerns with her teacher. Simultaneously, request an evaluation from a reading specialist. Also, request the school to screen your child for vision and hearing problems. Don't wait.

The hearing screening should be conducted by trained personnel, using a correctly calibrated audiometer; the vision screening should assess more than your child's ability to read an eye chart from a distance, as this can miss important problems. If the school won't honor your requests, privately have your child's hearing evaluated by an audiologist and her vision evaluated by an ophthalmologist or optometrist. Also read the special education chapters in this book. They describe how to resolve conflicts and the school's obligations to evaluate children for learning disabilities.

Difficulty Understanding What's Read. *Critical Question – Does your child have difficulty understanding what she reads?*

Some kindergartners and first graders have reading comprehension difficulties because their teachers stress word identification but virtually ignore comprehension; consequently, these children haven't learned that the aim of reading is comprehension—understanding—not word calling.

Such children need a balanced reading program, one that extends their word identification and word recognition abilities while stressing comprehension. Fortunately, their comprehension can often be improved by giving them extensive opportunities to discuss interesting stories they've heard or read, and teaching them simple comprehension strategies, like the one in Table 3.2.

TABLE 3.2: A SIMPLE COMPREHENSION STRATEGY

A SIMPLE COMPREHENSION STRATEGY: PREDICTING AND CHECKING
❍ The teacher shows the children the first page of a story, reads its title aloud, asks them what they know about the topic (e.g., snow), and then shows them one or two of the story's pictures.
❍ Then the teacher asks, "What do you think this story is about? …. What do you think will happen?" As he engages the children in discussion, he writes their answers on a flipchart.

○ Then the children read (or listen to the teacher read) the story for about 3 minutes. The teacher then stops them and points to an item on the flipchart. He reads the item. He then says, "Some of you said this would happen. Did it?" He does this for several items.

○ Then the teacher and the children discuss what happened in the story and why.

○ Then the teacher asks the children to keep or revise their predictions about the rest of the story. He records their new predictions on the flipchart.

○ The teacher reads the next few pages aloud, or has the children read them, discusses these pages with them, reviews their predictions, and asks for new ones.

Some children with good intellectual abilities have difficulty with comprehension because they've had limited practice with the English *spoken in schools* and emphasized in school books. Often, their experiences and vocabulary are sparse. For example, they may not know the meaning of *caboose* or *diesel* because they never heard the words, never saw a *caboose* or *diesel*, even in pictures. Such children can benefit greatly from language supports and programs that link vocabulary to interesting experiences directly related to the school's curriculum. Some, whose primary language is not English, will need formal, intensive programs that teach them the kind of English stressed in schools.

Other children have reading comprehension difficulties because they have underlying language and intellectual difficulties, despite a rich array of experiences. Generally, they need extensive language instruction and extra comprehension instruction that emphasizes how to apply specific comprehension strategies. Often, when teachers work with a reading specialist or a speech and language specialist to improve children's listening and speaking skills, children's language improves. For children with language problems, this provides a foundation for improved reading comprehension.

Finally, some children have comprehension problems because they don't have the time and energy to think about what they're reading. They struggle to identify or decode words. Fortunately, their odds of success increase if they're given:

- Direct, explicit, systematic instruction in phonological awareness (especially phonemic awareness), if it's a weakness.[35]
- Direct, explicit, systematic instruction in word identification and word recognition (e.g., applying phonics; applying knowledge of larger sound units, such as word families; developing sight vocabulary).
- Reading materials they find interesting.
- Reading materials on which they can quickly identify 95% to 98% of the words when their teacher works with them (generally, for word identification, this is their instructional level).
- Reading materials on which they can quickly identify 99% of the words when they

work alone (generally, for word identification, this is their independent level).
- Reading materials they can understand if they make moderate effort.
- Lots of easy, interesting reading.

If, however, struggling readers receive little direct instruction in word identification, or unskilled instruction, or are frequently required to read materials above their independent and instructional levels, failure is likely. In such cases, word identification problems impede comprehension and frequently energize resistance to reading.

Although we have described four sets of reasons, the causes of reading comprehension difficulties can be more complex. Some children, for example, have comprehension problems for several of the reasons listed. Plus they may have teachers who play down comprehension instruction or who mistakenly believe that teaching comprehension is simple: Just ask questions to assess understanding. Assessment is not teaching; simply asking questions fails to teach children explicit comprehension strategies as it neither tells nor shows them what they must do to comprehend. Thus, these children are not being taught how to comprehend. The good news is that teachers are becoming increasingly aware of comprehension's importance and how to teach it.

If you suspect that your kindergartner or first grader has reading comprehension difficulties, informally assess the possible causes; this knowledge will help you work with school personnel to develop effective interventions. To see if your child's reading program is balanced, ask her teacher to describe the program, request to observe a lesson or two, and examine the work she brings home. Is it dominated by decoding exercises, or does a fair amount of it stress comprehension? If she routinely gets homework, does it often engage her in enjoyable comprehension tasks, like watching a particular television show to get the gist of what's said, or having you read a story to her?

To see if your child's comprehension problems are caused by underlying language or intellectual difficulties, read a new, age-appropriate book to her and ask her to tell you what it was about. See if she explains the central idea, or gist, using sentence structure and words typical of her age. If she has difficulty with this, read her a page or two from the book and then ask her a few questions whose answers are right on the page. If, for example, the book says "Liam wore two hats," you might ask this literal question: "How many hats did Liam wear?"

You might also ask her to read aloud a section from a story she's recently read in school. Before doing so, review the chart in Table 3.3.

TABLE 3.3: PERCENTAGES FOR WORD IDENTIFICATION LEVELS

PERCENTAGES OF WORDS CORRECTLY IDENTIFIED WITHIN THREE SECONDS
Independent Level: ....99 to 100%
Instructional Level: ....95 to 98%
Uncertain—Perhaps Frustration Level: ....90 to 94%
Frustration Level: ....Less than 90%
Note: If, after three seconds, your child cannot identify a word, tell her to skip it and to keep reading.

As she's reading, silently count each word read correctly in three seconds. Compare this to the total number of words in the section and compute the percentage of words read correctly. Then, look at the chart above and ask yourself: Is she reading at her independent or instructional level? Or is her percentage lower? If lower than 95%, immediately investigate the situation: Instructional changes are probably needed. Why? Because she's probably reading— or struggling—at her frustration level. Regrettably, what many teachers consider children's instructional or independent levels are actually their frustration levels—the levels to avoid.[36]

As always, if you're unsure, but suspect a problem, formally request, in writing, an evaluation from a reading specialist. Save a photocopy of your request. As we've said often, but not often enough, better safe than sorry.

HIGH RISK INSTRUCTIONAL AND PROGRAM FACTORS

If your child has difficulty with any aspect of beginning reading, you need to examine several teacher and program factors. Unfortunately, accurate information about these can be difficult or impossible to get. Nevertheless, you must learn what you can as children's learning situations often cause or intensify their reading difficulties. Moreover, if your child begins to fall behind in reading, focusing on these factors becomes critical as struggling readers have little chance to succeed in reading without quality programs and quality teachers.

Teacher Problems. *Critical Question – Does your child's teacher fail to employ basic principles of effective reading instruction?*

Good teachers can help children with reading difficulties become good readers. In contrast, poor teachers can cause and intensify reading difficulties. As Sharon Walpole and Michael McKenna put it, "many children fail to learn to read because they receive poor instruction."[37]

In addition to answering chapter 2's questions about teachers, answering the questions below will help you determine if your child's receiving high quality instruction. To answer these questions, it's best to see what happens during reading instruction. If you can't, we suggest that you rephrase and use these questions to guide your conversations with your child's teacher, parents of children in the class, and school personnel who often visit the class, like the school's principal or reading specialist. Ideally, each question should earn a "yes."

- Is my child's teacher knowledgeable, skilled, and enthusiastic about reading?
- Is my child's teacher conscientious and flexible? Does he quickly adapt instruction to my child's needs?
- Daily, does my child get 90 minutes or more of reading and writing instruction? (This can include listening to stories, developing vocabulary, browsing though books, decoding unknown words, summarizing stories, writing notes to peers.)
- Are reading and writing woven into different subjects, like art and science, throughout the day?
- Daily, does my child spend considerable time reading materials she finds interesting and easy (independent level) or slightly challenging (instructional level)? If she can't

read words, does she have lots of opportunity to browse through and discuss books and listen to and discuss stories?

- Does the time my child spends reading materials she finds interesting and easy or moderately challenging far outweigh the time she spends on workbook-type exercises?
- If my child has difficulty learning specific words, sounds, or reading strategies, does her teacher adjust instruction to overcome the difficulties? If this doesn't work, does the teacher then teach my child the underlying or prerequisite skills she needs to learn these specific words, sounds, or strategies?
- Does instruction emphasize learning strategies—explicit, sequential steps—my child can use to identify unfamiliar words and comprehend text?
- Daily, when reading, is my child encouraged to apply her new word identification and comprehension abilities?
- Is reading taught to my child in small groups of five or fewer children, several times a week?
- Does the teacher, rather than an aide, provide the bulk of my child's instruction?
- Are reading groups flexible and temporary, so my child has good role models, makes friends with children of different achievement levels, and is not stigmatized for being in a lower achievement group?
- Does the teacher keep daily or weekly records of my child's reading progress?
- Does the teacher have realistic but ambitious expectations for my child?
- Does the teacher treat my child with respect? Does the teacher provide supportive comments and avoid criticizing her when she struggles?
- Is there a systematic, ongoing program to motivate my child when she's doing well and when she's having problems?

To encourage conversation, which, unlike debate, often results in greater understanding and cooperation, politely follow these questions with short, open-ended questions, such as "How?" or tentative comments, such as "I'm not sure I fully understand. If possible, please explain what you mean."

If the answers to your questions are negative, discuss your concerns with your child's teacher. First, listen to learn as much as possible about your child's program, then discuss her needs, and finally, if necessary, problem solve with her teacher. Avoid telling him how to run his class or criticizing him. When problem solving, ask questions that focus on your child's needs: "In class, what can be done to ensure that Alison has lots of chances to apply her new word identification skills?... In class, what can be done to ensure that Alison's not frustrated by what she's asked to read?" The strategies are understanding, not criticizing; discussing, not debating; problem solving, not winning. In later chapters, we'll discuss how to problem solve in small groups and what to do if you disagree with the teacher's program.

Problems with Out-of-the-Box Basal-Reading Programs and Narrowly-Oriented Programs. *Critical Question – Does your child's teacher fail to compensate for the weak-*

nesses of "out-of-the-box" basal-reader programs or narrowly-oriented reading programs like phonics and whole language?

Although reading instruction in many schools and classes is eclectic—teachers knowledgeably mix and match components of different programs and methods and adjust instruction based on children's successes and difficulties—instruction in many other schools and classes is dominated by basal-reader programs, phonics, or whole language. To understand how such dominance might affect your child, *these types of programs* are discussed below.[38]

Basal-reader programs. Basal-reader programs are the most comprehensive, complex, and common "out-of-the-box" commercial programs. To teach reading, they emphasize the use of specific reading books, called basal readers, for specific grades (e.g., first grade, fifth grade), as well as workbooks, skill sheets, software, accessories (e.g., flashcards), book tests, and teacher manuals for particular basal readers. Today, most basal programs for the primary grades support phonics instruction. Some advertise their compatibility with literature and whole language. With each succeeding grade, basal readers and workbooks get more difficult. If you sense that basal programs are like immense, complicated, five-story department stores, you're right.[39]

Although basal-reader programs can provide teachers with structure and reading activities, and can help improve the reading of many children, basal programs, *like all reading programs*, have or are associated with limitations that can cause or intensify reading difficulties, especially in the hands of teachers with little knowledge of reading. Here are six:

Limitation 1. The effectiveness of current basal-reading programs for at-risk or struggling readers has not been assessed by a series of ongoing, large, nationwide programs of rigorous, independent research. Therefore, their effectiveness for teaching such children is uncertain. Moreover, many struggling readers began their struggle with formal reading in basal-reader programs. The lesson is clear: Depending on basal programs *alone* to teach reading to such children is a mistake; it's like depending on medication that has yet to undergo widespread clinical trials.[40]

Limitation 2. Despite having many interesting and well-illustrated selections for children to read, many basal-reading programs do not provide an adequate variety of reading materials at each child's level and for each child's interests; this clashes with the fact that to become good readers, children must read lots and lots of different books they find easy and interesting. Thus, schools must supplement basal programs with extensive classroom and school libraries that offer a wide variety of interesting materials at each child's independent and instructional reading levels[41]—something many schools fail to do.[42]

Limitation 3. Schools often use basal programs inflexibly. Frequently, struggling readers must adapt to basal programs rather than schools adapting basal programs to their needs. Some struggling readers, for example, are in basal programs that advance too quickly and provide inadequate instruction or practice; for other children, the same programs crawl forward slowly and bore them by frequently repeating what they've already mastered. Both situations are destructive.[43]

Limitation 4. For some children, basal programs give inadequate attention to critical reading concepts and activities. In discussing reading programs in general—including basal programs—

Richard Allington, past President of the International Reading Association, asserted, "I've never encountered any product that, by itself, comprises even a full reading curriculum, much less a full literacy curriculum."[44]

Limitation 5. The tests that accompany basal programs often produce scores of questionable accuracy and relevancy. As a result, school personnel might place struggling readers in books that bore or frustrate them and develop lessons that emphasize the wrong skills. Instruction based on inaccurate or irrelevant information can harm rather than help struggling readers. In addition to frustrating or boring them, such instruction can prevent them from enjoying reading and from learning what's needed to become proficient readers.

Limitation 6. Many teachers lack the knowledge needed to adapt their basal-reading programs to children's instructional needs; such teachers tend to follow the manual, not knowing which of its many activities are inappropriate for their students, not knowing which should be stressed, not realizing that the manual—an inanimate object—is oblivious to the needs of their students.[45] Although this can harm all children, it can be especially harmful to struggling readers.

Phonics programs. To teach reading, many teachers and schools depend on commercial phonics programs. We have no trouble with teachers and schools using *quality phonics programs* as long as they recognize that phonics programs are narrowly oriented and should constitute only a fraction of a reading program. Teachers and schools should not depend on phonics programs. Consider the *often-ignored caution* of the Federally-funded National Reading Panel:

> Systematic phonics instruction should be integrated with other reading instruction to create a balanced reading program. Phonics instruction is never a total reading program.... Phonics should not become the dominant component in a reading program, neither in the amount of time devoted to it nor the significance attached.[46]

Note that we italicized the phrase *often-ignored caution*. Why? Because many teachers and schools overemphasize phonics, excluding or downplaying critical aspects of reading, such as comprehension and motivation. As the late Michael Pressley, Distinguished Professor in Teacher Education at Michigan State University, observed:

> Enthusiasm for phonics has often resulted in instruction that *only* covers lower-order word recognition skills (i.e., in contrast to higher-order comprehension and composition skills).... There are primary-level classrooms where there is little time left in the morning schedule after word-level instruction is completed. No one should read this chapter and conclude there is support for such instruction.[47]

And Pressley was right. Overemphasizing phonics, even good phonics programs, can impede progress in reading.

Also note that we used the phrase *quality phonics programs.* We believe that phonics is important, but that many commercial phonics programs are awful. Again, Michael Pressley:

> Quite frankly, many phonics programs ... are dreadful.... [They're] not much more than a collection of skill sheets and drills, providing little information to teachers about the skills that should be developed.[48]

If your child's teacher uses a phonics program, it's important to learn how much of your child's reading program is devoted to phonics, how extensively other components of reading—such as comprehension and motivation—are stressed, and, if she's having difficulty, how her teacher is adjusting her program to eliminate difficulties.

Whole-language programs. The opposite of phonics programs is whole-language programs that depend on immersing children in literature and "real" writing activities (e.g., writing letters to friends) and shunning or minimizing explicit, systematic phonics instruction.

Like all reading programs, whole-language programs have serious weaknesses. First, for philosophical reasons, they usually fail to explicitly and systematically teach children how to sound out unfamiliar words, the very type of instruction many struggling readers need. If they attempt to teach sounding-out strategies, the emphasis is often insufficient for struggling readers. This alone makes them narrowly oriented.

Second, whole-language proponents often disagree about the definition of whole language as well as instructional techniques and strategies.[49] When schools and teachers assert their reading program is whole language, other whole-language proponents may disagree. To say the least, this creates confusion.

Third, many whole-language programs are designed by teachers. Because such programs depend on teachers' knowledge of reading and writing as well as their philosophy, whole-language proponents assume the vast majority of teachers have the knowledge and skill to design and implement effective programs. The evidence doesn't support this.[50]

Fourth, proponents of whole language often assume that teachers have sufficient knowledge of reading disabilities and reading methodology and sufficient time and skill to adapt programs to the needs of struggling readers. Reality, however, often differs.[51]

Finally, independent researchers have yet to produce a large, compelling body of research that supports the superiority of whole language. Although some research suggests it can advance some children's reading comprehension and love of reading, research also suggests that some children find whole-language instruction a barrier to success.

Although many authorities characterize whole language as a philosophy rather than a program, some schools and teachers are ideologically wedded to it just as strongly as others are ideologically wedded to commercial phonics programs. In either case, instructional rigidity—the inability or refusal to adapt instruction to children's needs—hurts children. Thus, if your child's school or teacher is wedded to whole language, you need to ask questions similar to those we recommended for phonics.

A critical question: Can basal, phonics, and whole-language programs be effective? Yes.

The better ones can be. Their effectiveness depends on how and for whom they're used, how they're supplemented, how quickly they're altered or replaced to help at-risk and struggling readers overcome difficulties, how well the changes match the readers' needs, and how quickly additional instruction is given to readers whose progress in poor.

For parents, the important question is not whether these programs are generally good or bad, but the effects on their children. For example, whole language is a barrier to word iden-tification for many at-risk and struggling readers who need an intensive, explicit, systematic program of decoding and comprehension. In contrast, many children with superior decoding skills get bored in programs that emphasize decoding. They, however, often prosper in whole-language programs.[52]

The point is this: The success of any reading program depends on the knowledge and skill of teachers, their willingness and ability to adapt programs to children's needs, and the leeway and support they're given to supplement and adapt programs.[53]

Curriculum Problems. *Critical Question – Does your child's teacher spend a great deal of time "teaching to the test" or rushing through work, just to finish it?*

Despite public denials by many politicians and school administrators, teachers are under enormous pressure to "teach to the test." Often, this leads to narrow, rigid programs, programs unresponsive to the needs of individual children. Often, teachers don't teach what's not tested, even if it's critical to some children.

In some districts, one consequence of "teaching to the test" is the mandate that teachers rig-idly follow a calendar of scripted lessons. The rationale, which we find weak, is that this ensures proper instruction for all students and prepares them to pass the State or district's tests.

Concerned about the effects of such policies, Jonathan Kozol, an exceptionally astute advocate for quality education, told teachers that "very tightly scripted lessons [are] ... prob-ably useful to teachers who aren't very good [but] congeal the soul of wonderful teachers.... We no longer see our children as people with souls and spirits. We see them as products. And we overlook the secrets to unlocking a child's intellect."[54] Similarly, when Debbie Soran quit teaching after 16 years, she was asked why. Her answer: The new requirement—a scripted reading curriculum—was the "last straw." It robbed her of "joy" and her "professional voice in teaching."[55]

Despite the objections of many teachers, the tyranny of testing often compels them to rush through reading lessons at the expense of learning; if children don't learn what's taught, when it's taught, it's not re-taught or reviewed. Often, needed instructional changes are neglected. Pressure to follow particular scripts at particular times on particular days often results in neglect. It angers many teachers, who see themselves forced to ignore their students' needs.[56] It forces teachers to focus on test preparation—activities supported by many publishers but not by a compelling body of research—rather than giving children lots of chances to inde-pendently read easy, interesting materials. When combined, these practices virtually guaran-tee that children at-risk for reading disabilities and struggling readers who need instructional adjustments will continue to struggle and fail.

Two recently coined terms describe children who struggle academically because schools refuse to adjust or change what's taught (curriculum) or how it's taught (methods, instructional strategies): *curriculum casualty* and *instructionally disabled*. These terms are sad commentaries on instruction in some schools. In the last sentence the word *some* was used. It was used because schools and teachers differ. Many do put children's needs before the pressure to focus on tests and to unreflectively and irresponsibly rush through instruction at a predetermined pace. If your child is struggling, however, you can't just hope that her teacher puts children's needs first; you can't depend on luck—you need to find out what's happening in her class.

Instructional Problems. *Critical Question – Are instructional problems causing or adding to my child's reading difficulties?*

This question can be addressed by answering the questions below. Clearly, some of them overlap with previous discussions and questions. That's okay—overlap among teacher problems, curriculum problems, and instructional problems is expected. They're highly related. Thus, you may want to combine all our lists of questions into one master list.

Use our questions as a guide for observations, record reviews, discussions, and reflections. Use them to learn what's happening, not as weapons to interrogate or criticize. If you find difficulties, you might rephrase our questions and share some of your answers—respectfully, skillfully, and diplomatically—with your child's teacher. Although it's possible that he may get defensive, it's also possible that he'll welcome your information and use it to improve instruction. Ideally, each question should earn a "yes."

- Is the number of students in my child's class small enough for the teacher to give her the attention she needs?
- Are the other children in the class good role models? Does my child get along with them?
- Do the school and the class have the resources needed to help my child become a successful reader?
- Do the materials and tasks given to my child match her instructional and independent reading levels? Is she comfortable reading at these levels?
- If my child has difficulties, are instructional practices and materials quickly changed or adjusted to eliminate difficulties and help her make substantial progress?
- Are lots of appropriate, interesting reading materials, at various reading levels, readily available?
- Does my child get lots of daily practice applying newly learned skills, knowledge, and strategies to interesting reading materials?
- Is instruction explicit? Does the teacher explain and model what he teaches, including what my child should say to herself when applying new knowledge, skills, and strategies?
- Does my child have lots of opportunities to interact with peers in structured learning situations?
- Is instruction aimed at eliminating or minimizing the current causes of my child's reading difficulties?

- Is the pace of instruction quick enough to interest my child, but measured enough to avoid frustration?
- Does my child get extra, expert reading instruction, closely coordinated with her in-class instruction?
- If my child gets homework, is it interesting work that she can complete in less than 15 minutes, without difficulty?
- If my child gets homework, does it emphasize actual reading instead of busywork? (Actual reading: "Read this story, which you read so well in class, to your parents" or "Have your parents read this story to you." Busywork: "Copy these sentences 5 times.")
- Has my child received a high quality reading evaluation? If so, is instruction consistent with its findings and recommendations?
- Does the school quickly give my child and her teacher whatever support they need?
- Does my child get enough emotional and reading support in class?
- Is my child's progress in reading carefully monitored at least once a week? (Chapter 7 is devoted to monitoring.)
- Is information about my child's progress in reading sent to me frequently? Is the meaning carefully explained?

WHAT TO DO

If you think your child is at risk for reading disabilities, or you see her struggling with reading, stay calm and do three things: Learn all you can, ask about Response to Intervention (RTI), and make specific written requests.

Learn All You Can. By learning all you can about reading disabilities and how to use State and Federal education laws to help your child, the better you can help her. Having considerable knowledge about reading disabilities will help you make relevant, focused requests and will help you monitor her progress. Knowing the intent and the provisions of the laws will improve your chances of getting the services she needs, especially if her school refuses to provide them. When dealing with reading disabilities, knowledge is as important as air—you need it to ensure your child's academic success.

Ask About Response to Intervention (RTI). Although RTI is part of the *Individuals with Disabilities Education Improvement Act of 2004* (IDEA-2004), it serves both students with and *without* disabilities. In part, its purpose is to prevent both learning disabilities and unnecessary referrals to special education. It does this by screening all students for learning disabilities, such as reading disabilities, and instructing students at risk for learning disabilities with scientifically-based interventions targeted at remediating their difficulties.[57] It requires schools to frequently monitor the effects of such instruction on each student's progress and, if progress is poor, to provide the student with more intensive services, such as extra instruction, instruction in small groups, or individual tutoring. Thus, to receive RTI services, your child does not have to be eligible for special education.

IDEA-2004 does not require schools to offer RTI services. Nor does it require schools to use the same RTI model, eligibility standards for services, and instructional strategies. Consequently, it's important to ask school personnel if their school offers RTI and to explain how it works. If it's offered, we suggest that you consider RTI as part of a reading evaluation, but not a substitute for what we recommend about evaluations in this and subsequent chapters.

As we discuss in chapter 9, RTI is fraught with potential problems that have yet to be fully understood. Nevertheless, it has one major advantage over the old way that schools typically evaluated reading disabilities. The old way had students fail for many years before providing reading interventions. Ideally, RTI immediately offers quality interventions, evaluates their effectiveness, and adjusts instruction to overcome unforeseen difficulties. During this period, the student can also receive a formal reading evaluation.

Make Written Requests. Request a comprehensive reading evaluation that includes diagnostic teaching and in-class observations of her during reading and related instruction (e.g., science). Diagnostic teaching can identify which instructional strategies are effective for her. Observations can identify specific environmental and instructional factors that impede her learning and which might, if strengthened, improve it.

Also request that a qualified reading specialist provide extra reading instruction daily. This is not premature—it may take more than a month to complete the evaluation. In the meantime, your child may languish. Moreover, the results of instruction can provide valuable information to the evaluator.

For your child to get the most out of this instruction, it must be coordinated with what's taught to her in her general education class and how it's taught.[58] Failure to coordinate extra reading instruction with in-class instruction may confuse her, hindering progress.

If you cannot get the direct teaching services of a reading specialist, ask that one monitor your child's program and frequently meet with her staff to plan instruction. Instruction must focus on improving all underlying factors *currently* contributing to her difficulty (e.g., phonemic awareness or expressive language difficulties) and her specific reading difficulties (e.g., sounding out words).

The concept of *extra* daily reading instruction is important. Some schools, for example, offer pull-out reading instruction in which children at risk for reading disabilities and struggling readers leave their general or special education class for reading instruction. Often, this is not *extra* instruction; it's substitute instruction. Children at risk and struggling readers need much more than this. They need in-class reading instruction that effectively focuses on their needs, with materials they can comfortably handle, and *extra* reading instruction that supports and extends in-class reading instruction.

Waiting to see if reading improves by itself—without an evaluation and extra instruction that's carefully coordinated with your child's in-class reading instruction—wastes precious time. Children do not outgrow reading disabilities; without immediate help, they continue to fall further behind their peers. As at-risk children and struggling readers see their peers achieving and they see themselves falling further and further behind, anger, discouragement, demoralization, and other negative emotions begin to dominate, diminishing the likelihood of reading success. As the late Carrie Rozelle, founder of the National Center for Learning Disabilities, said of her son:

> Because he couldn't read he developed emotional problems.... He had difficulties with his brothers.... His books were torn up. There were lots of tears, lots of shouting, lots of anger.[59]

Simply put—don't wait. Make formal written requests for a reading diagnosis and for extra instruction.

KEEP IN MIND

We recommend that you keep in mind two warnings. They may sound counterproductive and counterintuitive, but following them may save you lots of time and prevent lots of grief. Simply put, don't waste time looking for the original cause and don't waste time looking for or demanding the best method or program. We'll explain.

Don't Waste Time Looking for the Original Cause. Professionals rarely know the original or exact cause of a child's reading disabilities. Some highly credentialed people, however, will claim they know; often, they have something to sell. Unless a clearly identified sensory or medical problem exists that fully and verifiably explains the problem, don't believe them—most serious reading disabilities have multiple causes, including invisible and historical ones. For example, you can't go back in time to see your child's class when she first started having difficulties. You may think you know what happened in her class, but unless you observed and took notes, you're probably wrong. And even if you're right, you probably missed other causal factors.

So, in most cases, you'll never know the original causes of your child's reading disabilities. Despite a strong feeling that you ought to know, it's usually not important. Surgeons don't need to know how a leg was broken to set it, and reading specialists don't need to know the original causes of children's reading disabilities to help them become highly proficient, highly motivated readers. To establish rapid rates of learning, reading specialists and teachers need to design reading programs that match children's current abilities, needs, and interests. To ensure progress, reading specialists and teachers need to continuously monitor children's progress and, at the first sign of difficulty, make responsive adjustments. This is far more important than knowing the original causes.

Don't Waste Time Looking For or Demanding the Best Method or Program. There's no *best* method or *best* program for teaching reading to at-risk or struggling readers. Why? Because children differ from one another, as do teachers. What works for one doesn't work for another. You may have heard from many parents and newspaper stories that whole language is terrible and that struggling readers learn only through intensive Orton-Gillingham (OG) phonics instruction. After all, OG worked for Nadine's child. But this simple logic—it's great because it worked for Nadine's child—is flawed. It ignores four very critical facts.

First, in educationally relevant ways, your child may differ from Nadine's. Second, it may not match the teacher's philosophy; forcing a teacher to use OG may demoralize him and provoke resistance. Third, the teacher may not be knowledgeable about or skilled in using OG. For a teacher highly motivated to master OG, developing adequate knowledge and skill may take years. Finally, research has yet to prove the clear superiority of any method—all have weaknesses. Thus, what was said about OG can be said about whole language, basal-reader programs, or any other method. That's why it's so important to continuously monitor progress and, if needed, make instructional adjustments.

Although many methods work for some children and teachers, all methods have weaknesses that require teachers to adapt them to the individual student's needs. Instead of focusing exclusively on the method, focus on factors most likely to influence reading success. Examine the questions listed in this chapter under Teacher Problems and Instructional Problems.

CHAPTER 3: CHECKLIST

BEGINNING READING INSTRUCTION: DOES MY CHILD HAVE DIFFICULTIES?

Your child has or is highly likely to have reading disabilities if she has difficulty recognizing letters and words, figuring out unknown words, or understanding what she hears or reads.

In addition to helping you determine if your child has or is at risk for reading disabilities, this list can help you begin to identify what needs to be stressed or changed in your child's reading program. But remember, this is an *informal* list and should be used only as a guide to identify possible difficulties. If you answer "Maybe" to any question, seek professional help to better understand your child's reading skills. If you check "Yes" to any question, meet with school personnel or other highly qualified professionals to better understand the situation and to begin devising a plan of action likely to increase your child's reading abilities. Whatever you do, if you check a "Yes," don't wait for your child to outgrow the difficulties or for your child's teacher to improve; the odds are against you and your child. You need to take informed action, now.

Compared to her classmates or children her age, does my child have difficulties:

○ Understanding concepts-about-print? Yes ☐ No ☐ Maybe ☐
○ Recognizing and naming letters? Yes ☐ No ☐ Maybe ☐
○ Recognizing and manipulating sounds
   (phonological awareness)? Yes ☐ No ☐ Maybe ☐
○ Understanding what is read aloud? Yes ☐ No ☐ Maybe ☐

Compared to her classmates or children her age, does my child have difficulties:

○ Paying attention in class? Yes ☐ No ☐ Maybe ☐

continues ...

○	On reading readiness or other reading tests?	Yes ☐	No ☐	Maybe ☐

Compared to her classmates or children her age, does my child have difficulties:

○	Identifying basic sight words?	Yes ☐	No ☐	Maybe ☐
○	Figuring out unknown words?	Yes ☐	No ☐	Maybe ☐
○	Understanding most of what she reads?	Yes ☐	No ☐	Maybe ☐

Does my child's teacher:

○	Lack the knowledge, skill, and enthusiasm needed to teach my child to read?	Yes ☐	No ☐	Maybe ☐
○	Fail to compensate for the weaknesses of reading programs?	Yes ☐	No ☐	Maybe ☐
○	Spend lots of time teaching to the test?	Yes ☐	No ☐	Maybe ☐
○	Move too quickly or slowly through the curriculum?	Yes ☐	No ☐	Maybe ☐
○	Frustrate rather than challenge my child?	Yes ☐	No ☐	Maybe ☐

ENDNOTES

---

1 "According to Poyner and Wolfe, the standardized reading curriculum eliminates the independence and flexibility of teachers to meet the needs of individual students and instead focuses on providing scripted lessons to groups of students with little concern for individual differences" (Yasik, A. E., 2007. Book review of Leslie Poyner and Pamela Wolfe's Marketing Fear in America's Public Schools: The Real War on Literacy. *Reading & Writing Quarterly: Overcoming Learning Difficulties, 23* (4), 417-423, p. 418). As a consequence, many children suffer needlessly.

2 The factors discussed in chapter 2 include your child's ability to understand oral language, to express herself, to pay attention, to follow directions, to remember things, to learn new concepts. You can find the list at the end of chapter 2.

3 Concepts-about-print is also called concepts *of* print.

4 We use the term letter recognition to mean that the child can point to a letter when someone names it; this is not as difficult as letter naming, which means that the child can name the letter when she sees it. The quicker the child can accurately name letters, the better: "Letter-name knowledge not only predicts reading acquisition but may also serve as an indicator of the intensity of remediation required to prevent reading failure among at-risk children.... Like letter-name knowledge, letter-naming fluency [the speed with which children accurately name letters] is associated with reading achievement and is a powerful predictor of later reading proficiency" (Rathvon, N., 2004. *Early Reading Assessment: A Practitioner's Handbook.* New York: The Guilford Press, p. 122).

[5] Rathvon, 2004.

[6] Catts, H. W., & Hogan, T. P., 2003. Language basis of reading disabilities and implications for early identification and remediation. *Reading Psychology, 24* (3), 223–246, pp. 226-227.

[7] Ehri, L., 2004. Teaching phonemic awareness and phonics: An explanation of the National Reading Panel meta-analysis. In P. McCardle & V. Chhabra (Eds.), *The Voice of Evidence in Reading Research* (pp. 153-186). New York: The Guilford Press, p. 165.

[8] Schools often have school nurses administer hearing screenings. For many children, this is satisfactory. However, if subtle hearing problems are suspected, evaluations are best done by an audiologist with a Certificate of Clinical Competence (CCC) from the American Speech and Hearing Association (ASHA).

[9] Sharon Walpole and Michael McKenna recommend that phonemic awareness instruction for kindergarteners and first graders "constitute 10 or 15 minutes of the literacy block and … be delivered to small groups, perhaps four to five children…. [Some children would need it for] part of the year, and a few [would need] more time" (Walpole, S., & Mckenna, M. C., 2007. *Differentiated Reading Instruction: Strategies for the Primary Grades.* New York: The Guilford Press, p. 36). In general, we agree. The children for whom we're recommending additional time with a specialist or a highly trained teacher are those for whom Walpole and McKenna's recommendations prove insufficient.

[10] Your child's teacher may not know much about phonological awareness instruction. Although consultation by a speech and language specialist or a reading specialist can help teachers, effective consultation takes considerable time, time your child cannot afford to lose. Moreover, in many schools, consultation is not available—for the most part, teachers are on their own. Thus we recommend additional instruction by a specialist.

[11] Syllables have two parts. The first part, the onset, is the part before the vowel. In the word *sit*, /s/ is the onset. The second part, the rime (not rhyme), refers to the vowel and consonants that follow. In *sit*, /it/ is the rime. Some teachers and specialists refer to rimes as patterns or phonograms.

[12] David Chard and Shirley Dickson offer a sequence of difficulty that may help you and school personnel find the right sound unit and the right skills. As you will see below, their sequence starts with the bigger units of sound and moves toward the smaller units, starts with the less complex and moves to the more complex:

- Rhyming songs [Biggest unit, least complex]
- Sentence segmentation
- Syllable segmentation and blending
- Onset-rime (parts of a syllable), blending, and segmentation
- Blending and segmenting individual phonemes [Smallest unit, most complex]
  (Chard, D. J., & Dickson, S. V., 1999. Phonological awareness: Instructional and assessment guidelines. *Intervention in School and Clinic, 34* (5), 261-270.)

[13] Ehri, 2004.

[14] We don't know why this is so. Linnea Ehri and Simone Nunes hypothesize that children may be more motivated in small groups and that small groups give them more opportunities to observe one another (Ehri, L. C., & Nunes, S. R., 2002. The role of phonemic awareness in learning to read.

In A. E. Farstrup & S. J. Samuels (Eds.), *What Research Has to Say About Reading Instruction* (pp. 110-139). Newark, DE: International Reading Association).

[15] No one can authoritatively tell you how long it will take your child to become proficient in phonological awareness. It may take two months, six months, a year, even more. Monitoring progress is key to determining if more instruction is needed. Keep in mind, however, that despite high quality instruction, some children make little progress. If, after several months of highly individualized, quality instruction that knowledgeably responds to your child's needs, she continues to struggle, we recommend that you meet with school personnel to determine if phonological awareness instruction should continue, the form it should take, or if it's time to try reading instruction that might minimize its importance. We speculate that Grace Fernald's Visual-Auditory-Kinesthetic-Tactile (VAKT) approach is such an alternative (Many textbooks describe this approach. One recently published description is found in McCormick, S., 2003. *Instructing Students Who Have Literacy Problems* (4th ed.). Upper Saddle River, NJ: Pearson Merrill Prentice Hall, pp. 438-440.)

[16] Howard Margolis and Patrick P. McCabe examined the literature on task difficulty. They reported the following: "Giving struggling readers tasks on which success is likely improves their academic prospects ... and influences their behavior. Gunter and Reed ... found that when students with emotional and behavioral disorders had the skills and knowledge needed to succeed on a task, correct responses increased and disruptive behavior decreased. Similarly, Gambrell, Wilson, and Gantt ... found that when students read assignments with minimal errors—assignments that were not frustrating—off-task behavior decreased" (Margolis, H., & McCabe, P. P., 2006. Motivating struggling readers in an era of mandated instructional practices. *Reading Psychology, 27* (5), 435-455, p. 441).

[17] We based this definition on one from an excellent dictionary of reading and writing: Harris, T. L., & Hodges, R. E. (Eds.), 1995. *The Literacy Dictionary: The Vocabulary of Reading and Writing.* Newark, DE: International Reading Association. If your local library does not have this dictionary, consider asking the librarian to order it. Over the years, it should prove invaluable.

[18] The *Mental Measurements Yearbook* is a comprehensive, widely respected source of test reviews. Here's the reference for the 2007 edition: Geisinger, K. F., Spies, R. A., Carlson, J. F., & Plake, B. S. (Eds.), 2007. *The Seventeenth Mental Measurements Yearbook.* Lincoln, NB: Buros Institute of Mental Measurements, University of Nebraska Press.

[19] For older children, for whom extensive, quality remediation has proven ineffective, it's often better to focus on teaching them how to compensate for their weaknesses. For example, if a 15-year old with good oral language abilities has had extensive, quality instruction in decoding unknown words, but has progressed to only a second-grade level, instruction should probably emphasize how to use text-to-speech software like Flamereader and TextAloud, which read electronic files (e.g., computer screens) aloud and can create files for MP3 players. Free limited editions of Flamereader and TextAloud are available at www.download.com.

[20] Joseph K. Torgesen, Professor of Psychology and Education at Florida State University and Director of the Florida Center for Reading Research, is a preeminent researcher on preventing and remediating reading disabilities. Recently he debunked the myth that children outgrow reading difficulties: "The evidence is in: The children who we hoped would be 'late bloomers' in reading rarely are. Their early and modest reading weakness impedes enjoyment and deters practice. Soon, their small

reading problems spiral into devastating ones" (Torgesen, J. K., 2004. Preventing early reading failure—and its devastating downward spiral: The evidence for early intervention. *American Educator*; retrieved 1/18/05, from http://www.ld.org/newsltr/0105newsltr/0105Feature3.cfm). Like the vast majority of reading authorities, Torgesen is an advocate for early, intensive, informed intervention.

[21] The technical term for this is *automaticity*, which *The Literacy Dictionary* defines as the "fluent processing of information that requires little effort or attention, as sight-word recognition" (Harris & Hodges, 1995, p. 16). Although many teachers help struggling readers identify words accurately, they fail to help them identify words quickly or automatically, in a fraction of a second.

During the first year of instruction, many good readers read sentences slowly, in a slightly choppy manner. By the end of second grade or the beginning of third, they begin to read passages of appropriate difficulty far more fluently.

[22] Most beginning reading programs use reading books that are geared to meet the reading abilities of average readers in the grade for which the book is geared. In first and second grades, these books, often called basal readers, emphasize the mastery of basic or common sight words, such as *a, an, up, go, the,* and *said.*

[23] Good readers are expected to learn far more sight words than just *basic* ones. For example, the New Jersey Reading Standards state that "by the end of Grade 1, students will develop a vocabulary of 300-500 high-frequency sight words and phonetically regular words…. By the end of Grade 2, students will develop a vocabulary of 500-800 regular and irregular sight words" (http://www.state.nj.us/education). Thus, to have a realistic understanding of your child's achievements, it's critical that you know what the State expects of her. Keep in mind, however, that individual districts may expect and require more.

[24] Actually, if they routinely struggle, the materials or tasks are too difficult and should be changed.

[25] Some authorities recommend that you wait five seconds. Unfortunately, there's not a compelling body of research to support three seconds or five.

[26] Some authorities would credibly argue that two seconds is too much time, that when reading, children must recognize words far more quickly. We're using two seconds as a rough gauge for parents to test their children.

[27] Although the developmental sequence is fairly firm, the time a child reaches a particular stage (or phase) may depend on her class' curriculum, the State's standards, and the leeway or ambiguity in the State's standards. For example, New Jersey's standards state that "by the end of Grade 1, students will decode regular one-syllable words and nonsense words (e.g., sit, zot) [and] use letter-sound correspondence knowledge to sound out unknown words when reading text…. By the end of Grade 2, students will decode regular multisyllable words and parts of words (e.g., capital, Kalamazoo)" (http://www.state.nj.us/education.). These standards offer great leeway.

[28] Walpole & Mckenna, 2007, p. 101.

[29] For most struggling readers in kindergarten and the primary grades, word identification and decoding, not comprehension, are their primary problems. Simply put, "the most salient problem for many poor readers is that they do not decode well" (Pressley, M., 2006. *Reading Instruction that Works: The Case for Balanced Teaching.* New York: The Guilford Press, p. 81). And without good decoding skills, and a large sight vocabulary, comprehension suffers.

[30] In the word unhappiness, *un* is the prefix, *happy* is the root word, and *ness* is the suffix. *Un* means not and *ness* means state or condition. Thus, unhappiness means a state or condition of not being happy.

[31] Graves, M. F., Juel, C., & Graves, B. B., 2007. *Teaching Reading in the 21st Century* (4th ed.). Boston: Pearson, Allyn & Bacon, p. 93.

[32] Daly, E. J., III, Chafouleas, S., & Skinner, C. H., 2005. *Interventions for Reading Problems: Designing and Evaluating Effective Strategies.* New York: The Guilford Press, p. 24.

[33] Savage, J. F., 2007. *Sound It Out! Phonics in a Comprehensive Reading Program* (3rd ed.). Boston: McGraw Hill, p. 9.

[34] McCormick, 2003, p. 221.

[35] The phrase systematic instruction is used frequently in reading instruction. The Florida Center for Reading Research provides an excellent definition: "Systematic instruction refers to a carefully planned sequence for instruction, similar to a builder's blueprint for a house. A blueprint is carefully thought out and designed before building materials are gathered and construction begins. The plan for systematic instruction is carefully thought out, strategic, and designed before activities and lessons are developed.... For systematic instruction, lessons build on previously taught information, from simple to complex, with clear, concise student objectives that are driven by ongoing assessment. Students are provided appropriate practice opportunities which directly reflect instruction" (Retrieved 11/13/07, from ww.fcrr.org/instruction/faq.htm#1).

[36] If she's read the material several times in school, and the materials were taught to her, she should correctly identify 99% of the words.

[37] Walpole & Mckenna, 2007, p. 164.

[38] The reason we used the phrase *these types of programs* is that schools use many different kinds of basal-reader programs, phonics programs, and whole-language programs. Phonics programs, for example, can differ dramatically from one another. Here's how the Federally-funded National Reading Panel described different phonics programs. Before reading this, take a deep breath: "In teaching phonics explicitly and systematically, several different instructional approaches have been used. These include synthetic phonics, analytic phonics, embedded phonics, analogy phonics, onset-rime phonics, and phonics through spelling. Although all explicit, systematic phonics approaches use a planned, sequential introduction of a set of phonic elements along with teaching and practice of those elements, they differ across a number of other features. For example, the content covered ranges from a limited to an elaborate set of letter-sound correspondences and phonics generalizations. In addition, the application procedures taught to children vary. Synthetic phonics programs teach children to convert letters into sounds or phonemes and then blend the sounds to form recognizable words. Analytic phonics avoids having children pronounce sounds in isolation to figure out words. Rather children are taught to analyze letter-sound relations once the word is identified. Phonics-through-spelling programs teach children to transform sounds into letters to write words. Phonics in context approaches teach children to use sound-letter correspondences along with context cues to identify unfamiliar words they encounter in text. Analogy phonics programs teach children to use parts of written words they already know to identify new words. The distinctions between systematic phonics approaches are not absolute, however, and some phonics programs combine two or more of these types of instruction. In addition, these approaches differ

with respect to the extent that controlled vocabulary (decodable text) is used for practicing reading connected text" (*Report of the National Reading Panel: Teaching Children to Read: An Evidence Based Assessment of the Scientific Research Literature on Reading and its Implications for Reading Instruction*. NIH Publication No. 00-4769. Washington, DC: U.S. Government Printing Office, p. 2-89). The differences among phonics programs are no greater than the differences among basal-reader and whole-language programs.

39 Publishers also change their basal-reader programs, depending on what's most marketable. Much depends on the requirements of larger States, like California and Texas. In one sales cycle, publishers may emphasize whole language and de-emphasize phonics, or vice versa. Right now, many publishers are de-emphasizing whole language and emphasizing phonics.

40 Although this limitation deals with basal-reader programs, we have yet to find a compelling body of research demonstrating that any commercial or packaged reading program is *consistently* and *highly* effective with a wide variety of children, *including* struggling readers. Thus, it was not surprising that in 2008 Johns Hopkins University School of Education's *Best Evidence Encyclopedia* reported that for upper elementary grades, middle school grades, and high school grades, no commercial reading programs demonstrated strong evidence of effectiveness. Many widely used programs, like Harcourt, Houghton Mifflin, and Wilson Reading demonstrated "insufficient evidence of effectiveness" or were not supported by qualifying studies (retrieved 1/3/2009, from www.bestevidence.org).

41 A child's independent level is the level of materials she can read without difficulty and without a teacher's help. Her instructional reading level is the level of materials she can read successfully with instruction and ongoing support from the teacher.

42 Richard Allington and Patricia Cunningham, two eminent reading authorities, assert that in order to become proficient, highly motivated readers, children need to read lots of easy, interesting books. Classroom libraries are key to this. Sadly, they often fall far short of the mark: "Well-designed classroom libraries work to increase the amount of reading that children do.... This wider reading results in better readers.... But most classroom libraries (90 percent) are not well designed nor well stocked.... Too often, classroom libraries have too few books, too little planning of the display, and little variety in either the difficulty or the types of books in the collections.... Children who find learning to read difficult are unlikely to find books in their classroom libraries that they can read comfortably.... Yet enormous amounts of easy and interesting reading are absolutely essential to developing effective reading strategies, to say nothing of appropriate attitudes and responses. When children struggle with the material they are reading, they cannot apply the strategies that good readers use, and they do not develop the habits and attitudes that good readers do" (Allington, R. L., & Cunningham, P. M., 2007. *Schools That Work: Where All Children Read and Write* (3rd ed.). Boston: Pearson, Allyn & Bacon, pp. 63-64).

43 Despite appearances, teachers may not be at fault. In some cases, schools mandate that teachers follow a specific schedule. For example, on Tuesday, November 13, 2008, all 1st-grade teachers may be mandated to follow script 23 for pages 12-19 in the Forest Book. As Gerald Duffy, an outstanding expert on reading, asserts, such practices block teachers from meeting the needs of all children: "We've learned that powerful strategy lessons cannot be scripted in the sense that a teacher can simply read the lesson from the manual. Effective teachers modify the explicit instruction they offer

from moment to moment based on the responses of the students they are teaching" (Duffy, G. G., 2003. *Explaining Reading*. New York: The Guilford Press, p. xiii).

44 Allington, R. L., December 2005/January 2006. What counts as evidence in evidence-based education? *Reading Today, 23* (3), 16.

45 In a sense, commercial basal programs (and phonics programs) are not entirely at fault. Expecting inanimate programs to know children and to make decisions about their needs is asking too much. A program is only a tool. And like any tool, it depends on the artisan. In the mind and hands of Michelangelo, a chisel produced the Statue of David. Lesser minds and hands have produced rubble.

46 National Reading Panel, 2000, p. 2-136.

47 Pressley, 2006, p. 180, italics added.

48 Pressley, 2006, p. 178.

49 Pressley, 2006, p. 17.

50 Dorothy Strickland, one of the nation's leading scholars on reading, noted that "Unlike a parent, who usually deals with one child at a time ... teachers find themselves in classrooms with as many as 30 or more students, all with varying needs and abilities. They ask how a single teacher can apply whole language principles with so many diverse individuals. In response, of course, one can point to the many teachers who are doing just that. Conversely, there are many others who will probably never be willing, because of philosophical differences, or [capability] of doing so.... Tremendous staff development [is] required to make the far-reaching changes asked of some teachers who wish to move toward whole language" (Strickland, D., 1995. Commentary on Whole Language found in Harris & Hodges, *The Literacy Dictionary*, 1995, p. 280).

51 In reviewing the research on the preparation of teachers to teach reading, Graham Neuhaus and his colleagues found that "many teachers do not have the knowledge and skills necessary to adequately teach reading" (Neuhaus, G. F., Roldan, L. W., Boulware-Gooden, R., & Swank, P. R., 2006. Parsimonious reading models: Identifying teachable subskills. *Reading Psychology, 27* (1), 37-58, p. 52).

52 After reviewing some of the more important research on reading instruction, Michael Pressley concluded that "students differ with respect to how much explicit decoding instruction they need— with the weaker readers benefiting more from decoding instruction, and the stronger readers benefiting more from holistic reading and writing" (Pressley, 2006, p. 180).

53 John Savage, Professor Emeritus of Education from Boston College, emphasized this point, a point you must remember when trying to prevent or remediate reading disabilities: "The teacher remains the key to effective classroom reading instruction. 'Time and time again, research has confirmed that regardless of the quality of a program, resource, or strategy, it is the teacher and learning situation that makes the difference'(International Reading Association, 2002)" (Savage, 2007, p. 183).

54 The Wisconsin Education Association, 2000 Convention; retrieved 1/26/06, from http://www.weac. org/News/2000-01/oct00/kozol.htm.

55 Winans, D., 2005. It's hard to stick around. *NEA Today, 23* (8), 41.

56 Howard Margolis and Patrick P. McCabe summarized one such incident reported in the New York Times: "Recently, in New York City, teacher perceptions of instructional rigidity reached a boiling point. The *New York Times* reported that teachers picketed the office of a regional superintendent

'over mandates they said had restricted their ability to teach, including minute-by-minute rules on conducting lessons.' In response to teacher chants of 'Let teachers teach!' the city's Deputy Chancellor for Education charged, 'We have been letting teachers teach for the last 40 years . . . and the kids haven't been getting where they need to be'" (Margolis & McCabe, 2006, p. 435). As a teacher of many New York City teachers, Howard has often heard them vehemently express resentment at having to follow a rigid calendar of scripts in a rigid manner. This, they believe, hurts their students. It slows the progress of higher-achieving students and overwhelms the lower-achieving ones.

[57] Many methods and programs that publishers and schools call "scientifically based" are supported by very little if any direct scientific evidence. Chapter 9 discusses this in detail.

[58] In schools, the phrases regular education class and general education class are often used interchangeably as are regular education teacher and general education teacher.

[59] Hevesi, D., 2007 November 12. Carrie Rozelle, 69, child advocate, dies; started a center for learning disabilities. *The New York Times*; retrieved 11/12/07, from http://www.nytimes.com/2007/11/12/us/12rozelle.html?.

CHAPTER 4
DIFFICULTIES IN SECOND GRADE AND ABOVE

To fully understand your child's reading difficulties, keep in mind everything we've said about beginning reading difficulties. Why? Because the difficulties we discussed in chapters 2 and 3 may still plague him. He may struggle with phonological awareness, or sight vocabulary, or decoding, or reading comprehension, or all of these and more. And he may be in an inflexible reading program that doesn't adjust instruction to his needs. Likely, this will frustrate and demoralize him.

Although this chapter reexamines some of the concepts in chapter 3—beginning reading problems—its emphasis differs. It's more focused on what children in grades two and above must do to succeed in reading. Knowing this will help you understand what a reading evaluation should assess. Regrettably, many reading evaluations ignore or superficially assess critical areas. Consequently, this chapter uses what we call the seven critical components of reading to explain what a reading evaluation should assess.[1] By knowing this, you'll understand if your child's program is built on a solid foundation, one you can *probably* trust—*temporarily*—to help him become a proficient, motivated reader.

Perhaps you wondered about the words *probably* and *temporarily*. We hope so. They convey two important but often ignored messages. The first, *probably*, means that educational (and psychological) evaluations can recommend what's *likely* to work. But *likely* means *uncertain*. Whereas chemists know for sure that mixing acids and bases will neutralize both, teachers can never be certain about a child's reactions to particular teaching methods. And teaching methods that were effective during a reading evaluation may prove ineffective in class. What's effective on Monday may be ineffective on Tuesday. Why? Perhaps the teacher is unfamiliar with the method. Perhaps her class has too many children. Perhaps, in class, the child is too anxious and distracted. Perhaps, during the evaluation, the child worked harder than usual. Perhaps on Tuesday his parents got into a terrible scream fest. Perhaps. Perhaps. Perhaps....

The second message, *temporarily*, refers to the evaluation's recommendations. If they prove successful, they become obsolete. By mastering his previous weaknesses, the child now needs different instruction, instruction that uses more advanced materials and emphasizes more advanced skills, concepts, and learning strategies. If, on the other hand, several weeks of expertly implementing the recommendations produces poor progress, all or part of the evaluation was likely incomplete or wrong. If so, it should be supplemented or abandoned.

This doesn't mean the evaluators were incompetent. It means that the best evaluations produce only educated guesses—hypotheses—about what will and won't work. More often than not, evaluations are accurate if knowledgeable, skilled specialists use quality measures and procedures to assess all critical needs. In such situations, inaccuracies, if any, are usually modest.

In essence, the best evaluations simply narrow possibilities; they identify what's likely—but not certain—to work. Don't let this uncertainty discourage you. Conceptually, there's a simple solution: The reading specialist and your child's teachers must continually monitor his progress, so, if needed, they can adjust instruction—quickly. That's why we devoted chapter 7 to one topic: monitoring.

Despite the temporary nature of formal reading evaluations, they're needed to figure out where to begin instruction. By zeroing in on critical questions—What are the child's instructional and independent levels? What does he know? What does he need to learn? What approaches and instructional strategies will likely produce success?—they dramatically improve the odds of success. As Eldon Ekwall and James Shanker made clear, "A thorough [reading] diagnosis is a prerequisite for the beginning remedial program."[2] Anything else is a blindfolded effort that shrinks the odds of success.

EXAMINE THE SEVEN COMPONENTS OF READING

Although not every reading evaluation needs to formally and thoroughly evaluate *the seven components of reading*, each component should be systematically considered to see if it should be evaluated thoroughly.[3]

The logic used to identify the seven components is straightforward. It answers the question: What do struggling readers have to *know* and *do* and *believe* to read successfully? A weakness in any of these areas can create serious reading disabilities. Here are the answers.

Sight Vocabulary. To successfully read fourth-grade materials, struggling readers must learn to reliably identify thousands of words quickly and effortlessly, without conscious analysis. Such words, identified within a second, are called *sight* words.[4]

Sight words form two categories: basic and other sight words. Basic sight words include common, high-frequency words that often comprise 50% or more of the words in a paragraph (e.g., *am, in, but, how, may, take, that*), including small abstract words with irregular spellings that cannot be sounded out by pronouncing the usual or highly predictable sounds of their letters (e.g., *the, was, come, have, said*).[5]

Other sight words are found just about everywhere. They're in newspapers, novels, and subject matter books, like books for health (e.g., *disease, plague*), science (e.g., *mammal, vertebrate*) and social studies (e.g., *epoch, revolution*). Clearly, other sight words are important. Just look at your own reading. For you to successfully and comfortably read this book, you must have an incredibly large vocabulary of sight words. After all, it's likely that in the previous sentence you quickly, automatically, without decoding, read *successfully, comfortably, incredibly,* and *vocabulary*. In contrast to many of the basic sight words (e.g., *in, of*), other sight words carry the text's primary meaning or message. For example, in the sentence "The elephants ran amuck," the primary message is carried by *elephants* and *amuck*.

As children move up the grades, they must learn to identify more and more words on sight, including words associated with subjects. In mathematics, for example, fourth graders may have to recognize *triangle* and *parallel*.

By the end of second grade, average readers have learned far more than 1400 words on sight; by the end of fourth grade, far more than quadruple this number.[6] This is an enormous but necessary task:

The books and other reading materials used by schoolchildren include well over 100,000 different words. The average child enters school with a very small reading vocabulary.... Once in school, however, a [good reader's] reading vocabulary is likely to soar at a rate of 3,000 to 4,000 words a year, leading to a reading vocabulary of something like 25,000 words by the time she is in the eighth grade and may be well over 50,000 words by the end of high school.[7]

For struggling readers to successfully read fourth-grade books, they must learn to identify—automatically, on sight—the vast majority of subject-matter words in these books, words like *calendar, contained, discovered, evidence, government,* and *harvest.* If they must sound out or work to identify 20% of these words, reading becomes a slow, unpleasant struggle with little mental energy left for comprehending. In other words, the purpose and pleasure of reading—understanding the text, thinking about its meaning, modifying and applying its ideas, enjoying its language—is lost if children must work or strain to correctly identify even 20% of words.[8] And what often amazes parents and teachers is that many struggling readers are overwhelmed when they must consciously work or strain to identify 6% to 9% of words.

Asking struggling readers to repeatedly read materials they find overwhelming or frustrating slows or halts their learning and erodes motivation for reading. Simply put, children, no matter their reading proficiency, need a steady diet of reading materials they read with ease, in which they recognize the vast majority of words on sight. This allows them to apply their decoding skills to a few important words. By having to decode only a few or a small percentage of words, they can improve their fluency, comprehend the text, and begin to move the newly decoded words into their sight vocabulary.

So how does a good reader develop a large sight vocabulary? By reading lots and lots and lots of easy and slightly challenging materials. By reading lots of interesting materials that don't frustrate him. By quickly sounding out (decoding) unknown words. By turning decoded words into sight words: "Words are often read initially through the application of various word analysis strategies [like phonics] .... [These words] become sight words after repeated exposure through reading."[9]

A problem for many struggling readers is that they read little, and thus decode little, and thus have little opportunity to develop a large sight vocabulary. To help solve this problem, later in this chapter we'll discuss a critical but often trivialized aspect of getting struggling readers to read more: motivation.

Decoding Skills. Struggling readers must quickly figure out words they cannot recognize on sight. This is called decoding.

To successfully decode written words, children must know that a word is one or more letters separated from others by relatively long white spaces, and they can use the sounds typically associated with printed letters to identify unknown words. Knowing that sounds are associated with written letters is the alphabetic principle.

Although children need to understand the principle, successful decoding requires them to know and do more. They must know the sounds of individual letters and letter combinations, such as *ai*, and quickly apply them to figure out unknown words. This is phonics.

Here's how a student might apply phonics. "Hmmm. I don't know this word, *t-e-l-l*. It looks like a word I know, *well*, and it starts with a *t*, which makes the *tuh* sound. It must be *tell*."

As students advance up the grades, they frequently encounter more complicated words composed of several syllables (e.g., *disagreeable*). To decode such words, they must often apply their knowledge of root words (*agree*), prefixes (*dis*), and suffixes (*able*), which is called structural or morphemic analysis. To identify the words, they may first have to divide words into syllables, which is called syllabic analysis.

Often, structural and syllabic analyses are combined. Here's an example. As a student encounters the word *disappearance*, he might decode it by thinking along these lines: "Hmm, *d-i-s-a-p-p-e-a-r-a-n-c-e* starts with *d-i-s*, which means *not*, like in *disagree*. I can divide *a-p-p-e-a-r* between the two *p*'s, so I get two syllables, */ap/* and */pear/*. I know that *a-n-c-e* is one of the suffixes we studied. It probably means action. The word's *disappearance*. It's like get lost, vanish, become invisible."

As you might have surmised, decoding can involve more than applying sounds to individual letters, letter combinations (*ai, ou, ph, wr*), syllables, root words, prefixes, and suffixes. It can involve meaning, such as knowing that word parts (e.g., the *dis* in *disappear*) and words have meaning and that meaning can help identify unknown words.

Decoding an unknown word by considering the meaning of the surrounding words might work like this: "I don't know what *t-e-l-l* says. One of the sentences says Jayne was listening. Another says Leslie was talking to Jayne. *Tell* starts with the letter *t* which makes the /t/ sound. *Tell* makes sense. It's probably *tell*." This is an example of using both phonics and the meaning of the surrounding words—context clues—to identify an unknown word.

But beware. Using context clues alone is a poor decoding strategy, used more by struggling than proficient readers. Alone, context clues produce high rates of inaccurately identified words. Joyce Jennings and her colleagues report that "words can be predicted from context only 10-20 percent of the time.... Poor readers tend to overuse context precisely because they do not have a large sight vocabulary and cannot decode quickly."[10]

By now, you may be saying, "This is a complicated, complicated process. Whew. There's so much to learn." And you're right.[11] But we're near the end. Stay with us because we need to discuss how some teachers, schools, and programs might inadvertently hurt your child's chances of success.

Decoding is not the parroting of rules, but the skilled application of knowledge. Unfortunately, some teachers, schools, and programs act as if this were false. They block progress by emphasizing the rote memorization and recitation of rules at the expense of teaching struggling readers how to quickly decode words by applying their knowledge of letters, sounds, phonics, structural analysis, syllabic analysis, and context clues. Often, they produce struggling readers who've memorized the rules, but never learned to apply them. The result: poor decoding skills.

Some teachers, schools, and programs add to struggling readers' decoding problems by embracing ideological extremes: They emphasize phonics or whole language to the exclusion of other strategies. Some whole-language proponents refuse to teach phonics and structural analysis in systematic, explicit, direct ways. As a result, struggling readers lose an irreplaceable opportunity to develop the decoding skills needed to become proficient readers—they're curriculum casualties. In contrast, some advocates of phonics act as if meaning—background knowledge and context clues—should be trivialized or shunned. Here too, struggling readers lose an irreplaceable opportunity to learn a critical strategy for decoding. They too become curriculum casualties. Neither extreme makes sense.

Clearly, if a struggling reader's decoding is weak, instruction must strengthen it. Instruction must teach him how to use phonics, word parts, and context to decode words so, with frequent exposure to and practice with these words, they become sight words. If it does not, reading will be a perpetual, laborious, frustrating struggle. The same holds true for reading comprehension. If a struggling reader has difficulties with reading comprehension, he must be taught comprehension strategies. Otherwise, reading will remain a frustrating, meaningless endeavor.

Vocabulary. To become successful readers, children must have a large listening and speaking vocabulary. If they don't know the meaning of many of the more important words they read, they won't understand what they read, even if they pronounce every word correctly.

If second graders don't know what a *locomotive* and *caboose* are, they'll have difficulty understanding, visualizing, and discussing this sentence: "The *locomotive* is pulling the *caboose*." They'll know the locomotive—whatever it is—is pulling something. But they won't know anything about the locomotive or caboose. Is the locomotive hungry or happy, tall or short? Is the caboose big or small, light or heavy? Are they friends? Are the locomotive and caboose on a road, on tracks, on grass, or on a sidewalk? And if eighth graders read "Initially, reconciliation was rejected," but don't know the meaning of *initially* and *reconciliation*, confusion will rule.

Thus, to understand what they read, children need large listening and speaking vocabularies.[12]

In addition, children need large listening vocabularies to match the words they decode to words in their listening vocabularies. This is because decoding often produces only rough approximations of the words in the text. If a second grader knows the meaning of *station*, *chugged*, and *train*," and he reads, "The train *choog...ed* into the station," his listening vocabulary and the context might help him realize that *choog...ed*, the rough approximation he sounded out, is *chugged*.

Similarly, if a child encounters the sentence, "I'll come home in an hour," and he cannot identify the word *come* on sight, he has to decode it. But *come* is irregularly spelled; it cannot be accurately decoded by following the often-taught rule, "In words with two vowels, the second being the final *e*, the first vowel usually has its long sound and the final *e* is not sounded."[13] Here, the rule doesn't apply; applying it produces /comb/. But he can use two other clues to help identify the unknown word: the first letter of come and the context or meaning of nearby words.[14]

Children's *listening* or *receptive vocabulary* is made up of the spoken words they understand; the words they use correctly in speaking or writing make up their *speaking* or *expressive vocabulary*. Usually, a child's listening vocabulary is larger than his speaking vocabulary. Thus, a child with a good speaking vocabulary usually has an even larger listening vocabulary, which helps him understand text. On the other hand, if his expressive vocabulary is below average, it suggests, but does not always mean, that his listening vocabulary is also below average.

Because vocabulary is so important to success in reading, school, and most things in life, parents, teachers, and schools should do whatever they can to help students enlarge their listening and speaking vocabularies. Schools, for example, might hold workshops for parents on how to foster vocabulary development. For many struggling readers, however, more is needed. One simple strategy is sharing information. Every few weeks the teacher might give parents information about an upcoming curriculum topic and a list of five to ten important, but difficult target words about the topic; the parents might then show their children videos on the topic and during dinner discuss the videos and target words.

As you may have surmised, vocabulary development does not require struggling readers to fill out countless workbook pages and memorize definitions—activities that produce few gains and sap motivation. Instead, to help struggling readers strengthen their vocabularies, parents and teachers can stress interesting, enjoyable activities, like playing word games, listening to and *discussing* good books, watching and *discussing* DVDs of historical events, taking and *discussing* digital photos of class trips, and *discussing* interesting experiences over lunch.

In the last sentence, notice how often we used the word *discussing*. Four times. A major way of helping a child strengthen his vocabulary is to give him lots of interesting experiences, and then *discussing* them with him. During the discussion, interject one or two important words he doesn't know—words he's likely to often see and hear or that are critical to his success in school. But be careful. Treating discussions like formal lessons or quizzes can easily dampen interest, weaken motivation, and arouse defensiveness. In contrast, enjoyable, interesting discussions in which the child feels safe and comfortable should improve his vocabulary.

Fluency. To become proficient readers, children must quickly and accurately read words, sentences, and paragraphs. The term used to describe speed and accuracy is rate of reading. When expression is added, the term is fluency.[15]

The opposite of reading quickly and accurately is reading slowly, inaccurately, and often laboriously. This strains short-term memory and makes reading an arduous, lengthy, and fatiguing task. Homework that average readers finish in 25 minutes might take children with fluency problems 75 minutes.

Not surprisingly, rate and fluency problems can add to struggling readers' comprehension difficulties. Sharon Walpole and Michael McKenna explain it this way: "Until a reader achieves fluency ... comprehension is apt to suffer because too much conscious attention must be directed at word identification and too little attention can be paid to comprehending what is read."[16]

So, how fast should children read paragraphs and the like? What's a good rate? Unfortunately, numerical answers are tricky. In 2000, Timothy Rasinski and Nancy Padak, two eminent scholars from Kent State University, suggested these rates for materials at or slightly below children's grades.[17] These figures are found in Table 4.1.

TABLE 4.1: RATES SUGGESTED BY RASINSKI AND PADAK

GRADE	NUMBER OF WORDS READ CORRECTLY IN A MINUTE
1st grade, second half	80
2nd grade, second half	90
3rd grade, second half	110

Six years later, in 2006, two equally eminent scholars, Jan Hasbrouck and Gerald Tindal, suggested substantially different figures.[18] These figures are found in Table 4.2.

TABLE 4.2: RATES SUGGESTED BY HASBROUCK AND TINDAL

GRADE	NUMBER OF WORDS READ CORRECTLY IN A MINUTE BY AVERAGE ACHIEVING STUDENTS
1st grade, winter	23
2nd grade, winter	72
3rd grade, winter	92

Rate figures, however, aren't absolute. If struggling readers are unmotivated to read, or bring little background to the materials, or have insufficient vocabularies to understand the materials, or feel highly anxious, or normally speak dysfluently, or are given materials with complicated sentence structures or materials that introduce several new concepts and have long sentences (like this one), their rate may suffer.

This lack of agreement on rates is not as critical as it may appear. Usually, a reading specialist can identify rate and fluency problems fairly easily by asking the child to read aloud while she listens and answers questions like these:

- On this specific material, was the child's reading rate much slower than that of other children at his instructional level?
- Was his reading smooth or choppy?
- Was his reading excessively arduous, as if he were struggling to identify the words?
- Was his reading flat and expressionless?
- Was his phrasing poor, as if he misunderstood the meaning of what he was reading?
- Did he read in a word-by-word fashion?

The bottom line is this: For struggling readers to become proficient readers, they must become fluent readers. If not—if reading is a slow, laborious, dreadful, and perplexing task, many will actively avoid it.

If this is so, when should fluency instruction begin for struggling readers with fluency problems? Paula Schwanenflugel and Hilary Ruston, two fluency scholars from the University of Georgia, provide excellent advice. Fluency instruction should *not* begin at a particular age or in a particular grade. It should begin at a particular stage:

> Once children have established a set of *sight words* that they can read readily and are able to decode most of the words they find in text, they are ready to receive fluency instruction. For most children, this phase occurs toward the end of first grade and throughout second and third grades as they confirm these skills through practice. There is a time for everything, and the time for fluency-oriented instruction is *after* children have developed their basic decoding ability.[19]

For struggling readers with mild to moderate word recognition and word identification difficulties, this may mean delaying fluency instruction until spring of second grade, when they've just developed sufficient sight vocabulary and can quickly decode words. For struggling readers with far more serious word recognition and identification difficulties, this may mean delaying fluency instruction until spring of third or even fourth grade. You can't rely on a time schedule to decide when to begin. It's a question of what struggling readers are ready for. Given that struggling readers differ greatly in their reading abilities, deciding when to begin fluency instruction must be based on observations of the child reading and data about his word recognition and identification abilities. A reading evaluation can provide this information.

Comprehension. Comprehending or understanding what's read makes reading important. This understanding is called reading comprehension.

If struggling readers have trouble comprehending what they're reading, they need to use strategies that unlock the meaning. But often, they don't because they don't know what strategies to use or they don't realize that they should read for meaning. Many are satisfied to just name the words.

Many struggling readers, especially those who focus on naming words, don't realize they must ensure that what they've read makes sense, not nonsense. They need to monitor their reading to correct substitutions like this, which substitutes *snoring* for *scoring*: "The boy hit the ball with his bat, *snoring* a run." But many wouldn't question *snoring*. They would continue reading, as if *snoring* made sense.

Many struggling readers don't realize that once they understand the material, they may have to use their new knowledge, which can be difficult. It requires remembering and applying. Consider this assignment: "You're going to write a composition about the principles of conflict management, which you just read about. Your composition should answer the question, "How can our government use these principles to prevent war?"

Like word identification, comprehension is complex, complex, complex. Successful comprehension depends on struggling readers applying their knowledge of sight vocabulary, word identification or decoding abilities, reading fluency, listening vocabulary, understanding of sentence structure (syntax), knowledge of the topic, memory, and knowledge of comprehension strategies. Equally important is the motivation of struggling readers, their desire to want to understand what they've read. Perhaps this is why most reading authorities consider reading an exceedingly complex mental activity that's never fully mastered.

But despite this complexity—the need to simultaneously know, juggle, apply, and consider so much—there's good news. Struggling readers, like most people, will likely work, and if necessary, work hard to understand material *if*—a mighty big word—they believe they can read the words, believe that with moderate effort they can understand the material, and believe it's interesting or important. Like most people, they'll likely ask themselves two critical questions:

- Can I succeed?
- Is reading worthwhile?

To help struggling readers improve their comprehension abilities, teachers can use many powerful instructional strategies. As an example, here's Edwin Ellis' RAP, a simple reading comprehension strategy that teachers can teach to struggling readers:

Read a paragraph
Ask yourself what it's about
Put the main idea and two details in your own words[20]

Of course, the effectiveness of any comprehension strategy depends on many factors, such as the struggling reader's sight vocabulary, word identification abilities, reading fluency, listening vocabulary, and background knowledge. Even the most powerful strategy will not work if the material is at the reader's frustration level and he knows little about the topic.[21]

Ideally, an evaluation should identify the struggling reader's levels of comprehension and, if they're low, the instructional methods and related resources likely to raise them.[22]

Study Skills and Independent-Work Skills. The term *study skills* means different things to different people in different grades. Thus, when school personnel use the term, it's important to ask what they mean.

Examining a partial list of skills illustrates why: following directions, alphabetizing by first letter, alphabetizing by first and second letter, outlining, note taking, using graphs, finding information in dictionaries or thesauruses or search engines, summarizing and synthesizing information, organizing information for reports, remembering what was read, studying for tests, mentally retrieving what was studied.[23] All differ, yet all are related. All are essential for working independently on classwork and homework and for succeeding in school. And when struggling readers have to work independently, all can cause nightmares.

Independent-work skills, often called self-regulatory skills, are inseparable from study skills.[24] For example, to successfully finish homework or classwork, children might have to use these study skills: find the right books, find the right chapters, find information in book indexes, interpret graphs and tables, take notes, classify and organize information by main ideas and supporting details, synthesize the most important information. But to successfully apply these, they'll have to use these and other independent-work skills: understand the requirements of the task; develop task-related goals; organize the task into manageable, sequenced activities; allocate sufficient time; concentrate on the goals and the activities; carry-out relevant activities; monitor progress; use substitute strategies if progress is poor; persevere to overcome difficulties; prevent and overcome distractions.

Because study skills and independent-work skills do not directly influence reading comprehension like word recognition and vocabulary do, many reading authorities do not consider them building blocks of reading. In this sense, they're right. Nevertheless, we view them as building blocks. Our reason: If struggling readers have poor study skills and poor independent-work skills, they can easily become overwhelmed by classwork and homework, even if the materials match their independent or instructional reading levels. This is because classwork and homework are typically independent tasks that students must complete by themselves. Not surprisingly, feeling overwhelmed, frustrated and distressed shatters a belief critical to overcoming reading disabilities: optimism, the belief that "If I try, I'll succeed."[25] Without optimism, motivation shrivels. In its place, parents and teachers must often confront what look like insurmountable obstacles to success: unique mixtures of apathy, anxiety, anger, resistance, resignation, and pessimism.

Motivation. We hope it's obvious: Motivation to read is critically important. It's as important to overcoming reading disabilities as food is to life. As Douglas Carnine, Jerry Silbert, and Edward Kameenui asserted, to make meaningful progress, struggling readers must be motivated:

> Unmotivated students will not receive the full benefit of increased instructional time, careful teaching, and a well-designed program. Without motivation ... the student will continue making the same errors and will perform poorly on new skills.[26]

And like all of reading's components, motivation is complex. But here, complexity is good. When you understand motivation's complexity, you begin to understand the sources of poor motivation, which offers clues for strengthening it.

Unfortunately, many teachers, administrators, learning consultants, and school psychologists ignore motivation, or blame struggling readers for their poor motivation, or dismiss the possibility of strengthening it, putting children in peril. They act as if motivation's an impenetrable boulder—once unmotivated, children can't be motivated.[27] They're wrong. Because motivation is complicated, much can be done, especially if school personnel understand its sources. Consider the following sources and solutions.

If struggling readers are poorly motivated because they find their reading materials boring or irrelevant, teachers can assign interesting or relevant materials. If assignments are too complex, teachers can simplify them, shorten them, and model the strategies need to succeed. If readers find the topic interesting, but the reading materials frustrating, teachers can give them easier materials, read the materials to them, or put them in pairs to help one another. If readers fear failure and typically quit after their first mistake, teachers can model how to succeed on the assignment, make sure it's relatively easy, and reward readers' effort, persistence, and correct use of learning strategies. If readers believe they lack the ability to read, teachers can employ all these methods, while teaching readers to make accurate, facilitative attributions: "I succeeded because I stuck to it and used the RAP strategy." Essentially, these strategies help readers believe that they can succeed; they help transform "I can't" beliefs into "I can."

But you're a parent, not a teacher. Why study these examples? Because they show that motivation's not an impenetrable boulder—poor motivation need not be *forever*. They give you suggestions to discuss with teachers. They show that teachers who understand the complexity of motivation, especially the sources of poor motivation, can kindle motivation. (For a motivation questionnaire that you and your child's teachers can use to identify the sources of poor motivation, visit our website: www.reading2008.com.)

Although some parents and school personnel may think that kindling motivation is a minor issue, it's not. Kindling motivation is critical for increasing the amount of reading that struggling readers do, reading that's critical for strengthening reading abilities. Without the motivation to read, and the optimism that they can succeed, struggling readers will read little, guaranteeing they'll fall further and further behind their age group. This is called the Matthew Effect: "As the rich get richer, the poor get poorer." Therefore, teachers have a primary responsibility, one that's achievable—to structure instruction to strengthen children's motivation to read, not their motivation to resist.

TWO MORE COMPONENTS: HOMEWORK AND SELF-CONFIDENCE

Why add two more? Aren't seven complicated enough? Yes – but if you don't successfully prevent or solve problems caused by homework and weak self-confidence, efforts to improve your child's reading may well prove useless.

Develop a Sensible, Productive Homework Policy. If you don't work with your child's reading specialist and teachers to develop a sensible, productive homework policy—one that regularly assigns homework on which your child will readily succeed—homework problems may well devastate his optimism and motivation, undermining all efforts to help him. As Lawrence Greene observed, the reasons for this devastation are straightforward:

> The prospect of doing homework can be intolerable to children who feel academically incompetent, frustrated, demoralized, and incapable of doing the assigned work. After having spent a miserable day in school, their teachers and parents now insist that they go home and spend an addi-

tional two or three hours being miserable. That many of these children try to evade their academic responsibilities is understandable. There is little incentive to children to record their assignments diligently when they believe that they will receive poor grades on their homework no matter how hard they try and that studying for tests is a futile exercise.[28]

In addition, homework assignments that are not submitted or are unfinished or sloppy often earn zeros, which lowers report-card grades, which intensifies the mental anguish of struggling readers. It's a self-defeating, destructive spiral of failure.

The key to dealing with the many problems caused by homework—homework that demands too much of struggling readers—is prevention. If homework must be assigned, teachers should make sure that with a reasonable, moderate effort, struggling readers can succeed on it.[29]

To identify such assignments, ask the reading specialist, as part of her evaluation, to describe the type of homework your child can independently complete, with moderate effort, without struggle or frustration, in reasonable time. Usually, a reading evaluation gives the specialist this information: the reading level, length, format, familiarity, complexity, and abstractness of assignments on which your child will likely succeed when working alone. After the specialist puts this in her report, it should become part of any plan to motivate your child and improve his reading.

If your child is eligible for special education under the *Individuals with Disabilities Education Improvement Act of 2004* (IDEA-2004), chapters 9, 10 11, 12, and 13 will help you modify his program so homework promotes success, not frustration and failure.

Develop a Plan to Strengthen Weak Self-Confidence. Unlike homework, self-confidence is hard to define. It's elusive. But it's so critical to success that you immediately know if it's weak. It's also critical to motivation, which in turn, is critical to reading achievement.

So, if your child's self-confidence for learning to read is weak, the school must develop a plan to strengthen it, while working to improve his reading. Without improved self-confidence for learning to read, he may give up. You'll know he's given up if he fights attempts to teach him to read, refuses to read on his own, or listlessly goes through the motions of learning, giving little thought to mastering what's taught.

To reverse this problem, ask the reading specialist (or the school psychologist) to evaluate your child's belief that he can succeed in reading. This belief is so important that it has volumes of research behind it and has a technical name: self-efficacy. If your child's self-efficacy for reading is weak, if he believes he can't succeed, he may well quit trying—so discuss this with the reading specialist, his teachers, and related school staff; then create a coordinated plan, for home and school, to strengthen his self-efficacy.[30]

The plan should give your child lots of work on which success is likely. Typically, this means that all reading should be at his independent level, the level he can readily succeed at when working alone, or at his instructional level, the level he can succeed at, with moderate effort, when his teachers work with him. The plan should teach him how to take credit for his successes, and how to constructively explain his failures. Such statements, called attributions, stress three processes: effort, persistence, and the correct use of learning strategies. It challenges dysfunctional attributions—"I'm too dumb to read"—by teaching facilitative ones—"I failed because I didn't follow the directions or make the effort. Next time I'll listen to the directions, make the effort, and ask questions about anything I don't understand."

The plan should also have you and your child's teachers link verbal encouragement to tasks on which success is likely. The plan might involve teaching your child relaxation methods for lessening anxiety, like slow breathing or progressive muscle relaxation. For more information about relaxation methods and self-efficacy, visit our website, www.reading2008.com. Feel free to share and discuss our information with your child's teachers and other school personnel. But be careful—sharing too much can overwhelm people, and if presented incorrectly, insult them.

THE PARENTS' ROLE
Although our description of the seven-plus-two components is complicated, it's only a sketch of what children must know, do, and believe to succeed. No wonder so many children, parents, teachers, and schools find reading so difficult.

Complications aside, at-risk and struggling readers are in a race against time: From the first day of kindergarten, many struggling readers have four years to succeed. Some have less. By the end of first grade, many who fall behind stop trying, thinking they're failures, thinking they're incapable: "Why try. I'm too stupid to read." The longer they struggle with reading, the lower their chances of succeeding. If by third grade they can't read third-grade materials with good word recognition, fluency, and comprehension, they'll likely struggle with reading in high school. This increases their odds of dropping out.[31]

To intervene successfully—to prevent, minimize, or reverse the consequences of falling behind—parents and teachers must know what the child can't do, and what's perpetuating it—his weaknesses. But this is not enough. They must also know what he's good at and what he likes, so they can use this to motivate him, and if needed, to sidestep or compensate for some of his weaknesses. Basically, they must know what to teach, how to teach it, and how to support him.

Understanding the seven-plus-two components of reading—sight vocabulary, decoding, listening and speaking vocabulary, fluency, comprehension, study skills, motivation, homework, self-confidence—is key to understanding your child's reading difficulties and what he needs to learn, do, *and* believe to become a successful reader. Knowing this will help you work effectively with the school to design a program that meets his needs. Knowing this will help you determine if his program will likely succeed. Not knowing this leaves everything to chance. And as so many people who lost money in Atlantic City know, chance is a lousy bet.

By this time, you probably feel overwhelmed, like we do when we read the instructions for our income taxes. Feeling overwhelmed is understandable—reading disabilities are complicated; if reading was simple, far fewer children would struggle. It's even more complicated if you're a teacher. But we're not asking you to be your child's reading teacher. Sometimes parents are wonderful teachers; often they're terrible, as their emotions dominate reason, causing endless arguments: "Pay attention. Don't forget what I told you. I said the 'e' can be long or short, like the 'i' and the other vowels. I told you five times. No, I'm wrong—I told you five thousand times. Try to care."

This is not the role we envision for parents, and we doubt it's one you want. Instead, we view your role as learning all you reasonably can about reading disabilities, so you can successfully set the stage for success. How? By helping your child develop the background he needs, by helping him develop awareness of sounds, by encouraging his language development, by collaborating with his teachers and other school staff, by knowledgeably negotiating and advocating for the services he needs to succeed, by supporting and reinforcing him, and by providing a home that encourages him to succeed, without creating needless stress. In later chapters, we discuss these and other ways you can set the stage for success.

A COMPREHENSIVE READING EVALUATION

Now that you're familiar with the seven-plus-two components, it's important that you ensure that your child has the building blocks for success—in all nine areas. But how do you ensure this, and how do you measure this, if you're not a teacher or reading specialist?

Like much in this book, it's difficult because you may lack easy access to critical information and because reading disabilities are enormously complex, so complex that those with graduate degrees in special education and reading and psychology, like Howard and Gary, always have much to learn about some aspects of reading (which forces us to ask critical questions and research the answers even harder). Nevertheless, you can get a good understanding of your child's abilities in all nine areas. Here's how.

Formally request, in writing, a comprehensive reading evaluation that examines all nine components,[32] answers questions like those below (which you'll have to adapt to reflect your child's age and situation), and offers a plan to monitor your child's progress. Part of the evaluation can include Response to Intervention (RTI), which we discuss in chapters 3, 5, and 9.

Sight Vocabulary

- How does my child's sight vocabulary compare to grade-level standards?
- At what grade level is my child's sight vocabulary?
- How large is his sight vocabulary?
- What common, high-frequency words does he have difficulty recognizing at sight?
- If his sight vocabulary is below that of average-achieving readers in his grade, exactly what is blocking him from developing a grade-level sight vocabulary? What can the school do to remove these blocks and strengthen his sight vocabulary? What research or related scholarship supports your recommendations?

Decoding

- Compared to grade-level standards, how well does my child apply decoding skills?
- At what grade level are my child's decoding skills?

- What decoding knowledge and skills does he have? With materials at his instructional level, how smoothly and effortlessly does he apply his knowledge and skills?
- What critical decoding knowledge and skills does he need to learn?
- What is blocking him from becoming far more proficient at decoding? What can the school do to remove these blocks and strengthen his decoding skills? What research or related scholarship supports your recommendations?

Listening and Speaking Vocabulary

- Compared to grade-level standards, how extensive are my child's listening and speaking vocabularies?
- At what grade level are my child's listening and speaking vocabularies?
- Does he know the meaning of common prefixes and suffixes as well as average-achieving students in his grade?
- When he reads materials at his instructional level, does he successfully figure out the meaning of unknown words by using surrounding sentences, dictionaries, other strategies, or by asking others?
- How interested is he in learning new words?
- If his vocabulary is below average, exactly what is blocking him from developing a far better vocabulary? What can the school do to remove these blocks and strengthen his vocabulary? What research or related scholarship supports your recommendations?

Fluency

- Compared to grade-level standards, is my child a fluent reader? Does he read at a relatively fast rate, in a smooth manner, with appropriate expression?
- If he has difficulty with fluency, what level materials give him difficulty? What types of materials (textbook-like or stories) give him difficulty?
- If he has difficulty with fluency, exactly what is blocking him from becoming a fluent reader, who reads grade-level materials at a relatively fast rate, smoothly, with proper expression? What can the school do to remove these blocks and improve his fluency? What research or related scholarship supports your recommendations?

Reading Comprehension

- Compared to grade-level standards, how well does my child comprehend what he reads? Does he have more difficulty with materials designed to convey information, like textbooks (expository materials), than with stories (narrative materials)?
- At what level can he successfully comprehend story-like or narrative materials?
- At what level can he successfully comprehend informational materials or expository materials?
- What strategies does he use to successfully comprehend what he reads? In addition to these, what strategies should he use to improve his comprehension?
- If he has comprehension difficulties, exactly what difficulties does he have?

Exactly what kinds of materials and questions give him difficulty?
To effectively comprehend, exactly what does he have to learn to do?

- If he has comprehension difficulties, exactly what is blocking him from developing far better comprehension abilities? What can the school do to remove these blocks and strengthen his comprehension abilities? What research or related scholarship supports your recommendations?

Study Skills and Independent-Work Abilities

- Compared to grade-level standards, how well does my child understand and use study skills?
- What study-skills strategies does he use successfully? In addition to these, what study-skills strategies does he need to acquire or better understand and apply?
- If he has difficulties with study skills, exactly what is blocking him from developing far better skills? What can the school do to remove these blocks and strengthen his skills? What research or related scholarship supports your recommendations?
- On what kinds of classwork can my child usually succeed if he works independently or with a partner?
- What kind of structure and support does he need to succeed when he works independently in class?
- If his independent-work skills are weak, what are the immediate causes? What can the school do to strengthen them so he will succeed if he makes a moderate effort? What research or related scholarship supports your recommendations?

Motivation

- What subjects and activities does my child like? What does he dislike?
- How motivated is he to learn to read?
- How motivated is he to read lots of materials or books by himself?
- If he's not highly motivated, what are the causes? What can the school do to remove or weaken these causes and strengthen his motivation, so he becomes a highly motivated, enthusiastic reader? What research or related scholarship supports your recommendations?

Homework

- What is my child's independent reading level for stories and textbook-like reading materials?
- On what types of assignments is he likely to succeed, if he works alone and makes a moderate effort?
- On what types of assignments is he likely to frustrate, if he works alone and makes a moderate effort?
- What types of assignments are likely to make him anxious?
- What types of assignments are likely to strengthen his self-efficacy?

- What types of assignments will strengthen his reading more than being read to and discussing the materials?
- In what ways can assistive technology, like speech-to-text software or text-to-speech software, help him with homework?
- If he has difficulties with homework or frequently fails to submit successfully completed assignments, what are the immediate, direct causes? What positive efforts can the school implement to improve the situation? If his self-efficacy for homework is weak, how can the school strengthen it? What research or related scholarship supports your recommendations?

Self-confidence (Self-efficacy)

- To learn to read, to work independently in class, to succeed on homework, what does my child have to believe about his abilities?
- Which of his self-efficacy beliefs are accurate? Which inaccurate?
- If his self-efficacy is weak in critical academic areas, what are the immediate causes? What can the school do to strengthen his self-efficacy, so he correctly believes that he will succeed if he makes a moderate effort? What research or related scholarship supports your recommendations?

In addition to these components of reading, you should also request that the evaluation report include:

- A chart with your child's listening level as well as his three reading levels: independent, instructional, and frustration. We'll call this a levels chart.
- A plan for closely and frequently monitoring and reporting your child's progress.[33]

INFLUENCING THE EVALUATION

Asking questions like those above and requesting that they're answered in your child's reading evaluation may well influence the nature of the evaluation as well as the care that school personnel give to conducting and interpreting it. Remember the old saying, "The squeaky wheel gets the oil"? Well, it's old but it's true—the squeaky wheel still gets the oil. In this case, it's your questions—asked respectfully, before the evaluation is planned—that get the attention of school personnel. It's your questions that establish your power as a knowledgeable, focused parent who expects a comprehensive, relevant, conscientious, and responsive evaluation, rather than a mechanical, unreflective one that sheds little light on your child's needs. It's your questions that necessitate action.

Like many parents, you may not want to ask questions, especially if you know little or nothing about educational research. Our advice: Ask anyway. If you get answers you don't understand, ask school personnel for clarification or examples, or ask outside experts. By asking questions, you're not putting school personnel on the spot. They're professionals, and as such, they should welcome thoughtful questions, they should know what they're doing, and they should have good reasons for their answers. Moreover, their answers should demonstrate a solid understanding of the professional literature, including research. Knowledge is a hallmark of professionals.

By asking questions, you can learn if your child's program is based on relevant research and related scholarship. Knowing this is critical, as many programs are based on habit rather than research and related scholarship. This mentality—"we've always done it this way"—is dangerous. It's one reason that the Federal law governing special education, IDEA-2004, states that each child's program "must be based on peer-reviewed research to the extent practicable." It's why the *No Child Left Behind Act of 2001* (NCLB) stresses the "use of effective methods and instructional strategies that are *based* on scientifically based research." It's why the National Information Center for Children and Youth with Disabilities (NICHCY) has a Research-To-Practice database (www.nichcy.org) for professionals and parents. Thus, it's important to ask school personnel for copies of the research or related scholarship on which they're basing your child's program. If they refuse, and also refuse to tell you the titles, authors, and sources, show them the quotes in this paragraph. Even better, highlight these quotes in IDEA-2004 or the NCLB, and show the laws to them—this can be astonishingly persuasive.[34]

Although IDEA-2004 uses the word "practicable," this is not as serious a loophole as you might think. The vast majority of what's recommended in the research and related scholarship on reading disabilities—tutoring; modeling; small groups; interactive instruction; explicit, systematic instruction; curriculum and homework adaptations; frequent, task-oriented feedback; minimal use of worksheets; logically sequenced curriculum that gradually moves from easy to difficult, from concrete to abstract, from short to long; brief practice sessions throughout the day (called distributed practice); strategies that strengthen confidence (self-efficacy) and motivation; lots of extra instruction from or closely supervised by teachers with credentials in reading (beyond that of general education teachers or special education teachers); opportunities to select books for recreational reading; opportunities to read lots of interesting materials at their independent and instructional levels; ongoing monitoring of progress; quickly-made instructional adaptations that overcome roadblocks—is highly practicable. Arguing against the practicality of such interventions is unlikely to withstand knowledgeable scrutiny.

KEEP IN MIND

Although the lists of questions in this chapter are important, keep in mind that our lists are not rigid scripts that must be followed, word-for-word. Some questions can be rephrased, others omitted. Much depends on your child's age, grade, and difficulties.

For example, if your child was considered a good reader until he started the seventh grade, you probably don't need to ask questions about sight vocabulary or decoding. He's probably quite skilled in these areas. Instead, you should focus on areas like vocabulary, fluency, study skills, and motivation.

In contrast, if he's beginning second grade, has good listening and speaking vocabularies, but since early first grade has struggled to recognize high-frequency sight words and to decode words that most first graders recognize readily, emphasizing study skills, like locating words in a dictionary and understanding their definitions is unimportant. He's not ready for this. Asking questions about study skills may divert attention from pressing questions like these: "Exactly what is blocking Joseph from developing a grade-level sight vocabulary? What critical decoding knowledge and skills does he need to learn? How can the school help him improve his sight vocabulary and decoding skills? How will the school measure his progress in these areas? How frequently?"

To help you determine which questions are most important for your child's grade and his general level of achievement, go to your State's NCLB website to see what children in different grades are expected to master in reading, writing, and mathematics. Keep in mind, however, that these standards differ from State to State, are often vague, and have, in many cases, deserved the criticism heaped upon them. Nevertheless, your State's standards will give you needed information about what your child should master. Our website, www.reading2008. com, provides links to standards from several States.

Once you have a quality reading evaluation in hand, one that has assessed every critical aspect of your child's reading (and perhaps writing), you and your child's school are in a good position to help him become a proficient reader. But a good position does not ensure success. You need to understand and do much more. The next chapter will help. It offers suggestions for making the reading evaluation work for you and your child.

ENDNOTES

[1] To many reading specialists, school psychologists, and special educators, the words assess and evaluate have different meanings. Assess is more limited; it refers to collecting, not interpreting information, not making recommendations. Evaluate includes assessing, interpreting, and making recommendations. Because the distinction can be important, we'll comment on it again in a later endnote.

[2] Ekwall, E. E., & Shanker, J. L., 1988. *Diagnosis and Remediation of the Disabled Reader* (3rd ed.). Boston: Allyn & Bacon, p. 55.

[3] The seven components are our formulation for discussing reading evaluations. Other experts offer different formulations for different purposes. One excellent formulation for curriculum is that of Michael Graves and his colleagues. Their "present-day literacy curriculum" has nine components: (a) knowledge about print and sounds, including phonemic awareness; (b) phonics; (c) fluency; (d) vocabulary; (e) comprehending and responding to narrative text; (f) comprehending and learning from expository or informational text; (g) the integration of reading and writing; (h) independent reading; (i) building connections between children's experiences and learning, between different subjects, and between school and life outside of school. More information about these components can be found in their textbook: Graves, M. F., Juel, C., & Graves, B. B., 2004. *Teaching Reading in the 21st Century* (3rd ed.). Boston: Pearson, Allyn & Bacon.

[4] Identify means quickly pronouncing the written word, orally or subvocally. If a child must work to sound out or decode a word, it's not a sight word. Usually, words a child sees and decodes numerous times become sight words, words that do not require a conscious effort to identify.

[5]   D. Ray Reutzel and Robert B. Cooter report that "just 109 words account for upwards of 50% of all words in student textbooks, and a total of only 5,000 words account for about 90% of the words in student texts"(Reutzel, D. R., & Cooter, R. B., 2000. *Teaching Children to Read* (3rd ed.). Upper Saddle River, NJ: Merrill Prentice Hall, p. 228).

[6]   As stated in chapter 3, New Jersey's reading standards state that "by the end of Grade 1, students will develop a vocabulary of 300-500 high-frequency sight words.... Building upon knowledge and skills gained in [Grade 1], by the end of Grade 2, students will develop a vocabulary of 500-800 regular and irregular sight words" (retrieved 2/1/08, from http://www.state.nj.us/education/aps/cccs/lal/horizontal/lal_hmatrix/reading/reading_vertical_d.pdf). The total over Grades 1 and 2 ranges from 800 to 1300 sight words. After Grade 2, New Jersey's reading standards do not mention numbers of sight words. The likely reason is that the sight word vocabulary of good readers takes off exponentially at this point, rising into the thousands, and increasing markedly year after year. It's impossible for teachers and parents to count these large increases.

[7]   Graves et al., 2004, p. 220.

[8]   "Words that are not recognized automatically will thwart the process of comprehending text" (Graves, Juel, & Graves, 2004, p. 220).

[9]   Lipson, M. Y., & Wixson, K. K., 2003. *Assessment and Instruction of Reading and Writing Difficulty: An Interactive Approach* (3rd ed.). Boston: Allyn & Bacon, p. 26.

[10]   Jennings, H. J., Caldwell, J. S., & Lerner, J. W., 2006. *Reading Problems: Assessment and Teaching Strategies* (5th ed.). Boston: Pearson Allyn & Bacon, pp. 205-206.

[11]   One indicator of decoding's complexity is the number of fuzzy synonyms for it. Here are some: phonemic recoding, word analysis, word attack, word identification.

[12]   "The importance of vocabulary as part of the process of learning to read cannot be overstated. Word knowledge constitutes the foundation of reading success. 'Research indicates that direct instruction in vocabulary can increase vocabulary learning and comprehension'.... Children who enter first grade with vocabulary deficits show increasing problems with reading, and they tend to fall further and further behind.... Children can hardly understand what they are reading without knowing the meaning of the words they read" (Savage, J. F., 2007. *Sound It Out: Phonics in a Comprehensive Reading Program*. Boston: McGraw Hill, pp. 176-177).

[13]   If children robotically follow the rule that in consonant-vowel-consonant-vowel words ending with e (e.g., *home*), the first vowel makes the long sound and the e is silent, they'll be wrong at least 40% of the time. Just look at the word *come*—it violates the rule, which is really not a hard-and-fast rule, but an unreliable guide. This (and similar topics) is discussed in Heilman, A. W., 2006. *Phonics in Proper Perspective* (10th ed.). Upper Saddle River, NJ: Pearson Merrill Prentice Hall, p. 103.

[14]   For an excellent understanding of phonics, which research shows benefits children, we suggest you read Heilman's (2006) book or one of these:

- Cunningham, P. M., 2004. *Phonics They Use: Words for Reading and Writing* (4th ed.). Boston: Allyn & Bacon.
- Savage, J. F., 2007. *Sound It Out: Phonics in a Comprehensive Reading Program*. Boston: McGraw Hill.

These books are small, but powerful—they take the mystery out of phonics and provide practical activities for teaching children to decode. Although we think most parents of struggling readers should not tutor their children, if you want to, these books can help.

15 The definition of fluency can provoke considerable debate. Paula Schwanenflugel and Hilary Ruston provide a brief, but helpful discussion of the debate:

> If you are confused about the meaning of the term reading fluency, you are not alone. A number of definitions of reading fluency in both the research and popular literature seem, at times, to conflict with each other. However, we would argue that this conflict is based more on the details of the definitions than on any inherent substance in them. Few researchers would argue that reading fluency is a single skill. Rather, it is the orchestration of a number of subskills, which, taken together, comprise reading fluency. The debate regarding the definition of reading fluency is more about which skills are important to this definition rather than what fluent reading ultimately 'looks like' in practice" (Schwanenflugel, P. J., & Ruston, H. P., 2008. Becoming a fluent reader: From theory to practice. In M. R. Kuhn & P. J. Schwanenflugel (Eds.), *Fluency in the Classroom* (pp. 1-16). New York: The Guilford Press, p. 2).

In discussing the definition, Schwanenflugel and Ruston then identify two sets of component skills: those somewhat controversial and those generally agreed upon. The generally agreed upon skills are phonics and blending, word reading efficiency (quick and accurate word reading), word reading autonomy (unintended but effortless reading of words, such as those on a television screen), and text reading fluency (quickly and accurately reading sentences, paragraphs and larger units of text with basic expression and basic comprehension). The somewhat controversial skills are good comprehension and expression.

As a parent, your role is not to get involved in the researchers' debate. Instead, it's to have school personnel clearly define what they mean by fluency. With an agreed upon definition, one that's shared by all involved in planning and carrying out your child's program, instruction will likely be more focused, more consistent, and more effective.

16 Walpole, S., & McKenna, M. C., 2004. *The Literacy Coach's Handbook: A Guide to Research-Based Practice*. New York: The Guilford Press, p. 53.

17 Rasinski, T., & Padak, N., 1996. *Holistic Reading Strategies: Teaching Children Who Find Reading Difficult*. Columbus, OH: Merrill, p. 70.

18 Hasbrouck, J., & Tindal, G. A., 2006. Oral reading fluency norms: A valuable assessment tool for reading teachers. *Reading Teacher, 59* (7), 636-644.

19 Schwanenflugel & Ruston, 2008, p. 13.

20 Ellis, E. S., 1996. Reading strategy instruction. In D. D. Deshler, E. S. Ellis, & B. K. Lenz (Eds.), *Teaching Adolescents with Learning Disabilities: Strategies and Methods* (2nd ed.) (pp. 61–125). Denver, CO: Love.

21 For an excellent summary of the research on comprehension strategies, see Willingham, D. T., 2006/7. The usefulness of brief instruction in reading comprehension strategies. *American Educator, 30* (4), 39-45, 50.

22 Note that we used the plural, levels. This is because children have several comprehension levels, such as their independent and instructional levels for narrative (story) materials and their independent and instructional levels for expository (textbook-like information) materials.

[23] The Literacy Dictionary defines study skills as "a general term for those techniques and strategies that help a person read or listen for specific purposes with the intent to remember" (Harris, T. L., & Hodges, R. E. (Eds.), 1995. *The Literacy Dictionary: The Vocabulary of Reading and Writing.* Newark, DE: International Reading Association, p. 245). Some experts might broaden the ending of this definition to "remember and, in some cases, apply."

[24] Gerald Duffy makes an important distinction between the words *skill* and *strategy*: "A skill is something you do automatically without thought. You do it the same way every time. Tying your shoe is an example ... [as is] instantly recognizing and saying a word such as 'the'.... A strategy, in contrast, is a plan. You are thoughtful when you do it, and you often adjust the plan as you go along to fit the situation. Planning a road trip is an example .... Making predictions is a strategy because good readers are thoughtful in using text clues and prior knowledge" (Duffy, G. G., 2003. *Explaining Reading.* New York: The Guilford Press, pp. 21-22). This distinction is important, especially when discussing reading comprehension and study skills. Many authors use the word *skill* to describe processes that are not automatic, that require a great deal of thought, judgment, and modification, such as outlining, following directions, creating a goal, monitoring progress, identifying main ideas, summarizing an article. So keep in mind that what sounds simple and automatic—a skill—may be a complex process that requires deep thought.

[25] Also called high or strong self-efficacy for a task. The specific task should be named, as a child can have high self-efficacy for one task, like reading silently, and low self-efficacy for a related task, like reading orally.

[26] Carnine, D., Silbert, J., & Kameenui, E. J., 1997. *Direct Instruction Reading* (3rd ed.). Columbus, OH: Merrill, p. 42.

[27] Actually, because of their failures and fears, struggling readers may be highly motivated to resist reading.

[28] Greene, L. J. (2002). *Roadblocks to Learning.* New York: Warner Books, p. 109.

[29] Some teachers assign large amounts of homework because they think it will positively influence academic achievement. For average-achieving children in the elementary and middle grades, its influence is weak to slight. For struggling readers, a steady stream of homework they find frustrating can be destructive. Moreover, no convincing body of research shows that typical home-work assignments—answering questions, filling out worksheets—motivates struggling readers to succeed in school or improves their reading. For an excellent review of the research, we encourage you to read, "Using research to answer practical questions about homework" (Cooper, H., & Valen-tine, J. C., 2001. *Educational Psychologist, 36,* 143–153). If your child gets large amounts of difficult homework, and you believe his teachers are unaware of the research, you might want to share with them this article as well as the homework articles listed on our website: www.reading2008.com. These articles show teachers how to modify homework so struggling readers will likely succeed.

[30] Because your child may have strong self-confidence in one subject, with one teacher, and weak self-confidence in another subject, with another teacher, developing a plan to strengthen his self-confidence may require the involvement of the school's reading specialist, school psychologist, and social worker, as well as your child's teachers and their teaching assistants. Furthermore, the chances of successfully strengthening your child's self-confidence or self-efficacy increase markedly if all staff

work together to reinforce the same behaviors, repeat the same messages, and use the same valid principles to structure and react to reading and writing assignments.

[31] Lyon, G. R., 1996. Learning disabilities. *Special Education for Students with Disabilities, 6* (1), 54-74.

[32] As stated in a previous endnote, an evaluation is more than an assessment. Evaluations provide insightful, trustworthy interpretations of findings (such as test scores), with instructional recommendations that logically reflect the findings, while assessments usually present data with little or no attempt to provide valid interpretations or logical recommendations. Although we have made this distinction, a distinction that is often important, many school personnel use the terms interchangeably, as if no difference exists. If you're unsure of what they mean when they use the terms, ask—the answer is important.

[33] If you don't request a plan to frequently monitor your child's progress, he may languish in a program that's wrong for him.

[34] Both laws can be downloaded from The Library of Congress-Thomas, http://thomas.loc.gov, or from the Department of Education, www.ed.gov.

CHAPTER 5
USING READING EVALUATIONS

Once the reading evaluation is finished and a report developed, the reading specialist usually meets with the parents and the child's teacher to discuss the evaluation's results and its recommendations.[1]

No doubt you will have many questions about the evaluation. What does it mean? Is it accurate and complete? What do its technical terms mean? Will its recommendations work? What can you do if you're unhappy with it? The suggestions below will help you answer these questions and use the reading evaluation to plan a program to markedly improve your child's reading.

UNDERSTANDING AND EVALUATING THE EVALUATION

The key to understanding and evaluating the evaluation is asking questions and making requests, *before and after* the evaluation is finished. The previous chapter focused on before; this chapter focuses on after.

Suggestion 1: Try to Understand the Evaluation—What Does It Mean? Ask questions, lots of them, until you fully understand what the reading specialist found and recommends. For example, if he and other school personnel use abstract technical terms to describe your child's difficulties, ask for straightforward definitions and simple, concrete examples. This isn't a sign of ignorance; it's a sign of intelligence.

Why? It's unlikely that you have a graduate degree in reading disabilities. Furthermore, different professionals use different terms to describe reading disabilities (e.g., dyslexia, hyperlexia, auditory dyslexia, visual dyslexia) and stages of reading development (e.g., logographic stage, stage of controlled word recognition). No set is universally accepted. Often, terms used by reading specialists, such as automaticity and strategic reading, are foreign to teachers. Thus, it's quite possible that your child's teachers don't understand the reading specialist's terms, but won't ask questions for fear of looking ignorant. So ask questions—questions lead to answers, which lead to better understanding, decision making, and action.

Questions also give you an opportunity to see if the reading specialist can explain his findings and their implications in explicit, straightforward ways and can give you examples that clarify whatever you find abstract, difficult, or just plain confusing. If he can, great—it inspires confidence. If he can't, and if he talks in roundabout ways, throwing in lots of jargon, be suspicious. He may have lots of words, but little knowledge.

Suggestion 2: If Necessary, Ask the Reading Specialist for Straightforward, Written Answers to Your Original Questions. If the reading specialist's written report did not directly answer all your original questions, such as those listed near the end of chapter 4, ask for a written addendum that answers them. Asking may reveal that he failed to gather the necessary information or think about the questions, and needs to do so.

If the reading specialist wants to provide only oral answers to questions his report failed to address, politely, respectfully, and firmly request written ones. If answers are oral, everyone will suffer from the natural inadequacies and tricks of human memory—they'll forget, they'll manufacture new memories, they'll act as if they listened to different evaluations. In all likelihood, this is not feigned or dishonest; it's just human memory expressing its limitations.

Moreover, you may eventually need a complete written report for other reasons, such as coordinating instruction with a private tutor, requesting special education eligibility, or, if your child becomes eligible for special education, developing an educational plan.[2]

Suggestion 3: If Necessary, Ask the Reading Specialist for a Chart that Lists Your Child's Listening Comprehension Level and Her Three Critical Reading Levels: Instructional, Independent, and Frustration. If you remember, chapter 4 recommended that before the evaluation you ask for a levels chart. Such a chart is critical. It's critical because it's a clear snapshot of what your child can do and what will frustrate her. In paragraphs, levels are easily overlooked; in charts, they stand out.

Thus, if, for any reason the reading specialist's report does not include a levels chart, ask him to revise his report to include one and to give you one at your meeting. Having the chart in hand at your meeting will help you to ask better questions and make better decisions.

Once you have a chart of your child's listening and reading levels, ask the reading specialist to explain their meaning. His explanations should conform to those below. The answers should inspire confidence or concern.

Generally, levels explain what your child can comfortably do and what frustrates her. If, for example, her instructional level for listening comprehension is 5th grade, she can usually understand 70% to 90% of 5th-grade materials read to her; probably, she'll understand 4th-grade materials even better. Sixth-grade materials, however, will frustrate her. In many respects, 5th-grade materials would be perfect for listening—they would challenge her just enough to interest her and advance her learning.

Similarly, instructional-level reading materials will challenge but won't frustrate your child. They're materials she'll succeed with and learn from—*if* her teachers provide direct instruction and ongoing support, and *if* she makes a moderate effort to succeed.

Independent-level materials are easier—they offer little word identification or comprehension challenge. Because they're easy, your child can focus most of her energy on the assignment's objective instead of struggling to identify words or unlock basic meanings. And, as the name suggests, when she has to work independently, doing homework or classwork, materials should be at her independent level.

In contrast, your child should not be asked to read materials at her frustration level. Frustration-level materials, as the name suggests, will frustrate her. Regularly assigning such materials to her will perpetuate struggle and failure, likely destroying her motivation, even if teachers provide frequent feedback and support.

Now comes a warning, one that sounds technical, unnecessary, and perhaps intimidating. As technical as it sounds, it's important. Here it is. When discussing the levels, make sure you get an answer to this question: Did the levels come from a norm-referenced test or an informal reading inventory?[3]

Here's the reason. Many reading and learning specialists find children's listening and reading levels by testing them on short, often unrelated items, to see how they compare to other children instead of seeing how well they've mastered common materials used in different grades.

The tests used to compare children to one another are usually standardized, norm-referenced tests; they report scores called grade equivalents. Although these tests produce other scores, grade equivalents are perhaps the most common scores reported, and also the most misleading. They appear to indicate what children can do—but they don't. They often exaggerate progress. For example, if your child earns a grade equivalent of 3.2 on a standardized, norm-referenced reading test, she may not be able to read 3rd-grade books. This is not a typo: We said she may not be able to read 3rd-grade books. In essence, grade equivalents fail to answer these questions:

- To make meaningful progress in reading, and to develop confidence (or self-efficacy) for reading, what level materials should teachers use to teach my child how to read (instructional-level materials)?
- What level materials should teachers assign my child when she works independently (independent-level materials)?

To answer these questions, reading specialists should administer tests that have children read graded passages, such as passages equivalent to those in the 3rd- and 4th-grade books used in your child's classes. In addition to administering such tests, called informal reading inventories (IRIs), the specialist should have your child read from books at different grade levels and observe her reading and completing assignments in class. With this information, you and her teachers will have a fairly good idea about materials that will moderately challenge, not frustrate her, that will strengthen her confidence, not destroy it.

So, ask for a chart of your child's listening and reading levels and ask how the levels were derived. To see if instruction is appropriate and to monitor her progress, to help her *beat the odds*, this information is critical.[4]

Suggestion 4: Ask How the Results of the Reading Evaluation Reflect Your Child's Response to Intervention (RTI) Performance. If your child was in an RTI program, she should have received several weeks or more of instruction that assessed her ability to gain from scientifically-based reading instruction. Moreover, her instruction should have been frequently monitored to accurately assess her progress so that you and school staff could see what did and didn't work.

When such instruction is well designed and well monitored, it can offer information that improves the value of an evaluation and the effectiveness of its instructional recommendations. RTI data may, for example, indicate that your child was motivated by frequent, positive comments that focused on her effort, but not by competitive games; that she liked reading and listening to stories, but not nonfiction; that she made good progress in word identification when instruction emphasized word families (like /ack/: back, hack, lack), but poor progress when it emphasized the sounds of individual vowels (like the short sound of /a/) and vowel combinations (like /ea/ or /oa/).

Given the value of well-designed and well-monitored RTI instruction, you and school personnel need to know how the RTI results compare to the findings and recommendations of the reading evaluation. If the evaluation and RTI are in conflict, and your child made good progress under RTI, go with what's already working—the RTI instruction. But if RTI instruction proved ineffective, and if the evaluation addressed the factors and questions listed in chapters 3 and 4, its findings, conclusions, and recommendations deserve respect. Keep in mind, however, that an educational evaluation can produce only hypotheses, hypotheses that require frequent and careful monitoring. This is the subject of chapter 7.

Suggestion 5: Ask How the Results of the Reading Evaluation Relate to Your Child's Performance on the State's No Child Left Behind (NCLB) Tests. The NCLB requires schools to test virtually all children in reading and mathematics in grades 3 to 8 and once in grades 10 to 12 and to use each child's test results to identify learning problems and improve instruction.

If your child does poorly on the NCLB tests, the National Center for Learning Disabilities recommends that you ask the first two questions below. The third is ours:

- What support and remediation will be provided?
- How will classroom instruction be adjusted?
- How does my child's NCLB test performance compare to the findings of her reading evaluation?

Often, data from another source, like an NCLB test, can strengthen your request for services. In the case of NCLB, the school will be judged "in need of improvement" if too many children have problems with reading and the school fails to make Adequate Yearly Progress (AYP). Many news media and politicians refer to this as "failing." For schools, "failing" can have severe consequences. Thus, if your child performs poorly on the State's NCLB test, the school may have added incentive to help her become a proficient reader.[5]

But, like much about reading disabilities, complications abound. Here's one. Jennifer Booher-Jennings reported that many schools, especially poorer ones, deny extra reading help to children with severe reading difficulties. Instead, these schools limit extra help to children who will likely pass the NCLB test if they get extra help. Because passing requires them to improve their scores only a little, they're called "bubble kids." The reasoning is flawed and heartless: The top students will pass without extra reading help; the bottom ones will fail, even with help, so don't waste money on them.[6] The only exception might be children in special education. If a child's Individualized Education Program (IEP)—a legally mandated document that describes her special education needs, her educational goals, and the services she'll get—specifies extra reading help, by law, the school must provide it.

Here's another complication. In many States, children who fail the State's NCLB reading test must repeat the grade. In the long term, retained children—even if they repeat only one or two grades—continue to suffer academically; moreover, if they're retained in elementary school, they're likely to drop out of high school.[7] Retention is so traumatic that many children report they'd rather go blind.[8] Unfortunately, in many States, once a child fails an NCLB test, parents have little say about retention. Thus, your best solution is to get your child the quality services she needs, as quickly as possible, to avoid this senseless, devastating threat.

Suggestion 6: If Necessary, Ask the School to Systematically Evaluate Any Behavioral or Emotional Difficulties Your Child May Have. Some struggling readers frequently have trouble paying attention, cooperating, following class rules, following class routines, getting along with peers; others are depressed or highly anxious. Some combine several of these characteristics. So ask the reading specialist if he saw indications of behavioral or emotional difficulties.

If he did, quickly get help. A reading evaluation is not enough. Ask the reading specialist to make a referral for an evaluation to the school's expert in working *with* teachers to help children improve their behavior or overcome emotional difficulties. In schools, the most effective interventions for improving behavioral and emotional difficulties stress the systematic and ethical use of behavioral principles, referred to as applied behavior analysis (ABA).[9] Typically, the school's ABA expert is a school psychologist or special educator.

If your child does have behavioral or emotional difficulties, and they're not evaluated and addressed quickly, they can frustrate efforts to improve her reading. Her behavioral or emotional difficulties might make her an outcast in school, trigger an unnecessary referral to special education, or rise to a level requiring intensive psychological or psychiatric help. Fortunately, early, knowledgeable, skilled intervention, built around ABA, can often improve the situation—markedly.

Improving the situation should begin with a relevant evaluation by an ABA expert, an evaluation that identifies the immediate, direct causes of the problem and sets the stage for remedying it. Usually, the expert examines the child's classroom to identify what might provoke the difficulties. Often, the solution focuses on changing some aspect of the class, like the difficulty of assignments.

Let's take the hypothetical but typical case of Luci. She "cuts up in class." During reading, she habitually calls out, taps her pencil incessantly, and talks loudly to her neighbors. She continually disrupts the class and exhausts her teacher. Her parents and her teacher know why: It's logical—she doesn't want to read. Logical? Perhaps. But what if they're wrong? What if she's highly motivated to read? Working to increase her motivation will waste precious time, energy, and hope. To avoid this common pitfall of erroneous assumptions, her behavior needs to be systematically evaluated to identify what's motivating her to "cut up."[10]

To find out what's causing Luci to "cut up," the school's ABA expert evaluates her behavior.[11] He systematically observes her in class; interviews her, her teacher, and her parents; and rates or quantifies her behaviors.[12] This may be all he needs to develop a highly probable, educated guess, or hypothesis, about what's causing the inappropriate behavior. The next step for him, her teacher, and perhaps her parents, is to plan and carry out a program to test the hypothesis. If the hypothesis says Luci needs to read easier materials, and easier materials solve the problem, further behavioral evaluations and interventions are unnecessary.

If easier materials don't solve the problem, and the reasons for Luci's behavior remain a mystery, the ABA expert needs to evaluate her more scientifically. In collaboration with her teacher, the expert needs to temporarily change or "manipulate" a few things in her class to identify the immediate, environmental causes of her behavioral difficulties.[13]

Changes might include giving Luci even easier materials to read, giving her fewer materials to read, shortening the time she spends on seatwork, simplifying directions, moving her to the front of the room, seating her next to students she likes, visibly praising nearby children for cooperating, frequently praising her for cooperating, frequently giving her valued rewards for following the class rules, letting her eat a snack, letting her take a 5-minute break during seatwork, letting her pick a study-buddy to work with, teaching her socially acceptable ways of asking for help. This process—systematically making and testing changes to identify the immediate causes of behavioral difficulties—is called a functional behavioral assessment (FBA). It's a problem solving approach, an experiment that systematically uses what's known about learning to identify immediate causes of behavior and resolve problems.

If knowledgeable, skilled professionals use FBAs systematically, and if the ABA plans derived from them are carried out faithfully, monitored carefully, and revised as needed, children's behavior and emotions often improve.[14] And sometimes dramatically. So, if you suspect that your child might be having behavioral difficulties or is emotionally distressed, request that an ABA expert systematically identify the reasons.[15] Often, the reasons are right there, but they're invisible. Part of the ABA expert's job is to make them visible (and manageable), so teachers and parents can address the right cause and solve the right problem.

Notice that the suggestions we made, like giving your child easier materials and frequently praising her for cooperating, are positive. Most interventions can and should be positive, which is far easier to do when you identify and address problems earlier rather than later.

Fortunately, schools and teachers have a wide array of positive behavioral approaches they can use to help children improve their behavior, such as teaching them to replace socially unacceptable ways of asking for help with socially acceptable ways. By carefully implementing and monitoring evidence-based approaches that address immediate causes, and emphasizing feedback that praises children for good effort and the correct use of specific strategies, ABA experts and teachers can help children replace destructive with constructive behaviors.

Although ABA is generally our first choice for school-based problems, we believe that counseling—if responsive to what happens in the struggling reader's classes—can help identify and solve the behavioral and emotional difficulties of some struggling readers.

Counseling should occur twice weekly, for 40 minutes per session. Please note that we specified the amount and frequency of counseling. Although there's no magic about "twice weekly, for 40 minutes per session," we did this to emphasize that many schools schedule counseling as little as once monthly for 20 minutes. If world-renowned counselors like Carl

Rogers, Sigmund Freud, or Virginia Satir counseled Luci for 20 minutes a month, without a miracle, counseling would fail. With a miracle, it still might fail.

For the counselor to begin understanding Luci's problems and for counseling to work, not only must the counselor be knowledgeable, skilled, and liked by Luci, but the sessions need to be long enough and frequent enough for the counselor and Luci to get to know one another and to adequately discuss the issues, without losing continuity and momentum. Also, for counseling to work, both diagnostically and therapeutically, it will probably require the counselor to periodically observe Luci in class, help her teacher modify instruction, help her parents properly reinforce her, and consult with her teacher and parents to ensure that everyone responds to her in a consistent, supportive manner that strengthens her self-confidence and prevents confusion.

All that said, if you believe your child is having behavioral difficulties or her reading is causing her emotional distress, ask for an ABA evaluation. If the school refuses, ask for a counseling evaluation. If the school refuses both, and she's not eligible for special education under the *Individuals with Disabilities Education Improvement Act of 2004* (IDEA-2004), or you think their evaluation was poor, seek outside help from an expert, such as a clinical psychologist, clinical social worker, or special educator *with extensive knowledge of* schools and applied behavior analysis. If such an expert is unavailable, seek help from a counselor with extensive knowledge of schools, instructional modifications, and struggling readers. Don't wait.

INSTRUCTIONAL RECOMMENDATIONS

Instructional recommendations are a critical part of reading and learning evaluations. In fact, using evaluative data to develop precisely targeted recommendations is a main reason for evaluating children.

The recommendations should be practical and powerful. Practical means they can be implemented in a quality way. Powerful means they can markedly improve your child's reading.

Suggestion 7: Ask the Reading Specialist Why He Thinks His Instructional Recommendations Will Work. Using particular approaches or strategies to teach a child during an evaluation is called diagnostic teaching. If possible, reading specialists should engage in diagnostic teaching. Without such teaching, recommendations are often guesswork, guesswork that may well be wrong. Again, questions can help. They can help you determine if the reading specialist engaged in diagnostic teaching and, if so, the results.

To determine why the reading specialist thinks his recommendations will work, we recommend that you ask him these questions:

- Did you teach my child using the approaches or strategies you're recommending?
- If so, how well did she respond? If not, why do you think they're likely to work?
- What does the research say about them? Can you share copies of the research?
- How will daily or weekly progress be monitored?

- What will the school do if, after a month of implementing the recommendations, progress is poor?

Unfortunately, it's often difficult or impossible for reading specialists to adequately engage in diagnostic teaching. In such cases, it's especially important to monitor children's progress.

Suggestion 8: Ask the Reading Specialist and Your Child's Teachers to Demonstrate How They'll Use Their Recommendations to Instruct Your Child. Simply put, this will tell you a lot about your child's program and might give you ideas about supporting her at home.

Many teachers and reading specialists would welcome such a request. Usually, demonstrating takes little time.

But some will resist. Resistance is telling: It tells you whether they care about helping your child and truly believe in parent participation. It's also suggestive. It suggests that they might not have the knowledge and skill to implement their recommendations.

Suggestion 9: Offer Suggestions for Instructing Your Child. After fully examining the recommended materials, approaches, and strategies, and attentively watching the demonstrations, feel free to comment on whether you think they'll work. Avoid absolute statements: "This won't work." Instead, share your reasons: "I don't think this will work because she struggled with a similar program that made her sound out individual vowels. Trying to sound out vowels confused her."

If, in addition to commenting, you feel comfortable making suggestions, make them: "Perhaps there are ways other than teaching her to use individual vowel sounds. Perhaps it might be better to teach her to use spelling patterns or word families. I read in a book by Caldwell and Leslie, two highly respected professors of literacy, that spelling patterns help kids who struggle with individual vowel sounds."[16]

Your suggestions may be particularly helpful, as you probably know a great deal about your child that school personnel don't.[17] You know her history. You probably know if she'll like books about polar bears, if she's likely to succeed on the type of homework they're recommending, and if she'll work hard for gummed stars. Share your information. Make suggestions. Your child's reading specialist and teacher may welcome your insight, knowing it may well save them and your child from the frustrations of trial and error.

Suggestion 10: Assess if the Amount of Instructional Time is Adequate. Ask *if* and *why* the amount of time planned for direct, explicit instruction and for easy, interesting reading is sufficient for your child to become a proficient reader. The following guidelines offer perspective on how much reading instruction and other reading is needed:

> Schedule sufficient instructional time to enable students to make more than a year's progress each year in all areas in which they are behind. For children who are behind, we recommend a morning language arts period

of 150 minutes, and if at all possible a 30- to 60-minute afternoon period. In addition, after-school and summer instruction should be scheduled for children who need even more extra instruction to reach grade level.[18]

As part of this, and sometimes in addition, your child should have plenty of opportunity to read materials she finds easy and interesting:

> Organize the classroom so that students have lots of time to read. The general guideline is that students should do 45-60 minutes of easy reading every school day. The time can be broken up, with 15 minutes during a designated free reading time, 7 minutes during a break in activities, and so on. But students do not learn to read unless they read a lot. And they cannot get better by reading difficult material. This is especially so for struggling readers. Therefore, students must have lots of time to read easy materials without interference from us and without focusing on skills or strategies.[19]

This is a lot of time. Many school personnel will say it's unrealistic. But without such time, it's likely that progress will be poor. Thus, for your child to make adequate progress in reading, additional reading instruction may have to be added before or after school or during other periods. Less time may have to be allocated to other parts of the curriculum. Reading might replace English. Subjects like social studies may have to be modified so reading instruction is emphasized—knowledgeably, skillfully, and systematically—through social studies books and discussions.

If the school personnel planning your child's program don't realize how much time struggling readers need to spend reading, show them the quotes above. If you need more support, show them Richard Allington's book, *What Really Matters for Struggling Readers: Designing Research-Based Programs*. Chapter 2's title says it all: *What Really Matters: Kids Need to Read a Lot*.[20]

Suggestion 11: Examine How Your Child's Program Components are Coordinated.
Unless the instructional recommendations and the other components of your child's program are coordinated, they're unlikely to work nearly as well as they should. Therefore, it's important to ask school personnel how everything will be *coordinated*, so that each part reinforces the others and gives your child sufficient practice, without prematurely introducing new strategies and concepts that might confuse her. A common acronym for coordination is ROCC: Struggling readers need a **R**ich, **O**rganized, **C**onsistent **C**urriculum.

When listening to their responses, listen for specific, concrete information, like "We meet every other Wednesday morning to jointly plan the upcoming two weeks." Be wary of vague generalizations, like "Oh, we follow the same curriculum, so we always know what's being taught."

If you get vague generalizations, ask specific questions, like these:

- How do you know if something was taught?
- How will you know if she mastered it?
- If she hasn't mastered it, how will you quickly coordinate efforts to help her catch up?

Remember that your questions have at least three purposes: To help school personnel develop a more appropriate and responsive program. To help you understand it. To help you gauge its potential effectiveness and, if necessary, influence it.

Suggestion 12: Ask School Personnel to Show You How to Reinforce at Home What Your Child is Learning in School. As we explain in the next chapter, at home you can help your child in many ways without becoming her teacher or tutor. For example, you can help her find pictures of ancient Rome, take her to story-hour at the library, read her a *Garfield Fat Cat* book, or praise her effort to complete homework.

In the long term, these actions can help your child immeasurably. They provide a foundation for a strong vocabulary and a positive attitude toward learning. In the short term, however, they're unlikely to help her unless they're carefully coordinated with what her teacher will soon teach or what's just been taught. So, it's important to ask her teacher what he'll be stressing over the next few weeks, and what he's just taught. It's also important to ask him to show you—not just tell you—how you can work with her at home to practice what he's already taught, in ways she finds enjoyable and motivating. Practice should emphasize knowledge, skills, ideas, and strategies that she's just about mastered. Although challenging, such practice should not prove frustrating.[21]

Reinforcing at home what your child is learning in school can also involve simple routines that over the years have proven effective. One is Topping's Paired Reading, a method that avoids teaching words or particular word identification strategies; instead, it focuses on practicing straightforward reading by having you and your child orally read together from the same easy reading material, such as a book that she's selected.

Here are a few more details. You stop reading aloud when she signals you to stop and you start again when she makes an error or hesitates on a word for five seconds. At this point, you say the word correctly, ask her to, and again begin reading together.

For Paired Reading to succeed, your child must select reading materials she can read successfully. With her teacher's help, this should be easy. Because Paired Reading creates success, your child is likely to find it enjoyable, therapeutic, and confidence-building.[22]

As you might suspect, learning how to implement Paired Reading requires school personnel to discuss it with you, demonstrate it, role play it, and answer your questions. Fortunately, many schools know that it's highly effective in improving word recognition and fluency; therefore, they hold Paired Reading workshops for parents.

AN INADEQUATE EVALUATION

If you think your child's reading evaluation's inadequate, you probably won't sleep well at night. So before you lose too much sleep, read the suggestions below. They suggest that you have the evaluation evaluated, request to observe your child in class, request an independent evaluation, or get a private evaluation.

Suggestion 13: Ask a Private or University-Affiliated Reading Specialist, One Without Financial Links to the District, to Evaluate the Evaluation. If you're unhappy with the answers you're getting—they're evasive, vague, contradictory, illogical, or dismissive— you may need to have the evaluation evaluated by a private, doctoral level reading specialist. You can find such a specialist by asking parents whose children have had reading problems, by asking your physician, or by searching the yellow pages. You can also search university websites for special education or reading faculty who regularly teach courses in reading disabilities or supervise the university's learning or reading clinic.

Fortunately, some university faculty are often quite generous with their time—they're often willing to volunteer an hour or so reviewing records and discussing your child's needs. For a modest fee, university clinics may be willing to review records (or evaluate your child), if they don't have conflicts of interest, such as contracts with your child's school.

A disadvantage of working with university faculty and clinics is that they may not be able to devote more than an hour or so to reviewing your child's records and evaluating the evaluation. Moreover, they're unlikely to meet with the school to discuss their findings.

In contrast, private reading specialists can usually devote whatever time is needed as they charge by the task or hour, which can be quite expensive. Once the private specialist finishes evaluating the evaluation, it may be a good idea for him to meet with you, the school's reading specialist, and your child's teacher to discuss his findings and recommendations. If he understands the law, as well as reading disabilities, and understands how to listen, develop trust, build rapport, negotiate, and problem solve, this may dramatically improve your child's program, her chances of succeeding in life, and your chances of getting a good night's sleep.

Suggestion 14: Ask to Observe Your Child in Reading and Related Subjects. Such an observation may provide you with critical, concrete information about your child's program and her reaction to it. Seeing and hearing gives you information you can't get from discussions or written reports. After your observation, ask yourself three questions:

- Did my child behave like she usually does?
- Did my child's reading and behavior match the findings of her reading evaluation?
- Is her teacher implementing the evaluation's recommendations in ways that will likely work?

Sometimes, school personnel don't want parents to observe their child's class, thinking their presence would dramatically change their child's behavior. If this is the case, ask the school to video her in reading and related subjects. Then together, in the school, you, the school's reading specialist, and your child's teacher can watch the video, with the specialist and teacher explaining what was happening.[23]

If the school refuses to let you observe your child's class or observe videos of her in reading, it's not paranoid to ask yourself, What are they hiding? What are they afraid of? After all, your child's future is in their hands. Schools argue, even plead for parent involvement. But how can you be knowledgeably and intelligently involved if you can't see what's happening? In this situation, words without pictures don't suffice.

So, if this is your situation, consider asking the superintendent of schools for permission to observe, or having a private expert, whom you hire, observe. If the district is evaluating your child for special education eligibility, or if she's already eligible and you're involved in developing an Individualized Education Program (IEP), observations are usually allowed.[24]

If, however, the district denies all observations, you have four options. One: Check with your State Department of Education. Ask them to send you the actual laws and portions of the State codes that govern parent observations. Two: Check your district's written policies; despite denial of your request, district policy may allow you to observe. Three: Hire an expert to evaluate your child. Often, schools will allow experts to observe as observations are critical to evaluations. Four: Hire an attorney who specializes in special education. But be careful: Some attorneys specialize in ten or more areas, meaning they don't specialize.

Suggestion 15: Ask the School to Pay for an Independent Evaluation. Independent evaluations are paid for by the district. They're a formal part of IDEA-2004, the Federal law that governs most of special education. Under IDEA-2004, you may formally request the district to pay for an independent evaluation—one conducted by a reading specialist, an ABA specialist, a school psychologist, or any other qualified professional who is not an employee of the district—if your child is being evaluated or reevaluated to determine her special education eligibility or to plan her program under IDEA-2004.

Under IDEA-2004, obtaining an independent evaluation is a formal process requiring you to show why the district's evaluation is inadequate. If you have solid reasons for thinking it's inadequate, and your child's being evaluated or reevaluated for special education, requesting an independent evaluation makes sense. It also makes sense if she's been receiving special education services for more than a few months, her progress has been poor, you requested an evaluation to identify barriers to progress, and you have solid reasons for thinking the evaluation is deficient.

The good news for both you and school personnel is that a highly competent professional evaluation can help everyone—it can improve everyone's understanding of your child's educational needs and the programs and strategies she needs to succeed in school. This can make school more productive and satisfying for her, for you, and for school personnel. In the long run, it can save schools lots of money by improving the effectiveness of instruction, thereby preventing the need for additional services.[25]

Nevertheless, districts may challenge your request by filing for an impartial due process hearing. This is court—it can be bewildering, frightening, expensive, and labor intensive. Because a request for an independent evaluation can trigger a legal challenge, and because such evaluations can be critical to a child's academic, behavioral, and emotional success, you should carefully balance the pluses and minuses of pursuing this course. If it looks as if a hearing will be required, it may be cheaper for you to pay for the evaluation. If you do, you can select any expert you want, not one the State or district must approve.

Suggestion 16: Have Your Child's Reading Evaluated Privately by a Doctoral-Level Reading Specialist. This can be expensive, very expensive, especially if the specialist interviews teachers, observes your child in school, tests her, conducts diagnostic teaching, and meets with school personnel to discuss the evaluation's results and plan the program.

So, if you have little trust in the school's evaluation, including its recommendations, and if the school refuses to pay for an independent reading evaluation, should you have your child privately evaluated? If there's no guarantee that your child's school will do a good job implementing or even trying to implement the recommendations of a private evaluation, should you have your child privately evaluated? If there's no guarantee that the private evaluation's recommendations, if implemented well, will result in excellent progress, should you have your child privately evaluated? To all three questions, our answer is absolute—*yes.*

Here's why: A good evaluation will help your child become a proficient, highly motivated reader. Without it, she has little chance. Moreover, many schools will do their best to implement the evaluation's recommendations in a quality way. And if they resist, and your child is sinking or making little headway, at least you have information that might compel them to create an adequate program. Lastly, the evaluation will help to guide tutoring, any other help you provide her, and your future decisions.

Sounds reasonable, but what if you don't have the thousands of dollars needed for a quality evaluation from a doctoral level specialist?

You have several options. One, seek an evaluation from a university reading clinic. They're usually inexpensive. Two, seek an evaluation and tutoring from a graduate program that requires its graduate students—usually teachers studying to become reading specialists—to evaluate and tutor struggling readers as part of their coursework. Three, seek the help of a charitable service organization, like the Masonic Lodges, who have dedicated themselves to helping struggling readers.[26] Four, seek out an expert, tell him what you can afford, and ask for help. Asking for help is powerful, especially with many reading specialists, who entered the field because they want to help. You may be positively surprised by their caring and generosity.

We recognize that not having enough money to get what your child needs is stressing and, in our eyes, unfair. No doubt the educational system is unfair and hurts untold millions of children. We know the options in the previous paragraph are not as good as having the money to easily pay for a comprehensive, high-quality evaluation from a doctoral-level reading specialist. But they're options, and they can work.

For more information on reading evaluations, we suggest you review chapter 4 and go to www.reading2008.com.

MONITORING

Recommendations from the best of evaluations are only educated guesses as to what will work with your child. They don't always work; sometimes they backfire. Thus, it's critical for you, the reading specialist, and your child's teacher to think of ongoing monitoring of her progress as an integral part of her evaluation.

As we said in chapter 4, before the evaluation, request that its report include a monitoring plan. After the evaluation, when you, the reading specialist, and your child's teacher meet to discuss the report, definitely, definitely, definitely discuss how and how frequently monitoring will occur and how you'll be informed of progress. Monitoring is so important that all of chapter 7 is devoted to it.

The following suggestions focus on your meeting to discuss the evaluation's findings and recommendations.

Suggestion 17: When Discussing Your Child's Evaluation Report, Ask School Personnel How and How Frequently They'll Closely Monitor Her Progress in Reading.

Sadly, once programs get underway, monitoring is often ignored. This is a big mistake, as no one will know if the recommended program is succeeding. If it's not, if progress is poor, the longer she stays in the program the lower her chances of becoming a highly proficient, motivated reader.

Poor progress means two things. First, the obstacles to progress must be identified. Second, to eliminate them, her program must be modified or replaced by a new one, with perhaps a new teacher. But identifying and eliminating obstacles is unlikely to occur unless her program is carefully and continuously monitored.

Careful and continuous monitoring does not mean daily or weekly standardized testing. Instead, it means probing children's progress by sampling their performance once or twice weekly and charting it over time. Depending on children's reading problems, reading levels, and ages, probes might stress oral or silent reading. What's critical is that the school has good reason, reason based on research, to believe that the probes accurately measure small increments of progress and quickly indicate difficulties. In other words, the probes for monitoring progress are valid.

Here's an example of a valid, simple, quickly administered, twice-weekly reading probe that teachers can use to evaluate progress: Count the number of words the child reads correctly in one minute of oral reading, from new, slightly easier than instructional-level reading passages. Graph the information. If, after four weeks of instruction and eight oral-reading probes, the graph's progress line falls or slants below the expected-growth line, investigate what's blocking progress.[27] Instructional changes are probably needed. On the other hand, if the graph's progress line rises above the expected-growth line, enrich the program and increase the challenge. Although comparing progress and expected-growth lines may sound complicated, it's not. Pamela Steckler, Erica Lembke, and Laura Saenz illustrate—in clear, simple ways— how to do this. You can download their document for free. It's from the 2007 U.S. Office of Special Education Programs' Summer Institute on Student Progress Monitoring.[28]

Here's another example of a valid, easy-to-administer reading probe that can be administered to groups of children: Have them silently read a passage with words missing and circle the missing words from short lists of words.[29] Calculate the percentage of correctly circled words.

Although simple, valid probes cannot fully diagnose problems, they can quickly warn of poor progress. Thus, this first step—frequently monitoring progress—is critical for ensuring progress.[30]

Once the "how" and "how often" of monitoring have been agreed to, it's time to ask "When will you send me the reports?" A satisfactory frequency is once weekly or twice monthly, depending on your child's needs and progress. The report can be a simple form, with spaces for teachers to provide the necessary information.

Suggestion 18: When Discussing Your Child's Evaluation Report, Ask Her Teachers to Send You Weekly Preparation and Progress Notes. Weekly preparation and progress notes can help you to coordinate your in-home support with your child's in-class instruction.

For example, if the teacher e-mails you a *preparation* note saying that your child's class will soon study ancient Rome, you and your child might watch and discuss videos about Rome. This gives you an opportunity to help her develop the background and vocabulary she'll need to identify words and comprehend text. If the teacher sends home a *progress* note saying that your child focused and persevered for 35 minutes in reading, you might tell her that you're proud of her effort. Your actions and comments—when tied to specifics—can add greatly to her success.

In an informal and non-threatening way, such notes help you to monitor progress. Usually, meetings to discuss the results and recommendations of a reading evaluation are a good opportunity to request preparation and progress notes.

If, however, you don't know what's happening in school, you're unlikely to show the right videos or link encouraging comments to your child's efforts. And making the link is not trivial—it's critical, because it gives you credibility with your child, shows her that everyone is working in concert, and tells her that she'll get the support she needs.

Fortunately, newspaper reports and self-serving politicians who paint teachers as lazy, uncaring hacks are usually wrong. Most teachers are dedicated professionals who strive to help children. Frequently sending preparation and progress notes home is an easy, efficient way for teachers to help you prepare your child for upcoming lessons and to monitor progress.

Suggestion 19: When Discussing Your Child's Evaluation Report, Ask School Personnel to Schedule Monthly Meetings to Discuss Her Progress and How You Can Help at Home. These meetings should last from 20 to 50 minutes and should focus on your child's progress, any difficulties she's having, how the school can help to overcome them, and how you might help at home, without becoming her teacher or tutor.

To ensure all the important points are covered, distribute a list of your most important questions a week or so before the meeting. Everyone who will attend should have the list, which might look like this:

- How did Elly do on her twice-weekly reading probes? What is the trend?
- Is Elly having difficulty with anything? If so, what is the immediate cause?

What can be done to help her overcome this difficulty?
- Is Elly having success with anything? If so, why? What can be done to ensure that her success continues? What can be done to extend her success to other areas?
- Recently, what has Elly found motivating?
- Recently, what's been weakening Elly's motivation?

Yes, the list looks short. But it's not. Because a list like this can take a long time to discuss, limit your questions to what's most important. If the list is too long, you'll probably get frustrated by the rush to squeeze lots of information into little time. Ironically, a long list guarantees one thing: superficial, incomplete answers.

As we previously said, monitoring is so important that all of chapter 7 is devoted to it. It provides lots of suggestions for how you and the school can work together to effectively monitor your child's progress.

KEEP IN MIND

Keep in mind that, to a large extent, evaluating your child's needs in reading, planning her program, monitoring it, and requesting changes requires you to seek answers to practical questions. Basically, the questions we keep recommending you to ask fall into four board categories:

- At what levels is my child functioning?
- What does she need to learn?
- To learn, what services and instructional approaches does she need?
- How do I know if progress is adequate?

But as we pointed out, you may not always have the knowledge to know if the school's answers are accurate and complete. This puts a tremendous burden on you, one that you can't escape, and one that you'll probably never fully satisfy, given the complexity of reading disabilities.

The burden: To learn all that you reasonably can about reading disabilities—how to instruct children with reading disabilities, how to monitor progress, how to quickly adapt or change ineffective practices and programs, how to support your child at home, and if she's eligible for special education, how to use the special education laws to meet her needs: academic, social, emotional, vocational, and recreational. To adapt one of diabetes education's main sayings, "the more you know about reading disabilities, the more likely your child will prosper."

Keep in mind that your burden is not unlimited. We described it as *all that you reasonably can* learn. We do not recommend that you study reading and learning disabilities 24 hours a day, sacrifice your family to it, or use this knowledge to become your child's key teacher or tutor. Instead, use your knowledge, and possibly the assistance of private professionals, to work with your child's school to plan her program, monitor it, make more informed and focused decisions, and perhaps get outside services, such as tutoring. And if necessary, use it respectfully—in an informed and rational way—to challenge poor or unsupported practices and recommendations.

To learn more about reading disabilities, visit our website, www.reading2008.com. It frequently updates information about the causes of reading disabilities, how to instruct struggling readers, how to motivate them, and how to monitor their progress.

ENDNOTES

---

[1]   If your child is eligible for special education under the *Individuals with Disabilities Education Improvement Act of 2004* (IDEA-2004), the procedures are more formal and prescriptive. Other people, identified in the law, will attend the meeting. This is discussed in later chapters.

[2]   If your child is found eligible under IDEA-2004, the plan is called an Individualized Education Program or IEP; if she's found eligible under *Section 504 of the Rehabilitation Act of 1973*, it's often called a 504 Plan.

[3]   Informal reading inventories are often called IRIs.

[4]   Although IRIs are important, they, like any test, only sample behavior. They need to be supplemented by the observations of knowledgeable teachers, and progress needs to be continuously monitored. As Marjorie Lipson and Karen Wixson so aptly said of IRIs, "In the hands of a skilled specialist, IRIs can provide a great deal of valuable information.... [However], the key to successful placement ... is the use of multiple indicators of performance on materials comparable to those in which the student is to be placed (Lipson, M. J., & Wixson, K. K., 2003. *Assessment and Instruction of Reading and Writing Difficulty: An Interactive Approach* (3rd ed.). Boston: Allyn & Bacon, p. 373).

[5]   Like all group-administered tests, NCLB tests have many problems; as such, they fall far short of what is needed to fully evaluate a child's reading difficulties. Thus, we recommend that you place more faith in a quality reading evaluation, planned and administered by a reading specialist, than in your State's NCLB test for reading.

[6]   Booher-Jennings, J., 2005. Below the bubble: 'Educational Triage' and the Texas Accountability System. *American Education Research Journal, 42* (2), 231-268.

[7]   Shane Jimerson is one of the nation's leading experts on the effects of grade retention. In summarizing the research on retention, he and Amber Kaufman noted that long term, retention did not improve academic progress of retained students. Moreover, "retained students are between 2 and 11 times more likely to drop out during high school than non-retained students" (Jimerson, S. R., & Kaufman, A. M., 2003. Reading, writing, and retention: A primer on grade retention research. *The Reading Teacher, 56* (8), 622-635, p. 626).

[8]   In their review of the literature, Shane Jimerson and Amber Kaufman reported, "By the time they were in sixth grade, children reported only the loss of a parent and going blind as more stressful than grade retention. This study was replicated in 2001 and it was found that sixth-grade students rated grade retention as the single most stressful life event, higher than both the loss of a parent and going blind" (Jimerson & Kaufman, 2003, p. 627).

[9]   Many parents are afraid of the word behavioral, thinking it means mechanistic or uncaring. We agree with Paul Alberto and Anne Troutman that applied behavior analysis is strongly supported by research and if correctly and ethically implemented, emphasizes the humane: "Teachers who learn and practice the principles of applied behavior analysis can help their students master functional

and academic skills in a systematic and efficient manner and can document their students' progress for parents and other professionals. They can manage behavior positively so that their focus remains on learning. They can teach students to get along with peers and adults and to make good choices. By providing learning environments that are safe, joyful, and successful, they can make enormous differences in students' lives" (Alberto, P. A., & Troutman, A. C., 2006. *Applied Behavior Analysis for Teachers* (7th ed.). Upper Saddle River, NJ: Pearson Merrill Prentice Hall, p. 22).

10 Although this is an example of "cutting up," a child who is extremely quiet and passive in a class can have just as many problems. Quiet children, however, are often ignored, as they don't disrupt class. They too may need the kind of help discussed in this section.

11 Some school systems have such specialists on staff; others hire them as consultants. As with any evaluation, if you think it's inadequate, you can request an independent evaluation of your child's behavior.

12 An expert can have a degree in school psychology, special education, or a related area.
But be careful: Few States have certification in applied behavior analysis. You want to be sure that the person has the proper training and a history of success in using applied behavior analysis.
Listen carefully to his vocabulary and examples. If possible, compare his vocabulary and examples to books on applied behavior analysis.

13 This is often referred to as manipulating variables, or manipulating educationally-relevant variables.

14 Faithfully carrying out and monitoring the effects of an ABA plan is often referred to as fidelity.

15 At the sake of being repetitious, we want to emphasize that extreme shyness, passivity, and disengagement are behaviors that must be addressed by knowledgeable, skilled professionals. Just because the behavior is not disruptive does not mean it should be ignored.

16 Caldwell, J. S., & Leslie, L., 2005. *Intervention Strategies to Follow Informal Reading Inventory Assessment*. Boston: Pearson Allyn & Bacon, p. 59.

17 And they probably know a great deal about your child that you don't. After all, they have much greater opportunity to see how she responds in class and how she compares to her peers.
Together, you and your child's teachers have clues to the mystery—how to help your child become a highly proficient, highly motivated reader who, with moderate effort, can successfully read more difficult books and complete more difficult assignments.

18 Carnine, D. W., Silbert, J., Kame'enui, E. J., & Tarver, S. G., 2004. *Direct Instruction Reading* (4th ed.). Upper Saddle River, NJ: Pearson Merrill Prentice Hall, p. 320.

19 Duffy, G. G., 2003. *Explaining Reading: A Resource for Teaching Concepts, Skills, and Strategies*. New York: The Guilford Press, p. 6.

20 Allington, R. L., 2005. *What Really Matters for Struggling Readers: Designing Research-Based Programs* (2nd ed.). Boston: Allyn & Bacon/Merrill.

21 This means that you should not have the primary responsibility for teaching her new, complicated concepts, like understanding paragraph patterns or using study strategies, and that you should not be teaching her concepts or skills that she's struggling with in class, like dividing words into syllables.

22 For an excellent description and discussion of Topping's Paired Reading, see Tierney, R. J., & Readence, J. E., 2005. *Reading Strategies and Practices: A Compendium* (6th ed.). Boston: Pearson, Allyn & Bacon, pp. 245-248. Earlier, less expensive editions of this book also discuss Paired Reading.

23 Many schools would reject your request, arguing that videoing violates other students' privacy. We don't understand this logic; these are the same students you would see if the class put on a play for parents or you visited the class. Moreover, the school, not you, has the video; you're watching it for only a short time. Nevertheless, the school may be right. The laws vary by State. In New York and New Jersey, for example, Howard was unable to get a clear answer on the legality of videoing volunteer graduate students teaching in their classes. The best answer we can give to our suggestion—as non-lawyers—is that you make the request of the school and check with your State Department of Education. The reason for checking is that this may be a gray area and schools may give you the wrong answer.

24 Every child found eligible for special education must have an Individualized Education Program (IEP), a written plan with mandated components, including these: "(a) a statement of the child's present levels of academic achievement and functional performance; (b) a statement of measurable annual goals; (c) a description of how the child's progress toward meeting the annual goals will be measured and when periodic reports on the progress ... toward meeting the annual goals ... will be provided; (d) a statement of the special education and related services and supplementary aids and services ... to be provided to the child, or on behalf of the child" (Public Law 108-446, IDEA-2004, Section 614). In order to accurately gauge "the child's present levels of academic achievement and functional performance"—which is the foundation for everything else—assessment principles require observations. If the school prohibits observations, you might want to share with them these two quotes that emphasize the importance of observations: (1) "As part of an initial evaluation (if appropriate) and as part of any reevaluation ... the IEP Team ... must ... review existing evaluation data on the child, including ... classroom-based observations; and ... observations by teachers and related services providers" (IDEA-2004, 34 CFR § 300.305); (2) "Although much information can be obtained through talk and testing, no other single tool can provide such in-depth information about the learner's actual use and application of knowledge and skill as observation. No other tool can demonstrate so clearly whether the reader is both skilled and motivated" (Lipson & Wixson, 2003, p. 100).

In the preceding paragraph, we gave you the reference 34 CFR § 300.305. This refers to the regulations for IDEA-2004; 34 CFR stands for Title 34 of the Code of Federal Regulations; § stands for section, which in this case is section 300.305. You can download a copy of the regulations from our website: www.reading2008.com.

25 Over the years, ineffective instruction causes academic problems, or intensifies them, forcing districts to spend money on expensive remedial or special education services, services that children would not need had instruction been effective. For example, each child placed in special education because of ineffective instruction may cost districts an extra $12,000; likewise, each child retained may cost an extra $12,000.

26 The Masonic Lodges use the term dyslexia to describe struggling readers. Don't be upset by the word; it's ill-defined.

27 In this example, we used our own terms. Generally, what we call a progress line is called a trend line; what we call an expected-growth line is called a goal line.

28 Pamela Steckler, Erica Lembke, and Laura Saenz present a sophisticated and highly valuable set of procedures and decision rules for monitoring a child's reading and deciding if program changes

are needed. They illustrate, using simple terms and simple graphs, how to collect valid information about a child's progress, how to compare it to her annual goals, and how to quickly decide if program changes are needed. Their document, which is well written, easy to read, and illustrates numerous measures of progress as well as oral reading rate, can be downloaded for free and is worth studying. Here's the information you need: Steckler, P. M., Lembke, E. S, & Saenz, L., 2007. *Advanced Applications of CBM in Reading: Instructional Decision-Making Strategies*. Washington, D.C.: U.S. Office of Special Education Programs; retrieved 8/20/07, from http://www.studentprogress.org/summer_institute/2007/Adv%20Reading/AdvancedCBMReading2007.pdf.

[29] This is called a maze or maze-fluency procedure.

[30] In the first edition of her excellent textbook, *Classroom Assessment for Students with Special Needs in Inclusive Settings* (2002, Upper Saddle River, NJ: Merrill Prentice Hall), Cathleen G. Spinelli clearly explains how to use and interpret these and other monitoring procedures. Spinelli's book is an excellent reference that you should keep handy. To save money without sacrificing quality, we suggest that you buy the first edition rather than the second. Although the second is more current, the first has what's needed.

CHAPTER 6
HELPING AT HOME

You're frustrated. Your child won't read. He won't do his homework. He looks depressed. Sobbing, he mumbles: "I hate school." You know this has to change, but what should you do? Should you leave him alone and hope for the best? Should you force him to read and finish his homework? Should you get him a tutor or should you teach him to read?

Unfortunately, these solutions often fail. We'll tell you why and then show you how to help your child develop the background skills and abilities needed to succeed. We will also show you how to support and motivate him.

SOLUTIONS THAT USUALLY FAIL: COMMON QUESTIONS

Should I Leave My Child Alone and Hope for the Best? No. When children have reading problems, they need effective instruction. Leaving your child alone—not getting him effective instruction—will aggravate his problems as he'll fall further behind his peers. For you, the question becomes "How can I get him the instruction he needs?" You can find the answers in the previous chapters and in those that follow.

Should I Force My Child to Read Whatever is Assigned? No—not if the materials frustrate him. Regularly forcing children to read frustrating materials produces despondency, depression, resentment, and resistance. This will hurt your child and will not improve his reading. Instead, to become proficient, he needs to read lots of easy, comfortable materials and think about what he's reading and how it relates to his life and interests. This requires him to believe he can succeed, to have adequate self-efficacy—the belief that "I can succeed."

In all likelihood, adequate or high self-efficacy—which you might call confidence—will motivate your child to try. It usually motivates children to complete their work and master subjects. This is especially true if they find the subject and reading materials interesting and slightly-to-moderately challenging (but not frustrating), or if they think the work will help them achieve a goal they value.

Should I Reward My Child? Yes. Rewards can motivate children to read, to finish their homework, and to master school subjects. But artificial rewards—stickers, money, toys, free time, music downloads—usually work well only when children find that moderate effort produces success, that their reading materials and writing tasks are easy-to-moderately challenging, and that rewards are frequent and worth the effort.[1]

Artificial rewards backfire if the work is too difficult, if the time between the behavior and the reward is too long (e.g., more than a few hours), if parents don't pair rewards with kind, friendly, encouraging words and smiles, and if, after children's repeated successes, parents don't gradually replace artificial rewards with more natural ones, like playing Monopoly© together. Once artificial rewards have motivated children to read, and they find reading enjoyable and valuable, parents should gradually eliminate artificial rewards—reading interesting materials becomes the reward.

Should I Get My Child a Tutor? Perhaps. If tutors coordinate their efforts with classroom instruction, if they are highly knowledgeable about teaching reading to struggling readers, if they can skillfully apply their knowledge, and if they can relate well to children and build their confidence or self-efficacy, they can be extremely effective. If you find such a tutor, hire her.

Often, however, the four "ifs" are major problems that make tutoring ineffective, even damaging. Many tutors ignore what's taught in class—they teach struggling readers different strategies, confusing them. Moreover, tutors sometimes emphasize strategies that contradict the teacher's.[2]

Many tutors, including special education teachers with advanced degrees, know little about reading disabilities or how to teach struggling readers; some have the knowledge but not the skill. Consequently, they make tutoring difficult, boring, irrelevant, confusing, and emotionally draining. And many, knowing little about how to increase struggling readers' confidence or self-efficacy, miss opportunities to help them develop the confidence critical to success in school.

To complicate the situation, tutoring services frequently change tutors, giving struggling readers new tutors every few sessions, destroying insight, rapport, and continuity, as well as struggling readers' confidence that they can succeed.[3]

Should I Teach My Child to Read? This is difficult to answer, especially if you don't have enough money to hire a quality tutor for the number of sessions your child needs. Although it's impossible to predict the number of sessions needed, struggling readers may need several sessions a week for several months or years.

When parents try to teach their children to read, they often fail, making the situation worse. They fail for four reasons.

First, teaching reading to a struggling reader is a highly complex job, one that requires both supervised practice and considerable theoretical and technical knowledge. It can frustrate anyone, even people like us, with doctorates in reading and clinical psychology. Second, when you're frustrated, you may say things to your child that you'll regret and he'll remember. Once said, words cannot be taken back, despite apologies. Continuing to say things that hurt your child may destroy your relationship. Third, he may have difficulty relating to you as a teacher; he may respond and concentrate better when tutored by professionals. Finally, you may have difficulty coordinating your lessons with his teacher's or may not have time to tutor him several hours a week. Despite these problems, some parents have successfully taught their children to read; unfortunately, many have made their children's problems worse.

If you're committed to teaching your child to read—to teach him new concepts and skills, in formal, structured ways—we recommend that you do four things: coordinate what you're doing with his teacher; consider emphasizing the instructional suggestions in the next section; study one of the books about tutoring listed on our website, www.reading2008.com; and make sure he thinks your sessions are fun and emotionally satisfying.

Should I Have My Child Sound Out Words? If you think your child can easily and accurately sound out a word or two, remind him to do so. This is guidance, not tutoring. But if you expect that he'll struggle to sound out a word, will take more than five seconds, or will be embarrassed, quickly tell him the word so he can continue to read for meaning. Moreover, telling him the word can teach him the word. Remember, to motivate children to read, reading must be an enjoyable, easy activity that interests and informs, rather than embarrasses.

Sounds good, but what if he struggles with or must sound out lots of words? Should I encourage him to sound them out? No. Instead, read the sentence or paragraph to him and then, immediately have him read it. Try this for several sentences or paragraphs. If he still makes many mistakes or has to sound out many words, read the material to him, or have him read something easier, or stop reading.

Why? The material is too difficult. As Richard Allington noted:

> When a 9-year-old misses as few as two or three words in each hundred running words of a text, the text may be too hard for effective practice.... It is the high-accuracy, fluent, and easily comprehended reading that provides the opportunities to integrate complex skills and strategies into an automatic, independent reading process.[4]

INCREASING THE LIKELIHOOD OF SUCCESS: SEVEN PRINCIPLES

You've read the bad news, Now, here's the good news: You can dramatically increase your child's chances of success by following these principles.

Principle 1—Set the Stage for Reading, Emotionally and Physically. In general, children are much more motivated to try new things, to seek challenges, and to overcome difficulties when they feel emotionally comfortable and believe that no matter what the outcome, if they try, they'll have their parents' support. Thus, to encourage reading, children need to know that they will not be "put down" for making mistakes, not be "nagged" to get everything perfect, not be compared to others, and not be forced to do what they find too difficult. They need to know that they can choose much of their reading material, that they have a comfortable place to sit when reading, that they can get whatever help they need without being instructed or tested "all the time," and that everyone in the family regularly reads for information and pleasure. They need to see a house full of books and magazines, in which family members read and share and discuss what they read, and even have friendly debates about what they read, without demeaning or attacking one another.

Is this ideal? Yes. Practical? Not always. Is it something you should try to achieve? Yes. Will it solve all your child's reading difficulties? No—but it will make him more receptive to instruction and motivate him to want to read. After all, children usually emulate their parents' values and behaviors. As Harry Chapin both celebrated and lamented in the song *Cat's in the Cradle*, the son had grown up just like the father.

Because what you model is often what you get, you should model good health habits, especially exercise and sleep.

You should encourage your child to fall asleep and wake up at regularly scheduled, sensible times. Why? Restless, superficial sleep, or an inadequate amount of sleep can intensify learning and memory problems and make you and your child irritable. In contrast, enough *restful* sleep increases the likelihood that you and he will focus more sharply, think more clearly, remember more, and maintain a better disposition.

You should also make sure he gets enough enjoyable exercise, as it may well improve his emotional state and help him deal with the stresses of reading disabilities. As Michael Sachs, professor of psychiatry at Weill Cornell University Medical College, advised:

> Exercise can be a powerful method of relaxation, and it can help people deal effectively with the stress of daily life. In various studies, researchers have found that exercise can decrease anxiety and depression, improve an individual's self-image, and buffer people from the effects of stress.... Exercise comes in a wide variety of types: aerobic and non-aerobic, solitary and group activities, competitive and noncompetitive sports, endurance activities and those that are based on skill.... Any of these activities ... can help you feel more focused and relaxed, as long as you pick an activity that fits your personality and physical abilities—and [it is] one that you enjoy.[5]

But remember, exercise should be something your child enjoys. It should match his age, abilities, and interests. It should relieve stress, not add to it.

Later, when we discuss the seventh principle, *Hone Your Parenting Abilities*, we'll delve further into "setting the stage."

Principle 2—Help Your Child Develop a Rich Background and a Strong Vocabulary.

Reading is understanding, understanding that depends on the richness of the struggling reader's experiential background and the depth and breadth of his vocabulary.[6] Even if your child struggles to recognize basic sight vocabulary—common words like *in, on, of, for, the, why, was, there, where*—you can prepare him to understand what he reads when he's no longer frustrated by word recognition.

Because reading comprehension depends on the reader's experiential background and vocabulary, preparing him to comprehend what he reads is straightforward: Help him develop extensive knowledge of the world and a large vocabulary. Together, they'll make understanding, or reading comprehension, easier. Here are several suggestions.

Tie vocabulary to lots of instructionally-relevant experiences. By requesting and reviewing the curriculum for your child's classes, you might plan experiences that give him the background and vocabulary needed to fully understand the curriculum. For example, if his 7th-grade class will spend the next two months studying fresh water ecology, you might take trips to different fresh water sites (e.g., lakes, streams, marshes, reservoirs, municipal water plants), take pictures (if allowed), let him take pictures, get picture brochures or postcards, and discuss what you saw. Let him explain things to you. The more he explains, the more he's likely to learn. The more he explains, the better you'll understand what he still needs to learn.

If you've taken pictures, you might jointly plan and record a narrative to explain them. Before doing this, you should use and discuss the vocabulary his teacher will stress. If your child is ready to learn about prefixes, informally stress those that reveal the meanings of the words his teacher will stress.

Assume, for example, that his teacher tells you the curriculum will stress these words: aquatic, ecology, hydrology, submerse. You might stress that the prefix *aqua* in *aquatic* means water, *eco* in *ecology* means habitat or environment, *hydr* (or *hydro*) in *hydrology* means water, *sub* in *submerse* means under or beneath. Because these words and prefixes relate to a theme, they're probably easier to learn than ones chosen randomly.

If your child finds prefixes frustrating, stop teaching them; stick to teaching full words, like *pollution*: "Brian, let's look for garbage or spilled oil in this lake. This kind of pollution ruins lakes." But continue to avoid drill and frustration. Make new words interesting and moderately challenging: "Brian, you're right. Yesterday's rain filled the lake. Rain is called *precipitation*. Let's ask the park ranger what lots of *precipitation* does to streams. Then, let's ask him which stream to see."

Take video and still pictures of your neighborhood. All neighborhoods are rich with picture-taking opportunities that can encourage discussions—discussions that develop language and, in particular, vocabulary. Take advantage of such opportunities, as they give your child images he can relate to, intellectually and emotionally. Here are a few possibilities: houses, traffic, streets, stores, fences, schools, animals, garbage, playgrounds, sandlots, bus stops, police cars, supermarkets, ball games, street signs, construction workers, construction equipment.

Read to your child daily. Read what he finds interesting and relevant. Let him choose the books, stories, or articles, even if he asks you to read the same ones again and again. After all, choice motivates.

Discuss what you read to him, without making it a test or an inquisition. Tell him the meaning of new vocabulary, ask him what words he'd like to learn, discuss the book's pictures, show and discuss similar pictures, role play meanings, use the words in daily conversation, take him to places like those in the book.

If he likes a book about circuses, take him to one; take lots of pictures, and use them to develop vocabulary: tent, ring, arena, comics, clowns, troupe, acrobats, costume, big top, cavalcade, performance, feats of skill. Use words like "exhibition," "sensational," and "frenzied" if he can understand such abstractions; if he can't, focus on new, more concrete words that you can illustrate, words like *clowns* and *livestock*. Remember—make words interesting; make them fun.

Show and discuss instructionally-relevant videos. Not all pictures have to be home videos or stills, not when there's PBS and the like. If your child's class is studying Lewis and Clark, the two of you might watch and discuss the PBS DVD, *Lewis & Clark: The Journey of the Corps of Discovery*; if they're studying the Earth's origins, the two of you might watch and discuss the PBS DVD, *NOVA: Origins*. Exciting, well-produced, relevant videos can be borrowed from the library, rented, or purchased.

Watching and discussing videos is an excellent way to build background and vocabulary while heightening motivation and preparing children for school discussions and activities. When children develop knowledge about a subject before studying it in school, they'll better understand it, whether they listen to a lecture, engage in a discussion, or read about it in school.

Although videos can be highly effective, heed three guidelines: First, use videos that match your child's intellectual abilities; videos that are too easy or too difficult will quickly cause attention to wane. Second, connect the videos to vocabulary: Use videos as springboards for conversations that build critical vocabulary. Third, discuss videos as soon as possible. Children forget. Thus it's best to watch a video with your child and discuss it immediately, while it's fresh in his memory.

Discuss his interests and concerns. Focusing on your child's interests and concerns creates a wonderful opportunity to develop concepts, vocabulary, and other language skills.

When possible, take advantage of newspapers and magazines (e.g., the *Weekly Reader* for younger children; *Upfront*, the *New York Times'* current events magazine for teenagers). If, for instance, your child starts saying, "No reason for me to bike on the sidewalk. With a helmet, the street's not dangerous," you might read a few brief articles to him, or give him one or two that he can readily read. Now you have something to discuss, something that's important to him.

But be careful. Don't be imperious, don't be authoritarian, don't be dismissive—listen to understand his views. Understanding is not agreement. Remember, you can't change his mind—only he can. So, ask him what the articles say about the safety of riding bikes in the streets: the plusses, the minuses, the precautions. Make the discussions fun, not battles. And remember, you're still the parent—you make the final decision. But despite your authority, you're far more apt to succeed if he feels he was fully understood and treated fairly.

Not all discussions need to focus on controversial or emotional topics, like bike riding in the street. Your child might want to discuss wild animals, magic tricks, the Hubbell Telescope, a new movie, planning a hike, a comic book hero, or how to improve his basketball skills. The strategy is to discuss a topic, use the discussion to encourage him to read about it, or listen to you read about it, and discuss it further. Use the topic to be with him, to value his interests, to spur further investigation, and to informally improve his language skills, including relevant vocabulary.

Principle 3—Informally Help Your Child Develop Fundamental Knowledge and Skills. No doubt about it—parents can and should help their children acquire the knowledge and skills critical to reading. Their question is, "How can we help our child so he learns what's taught and likes learning?" The answer lies in five words: *informal, incidental, fun, frequent, relevant.*

Informal means easy, casual, relaxed, comfortable, and unceremonious: Not paper and pencil tests, not drill-drill-drill, not demands for continuous improvement, not the attitude "you do this or else!" Informal means taking advantage of *incidental* opportunities, like walking and seeing an opportunity to play a rhyming game:

- Grandfather: "Look Ryan, there's a gigantic tree."
- Grandmother: "I wonder what word rhymes with tree?"
- Grandmother: "I know one: bee. Ryan, if you want to play, give me a rhyming word?"
- Ryan: "See."
- Grandfather: "Okay, Ryan. You be the leader now.
  Tell us a word and we'll give you some rhyming words."
- Ryan: "Red."
- Grandmother: "Bed."
- Grandfather: "Fed."
- And so on ....

Such activities should be *fun*: amusing, interesting, and lighthearted. They should be slightly challenging, not frustrating. If your child fully engages in them and keeps trying, he probably finds them slightly challenging. If he refuses to engage, engages superficially, or soon loses interest, they're probably too easy or too difficult.

Such informal, incidental activities should build on developed or emerging skills and concepts. The rhyming game worked with Ryan for four reasons: He knew what rhyming meant; he had previously rhymed words successfully, though not perfectly; he would likely succeed because his rhyming skills were fairly well developed; he felt safe enough with his grandparents not to fret about mistakes.

Although the rhyming game was instructional and would likely benefit Ryan, it was informal. Ryan didn't have to review previous work, sit for 20 minutes, attend to a prescribed curriculum, answer specific questions, complete an assignment, correct his errors, or succeed on a mastery test; instead, he had a choice—he could have provided a rhyming word, if he wanted. And if he didn't want to, all was fine—he knew he wouldn't be coaxed or nagged.[7]

For incidental activities like this to solidify learning, they need to occur *frequently*: Several times a week or several times a day—frequently enough to give children enough practice to ensure mastery. Fortunately, almost any event or object can be used as an incidental opportunity for practice.

To know if you're creating enough of the right incidental activities, answer these questions: Does my child enjoy these activities? Does he fully involve himself? Is he getting better at them? Is he getting just about every answer right? Is he confident? Once he's highly successful, start emphasizing other knowledge or skills that he's well on his way to mastering. All he needs is a little practice and feedback.

Implied in what we've said about incidental activities is awareness and planning. You need to look for or create opportunities and have an activity or two in mind. Ryan's grandparents were looking for opportunities to play a game that would ask him to produce rhyming words. If his rhyming skills were less developed, they might have planned an easier activity, such as asking him to identify, not produce, a rhyming word: "Ryan, which word rhymes with *tree*: *basketball* or *see*?"

When creating incidental opportunities and activities, ask yourself, "Is the activity *relevant* to reading success?" If learning something will improve your child's reading, it's relevant. If it's unlikely to improve his reading, it's not.[8] For a list of websites and other resources that identify relevant skills for preschoolers and older students, visit our website, which is, www.reading2008.com.

The first key to selecting relevant knowledge and skills is to identify what your child needs to know or do in order to succeed in and enjoy reading. The second key is to identify what he knows and can easily do, so you stress what's *slightly* but not dramatically new.

Why slightly? To ensure that tasks are moderately challenging, rather than frustrating and discouraging. For example, once Ryan rhymes words quickly and accurately, his parents or grandparents might create incidental games that ask him to manipulate smaller units of sound:

- Mother: "Ryan, here's some new pictures of the family. Here's one in which you're running in the park. Looks like you had fun." [Ryan spends a few minutes looking at and commenting on the pictures.]
- Mother: "Let's play a game. I'll say some words that start like *running*. They start with the /r/ sound. When I say the word, you make the beginning sound, but stretch it out like this: *rrrrrunning*. Here we go: *read* …. Here's another: *round* …. Here's another: *ring* …."[9]

Later, when Ryan is highly adept at stretching the beginning sounds of words, his parents might extend the concept:

- Father: "Ryan, I'm going to say three words that start like *run*, with the /r/ sound. Here I go: *rabbit … rain …. road*. Now, let's play detective. Tell me which of these two words starts like run. *Platypus* or *Ryan*?…. Here's another two: cake or read?…. Here's another two: radio or zillion?…."

The third key is to keep it manageable. Ryan's grandparents and parents didn't overwhelm him. They stressed only a few concepts or skills, ones on which he would likely succeed if he made a moderate effort. Research has shown that it's more productive to focus on a few, rather than a wide variety of sound manipulations.

To illustrate these keys, the end of this paragraph lists Hallie Yopp and Helen Yopp's sequence for phonemic awareness instruction. Their sequence aims to make instruction relevant, manageable, and successful. Although it focuses on helping children identify and manipulate large *and* small units of sound, it starts with large, easier units and sequentially moves to the small, more difficult ones. To increase the likelihood of success, children need to succeed on the large, easier units before they're asked to identify and manipulate the small, more difficult ones.

Here, from the easiest (activity 1) to the most difficult (activity 4), is Yopp and Yopp's sequence:

1. Activities that focus on rhyme—the easiest.
   Teacher or parent: Let's think of something that rhymes with *cow*.
   A correct response: (now)
2. Activities that focus on syllable units.
   Teacher or parent: Clap twice for Harry's name.
   Correct Response: Har (clap)—ry (clap)
3. Activities that focus on parts of syllables.[10]
   Teacher or parent: Say just the first part of *brown*.
   Correct Response: (/br/)
4. Activities that focus on phonemes—the most difficult.
   Teacher or parent: Let's put these sounds together: /ch/—/ā/—/n/
   Correct Response: (chain)[11]

You can play dozens of phonological and phonemic awareness games with your child. But to succeed, you must remember they're games—games should be fun, not tests or trials or inquisitions. Resources for helping your child develop these skills are listed on our website, www.reading2008.com.

What's most important about Principle 3 is not the discussion of phonological awareness and, its component, phonemic awareness. Yes, they're important for children to master—mighty important. But for parents who want to help their struggling reader at home, what's most important, and what applies to just about any aspect of reading that parents try to encourage or reinforce, is the meaning behind these five words: *informal, incidental, fun, frequent,* and *relevant*. So ask, is what you're doing to strengthen your child's fundamental knowledge and skills *informal, incidental, fun, frequent,* and *relevant*?

Principle 4—Prevent Homework Problems. Many struggling readers become despondent or depressed about reading. They think they'll never learn to read. They're also embarrassed and confused by their reading difficulties—they can't understand why other children read so easily, but they can't. Consequently, they lose their enthusiasm for reading. Said one struggling reader, "I'd rather drink vinegar [than read]."

At home, family arguments about reading often involve homework, homework that struggling readers find confusing, overwhelming, and frustrating. Often, assignments that average-achieving children finish in 30 minutes take struggling readers quadruple this time—and they get lots of items wrong or fidget away the time or throw tantrums or cry in defeat or do all of this and more.

The key to solving this problem and motivating your child is prevention.

Prevention requires discussing your child's homework problem with his teachers and reaching agreement that they will assign only homework on which he can succeed without frustration, and that they'll give him feedback about his homework successes. Often, success plus feedback can strengthen motivation and get children to finish their homework without tears, fights, or tantrums.

It's easy for teachers to identify homework on which your child can readily succeed. All they have to do is assign homework at his independent level. At this level he can quickly and correctly read 99% of the words and understand 90% of the material without anyone's help, correctly and legibly write answers to 90% of questions without undue effort, and efficiently organize the work and his efforts. Independent-level assignments give your child needed practice, one of homework's major purposes, and dramatically increase the likelihood of success, which increases motivation.[12]

To illustrate how homework might be modified, let's look at how teachers might replace worksheet-like or question-and-answer writing assignments with more enjoyable activities that stress actual reading.

- *Student read-alouds.* Your child reads a short book or story aloud to you. He does this after he has practiced it in school and can read it correctly, with good phrasing.
- *Parent read-alouds.* You regularly read aloud books or stories that interest your child and perhaps arouse his curiosity and challenge him intellectually. This is critical to strengthening his motivation and development as most books read by struggling readers are far below their intellectual and developmental levels. Consequently, they're boring. Moreover, they lack the concepts and vocabulary struggling readers need to learn to comprehend class discussions and more difficult reading materials. By reading relevant, interesting, challenging materials to your child, you're telling him that he's intelligent and that he can learn—beliefs critical to motivation.
- *Paired reading.* As we discussed in chapter 5, Paired Reading has you and your child read a selection in unison; you keep reading together until he gives you an agreed-upon hand signal to stop while he keeps reading; you read along silently until he makes an error or struggles on a word; at this point, you start reading aloud, in unison, from the difficult word. You don't try to correct him or teach him to sound out difficult words. When it's over, you praise him for the things he did well and invite him to read a little more: "Matthew, you did it. You read two pages and read just about all the words correctly. Let's try another page."
- *Silent reading.* Your child sits in a comfortable place and silently reads some books that he wants to read, books at his independent level. (If occasionally a book or article interests him greatly, it may be slightly more demanding than independent-level materials.) You might read the same books and then discuss them with him. Be careful, however, that the discussion doesn't turn into an inquisition, in which you're testing him. Discussions are give-and-take and go where the parties want.

These activities will work for many, but not all, struggling readers. Some, especially older ones, want homework that looks like everyone else's. If so, consider asking the teacher to:

- Assign the same topic, but with materials at his independent reading level. (If this proves difficult, read the materials to him, or record them on a simple digital recorder.[13])

- Assign him only a small portion of the work, as the full assignment will take him too long. Thus, if the class has to answer 20 questions, he's asked to answer only five (at his independent reading and writing levels). He can answer more questions for extra credit.[14]
- Allow him to stop work after 30 minutes of reasonable effort, or however long the teacher expects the work to take the average-achieving student. As long as you sign a brief statement saying his effort was reasonable, whatever he finishes is sufficient and will not lower his grade. If he's eligible for special education and has an Individualized Education Program (IEP), make sure it describes this accommodation.
- Assign homework buddies to help one another. If work is at their proper independent level, few difficulties will arise.

By modifying homework to produce success, optimism, and, with some luck, enjoyment, your child will likely be more motivated to read and do his homework. After all, belief that success is likely (and worthwhile) is highly motivating.

On our website, www.reading2008.com, you can find information on preventing and resolving homework difficulties, as well as motivating struggling readers to complete their homework. If you have good working relationships with your child's teachers, you may want to share these with them.

Principle 5—Help Your Child Develop Realistic, Effective Beliefs. Many struggling readers resist reading, believing they'll inevitably fail because they lack the ability to become good readers. In other words, they have low rather than high self-efficacy or confidence for learning to read.

Many researchers and teachers correctly believe that without sufficiently high self-efficacy for reading, struggling readers won't make the effort needed to learn to read. At the first signs of difficulty, they'll quit. After all, when failure is certain, trying is futile.

If this is what your child believes, you must help him develop sufficiently high but realistic self-efficacy for reading. In other words, confidence that moderate effort will produce success.[15]

Fortunately, research suggests that the following guidelines—matching work to abilities, linking new work to recent successes, rewarding (reinforcing) effort and persistence, teaching children to make facilitative attributions, helping them identify or create personally important, achievable goals—can help turn pessimism into optimism, thereby strengthening self-efficacy, which in turn, should strengthen motivation for reading.

Match work to abilities. For these strategies to effectively change "I can't" into "I can" beliefs, your child must succeed on the very types of tasks he expects to fail. To accomplish this, you may have to work with his teachers to ensure that classwork is at his instructional level and homework at his independent level, and that his work is neither too complex nor too lengthy. (Chapter 8 offers many suggestions for working with teachers.) Because such work is challenging rather than frustrating, moderate effort produces success.

If work is at your child's proper instructional and independent levels, if it's interesting, and if it's short enough for him to handle, he'll probably work to succeed, especially if you make encouraging remarks. However, if typical work is too easy, it may easily bore him and communicate, "We don't think you're intelligent." If it's too hard, it will frustrate him, erode confidence, and easily destroy motivation. Mismatched work guarantees that low self-efficacy and reading difficulties will continue, and will likely intensify.

Link new work to recent successes. Once your child has recent successes to draw on—such as orally reading a second-grade passage or writing brief answers to questions from his social studies text—you can help him link his new work to his previous successes.

Start by explicitly showing and asking him how the new work resembles his recent successes; then remind him what he recently did to succeed: "Warren, this story comes from the same book you read so well last week. Look, it's also about Lewis and Clark. You did well on the Lewis and Clark story because you previewed it before reading it. You can do that again." Emphasizing similarities builds confidence. Warren might well think, "I know a lot about explorers. I already understand parts of this book and I know how to preview. I succeeded once. I can succeed again."

Reward effort, persistence, and success. Work that matches your child's abilities gives you opportunities to reward his effort, persistence, and success, and make the link between them. When tasks are moderately challenging, "effort feedback" can strengthen his self-efficacy—his belief about his ability to succeed—and motivation, while improving achievement: "You worked hard on your homework for more than 20 minutes and carefully checked your answers. By correcting two of them, you got everything right. Good job."

But some struggling readers need more than praise—first they need physical or visible "do, see, or touch" rewards, rewards so powerful that to earn them they're willing to change their behavior: They're willing to read and to complete their homework.

When rewarding your child for reasonable effort, remember that what's a powerful reward for younger children may be insulting to older ones; what's powerful for one teenager may be worthless to another. So, for hints about what's rewarding, look and listen for what your child wants. Note what he watches on television, what he wants to buy and do, who he talks to, and what he talks about. Then experiment to see what he finds rewarding—what motivates him, albeit temporarily, to read and to finish his homework. For younger children it might be stickers or playing catch; for older ones, it might be a music download or free time to hang out with friends.

The problem with rewarding your child with artificial, extrinsic rewards, like toys and stickers and music, is that to keep him reading and doing homework, you have to keep rewarding him. To reduce the frequency of or eliminate the need for such rewards, and to motivate him to continue reading and doing homework, you need to adhere to the reinforcement principles listed in Table 6.1.

TABLE 6.1: REINFORCEMENT PRINCIPLES

- *Start small.* Use the smallest, most natural rewards your child will work for, like playing catch or helping you prepare dinner.

- *Start by rewarding all reasonable efforts and correct use of strategies.* Start by rewarding your child every time he makes a reasonable effort, persists, or correctly uses a learning strategy. Briefly tell him why he earned the reward: "Mel, you worked on this for 15 minutes straight. You used the learning strategy your teacher taught you. Great job. You earned 10 minutes of telephone time with Wilson."

- *Vary rewards.* This avoids boredom. Let your child choose from several rewards acceptable to you. When possible, substitute more natural rewards, like going to the movies as a family, for more artificial ones, like stickers.

- *Praise success.* Give task-specific praise when giving rewards: "Mel, you finished that paper by 4:30, just like you said you would. And it reads well; it makes sense. Want to shoot some baskets?"

- *Reward less often over time.* Gradually thin out the frequency of artificial rewards by reinforcing fewer instances of correct behavior. But be careful: Go slow—do not reduce the frequency too quickly. Once your child is reading and doing homework regularly, you might stop rewarding every success and begin to reward every second success for three weeks, then every fourth for three weeks, and so on.

- *Make success visible.* Keep a visible record of your child's successes, so he sees them pile up. If he has word-identification problems, make a word wall on which he writes every new word he's mastered. If he has comprehension problems, keep a large chart of the percentage of assignment-items he answered correctly. Or if you're not sure of what to record, make a port-folio of his best work, label it "best work," and add to it every few days.

- *Gradually raise the standards for rewards.* To produce successes that you can reward requires work that matches your child's abilities. It may also require you to start with lower standards, standards that you raise gradually.

  If, for example, you and your child's teacher want him to "earn a 'B' on five consecutive homework assignments at his independent level," and the requirements for earning grades are explicit, you and his teacher might initially reward him for each assignment on which he earns a "C." Once he submits "C" work for five consecutive assignments, you both raise the standard for earning rewards to the next level, "C+," and stop rewarding "C" work. You follow this strategy of gradually increasing the standard for rewards—in line with his successes—until he achieves "Bs" on five consecutive assignments.

  This strategy, called "shaping," starts by rewarding your child at an easy level and, with his successes, gradually increases the requirements for earning rewards. Shaping makes success manageable by tying rewards to realistic, but increasingly demanding standards until your child routinely achieves the targeted behavior.

Teach your child to make facilitative attributions. Success also gives you opportunities to teach your child why he was successful, to name the reasons. Such explanations, called attributions, can simplify the reasons for success and failure and can influence your child's future beliefs and actions, including effort and persistence.

Many parents and teachers unintentionally harm children by attributing success to intelligence, which many children and adults incorrectly believe is innate and fixed. If children think that intelligence is responsible for their successes, they usually think it's responsible for their difficulties and failures, leading to the infamous but all too common statements: "I'm dumb.... I'm stupid.... I'm a loser."[16]

So what attributions should parents and teachers teach? The answer: effort, persistence, and the correct use of learning strategies.

By *consistently* teaching your child to attribute his successes to effort and persistence and to using the learning strategies emphasized in school—such as the word-identification strategy of first sounding out the beginning letters of a word, then looking for a familiar spelling pattern, then reading and thinking about the rest of the sentence, then spending a few seconds trying to identify the word from the known parts and the meaning of surrounding sentences, and finally, asking for help if the word remains unknown but possibly important—you're teaching him to attribute success to factors he can control and replicate: "I succeeded because I tried very hard. I stuck to it. I followed the steps on my cue cards."

This also teaches him to attribute failure to factors he can control and change: "I did poorly because I didn't try hard enough. I didn't follow the cue cards. Next time I'll try harder and follow the steps on my cue cards." By focusing on effort, persistence, and strategy use, your child doesn't have to worry about innate intelligence or being smart. Instead, he can focus on the behaviors that produce success.

By *consistently* attributing his success and failure to controllable factors—his effort, persistence, and correct use of learning strategies—you help him create and strengthen the optimistic belief that he's in control. If his homework is at his independent level, and support is available, you can *frequently* reinforce constructive attributions, thus helping your child rid himself of the lingering, disastrous thought—"I'm dumb."[17]

Principle 6—Help Your Child Identify Personally Important, Achievable Goals. Perhaps nothing is more motivating than combining personally important goals with the belief that they're achievable. But not every goal is motivating. Not every goal strengthens self-efficacy. For goals to positively influence self-efficacy and motivation, they need to be:

- Personally important to your child
- Short-term and specific
- Achievable

Moreover, to sustain motivation, your child needs credible feedback that he's making substantial progress toward achieving his goal.

Your child's specific, concrete, short-term goal might be, "To get a 'B' on next week's reading test." His long-term goal might be, "To get a 'B' in reading on my report card." Although the two kinds of goals work hand-in-hand, short-term goals are usually more motivating as they're more quickly achieved.

If, with moderate effort, your child is likely to achieve his short-term goal by carrying out a few simple strategies, encourage his efforts: "Oscar, I think you can get a 'B' on next week's test if you spend 30 minutes a night studying silently, without television or music; underlining the words you don't know so we can discuss them; and using the SCAR strategy your teacher taught you for figuring out the meaning of unknown words. Look at your SCAR cards. The S stands for **S**ubstitute a synonym, the C for **C**heck it out, the A and R for **A**ccept or **R**evise."

If success is unlikely, help him identify a new goal or modify the unrealistic one, so he won't be frustrated, so he can quickly achieve his new goal.

Make sure your child's short-term goal is specific and concrete, so he quickly knows if he's making adequate progress. Getting a "B" on next week's test is specific and concrete. He'll quickly know if he's successful. In contrast, "Improving my reading" is too fuzzy and too prone to misinterpretation. It's also endless.

Even with specific, concrete short-term goals, many struggling readers need feedback, feedback to keep them optimistic and motivated. Without frequent, explicit, visible feedback that they're making progress, they often get discouraged and retreat from reading. To give feedback, try these simple ideas:

- Chart your child's successes.
- Comment on what he did well: "You used SCAR the right way. You figured out the meaning of prescription. Nice job."
- Occasionally, celebrate his success: "You were supposed to study for 30 minutes. Instead, you studied for 40. You focused. Take a break. Want to play Monopoly©?"

Rewards, like playing Monopoly©, are feedback. But be careful. Don't provide external rewards, like money or tokens, when your child voluntarily engages in activities that motivate him, activities he believes will help him achieve a personally important goal. Children often view rewards for doing what they like as bribery. In such cases, rewards can backfire.

Principle 7—Hone Your Parenting Abilities.[18] All parents have difficulties with their children, whether or not they have reading disabilities. All parents—including Howard and Gary—have to keep honing their parenting abilities.

For parents of struggling readers, honing parenting abilities is especially critical. For them it's especially important to develop an insightful, research-based perspective on parenting. Why research based? Because habits and intuitions are often wrong: What works with academically successful children often fails with struggling readers. Why? We don't always know.

What we do know, however, is that many struggling readers have frequent and intense motivational, social, emotional, and behavioral problems. We also know that well-designed research, conducted by impartial researchers, can point parents in the right direction.

One particularly well-researched, well-written book, by an outstanding authority on child and adolescent development, is Laurence Steinberg's *The 10 Basic Principles of Good Parenting*.[19] Steinberg's principles relate to everything in this chapter. By following his principles, you can create the emotional atmosphere and structure needed for our recommendations to work. In essence, you can "set the stage" for increasing the likelihood of success. Here, briefly, are five of his principles.

Behave as if what you do matters. Because it does: Your child watches and imitates you. If, when frustrated, you slowly count to a hundred, take a walk, or listen to music, he's apt to do the same. Similarly, if you scream and pity yourself, expect the same. So think through your actions—plan ahead and then act as you want your child to. If you want your child to admit mistakes and apologize, admit yours and apologize. As Steinberg says, "You are on stage all the time, and your child is in the audience, right there in the front row of the orchestra section."[20] In other words, the best gift you can give your child is your behavior.

Involve yourself in your child's life. This means you have to spend time with your child, pay attention to him, listen to him, and sometimes—if it's consistent with your rules and values—do what he wants. To truly be with him, you can't be thinking of work or other obligations, or counting the seconds until it's time to do something "more important." Rarely is anything more important. Nor should you always be his teacher. Together, you should have fun.

Involvement also means knowing his friends and participating in school functions. You can get to know his friends and their values by having his friends over your house or taking them to ball games and listening inconspicuously to their conversations. Knowing them gives you the information you need to encourage him—not force him—to spend more time with some children and less with others.

You can participate in school by attending parent-teacher conferences, PTA meetings, and the like. You can ask you child's teachers how you can help with homework without doing it for him.

You can do all this—be involved—without being intrusive. When your child can do something for himself, let him. If he's about to make a mistake, and the consequences are not dire, let him; then show him how to learn from it.

Establish rules and set limits. Rules give your child something all children need: structure and limits. To be effective, however, he must believe that family rules make sense and are administered fairly. This can be tough on you. It means that:

- You can't be arbitrary.
- You have to enforce the rules, unless there's a compelling reason not to.
- Over time, you may have to gradually relax or modify some rules.
- Your child will sometimes get angry at you.

But, as Steinberg says and as we've experienced, "It's okay for your child to be angry at you.... It really is. Usually anger fades pretty quickly.... Believing that rules are fair and sensible is what gets children to comply."[21]

When conflict arises over a rule, calmly listen to your child so that you fully understand his views and reasoning. In some situations, it's best to problem solve with him, to develop a better rule that satisfies both of you.

Use rules to support your child's natural quest for independence. Slowly, almost imperceptibly, relax some rules or substitute new ones, so the rules reflect your child's increasing maturity. Carefully monitor their effects.

Relaxing and substituting rules—in a fair and rational way—tells your child that you respect him and his quest for independence. Happily, you're likely to earn his cooperation, though sometimes grudgingly.

Help foster your child's independence. Steinberg makes clear that to develop a sense of self-control and self-direction, "Children need a mixture of freedom and constraints.... [You always need to] maintain some balance between granting freedom and imposing limits."[22] To keep this balance, you need to:

- Avoid power struggles over little things: If he wants to read a *Thomas the Train*© book for the 23rd time, but you want him to read a more sophisticated one, let him read *Thomas*. In all likelihood, he'll soon gravitate to more sophisticated books.
- Let him decide between items or activities you've preapproved:
  Ask him if he wants to drink apple juice, orange juice, or grapefruit juice.
  Here, any preapproved choice is fine.
- Praise his decisions on preapproved items or activities: "Mel, waiting two days for the jeans sale was a good decision. You saved yourself $25 and picked a nice color.
  Now you have money for the movies."
- Help him think through decisions: If he wants to do homework after the Phillies' game, ask him to list the advantages and disadvantages of doing it before and after.
- Let him learn from his mistakes, as long as they're not dangerous or illegal:
  Let him spend his last ten dollars on a toy he'll tire of quickly; once he tires, discuss how he might have better spent the money.

Be consistent. Consistency is not rigidity. Consistency means that on important things, like crossing the street, you always insist that your young child holds your hand and that, at a minimum, your older child listens for cars and looks both ways. It means that you maintain household and sleep schedules, although, as your children get older, you agree to later bedtimes. Schedules are not harsh: "Familiar routines make children feel safe and secure, because they feel more in control when they know what to expect.[23] In a two-parent family, it also means that you and your partner discuss differences privately, and then support your agreement, even if you don't like it.

Rigidity screams "no exceptions," even if circumstances warrant them. If, for example, the family's rule says that homework must be finished and checked before your child sees his friends, and today he did his best to complete homework that was simply too difficult, and you couldn't check it because your neighbor's St. Bernard ate it, rigidity demands that he can't see friends, even if they invite him to play ball.

In contrast, consistency says that when—for understandable and justified reasons—a rule is ignored, briefly discuss what could be done differently, and then, let him play ball. Consistency also says it's smart to revise rules that backfire—it shows you're a thinking, sensible parent: "The more your authority is based on wisdom and not power, the less your child will challenge it."[24]

For more information on parenting, with insightful examples and interesting discussions, we recommend that you study, think about, and discuss Laurence Steinberg's book, *The 10 Basic Principles of Good Parenting*. As parents and grandparents, it helps us.

KEEP IN MIND

Keep in mind that no book, including this one, knows you or your child or your household. No book knows what you're good or bad at, what you like or dislike, and the different pressures that hammer away at you. No book can tell you what to do. At best, a book can suggest.

With this in mind, we suggest that you:

- Study this chapter.
- Study the resources we've discussed.
- Study the resources on www.reading2008.com.
- Discuss possible solutions and activities with people you trust, including your child's teachers and other experts.
- Try to avoid the pitfalls of *Solutions that Usually Fail*, which we discussed at the beginning of this chapter.
- Study the ideas in *Increasing the Likelihood of Success*, which is near the beginning of this chapter. Try those that might work.
- Remember, all instruction and all interventions are experiments that need monitoring, which the next chapter focuses on.

As you try new ideas, keep this in mind: If something works, stick with it and keep improving upon it, as long as it works, as long as it achieves its goals; if it doesn't work, modify it, and try the modification; if it still doesn't work, abandon it, and try something else that has a good chance of working. Above all, be optimistic, keep learning about potential solutions, and keep improving your parenting skills.

ENDNOTES

[1] A reward is something a child will actually work to get, not what a parent or teacher thinks he'll work for. If you believe something is rewarding to your child, but he won't work diligently to get it, he may not think of it as rewarding, or the delay between doing what he's asked to do and getting the reward is too long, or what he's asked to do is simply too difficult. For a more detailed discussion, visit our website: www.reading2008.com.

[2] You might remember ROCC from chapter 5. To avoid confusion and to get adequate practice and reinforcement, struggling readers need a **R**ich, **O**rganized, **C**onsistent **C**urriculum.

[3] If done right, tutoring can be one of the most effective forms of instruction. In summarizing one of the more important studies on tutoring, here's what the late Michael Pressley, a leading scholar on reading disabilities, concluded: "There is a very, very important message in Vellutino et al.'s [study]: Until there is an intensive effort to teach a child to read words using a systematic approach, it is a huge mistake to assume that the child cannot learn to read because of biological differences.... It should not be missed, however, that the instruction that worked in Vellutino et al. ... was daily one-to-one tutoring for a semester or more ... Such intensity permits careful monitoring of specific difficulties and tailored instruction. That the control in the study was small-group instruction consistent with the school district's normal approach to remediation makes clear that instruction short of intensive one-to-one tutoring is just not as effective.... Such tutoring can turn struggling readers around" (Pressley, M., 2006. *Reading Instruction that Works: The Case for Balanced Teaching.* New York: The Guilford Press, pp. 74-75).

[4] Allington, R. L., 2002. What I've learned about effective reading instruction. *Phi Delta Kappan*, 740, 742-747, p. 743.

[5] Sachs, M. H., 1993. Exercise for stress control. In D. Goleman & J. Gurin (Eds.). *How to Use Your Mind for Better Health* (pp. 315-330).Yonkers, NY: Consumer Reports Books.

[6] Underlying difficulties in understanding spoken language can also affect reading comprehension. If you suspect that such difficulties, like understanding the structure of sentences (called syntax), are impeding your child's reading comprehension, have a language specialist evaluate his language abilities.

[7] Like success, choice is a major motivator. When present, it encourages high levels of engagement; when missing, it can arouse resistance. This is why restaurants have menus, toy store isles have thousands of toys, and single screen theaters have been vanquished. So, when you can offer choices—choices that are acceptable to you—do so. For enlightening discussions about how choice motivates academic engagement, such as reading, you might want to read one of these: (a) Allington, R. L., & Johnston, P. H., 2001. What do we know about effective fourth-grade teachers and their classrooms? In C. Roller (Ed.), *Learning to Teach Reading: Setting the Research Agenda* (pp. 150– 165). Newark, DE: International Reading Association; (b) Pintrich, P. R., & Schunk, D. H., 2002. *Motivation in Education: Theory, Research and Applications* (2nd ed.). Englewood Cliffs, NJ: Prentice Hall Merrill.

[8] These are not frivolous questions. To improve children's reading, some schools and teachers emphasize knowledge, skills, and activities that have very little importance for improving reading. In other words, if children acquire the targeted knowledge and skills and master the activities, their reading will not improve.

[9] To stretch and hold the beginning sound of a word, look for a sound that can be stretched. The /r/ sound can be stretched, but not /k/. Sounds that can be stretched and held are called continuants; those that cannot be are called non-continuants. Continuant sounds include /f/, /l/, /m/, /n/, /r/, /s/, /v/, /w/, /y/, /z/, /th/, /sh/. For a wonderful article on playful activities to support phonemic awareness, see Yopp, H. K., & Yopp, R. H., 2000. Supporting phonemic awareness development in the classroom. *The Reading Teacher, 54* (2), 130-143. Many of these activities can be adapted by parents to present as incidental, informal games.

[10] Like many reading authorities, Yopp and Yopp (2000) divide syllables into two parts. The first part, called the onset, is the consonant preceding the vowel. The second part, called the rime, is the vowel and any consonants following the onset. All syllables contain a vowel sound.

[11] Yopp & Yopp, 2000, p. 133 (with a minor modification).

[12] Assigning homework that is more difficult than a struggling reader's independent level is assigning work that he cannot succeed on, independently. As homework is, in theory, independent work, such assignments are unethical as they produce—whether knowingly or not—failure, frustration, and, in many cases, alienation from school. Whatever a teacher's reason for assigning homework more difficult than a struggling reader's independent level, the reason is unjustified. Arguing that it's school policy is the same as arguing that schools require teachers to set-up struggling readers for failure and frustration. In our eyes, homework is a crucial matter, as we have often seen poorly designed assignments damage the self-efficacy of struggling readers, increase resistance to school work, and create family fights.

[13] Digital recorders are far easier to use than cassette recorders. They don't require cassettes, can transfer files to computers, produce files that can be played on computers, and are inexpensive. Howard's favorite is his Olympus WS-100®, which holds some 25 hours of recordings and costs about $75.00. Many struggling readers over age ten like them because they're easy to use and are age appropriate.

[14] Five questions can be far too demanding if the reading level of the materials is far above the struggling reader's independent level. At a much higher level, one question can be overwhelming.

[15] For a detailed discussion of self-efficacy, visit our website, www.reading2008.com. It contains several publications on how to strengthen the self-efficacy of struggling readers.

[16] In discussing the results of one of her studies on praise, Carol Dweck of Stanford University raised an alarm: "We took ordinary children and [inadvertently] made them into liars, simply by telling them they were smart.... Telling children they're smart, in the end, made them feel dumber and act dumber, but claim they were smarter.... That's the danger" (Dweck, C. S., 2006. *Mindset: The New Psychology of Success*. New York: Random House, pp. 73-74).

[17] Note how this section uses the words *consistently* and *frequently*. The reason: Repeating attributions frequently is critical; without doing so, little will change. As George Lakoff, Goldman Distinguished Professor of Cognitive Science and Linguistics at the University of California, Berkeley, asserts, "When [words and phrases]... are repeated every day, extensive areas of the brain are activated over and over, and this leads to brain change. Unerasable brain change. Once learned, the new neural structure cannot just be erased.... And every time the words are repeated, all the frames and metaphors and worldview structures [associated with these words] are activated again and strengthened—because recurring activation strengthens neural connections" (Lakoff, G., 2007. What Orwell didn't know about the brain, the mind, and language. In A. Szanto (Ed.), *What Orwell Didn't Know* (pp. 67-74). New York: Public Affairs, pp. 70-71).

[18] We used the word *hone*, not *perfect*. Our concern is that perfect is an illusion that no human can achieve, certainly not in parenting.

[19] Steinberg, L., 2004. *The 10 Basic Principles of Good Parenting*. New York: Simon & Schuster.

[20] Steinberg, 2004, p. 15.

[21] Steinberg, 2004, pp. 92-93.

[22] Steinberg, 2004, p. 108.

[23] Steinberg, 2004, p. 131.

[24] Steinberg, 2004, p. 141.

CHAPTER 7
MONITORING PROGRESS

Now that you have a clearer understanding of reading problems and your child is in a program to improve her reading, you may think that her success is ensured. You could be wrong, dead wrong!

Why? Because even a well-designed program, based on a highly competent diagnosis, may not work. As Joseph Witt and his colleagues noted, "Trying to predict which interventions will work well for individual students has not been a fruitful endeavor."[1] Thus, to improve your child's odds of success, you need to ensure that her progress is carefully and frequently monitored. If progress is poor, monitoring allows her program to be quickly adjusted or replaced. Inadequate or infrequent monitoring may condemn her to an ineffective program, one that wastes irreplaceable instructional time and causes continued frustration and failure.

Unfortunately, schools often fail to carefully and frequently monitor children's progress.[2] Testing children with reading disabilities a few times a year, especially with standardized tests, is insufficient.[3] Grades are also insufficient—often they're based on impressions, not valid, impartial information. So, how can you increase the odds that teachers and other school personnel will carefully and frequently monitor your child's progress?

The answers are complex. They require you to understand some of the dynamics of schools and to become actively involved in your child's reading program. Specifically, they require you to:

- Understand the pressures felt by your child's teachers and other school personnel, such as administrators, learning consultants, and school psychologists.
- Understand their backgrounds in reading disabilities.
- Treat everyone with genuine respect.
- Work with them to develop an in-school monitoring plan.
- Directly monitor your child's progress.
- Regularly discuss your child's progress with her teachers and other school personnel.

This list may seem overwhelming. But, don't fear. As you begin to understand the information and strategies in this chapter, you increase the odds of working effectively with school personnel to monitor your child's progress.

PRESSURES FELT BY TEACHERS AND OTHER SCHOOL PERSONNEL

Teachers and other school personnel are often under tremendous pressure to improve achievement test scores, follow school procedures, avoid setting precedents, and minimize expenses. Regardless of whether the pressure is obvious or subtle, early in their careers, many teachers and other school personnel learn to avoid precedent setting and costly recommendations, such as 50 minutes a day of one-to-one tutoring by a reading specialist. Consequently, many censor their true recommendations or gradually come to embrace the belief that, at most, children should get limited services.[4] Many come to believe that public schools, with their limited resources, can't really help children with serious learning problems. Many believe that giving intensive services to one child robs others of services.

Often, teachers and other school personnel follow whatever administrators deem appropriate, even if past results have been poor. Like many administrators who allow short-term financial constraints to dominate their decisions, many teachers and other school personnel fail to realize that denying children the programs and services they need to become proficient readers will produce poor test scores and skyrocketing costs. They don't realize, for example, that retention is far more costly and far less effective than preventative or remedial tutoring,[5] and that special education evaluations are costly and often fail to provide the information needed to improve instruction and achievement. Thus, you shouldn't be surprised if school personnel challenge the kinds of programs and services needed to improve your child's reading.

Under the *No Child Left Behind Act* (NCLB), schools and teachers are judged by their students' scores on standardized achievement tests. Because many teachers feel pressured to teach to the test[6] and to cover specific material by a particular date, many struggling readers are:

- Forced to frequently read materials and complete assignments at their frustration level rather than at their proper instructional and independent levels.
- Not taught the prerequisite skills and background knowledge they need, guaranteeing failure.
- Taught through whole-class instruction that ignores their particular learning needs.
- Denied adequate opportunity to stretch their minds in ways that are personally and intellectually satisfying. For example, they may not have opportunities to work on moderately challenging group projects, read materials on which they can succeed, listen to intellectually challenging stories.

Any one of these can cause failure and trigger strong emotions, such as anger, despair, and depression. Any one of these can destroy motivation for learning.

In most schools, time is precious, scheduling is difficult, and people must do far more than is reasonable. Thus, teachers and other school personnel often resist instructional and programmatic suggestions, however well justified, because they consume precious time. Even if they don't resist, teachers and other school personnel often fail to monitor progress because they feel pressured by competing demands. Time and pressure are issues because schools fail to hire adequate numbers of qualified teachers and support staff.[7]

Time and standardized test pressures add to three other problems that intensify the reading difficulties of struggling readers:

- Many general education teachers want special education teachers and reading specialists to take full responsibility for teaching reading and writing to struggling readers. When reading instruction is limited to time in pull-out programs, programs in which struggling readers leave their general education classrooms for instruction in separate resource or reading rooms, they typically get far less reading instruction than they need.

- Many general education and special education teachers have little time to jointly plan struggling readers' reading programs. Thus, these teachers may emphasize different reading strategies and not reinforce each other's instruction. This adds to struggling readers' confusion about reading and denies them adequate opportunity to practice and apply critical reading skills.

- Many schools believe it's a waste of time to teach reading to children who are far behind and, even with extra help, couldn't pass NCLB tests. Better, they think, that they focus efforts on children who had almost passed, who, with a little bit of help, could pass. These are the "bubble kids."[8] As Gerald Bracey, an insightful educational critic, noted, the pressure to focus on the "bubble kids" is tremendous: "With the bubble kids getting laser-like attention, though, and the sure-to-pass and sure-to-fail students getting none, we could easily see rising pass rates and falling scores."[9] Because of NCLB pressures, some schools have made shameful decisions: To abandon many of their students.[10]

Before blaming teachers, it's important to understand that teaching is a complex, demanding, often overwhelming job that receives little financial support or public respect. On the whole, teachers work hard, very hard. They spend far more time planning and teaching than teachers in most industrialized countries, even those with longer school years. In addition to quitting in great numbers because of large classes, unsafe schools, professional isolation, long work hours, demeaning treatment, and poorly motivated students, many leave because of inadequate preparation time, little influence on educational decisions, and frequent interruptions to their teaching. Many feel helpless to change the system or to get children what they need.

From this gloom a lesson emerges: To advocate effectively for your child, you need to understand the pressures felt by teachers and other school personnel—understand so you can genuinely empathize with them, and, if feasible, reach agreement on how to monitor your child's progress. The better you understand their situations, the more likely your requests or recommendations about monitoring will match their needs, abilities, and situations, and thus be accepted.

PEOPLE'S BACKGROUNDS IN READING DISABILITIES

Reading disabilities is an extremely complicated, rapidly changing field that requires expertise in many aspects of counseling, psychology, group dynamics, and special education, as well as reading. It takes years of graduate study and supervised practice for reading specialists to develop the knowledge and skill needed to design, implement, monitor, and evaluate reading programs that meet the academic, social, and emotional needs of struggling readers. Even with such study and practice, as well as advanced degrees in reading, many reading specialists lack the knowledge and skill needed to address the more complicated, persistent problems of struggling readers.

Despite the complexity of reading disabilities, professionals with virtually no directly relevant graduate study—learning disabilities specialists, school psychologists, special education teachers—often have total responsibility for diagnosing and remediating difficult reading problems. Many have taken only one or two courses in reading, and none that emphasized complex reading disabilities. Many have no more expertise than average classroom teachers.[11] Consequently, struggling readers are often harmed. In a sense, it's like asking general practitioners or orthopedic surgeons to perform open heart surgery; needlessly, many patients will die.[12]

Despite their lack of expertise in reading disabilities, general education teachers and special education teachers need to play a prominent role in teaching reading to struggling readers. After all, struggling readers work with these teachers most of the day. The key is to blend the expertise of these teachers with the reading specialist's.

If the reading specialist instructs your child, the specialist should coordinate instruction with your child's teachers. This involves both observing your child when she's reading, writing, and speaking in her other classes, and meeting regularly with her teachers to discuss her progress and plan her reading program. If the specialist cannot instruct her, the specialist should, at a minimum, assess her; work with you and her teachers to plan and monitor her reading program; observe her in class during reading and related instruction; observe her in other subjects that emphasize reading, such as science and social studies; and consult with her teachers. The more difficulty your child is having, the more frequently the specialist should observe her in class and consult with her teachers. Eighty minutes per week of observing and consulting is not excessive.

In sum, if your child is struggling with reading, there is no substitute for the continued involvement of a highly knowledgeable, highly skilled reading specialist. In echoing numerous reading experts, Douglas Carnine, Jerry Silbert, and Edward Kameenui assert:

> The more severe the student's deficit, the more careful the instruction must be. The instruction of remedial students must be monitored quite carefully by highly trained teachers.... Many remedial readers need the help of the *most highly trained professional*, because they have developed serious confusions that must be carefully and consistently corrected.[13]

GENUINE RESPECT
At all times, remember these principles:
- People need to be treated with respect.
- People need to be listened to and feel understood.
- People like to be acknowledged for their accomplishments.
- People defend themselves when criticized.
- People get demoralized or angry when constantly criticized.
- People get angry when they believe they're being treated unfairly.
- People get angry or despondent when they're blamed for things they can't control.

Why keep these principles in mind? When you understand and remember them, you're likely to treat people with respect, a key to gaining cooperation.

Treating people with respect doesn't mean you have to agree with them. It means that you view them as important, listen carefully to what they say, and try to understand their views, their feelings, and the reasons for their opinions and actions. By focusing on the merits of their ideas, and asking information-seeking *why* questions, *how* questions, and *what-if* questions, you're laying the foundation for a solid working relationship. Table 7.1 offers examples.

TABLE 7.1: QUESTIONS

> *A Why Question:* Why do you want to use whole language rather than direct instruction?
>
> *A How Question:* How will you implement whole language in social studies, when Sue has to read textbooks?
>
> *A What-If Question:* You've made some good points about why whole language might work. What if we try it for a month and the monitoring data show that progress is poor? Can we meet to plan a different kind of program?

In addition to listening to understand, a simple but powerful way to communicate respect is to focus on people's accomplishments. For example, a note to the principal complimenting your child's teacher for helping her master some difficult sight words can work wonders. So can a note from your child, thanking her teacher for the after-school help he gave her. Table 7.2 offers a simple example.

TABLE 7.2: A SAMPLE NOTE

> Dear Mr. Patrick,
>
> Thank you for spending time with me after school, teaching me how to break words into syllables. What you did will help me become a better reader.
>
> Sincerely,
>
> Megan

Emphasizing the positive—when it's obvious and well deserved—reduces defensiveness and creates respect, making cooperation more likely.

AN IN-SCHOOL MONITORING PLAN

In the final analysis, you are your child's best advocate. You're the person with the 24-hour-a-day, life-long perspective. At most, your child's best teachers will work with her for only a few years. Thus, to advocate effectively for her, you have to be ever-present; you have to know how she's progressed over the years and how she's doing now. If she's having problems, you can't wait for them to escalate before requesting changes in her instruction or program. You need to work with her teachers and other involved school personnel to ensure that they have a plan to frequently monitor her progress.

Below are suggestions for developing and carrying out a plan to monitor your child's progress in school. You can use some or all of them, depending on your situation. Although the first three are legally mandated for the Individualized Education Programs (IEPs) of children classified as eligible for special education under the Federal *Individuals with Disabilities Education Improvement Act of 2004* (IDEA-2004)—and not mandated for other children—they're sound educational suggestions that can help all struggling readers.[14] Thus, you should consider adapting them to your child's needs if she's not classified as eligible for special education under IDEA-2004.[15] Sadly, if your child is not eligible, Federal law gives you little legal leverage. But little doesn't mean "none." It means that you must learn about your State's laws and regulations, as well as its written policies and those of the district. It also means that you must cultivate positive, genuine relationships with school personnel and learn about their values, their professionalism, and the pressures they face.[16]

With these thoughts in mind, here are five suggestions:

- Make sure your child's IEP has annual goals that are measurable.
- Make sure your child's IEP describes exactly *how* the school
  will monitor progress.
- Make sure your child's IEP specifies *when* they will monitor progress and report
  the results to you.
- Request a portfolio that describes your child's progress.
- Request once weekly or twice monthly progress reports.

Make Sure Your Child's IEP has Annual Goals that are Measurable. If your child is eligible for special education under IDEA-2004, she must have a written plan called an IEP. IDEA-2004 requires that the IEP Team, which consists of you, your child's general education and special education teachers, and other school personnel listed in IDEA-2004's regulations and your State's special education code, jointly write the IEP.[17] The IEP must contain:

> A statement of measurable annual goals, including academic and functional goals designed to ... meet the child's needs that result from the child's disability to enable the child to be involved in and make progress in the general education curriculum; and meet each of the child's other educational needs that result from the child's disability.[18]

The importance of measurable annual goals should not be underestimated as they form the basis for related services, such as individual tutoring, and for monitoring. If goals do not justify related services, like individual tutoring, the school need not provide them. With school budgets getting substantially tighter, denial of services will likely become more common. As the Superintendent of the Newhall School District in California recently said about diminishing budgets and State aid: "All too often policy decisions—or the lack of hard choices—that are made at the State level fall on the shoulders of children and the dedicated people who work with them.... We don't want to implement these cuts to services for our students and we want the Legislature to find another solution."[19]

Given possible difficulties in getting needed services, it's essential that your child's goals are important, realistic, and ambitious.[20] As such, they provide justification for whatever services your child needs to make meaningful progress in reading.

Goals also form the basis for monitoring: Without explicit, measurable goals, it's impossible to measure progress accurately. Put another way, without explicit, measurable goals it's impossible to know what to measure and how to measure it. Without such goals, school personnel may well disagree with one another and with you about the adequacy of progress.[21]

To ensure that each goal is measurable, ask for several short-term objectives that logically reflect small steps toward achieving each goal, small steps that clearly indicate whether your child's rate of progress is adequate to achieve her goals. Short-term objectives target what your child can achieve—without becoming frustrated or stressed—in one marking period. So, if one of your child's reading goals is to quickly recognize, by the end of the 4th or last marking period, all the sight words in the Dolch Word List, a published list of common words, each marking period would have one objective. Table 7.3 offers a clear, measurable set of objectives to assess mastery of the Dolch List.

TABLE 7.3: CLEAR, MEANINGFUL OBJECTIVES

Objective 1: Given *50 of the 200* sight words that Sue did not know when tested with the Dolch Word List in the second week of school, she will correctly pronounce each of these *50 words* when they're individually presented on flash cards. She will correctly pronounce each word within one second of exposure on five consecutive school days by the end of the *1st marking period.*

Objective 4: Given *200 of the 200* sight words that Sue did not know when tested with the Dolch Word List in the second week of school, she will correctly pronounce each of these *200 words* when they're individually presented on flash cards. She will correctly pronounce each word within one second of exposure on five consecutive school days by the end of the *4th marking period.*

From the objectives in Table 7.3, we hope it's clear that measurable short-term objectives have five parts:

- The behavior to be observed: Sue will correctly pronounce each word.
- The name of the student who will perform the behavior: Sue.
- The criteria for mastery: Correctly pronounce each word within one second of exposure, on five consecutive school days.
- The conditions under which the behavior will occur: Words will be individually presented on flash cards.
- The target date for attainment: End of a specified marking period.

Generally, objectives with these five parts are directly and readily measurable. By including a reasonable target date, one Sue can meet if she makes a moderate effort, both teachers and parents can readily determine if progress is sufficient. By measuring the objectives, teachers are measuring the goal: Once the last objective is achieved, the goal is achieved.

One of the downsides of IDEA-2004 is that it eliminated the Federal requirement that all IEPs contain measurable short-term objectives. As a result, many States have eliminated the requirement.[22]

If your State no longer requires short-term objectives, you can still ask the IEP Team, on which you're a full-fledged member, to include them. If it refuses, insist that your child's IEP include other valid ways of measuring progress toward achieving her annual goals. Even without short-term objectives, IDEA-2004 requires this. After all, if an IEP Team will not use valid procedures to monitor a child's progress in meeting her "measurable annual goals,"[23] it's negating its obligation to measure progress and nullifying one of IDEA-2004's basic principles: To properly inform parents of their child's status and progress so they can make informed decisions. It's also negating its responsibility to adjust instruction so the child achieves her IEP goals. In line with this, note what the U.S. Third Circuit Court concluded:

> A school district that knows *or should know* that a child has an inappropriate IEP or is not receiving more than a de minimis [trivial] educational benefit must, of course, correct the situation.... If it fails to do so, a disabled child is entitled to compensatory education.[24]

Also note that the Federal regulations for IDEA-2004 make clear that schools must provide children, and those who instruct them, with the educational resources they need to achieve the IEP's goals:

> [The IEP] must include... a statement of the special education and related services and supplementary aids and services... to be provided to the child, or on behalf of the child, and a statement of the program modifications or supports for school personnel that will be provided to enable the child—to advance appropriately toward attaining the annual goals; to be involved in and make progress in the general education curriculum.[25]

If the IEP Team refuses to develop measurable short-term objectives, what can you do? Make sure that all of the IEP's goals are measurable. To do this, create a series of short-term objectives, and request that the IEP Team use your last, most ambitious objective as a goal.

Look at Table 7.3 again. When comparing its short-term objectives, note that only the *italicized* parts differ and that Objective 4, the last objective, is far more ambitious. Make this into your measurable goal.[26] Although this "work-around" strategy is less effective than having explicit short-term objectives for each marking period, it's far better than settling for vague goals.

If the IEP Team disagrees with your suggestion, and they offer a vague goal (e.g., Sue will improve her sight vocabulary), what should you do?

Consider using Objective 4—the one that increased the requirement from 50 sight words to 200, from a time span of one marking period to four—as your criterion for the specificity needed to make an annual goal measurable. Once you have a clear image of the degree of specificity needed, the degree illustrated by Objective 4, work cooperatively with the Team to make their goal measurable. Do this by asking questions to make the goal concrete and specific. Use questions like these:

- How many new words will Sue learn?
- How will we identify these words?
- How can I get a list of these words so I can help her at home?
- How quickly will she have to say them once they're presented?
- How will you present the words? When can you show me how?

It's important that the IEP's goals be so explicit that you and the other members of the IEP Team can readily agree—no later than the end of each marking period—if your child is making meaningful progress toward achieving her goals.[27] This helps to ensure that progress can be accurately monitored and that any needed changes can be made—quickly. Anything less risks your child's future.

But what do you do if your child is ineligible for special education under IDEA-2004? Ask for reconsideration or for an eligibility re-evaluation. Because IDEA-2004 and its regulations fail to provide the specificity needed for widespread agreement, schools and their evaluation and eligibility groups often use vague criteria, which can create disagreement among school personnel.[28] Asking for reconsideration or a re-evaluation can occasionally result in schools agreeing—for legitimate reasons—to eligibility.[29]

If, however, the IDEA-2004 group does not agree to eligibility, ask the school to consider eligibility under *Section 504 of the Rehabilitation Act of 1973* (Section 504).[30] In practical, not legal terms, this often means that your child's reading disability is not as severe as the school requires for IDEA-2004 services. If the school's 504 Team, which is usually the same as the IDEA-2004 group, agrees to eligibility, request a Section "504 Plan." In developing it, we suggest that you ask the school to use its IEP form, or, if their form is poor, the U. S. Department of Education's.[31] If the 504 Team is unsure of the legalities, you might share this Section 504 regulation:

> Implementation of an individualized education program [IEP] ... is one
> means of meeting the standard.[32]

The reason for requesting the district to use its IEP form is that school personnel are familiar with it, and it likely has places for goals and services. It may even have a place for short-term objectives. In any case, request measurable goals and short-term objectives: It's good educational policy that can improve learning.[33]

If, in developing the plan, the school's 504 Team refuses to use short-term objectives, ask relevant questions: "Why? Without measurable goals and short-term objectives, how can you ensure that my child's program will focus on her needs and that she's making excellent progress in becoming a highly proficient reader? How can you ensure that she'll pass the State's No Child Left Behind tests?" Often, the goals and objectives questions remind Team members of their professional knowledge and obligations. The NCLB question reminds them that annually they will be publicly and administratively judged by the percentage of students who pass these tests.[34]

One caution about Section 504:

> [It does] not require public schools to provide an educational program that is individualized to meet the needs of a disabled child with the goal of enabling the child to become independent and self-sufficient.... A Section 504 plan does not have the protections available to the child who has an IEP under the IDEA.[35]

Despite its many limitations, Section 504 can be of great help. You can find additional information about Section 504 in chapter 12 and on our website, www.reading2008.com.

Make Sure Your Child's IEP Describes Exactly *How* the School Will Monitor Progress. IDEA-2004 has a powerful provision to ensure that your child's school will monitor her progress in reading. Specifically, it requires IEPs to state "*how* the child's progress toward meeting the annual goals ... will be measured."[36]

This requirement—a statement of *how* progress will be measured—implies that the school must specify *what* they will do to collect data. Note that the *Concise Oxford Dictionary* defines "how" as "in what way or by what means." It also implies the need to identify *what* data they will collect. To illustrate *how*, again examine Objective 4 for Sue, which became her word recognition goal:

> *Word Recognition Goal:* Given *200 of the 200* sight words that Sue did not know when tested with the Dolch Word List in the second week of school, Sue will correctly pronounce each of these *200 words* when they're individually presented on flash cards. She will correctly pronounce each word within one second of exposure, on five consecutive school days, by the end of the *4th marking period.*

For Sue's goal, presenting a selected group of words to her on flash cards, one at a time, is *how.*

Now, let's look at the goal in Table 7.4. If Kelly reads orally and meets the Qualitative Reading Inventory's (QRI) criteria for instructional level, she will achieve this IEP goal—but only partly. To achieve the full goal, she must also read silently and meet the QRI's instructional level criteria for silent reading.

TABLE 7.4: KELLY'S READING GOAL

Reading Goal: By the end of the *4th marking period*, Kelly will achieve a 4th-grade instructional level for oral reading and for silent reading on the Qualitative Reading Inventory (QRI). The criteria for instructional level will be that specified by the QRI.

READING OBJECTIVES

Reading Objective 1: When *orally* reading previously unread selections of 200 or more words from a 3-1 basal reader, Kelly will achieve, without help, an *independent* level (99% of words correctly recognized in context; 90% of questions answered correctly) on three successive occasions by the end of the *first* marking period.

Reading Objective 2: When *orally* reading previously unread selections of 200 or more words from a 3-2 basal reader, Kelly will achieve, without help, an *instructional* level (95% of words correctly recognized in context; 70% of questions answered correctly) on three successive occasions by the end of the *second* marking period.

Reading Objective 3: When *silently* reading previously unread selections of 200 or more words from a 3-2 basal reader, Kelly will achieve, without help, an *independent* level (90% of questions answered correctly) on three successive occasions by the end of the *third* marking period.

Reading Objective 4: When *orally* reading previously unread selections of 200 or more words from a 4-1 basal reader, Kelly will achieve, without help, an *instructional* level (95% of words correctly recognized in context; 70% of questions answered correctly) on three successive occasions by the end of the *fourth* marking period.

Reading Objective 5: When *silently* reading previously unread selections of 200 or more words from a 4-1 basal reader, Kelly will achieve, without help, an *instructional* level (70% of questions answered correctly) on three successive occasions by the end of the *fourth* marking period.

Reading Objective 6: On the QRI, Kelly will achieve, without help, a 4th-grade instructional level on a previously unread passage she reads orally and on one she reads silently. She will achieve this standard with different passages for oral and silent reading by the end of the *fourth* marking period.

In reviewing the examples of Sue and Kelly, it's important to note that they deal with relevant, objective, simple, specific data, data that directly measure the objectives and goals. Such data can be extremely helpful: They can clarify progress and prevent problems. As Table 7.5 shows, when driving a car, such data can keep you from getting lost and can help you get directly to your destination. And as you'll soon see, so it is with monitoring progress in reading.

TABLE 7.5: NEED FOR RELEVANT, OBJECTIVE, SIMPLE, SPECIFIC DATA

Without Relevant, Objective, Simple, Specific Data: "You'll have to keep driving. Then, go a little bit farther and make a turn. I'm not sure what the road's called. But sooner or later you'll see a house."
continues...

> *With Relevant, Objective, Simple, Specific Data:* "It's 9 miles from here. After going 8.9 miles west on River Road, you'll see a big red barn on your right. A tenth of a mile after that, make a right turn onto Oak Tree Road. It's the first house on your right."

Many schools, however, don't value *Relevant, Objective, Simple, Specific data,* which we call *ROSS* data.[37] Many IEPs don't call for its collection. Thus, you must ask that your child's IEP require the collection of ROSS data, like that in the previous examples: For Sue, the ROSS data are the number of words she correctly and quickly reads; for Kelly, it's the percentage of accuracy she achieves for word recognition and comprehension.

So, if you think your child's IEP does not adequately provide for monitoring her progress, make your concern clear. Tell it to her IEP Team. Ask that her IEP require the use of relevant, objective, simple, specific data to frequently monitor her progress.

You are a full-fledged member of the IEP Team. You have the right to express your concern to the Team. And the Team must consider it. Look at these IDEA-2004 regulations:

- The school "must ensure that the IEP Team for each child with a disability includes—the parents of the child."[38]
- The IEP Team "must consider… the concerns of the parents for enhancing the education of their child."[39]

These regulations, however, do not mean that the school must agree to collect ROSS data. It's a decision that the entire IEP Team, including you, makes.

If you're unsure about your child's progress, and the school refuses to provide you with ROSS data, politely ask to see the data the school has collected to measure progress. After all, the school should frequently collect data to gauge progress: Without data, progress cannot be measured, just as the severity of anemia cannot be measured without analyzing blood. In line with this, IDEA-2004 requires that the IEP Team, of which you're a member:

> [Review] the child's IEP periodically, *but not less than annually,* to determine whether the annual goals for the child are being achieved; and … [revise] the IEP, as appropriate, to address … any lack of expected progress toward the annual goals … and in the general education curriculum.[40]

So, both logic and adherence to recommended professional practices require schools to collect data to detect "any lack of expected progress toward the [IEP's] annual goals … and in the general education curriculum."[41]

That said, consider this situation and the warning at the end. One of your child's IEP goals says that "When reading a story from a third-grade reader, she will correctly pronounce 95%

of the words; she will achieve this standard with different stories on 3 successive occasions." To check on your child's progress, you might ask to see the data that was collected to measure it. Such data are easy to collect and easy to understand. If the teaching staff has met its obligations, and has carefully monitored her progress, this information should be readily available. If it's not, an alarm should sound, warning you that her program and progress may be poor.

To rectify the situation, request —in writing—a meeting with her IEP Team. In your request, specify the reason. Here's one way of phrasing it: "I want to meet with the IEP Team to ensure that the school is collecting relevant, objective monitoring data on my child's progress in meeting her reading goals. Knowing the degree to which she's progressing will help her teachers, her IEP Team, and me to make more informed decisions."

In the rare instance that the school does not respond to your request to review progress data, politely ask again, by e-mail or certified letter.[42] In your request, you might include this statement from IDEA-2004's regulations:

> The parents of a child with a disability must be afforded ... an opportunity to inspect and review all education records with respect to—the identification, evaluation, and educational placement of the child; and ... the provision of FAPE [free appropriate public education] to the child.[43]

And what are education records? IDEA-2004 uses the definition in the *Family Educational Rights and Privacy Act of 1974* (FERPA), which, in part, defines records as "files, documents, and *other* materials which ... contain information directly related to a student; and ... are maintained by an educational agency or institution or by a person acting for such agency or institution."[44] The word *other* makes the definition broad. It may even include notes that a teacher puts in your child's file or sends to a guidance counselor, principal, or support teacher.

By now we hope it's obvious that measurable goals, with explicit criteria, are needed for goal monitoring to be relevant, accurate, and straightforward. Measurable goals, like those for Sue and Kelly, make it fairly easy to identify relevant ways of monitoring progress and stating, in the IEP, *how* progress will be measured. In contrast, vague, poorly written goals, like "Sue will improve her word recognition" or "Kelly will improve her reading test scores,"[45] prevent relevant, accurate, straightforward monitoring. They make it impossible to specify exactly how goals will be measured and the criteria for success. Such goals can cause lots of guesswork, disagreement, and conflict—and perhaps, condemn your child to a difficult, corrosive situation.

Make Sure Your Child's IEP Specifies When the School Will Inform You of Progress.

Not only does IDEA-2004 require the IEP to state *how* progress will be measured, it requires it to state "*when* periodic reports on the progress the child is making toward meeting the annual goals ... will be provided."[46] Knowing *when* you will receive progress reports is as important as knowing *how* the school will gauge progress. If you wait until February to learn of your child's progress, and it's poor, she's lost irreplaceable time.

During this time, she may have become frustrated, angry, demoralized. This may have destroyed her motivation for reading and other school work. By February, she may hate school. Thus, it's critical that her IEP state when—*how frequently*—the school will give you accurate, meaningful reports about her progress.

But how frequent is frequently enough? Once, twice, or three times a marking period may be inadequate. Daily or weekly monitoring may be needed. As Edward Shapiro, Iacocca Professor of Education at Lehigh University, wrote, monitoring should be "continuous." This allows schools to quickly make needed changes in instruction.[47] Put another way, the more serious your child's reading disability, the more frequently you and her teachers need information about her academic, social, and emotional progress.

Monitoring the progress of struggling readers daily, weekly, or twice-monthly is as important as monitoring the glucose levels of diabetics several times daily. Howard checks his frequently. He uses this information to adjust his diet and exercise and reap the benefits: no hyperglycemia, no hypoglycemia, better health.

Like monitoring the glucose levels of diabetics, the lesson for monitoring the progress of struggling readers is clear—frequent monitoring is powerful and beneficial[48]; infrequent monitoring is destructive. Thus, if your child's eligible for special education, we urge you to insist, politely, that her IEP or Section 504 plan[49] specify that her progress will be monitored frequently and the results reported to you frequently. Although frequency is a judgment call, usually, the greater the frequency, the greater the benefit.

Some school personnel argue that frequent monitoring wastes time and interferes with instruction. They're wrong. It's a part of instruction that makes instruction more efficient, as it tells everyone if progress is poor, if instruction needs to be changed. Think of how much time is wasted if progress is not frequently monitored, if instruction is not working, if instruction is not changed, if the struggling reader remains in the program for the entire school year. In medicine, failure to daily take the temperature and blood pressure of a feverish patient with chronically high blood pressure would be called malpractice. We hope the analogy is clear.

Monitoring need not interfere with instruction. With measurable goals and, even better, measurable short-term objectives, it can become part of instruction. Look at the goals and monitoring strategies in Table 7.6.

TABLE 7.6: GOALS AND MONITORING STRATEGIES

EXAMPLE 1

Goal: Given 200 of the 200 sight words that Sue did not know when tested with the Dolch Word List in the second week of school, Sue will correctly pronounce each of these 200 words when they're individually presented on flash cards. She will correctly pronounce each word within one second of exposure on five consecutive school days by the end of the *4th marking period.*

Monitoring Strategy: Every day, during instruction, when Sue is presented with flash cards, check those words she pronounced correctly, within one second of exposure.

Comment: Having Sue pronounce targeted words is part of instruction. Counting the number of words pronounced correctly is a simple monitoring task that can readily be completed during instruction. The entire process takes only a few minutes and can be completed by a teaching assistant. The form in Table 7.7 shows how ROSS data can be recorded easily and quickly.

EXAMPLE 2

Goal: By the end of the *4th marking period*, Kelly will achieve, without help, a *4th-grade instructional level* for oral and silent reading on the QRI. The criteria for instructional level will be that specified by the QRI.

Monitoring Strategy: Every two weeks, have Kelly *silently* read a passage at her *current instructional level*; midyear this may be 3rd grade as the aim is to reach 4th grade by year's end. Compute the percentage of questions she answers correctly. Every two weeks, have Kelly *orally* read a passage at her current instructional level. Compute the percentage of words she pronounces correctly and the percentage of questions she answers correctly.

Comment: Having Kelly silently and orally read instructional level passages should be part of her instruction, as should computing her percentages of accuracy. Computing percentages takes only a few minutes and can be done by a teaching assistant.

TABLE 7.7: SUE'S PROGRESS IN MASTERING SIGHT WORDS

Goal: Given *the 200* sight words that Sue did not know when tested with the Dolch Word List in the second week of school, she will correctly pronounce each of these *200 words* when they're individually presented on flash cards. She will correctly pronounce each word within one second of exposure on five consecutive school days by the end of the *4th marking period.*

continues...

139

Background: Present only the words that Sue has been taught, but has not yet mastered. Keep in mind that by the end of the year, she should have mastered all 200 words. Thus, mid-way through the year she should have mastered about 100 words. If she can comfortably progress at a faster rate, she should be challenged to do so.

Directions: Put a check (√) to the right of any word Sue correctly identifies in 1 second. Leave the right space blank if she takes more than 1 second to identify the word or identifies it incorrectly. Do not tell her any of the words.

WORD	DATE — √ = Right	WORD	DATE — √ = Right	WORD	DATE — √ = Right	WORD	DATE — √ = Right	WORD	DATE — √ = Right
all		all		all		all		all	
after		after		after		after		after	
always		always		always		always		always	
been		been		been		been		been	
best		best		best		best		best	
carry		carry		carry		carry		carry	
did		did		did		did		did	
four		four		four		four		four	
full		full		full		full		full	
give		give		give		give		give	

The......below indicated that the rest of the 200 words should be listed as they are taught. Not all need to be listed at the beginning of the year.

......		......		......		......		......	
......		......		......		......		......	
......		......		......		......		......	

The monitoring strategies for Sue and Kelly are embedded in instruction—they're part of instruction, a part that uses ROSS data to inform Sue and Kelly's teachers and parents if the two struggling readers are making adequate progress. Do the monitoring procedures take excessive time or interfere with instruction? No. Do they provide information likely to keep instruction heading in the right direction? Yes. Will they provide relevant and reliable data that can quickly warn teachers and parents if instruction needs to be examined and perhaps changed? Yes.

We have a phrase for one situation in which ROSS data are not collected or considered: a report card only mentality.

We call it a "report card only mentality" because the only data on which the struggling reader's report card grades are based are the teacher's subjective impressions. Often, subjectively-based report cards tell parents of struggling readers that their children are making fine progress in reading—when they're not. Rarely are the teachers dishonest. They're probably dedicated, honest people who believe what they say. But what they believe is often wrong because it's impressionistic, it's subjective, it's not based on objective data, like ROSS data.

So, what do you do if monitoring will likely be subjective? We recommend that you politely insist that the school send you ROSS data and interpretations of their meaning *once weekly or twice monthly.* Although the school may not be legally obligated to do so, it's a well-supported, excellent educational practice that many professionals call "best practice." This request is not as outlandish as it may sound. Many professionals want good relationships with parents, many admire professional knowledge, many want to do the best job possible, many want to apply "best practices."

Should school personnel ask you why you want them to use ROSS data to frequently monitor your child's progress, calmly and respectfully say something like this: "The more frequently you monitor my child's progress, using relevant, objective, simple, and specific data, and the more frequently you report this information and its meaning to me, the quicker we can identify and eliminate roadblocks to progress and the more effectively I can help my child at home. Such information will also help you determine if instructional or program changes are needed. I guess this is what the experts call a win-win situation."

Request a Portfolio That Describes Your Child's Progress. A portfolio is an organized collection of a child's work gathered over time to illustrate progress and identify current educational needs. Typically, the child and the teacher place items in the portfolio. Depending on the purpose of the portfolio, items usually represent the student's typical or best work. Common items include drawings, marked worksheets, marked spelling tests, dated recordings of a child's oral reading, marked drafts of compositions and final compositions, and graphs of oral reading fluency that specify the number of words correctly read per minute.

To assess the reading progress of struggling readers, it's important that the teacher date each item and provide written explanations or scoring guides with performance standards, called rubrics, that indicate what the items say about the reader's progress and educational needs. Table 7.8 is a typical rubric. Items in the portfolio should be grouped by subject or type of assignment.

TABLE 7.8: RUBRIC FOR ORAL READING FLUENCY[50]

Name:
Grade:
Date:
Level of Passage Read:
Evaluator:

Directions: This should be used for students whose instructional level is beginning 3rd grade or above. Before meeting with the student, study the descriptions below. Immediately after the student reads a passage aloud, check one of the descriptions below. To assure accuracy, you might record the student reading.

_____ Level 4: Reads primarily in larger, meaningful phrase groups. Although some regressions, repetitions, and deviations from text may be present, those do not appear to detract from the overall structure of the story. Preservation of the author's syntax is consistent. Some or most of the story is read with expressive interpretation.

_____ Level 3: Reads primarily in three- or four-word phrase groups. Some smaller groupings may be present. However, the majority of phrasing seems appropriate and preserves the syntax of the author. Little or no expressive interpretation is present.

_____ Level 2: Reads primarily in two-word phrases with some three- or four-word groupings. Some word-by-word reading may be present. Word groupings may seem awkward and unrelated to larger context of sentence or passage.

_____ Level 1: Reads primarily word-by-word. Occasionally two- or three-word phrases may occur, but these are infrequent and/or they do not preserve meaningful syntax.

Comments (Optional)

Maintaining portfolios is a common educational practice that many textbooks on reading recommend. One reason is that portfolios provide teachers with a great deal of diagnostic information to guide instruction. As Sandra McCormick noted:

> The portfolio has become a popular idea …. Based on the portfolio, the teacher can evaluate amount of reading, changes in oral reading strategies, comprehension, growth in word knowledge, students' perceptions of their own growth and needs, skills in various types of writing, types of books enjoyed, and other areas crucial for instructional decisions.[51]

Consistent with IDEA-2004's requirement that the IEP state how your child's progress toward achieving her goals will be measured, you may request that the school keep a portfolio. Meeting regularly with your child's teacher to discuss the portfolio's items provides an effective way of monitoring and analyzing her progress, and identifying and solving problems before they become unmanageable.

If your child's teacher has not kept a portfolio of her work (and he may have good reasons for not doing so), you might ask him to send you work samples, at least twice monthly, with explanations of what they signify about her progress.[52] You can then organize your own portfolio. Your portfolio, arranged by date and by topic, can help you understand the nature of your child's program, gauge progress, and pinpoint difficulties. It can help you communicate more effectively with school personnel, especially when discussing modifications to your child's program. And it may well convince school personnel that your points and suggestions are supported by powerful information, information they forgot or failed to notice.

Request Once Weekly or Twice Monthly Progress Reports. To report progress, many teachers like to use rating forms that they can complete quickly, with fairly good accuracy. Given their many obligations, this makes sense. However, the rating forms may not be completely relevant to your child's needs.

If school personnel suggest using a rating form to communicate weekly progress—which may be a good idea—make sure it assesses your child's progress in all areas of need. For example, if your child reads slowly and laboriously, make sure the rating form assesses her reading fluency. Our website (www.reading2008.com) has simple rating forms that teachers can adapt to your child's needs.

In addition to specifying your child's weaknesses, rating forms should specify her strengths. This provides balance for you and the teacher, and helps your child to see herself as more than a "list of problems."

Whether or not your child is in special education, ask her teacher to continually monitor her educational weaknesses and strengths—such as listening comprehension, phonological awareness, listening and speaking vocabulary, word identification, word recognition, reading comprehension, reading fluency, study skills, composition writing.

When monitoring her weaknesses, her instructional level should be the standard against which progress is judged. If she's in special education, and her IEP contains realistic short-term objectives that reflect what she can accomplish with moderate effort, these are the instructional levels that should be used as criteria for monitoring her progress. Using the right instructional level eliminates the problem of comparing your child to grade-level standards, a practice that often leads to poor reports, despondency, or resentment.

Although rating forms can be helpful, they have a major weakness: they're subjective. Basically, they quantify teachers' impressions. Consider this teacher's response to a checklist on Sue's ability to recognize words from The Essential Primary Grade Sight Word List[53]: "Sue did very well." It says very little and can easily be misinterpreted. Did Sue master 3 words, 5, 10, 20? Now consider this data-based response: "This week, on 5 of 5 consecutive days, Sue correctly pronounced 14 of the 18 words we introduced on Monday. She succeeded on these words: about, from, enough.... She had difficulty with these words: another, green, people, terrible." Teachers can easily save time by making this into a form they use for weekly reports: "This week, on 5 of 5 consecutive days, Sue correctly pronounced ____ of the ____ words we introduced on Monday. She succeeded on these words: _____. She had difficulty with these: _____."

Because impressions are often unreliable and often fail to convey accurate information, it's important to ask for actual data, especially if your child's reading problems are severe. This is not creating a burden for teachers—it's a necessary step in teaching children with severe reading problems. As William Rupley and Timothy Blair asserted:

> Directly related to continuous diagnosis [monitoring] is the teacher's ability to keep accurate records.... Continuous diagnosis holds no meaning without it.[54]

Table 7.9 is an example of a simple data-based report that teachers can adapt to children's needs and share with parents. It can be downloaded from our website, www.reading2008.com.

TABLE 7.9: WEEKLY PROGRESS REPORT FOR READING

WEEKLY PROGRESS REPORT FOR READING

Name: _____   Date of Report: _____

- Word Recognition and Fluency: Number of words correctly pronounced during 1 minute of oral reading of a previously unread 3rd-grade passage.
- Reading Comprehension: Percentage of questions correctly answered from memory after reading a previously unread 250-400 word selection from a 3rd-grade reader.
- Vocabulary: Number of targeted vocabulary words used correctly (Maximum: 7)

continues...

WORD RECOGNITION AND FLUENCY	READING COMPREHENSION	TARGETED VOCABULARY WORDS
• Number of words correctly pronounced: _____ • Percentage of words correctly pronounced: _____%	• Number of questions asked: _____ • Number answered correctly: _____ • Percentage correct: _____%	• Words used correctly: 1) 2) 3) 4) 5) 6) 7)

NOTABLE ACHIEVEMENTS	DIFFICULTIES OR OBSERVED FRUSTRATION

Dear Parent,

If you would like me to phone you, please write your phone number:

(_____) _____.

What are the best times, after 2:30 pm? _____, _____.

Thank you,

E. McCormick

Fourth Grade Teacher

Respect Teachers' Suggestions. As these strategies illustrate, to get a clear picture of your child's progress, teachers can use simple strategies that take little time. Your child's teachers, however, may suggest other strategies. And this is fine, *if*—and this is a big *if*—their strategies give you an accurate, comprehensive picture of your child's progress and *if* they provide you with frequent reports. Anything less reduces your child's chances of *beating the odds.*

DIRECT MONITORING

If you believe that the in-school monitoring is inadequate, you can directly monitor your child's progress. Here are several ways:

- Observe your child's success with homework.
- Have her read orally for one minute a week.
- Read to her and informally check her comprehension.
- Observe her in class.
- Get a private evaluation.

Observe Your Child's Success with Homework. For parents, homework assignments can be diagnostic. They give you clues about how well your child's teachers understand her needs and their willingness to regularly adjust the level and complexity of work to meet those needs. They help to answer the question, "Are classwork and homework moderately challenging or frustrating for my child?"

Ideally and practically, homework should be at your child's independent level of functioning. She should be able to complete her homework successfully, by herself, in reasonable time, without frustration. Assignments should be such that she expects to achieve success with moderate effort.

If this is not the case, you need to discuss your child's homework with her teachers. It will tell you a great deal about her program and her teachers' willingness and ability to address her reading needs. If she struggles with homework, ask that it be modified so moderate effort produces success. Some teachers will devise solutions. Others will resist. Both responses are telling.[55]

By examining the nature, difficulty, and complexity of your child's homework, her ability to successfully complete assignments independently, and her teachers' written comments or grades, you can develop a fairly accurate picture of her academic program, her current reading and writing abilities, and her work habits and motivation to succeed in school. Keeping a folder of her homework assignments—completed and uncompleted, marked and unmarked—gives you a running record of her successes and difficulties. If you organize them by date and subject, they can prove valuable in planning her program and, if necessary, provide powerful justification for revising it.

Have Your Child Read Orally, One Minute a Week. If your child is in elementary school, the number of words she reads correctly—in one minute of oral reading per week—is a good gauge of progress, especially if you look at the trend over several weeks. As Jan Hasbrouck and Gerald Tindal concluded, the number of words orally read correctly in one minute "has been shown, in both theoretical and empirical research, to serve as an accurate and powerful indicator of overall reading competence, especially in its strong correlation with comprehension."[56]

If the number of words read correctly increases over several weeks, your child's probably making progress; if, over several weeks, the number stays steady or decreases, progress is probably inadequate. As Terry Overton concluded, when three consecutive samplings fail to show progress, "instruction should be adjusted."[57] Although this standard differs from that of Steckler and her colleagues, which we discussed in chapter 5, the situation is different. You're doing this at home, once, not twice a week, without graphing progress and expected-growth lines. In this situation, we agree with Overton. If you see poor progress over three consecutive samplings, ask for a meeting with school personnel to discuss your child's reading program. The meeting should focus on what's blocking progress and what changes should accelerate progress.

To begin oral reading, select a book (or set of books) at an instructional level your child finds somewhat easy. Stick with the book(s) for three to six months, or until she finishes it, or until she wants another book at this level. The instructional level is the level (e.g., 3rd grade) at which she reads comfortably, without the teacher's help. At this level she identifies most words accurately, easily, and quickly (about 95% to 98% of words), correctly answers most questions about what she reads (70% to 90%), and reads fairly fluently. If she's uncomfortable reading at this level, drop to easier levels, one at a time, until she's comfortable. You might drop from beginning 3rd grade to end of 2nd; if end of 2nd is too difficult, drop to beginning 2nd.[58] Her instructional level and titles of appropriate books should be available from her teacher or the school's reading specialist.

Every week, record your child as she orally reads a previously unread selection from the book.[59] Start at the book's beginning and sequentially work toward the end. If she becomes stuck on a word for three seconds (silently count one Mississippi, two Mississippi, three Mississippi), tell her the word and go on.[60] Don't correct her reading or ask her questions about the selection. When she's read aloud for 60 seconds, tell her to stop. Count the number of words read correctly, including self-corrections; count as wrong any words you told her. Then put the number correct on a chart.

The process should be fun. To make it fun, you might read from a book while your child records you. Then you might listen to it together. While reading, you might even stumble on a few words and correct yourself, or ask her to correct you.

Read to Your Child And Informally Check Her Comprehension. Reading aloud to your child is a highly enjoyable and productive activity that can create or strengthen interest in reading and help her develop the background knowledge and vocabulary she needs to become a successful reader. In summarizing much of the research about reading aloud to children, Marjorie Lipson and Karen Wixson, two noted literacy authorities, identified many benefits: improved vocabularies, improved understanding of the special language of books, improved knowledge of literacy conventions, improved knowledge of the linguistic aspects of reading. Of particular importance is the influence that read-alouds have on critical thinking: They "teach children to question the meaning of text and encourage them to begin to think and use language in ways that will later be critical for school success."[61] So—read aloud to your child: it's simple, it's powerful.

In addition to these benefits, reading to your child and discussing the text with her helps you monitor her progress. It gives you a fairly accurate idea of what she can understand when she's not frustrated by word identification and word recognition difficulties.

Ideally, you should choose books that match your child's interests and intellectual abilities.

After reading aloud, try to promote energetic, interesting discussions and further explorations of the topic. You might ask some questions. If so, make sure not to grill her. Instead of asking questions that have one right answer, ask open-ended questions that encourage interesting discussions: "If you were Linda, and a fiery ghost shrieked at you, what would you do? I wonder what Tim was thinking. Have any ideas? What else do you think kids would like to learn about ghosts?" When asking questions, try to remember Patricia Cunningham and Richard Allington's advice:

> Open ended questions allow for a range of responses, all potentially correct. Such questions serve to begin a conversation about the material read. In many respects the goal is to create the kind of conversations that adults typically engage in when discussing something they have read. Adults do not interrogate each other.... Instead, they discuss, they converse. The goal is to share understandings and through this to gain an even better understanding of the material read.[62]

All or part of the conversation might involve other family members or a few of your child's friends who are well behaved and have similar interests. For example, if you've read her and her friends a book about dinosaurs, you might buy them model-building kits of dinosaurs and show them a video about dinosaurs. After reading the book, building the model, and watching the video, you might ask what they found interesting or surprising about them. In addition to arousing curiosity, sharpening reasoning, and making reading an enjoyable social activity, the conversation should give you a wealth of information about your child's intellectual and listening comprehension abilities.

If, over time, your child becomes apathetic about read-alouds, have someone else, whom she respects, read to her. If this doesn't improve the situation, meet with school personnel to identify the causes of her apathy. It's quite possible that she's discouraged about reading, tired of school work, and needs a short vacation from reading. It's also possible that she needs an intensive, well-designed program to increase or maintain motivation for reading. Such programs need to be carefully coordinated between school and home, and need to systematically apply scientifically-supported motivational principles. These include:

- Letting your child choose what's read to her. This might involve her freely choosing books at a library or book store or from alternatives you provide. This latter strategy is called managed choice.
- Letting her earn a vacation day in which she does something special, something that she enjoys.
- Letting her invite friends to her read-aloud.
- Letting her earn rewards for attending to what's read. For this to work she must truly value the rewards and they must be acceptable to you.
- Phasing out rewards gradually. This is easy to do when children find books interesting.

- Telling her that her success in listening is attributable to her effort and her decision to listen.
- Giving her experiences that connect the read-aloud materials to the world; if, for example, you read her a book about dinosaurs, take her to a museum that has paintings, skeletons, and sculptures of dinosaurs.

If your child has trouble understanding read-aloud selections that match her age and interests, discuss this with school personnel. Don't wait: She may have listening comprehension or related problems that need professional attention.[63] How important is listening to reading? Children who struggle to understand what's read to them usually struggle to understand what they read, even if their word recognition is excellent. So, ask for help. Listening comprehension problems don't disappear by themselves. They suggest that progress in school—in any subject that involves more than minimal listening or reading—will be difficult. Thus, her program, and if she's in special education, her IEP, must knowledgeably and systematically address her listening problems.

Observe Your Child in Class. Although parents don't usually observe their child in class, doing so provides valuable information. Once you see how the class is organized and operated and how your child behaves, you can better understand the nature of her program, the demands she faces, and her teacher's comments and concerns. By observing, you also establish a psychological presence that says, "I'm very interested in my child's welfare and will actively participate in her education." When you combine observations with knowledge of reading problems and treat school personnel with respect, you create a powerful, positive image in the minds of most teachers and other school personnel.

If you observe, it's important to do so more than once as what you first see may be atypical. The first time, your child may be self-conscious; the second time, less so. Generally, the second or third observation provides a more typical picture.

Before observing, ask the teacher where you should sit, and if he wants you to focus on anything special. Unless told otherwise, try not to interact with the children and don't help out. Try to be invisible.

One way to observe regularly, without bringing undue attention to yourself, is to volunteer in your child's class. This provides an excellent opportunity to help while learning more about your child's school, program, and progress. After a while, people will tend to think of you as "one of us" and will likely speak to you more openly. By volunteering, you can contribute a lot and learn a lot.[64]

When observing, ask yourself these questions:

- Does my child usually find her work moderately challenging?
- Daily, does she meet with lots of success?
- Daily, is the class and is curriculum intellectually stimulating?
- Daily, does she get more than 40 minutes of direct reading instruction from a highly qualified professional?

- Daily, does she have many opportunities to read interesting, easy-to-moderately challenging materials?
- Throughout the day, are reading and other language activities, such as writing, stressed?
- Several times weekly, do children share what they read, without engaging in round-robin reading (in which they take turns reading aloud, one after the other)?[65]
- Several times weekly, do children share their writing?
- Daily, does she get lots of opportunities to practice what's taught?
- Throughout the day, does she get whatever help she needs, when she needs it?
- Several times weekly, is she taught in small, interactive groups, in which children discuss topics, ask each other questions, and work together?
- Usually, does the teacher treat the children with respect and focus on the positive?
- Throughout the day, is the class well organized?
- Throughout the day, is the teacher clearly in control of the class?
- Throughout the day, do the children know exactly what they're supposed to do?
- Throughout the day, are the children actively engaged in different academic activities?
- Several times daily, are the children given time to rest, play, and socialize?

Ideally, each answer is "yes." But remember, your information will be imperfect. You may not be able to answer each question with certainty. But after two or three observations, you should have a fairly good understanding of your child's class, teacher, and program. This can be of enormous help in working with the school to support or improve her reading.

Get a Private Evaluation. If your child's progress is poor, or you lack information to judge it, or your child is becoming increasingly resistant or emotionally upset about reading, get a private evaluation from a reading specialist not affiliated with local school districts. Seek a specialist with a graduate degree in reading, preferably a doctorate. Beware of specialists whose primary credentials are certifications from private companies that sell specific reading materials.

Before hiring the specialist, interview him. Ask questions and listen to find out if he understands the culture and the procedures of schools, the IEP process, and all relevant State and Federal special education laws, such as IDEA-2004 and Section 504. Since he may need to attend IEP meetings and work with administrators, IEP Team members, and general and special education teachers, try to assess his listening, trust building, and problem solving skills. Evaluate his respect for school personnel, willingness to explore alternative solutions, willingness to judge ideas on their merits, dedication to getting your child an effective program, and willingness to monitor your child's progress. In sum, you need to assess his knowledge of reading disabilities, your child's rights, and his ability to work with others to solve problems.

Involving a private specialist may prove highly beneficial. It may provide fresh insight into the current causes of your child's disabilities. It may generate ideas that foster progress. It may spur the school to do far more than planned. Minimally, it informs school officials that your child is important to you and that you'll be actively involved. Nevertheless, specialists are expensive. At $150 to $250 dollars an hour for record reviews, travel, observations, research, reports, meetings, and phone calls, bills can easily exceed $8500, an amount most families can't afford. If this is your reality, you might ask the IEP Team to have the school's reading specialist use a structured instructional-observation system like TIES-II (*The Instructional Environment System II: A System To Identify A Student's Instructional Needs*) to observe your child.[66]

Once the school gives you its specialist's report, you might share it with professionals you trust. Often, local child advocacy groups can link you to experts willing to volunteer an hour or so of service. If you can't get an expert to volunteer, you might black-out all identifying information on the expert's report; then ask a college professor to have his graduate class critique it and offer suggestions.

Another alternative to hiring an expert is to formally request an independent evaluation, including an observation, paid for by the district. If your child is eligible for special education under IDEA-2004, you may be entitled to this. Under IDEA-2004, this sounds better than it is, so be *careful*. Why be careful? In actuality your request charges that the school's evaluation is inadequate. As such, you may provoke resentment. The school might challenge you by initiating a formal due process hearing, meaning they're taking you to court. Here are some of IDEA-2004's relevant regulations:

- An "independent educational evaluation means an evaluation conducted by a qualified examiner who is not employed by the [school]."
- "A parent has the right to an independent educational evaluation at public expense if the parent disagrees with an evaluation obtained by the [school]."
- An independent evaluation "must be considered by the [school], if it meets [the school's] criteria."
- "A parent is entitled to only one independent educational evaluation at public expense each time the [school] conducts an evaluation with which the parent disagrees."
- "If a parent requests an independent educational evaluation at public expense, the [school] must, without unnecessary delay, either ... file a due process complaint to request a hearing to show that its evaluation is appropriate; or ... ensure that an independent educational evaluation is provided at public expense." If a hearing is held, the school can challenge the appropriateness of the parent's evaluation.[67]

This last regulation may prove costly. Logically, if the school initiates a formal hearing to show that an independent evaluation is not warranted, you'll have to hire an expert to show why it is, why the school's evaluation is inadequate.

DISCUSSING PROGRESS AND PROBLEMS WITH SCHOOL PERSONNEL

Although valid monitoring strategies generate valuable information, they don't *automatically* offer ongoing opportunities to quickly resolve problems. And quickly resolving problems is critical, especially if progress is poor.

Overcoming poor progress requires a lot from everyone. It especially requires that you regularly *meet* with your child's teacher and other involved school personnel to discuss your child's progress and problems and to refine her program until progress is satisfactory. Once satisfactory, it requires you to continue *meeting* with school personnel to monitor progress and intervene quickly when difficulty arises.

As obvious as the next statement sounds, it's important and it's often ignored: Several months of progress does not guarantee continued progress. It can be an aberration. Commenting on a lengthy study of small-group instruction and individualized tutoring, Frank Vellutino and his colleagues underscored this point: Although many students at risk for or with reading problems maintained their gains, some didn't.[68]

But meetings take time. Why not phone calls? If necessary, phone calls will do, but face-to-face meetings foster better communication and better personal relationships: they make small-talk easier, allow you to see the teacher's facial expressions and body language,[69] make it easier to jointly examine and discuss your child's work. Through regular meetings, in which you develop good interpersonal relationships, you increase your personal influence and create ongoing opportunities to quickly solve new problems.

If, however, you've had several meetings with your child's teacher, but progress remains inadequate, request that the school's reading specialist attend these meetings. If your child is eligible for special education under IDEA-2004, also request that an IEP Team member attend, preferably the one you think is most knowledgeable about reading and most interested in your child's success. Together, the group members may have the knowledge and resources to implement and monitor potential solutions.

Another reason for regular meetings with school personnel is to closely coordinate your efforts with your child's curriculum. By asking what will be taught to her over the next "two to three weeks," you learn what vocabulary and concepts to stress at home so she's ready for the upcoming topics. For example, if you learn that her class will soon study the senses, you might want to show her the PBS video NOVA: Mystery of the Senses: Smell or NOVA: Mystery of the Senses: Sight. Discussing one of these DVDs at diner might reinforce particular concepts and vocabulary. By coordinating efforts, in two- or three-week blocks, you'll emphasize the right concepts, without needing to rush or pressure your child. This increases her chances of success, by giving her the necessary vocabulary, vocabulary that will make every aspect of reading easier, even decoding.

Despite the enormous value of regularly scheduled discussions, some schools don't like to schedule frequent meetings or phone discussions. One reason is time—a precious resource that schools protect zealously. Nevertheless, if your child's progress is poor, frequent discussions are essential. Moreover, they save time by preventing or solving problems. So, in a respectful but emphatic way, insist on discussions.

If your child is eligible for special education under IDEA-2004, request that the IEP ensure regularly scheduled meetings. Request that it include a statement like this: "Sue's classroom teacher and reading specialist will meet with Mr. and Mrs. Asher for 45 minutes a month to discuss Sue's progress, coordinate efforts, and try to solve unexpected problems. If needed, additional time will be scheduled."

At all meetings, focus on the issues and treat people with respect. Act in concert with the principles listed earlier in the chapter:

- People need to be treated with respect.
- People need to be listened to and feel understood.
- People like to be acknowledged for their accomplishments.
- People defend themselves when criticized.
- People get demoralized or angry when they're constantly criticized.
- People get angry when they feel they're being treated unfairly.
- People get angry or despondent when they're blamed for things they can't control.

Before your meeting, develop a short agenda with your child's teacher. Then ask the meeting's organizer to:

- Distribute the agenda to all relevant parties a week before the meeting; this gives people time to think about the agenda and assemble whatever information is needed.
- Invite school personnel who must decide about the items on the agenda; without their attendance, problems will persist.
- Make sure there's time to fully discuss each item; meetings fail if people feel rushed.

THE SCHOOL'S WILLINGNESS TO MONITOR

If your child is eligible for special education under IDEA-2004, you have numerous protections for developing and monitoring her IEP. If, however, she's ineligible, you have far fewer, if any, compelling rights. Nevertheless, you should still request that the school implement ongoing monitoring procedures. As William Rupley and Timothy Blair, two distinguished professors of literacy, noted:

> The effective teacher of reading continually diagnoses [monitors] each student every day, either formally or informally. Without this step ... inadequate instruction will always follow. Initial diagnostic decisions on students must be continually evaluated and [if student progress is poor]... appropriate changes made in the corrective procedures.[70]

Out of professionalism and a genuine desire to help your child, some schools will painstakingly monitor her progress. Others will dismiss the request as difficult, unrealistic, or unnecessary. Some may agree, but remain vague about how they'll monitor progress. Still others may agree, provide explicit detail, but not follow through. Sadly, as Frank Gresham, Amanda VanDerHeyden, and Joseph Witt have noted, poor monitoring is common: "Schools have never been overly conscientious about keeping data on intervention integrity or even effectiveness.[71]

Perhaps *sadly* is too weak a word, as struggling readers can suffer devastating consequences. Simply put, struggling readers have little chance of making adequate progress in schools that fail to frequently monitor reading progress and revise instruction to meet their immediate needs. Their chances of success increase markedly when progress is monitored and the ensuing data guides instruction. Here, for example, is what Jack Fletcher and his colleagues concluded about curriculum-based measurement (CBM), a widely researched, relatively easy-to-implement form of monitoring that's taught in many teacher-preparation programs. The language may be intimidating, but the message is important, important enough to show to school personnel:

> A large set of controlled investigations provides corroborating evidence of dramatic effects on student outcomes in reading, spelling, and math when teachers rely on CBM [curriculum-based measurement] to inform instructional planning. When this form of progress monitoring is used to assess the effects of validated interventions on individual students with LDs [learning disabilities] and to revise programs responsively to those data, positive academic outcomes for students with LDs are more likely.[72]

Unfortunately, resistance to monitoring indicates that those in power know little about reading problems or care little about struggling readers. If this is the case, as daunting as the next suggestion may be, it's critical: Do whatever is legal and ethical to ensure that your child's program is monitored effectively; if progress is poor, quickly initiate changes—changes supported by research in peer-refereed journals.

KEEP IN MIND

Keep in mind that disagreements are natural. No matter how well intentioned people are, disagreements will arise. They're part of life. The problem is not disagreement, but how it's handled. Too often, people disparage those with whom they disagree and try to force them to submit, to accept solutions they don't like. Frequently, this generates resentment, resistance, and retaliation. In the next chapter, we describe some specific steps for collaborating to resolve disagreements and solve problems.

ENDNOTES

[1]   Witt, J. C., Elliott, S. N., Daly, E. J., III, Gresham, F. M., & Kramer, J. J., 1998. *Assessment of At-Risk and Special Needs Children* (2nd ed.). Boston: McGraw-Hill, p. 51.

[2]   We suggest you read one of these: (a) Etscheidt, S. K., 2006. Progress monitoring: Legal issues and recommendations for IEP Teams. *Teaching Exceptional Children, 38*, 56-60; (b) Pemberton, J. B., 2003. Communicating academic progress as an integral part of assessment. *Teaching Exceptional Children, 35*, 16-20.

[3]   Spinelli, C. G., 2006. *Classroom Assessment for Students in Special and General Education* (2nd ed.). Upper Saddle River, NJ: Merrill Prentice Hall.

[4]   This is referred to as cognitive dissonance. In an exceptionally fine and authoritative book on the subject, *Mistakes Were Made (But Not By Me)*, Carol Tavris and Elliot Aronson define cognitive dissonance as "a state of tension that occurs when a person holds two cognitions (ideas, attitudes, beliefs, opinions) that are psychologically inconsistent" (2007. New York: Harcourt, p. 13). Until people reduce these clashing beliefs, they suffer mental discomfort. Thus, if teachers feel obligated

to and frequently make recommendations consistent with school policy—recommendations that clash with their core beliefs—many of these teachers will abandon their core beliefs and embrace the school's policies as their beliefs. They'll do this, probably unconsciously, to reduce or eliminate their mental anguish. This does not mean they're "bad" people. Instead, it means they do what all people do: work to eliminate cognitive dissonance, seek consistency, and justify their actions.

[5] Here are two of *many* resources on this topic: (a) Bowman, L. J., 2005. Grade retention: Is it a help or hindrance to student academic success? *Preventing School Failure, 49* (3), 42-46; (b) Margolis, H., 1998 May 12. There's a better way than social promotion or retention. *The Baltimore Sun*, p. 9A (available from The Baltimore Sun archives at www.baltimoresun.com).

[6] In their discussion of teaching to the test, Betty Higgins, Melinda Miller, and Susan Wegmann identify many of the problems created by pressures to raise test scores: "The focus is now on account-ability rather than the diagnosis of learning for instructional purposes …. Decisions about promotion or retention are attached to student success or failure on some State-mandated tests…. Many teachers change their literacy curricula in order to train students to take the test, and standardized tests drive the curricula in many States. Rather than focusing on meaningful learning experiences, many schools spend a lot of time preparing students to take State assessments by engaging them in test-like activi-ties…. This change—from teaching for learning to teaching for the test—results in a narrowing of the curriculum, loss of instructional time, and loss of teacher autonomy" (Higgins, B., Miller, M., & Wegmann, S., 2006. Teaching to the test... not! Balancing best practice and testing requirements in writing. *The Reading Teacher, 60* (4), 310-319, p. 310, references removed).

[7] An examination of State and school budgets often illustrates the scarcity of resources. One of many recent examples is California's devastating budget cuts: "Gone for the foreseeable future are the governor's ambitions to overhaul public schools; instead he is proposing cuts that educa-tion officials say would *devastate* schools" (Zapler, M., 2008 January 12. Budget crisis crimps Schwarzenegger's grand plans. *Mercury News*; retrieved 1/17/08, from http:/www.mercurynews.com/fdcp?1200598694248; italics added). In the spring of 2008, more than 20,000 California teachers received letters stating their positions would be cut—they would be fired.

[8] Booher-Jennings, J., 2005. Below the bubble: 'Educational Triage' and the Texas Accountability System. *American Education Research Journal, 42* (2), 231-268.

[9] Bracey, G., 2005. Tips for readers of research: Handle pass rates with care. *Phi Delta Kappan, 87* (4), 333-335, p. 335.

[10] Rothstein, R., Jacobsen, R., & Wilde, T., 2006. 'Proficiency for All' – An oxymoron. Paper prepared for the Symposium, *Examining America's Commitment to Closing Achievement Gaps: NCLB and Its Alternatives*, sponsored by the Campaign for Educational Equity, Teachers College, Columbia University, November 13-14, 2006.

[11] This is not a criticism of classroom teachers or the disciplines mentioned as no one is expert in everything. For example, we are experts in reading disabilities and clinical psychology, but we are less knowledgeable about teaching science than first-year elementary school teachers. Our exper-tise in teaching science is so poor that we would be inadequate science teachers—any child who depended upon us for quality science instruction would be at risk.

[12] Two common examples of how insufficient expertise affects decision making are (a) using grade

equivalents from standardized tests to assign struggling readers to reading groups and reading materials; and (b) using readability formulas to assign struggling readers to reading materials. To most non-reading professionals, these practices make sense. To reading specialists, they don't. When used like this, grade equivalents and readability formulas typically create ongoing frustration for struggling readers. Not surprisingly, ongoing frustration obstructs reading achievement and deadens motivation and enthusiasm for reading.

13 Carnine, D., Silbert, J., & Kameenui, E. J., 1997. *Direct Instruction Reading* (3rd ed.). Columbus, OH: Merrill, pp. 41-42, italics added.

14 In chapter 5 we briefly described an Individualized Education Program (IEP) as a legally mandated document for children eligible for special education under IDEA-2004; the IEP describes a child's special education needs, educational goals, and required services. In later chapters we'll provide far more information.

15 The reason we use the phrase "eligible for special education under IDEA-2004" is that some children are eligible for special education under *Section 504 of the Rehabilitation Act of 1973* (Section 504). Because Section 504 is a civil rights act that aims to ensure opportunity and IDEA-2004 aims to ensure benefit, children ineligible under IDEA-2004 but eligible under Section 504 have far fewer protections. For example, Section 504 does not require schools to specify goals or to tell parents when and how they will monitor progress. Section 504's sparse detail makes enforcement difficult, even if a child's progress is poor. Chapter 12 discusses Section 504 in greater detail.

16 Had you the strongest laws possible, we would still recommend that you cultivate positive, genuine relationships with school personnel and learn about their values, their professionalism, and the pressures they face. Although laws are critically important, this, not laws, can be the source of your greatest influence.

17 Your child may attend IEP meetings. Many authorities encourage this, believing it promotes self-advocacy. However, it can have serious drawbacks, such as self-censoring of needed discussions.

18 The regulations for IDEA-2004 are published in the Code of Federal Regulations, which is abbreviated as CFR. The citation for this quotation is 34 CFR § 300.320.

19 KHTS, 2008 April 27. Newhall School District Planning For Budget Cuts In 2008-2009; retrieved 4/27/08, from http://www.hometownstation.com/index.php?option=com_content&task=view&id =12481&Itemid=1768

20 Ambitious goals are moderately challenging. If your child is in a well-designed program, staffed by knowledgeable, skilled, and motivated teachers, she should achieve these goals without frequent frustration.

21 Goals are essential for monitoring progress. Research has shown that when progress toward achieving a goal is accurately monitored and monitoring results are used to formulate instruction, "students achieve more, teacher decision making improves, and students tend to be more aware of their performance" (Steckler, P. M., Lembke, E. S., & Saenz, L., 2007. *Advanced Applications of CBM in Reading: Instructional Decision-Making Strategies*. Washington, D.C.: U.S. Office of Special Education Programs; retrieved 3/1/08, from http://www.studentprogress.org/summer_institute/2007/Adv%20 Reading/AdvancedCBMReading2007.pdf, plate 6.)

22 Nevertheless, even in States that don't require short-term objectives in all children's IEPs,

the IEPs of a tiny percentage of children must have them. Generally, these are children with severe or profound cognitive or physical disabilities for whom standardized tests are not valid.

[23]   34 CFR § 300.320.

[24]   M.C. on behalf of J.C. v. Central Regional School District, U. S. 3rd Circuit Court, 1996.

[25]   34 CFR § 300.320.

[26]   It is best to limit goals to two per area of need. The reason is simple: Too many goals become unmanageable and reduce the importance of each goal. Our goal of using flashcards to assess mastery of sight words on the Dolch Word List might be criticized as too narrow. In some cases, the criticism would be correct; in some, incorrect. In the final analysis, it depends on the IEP Team's interpretation of the data and its projection of what the child can master in a year. For some children reading at this level, a more ambitious and appropriate goal for assessing word recognition might focus on recognizing words in paragraphs: When orally reading new *2nd-grade* narrative passages of 150 or more words, Sue will accurately recognize *95% of the words*; she will achieve this criterion with new passages on 3 successive occasions by the end of the *4th marking period*.

[27]   Although goals must be measurable, they must also be relevant and important. IEP Teams sometimes use goals that are easily measurable, but irrelevant and unimportant. Thus, it's important to ask these questions: Would emphasizing this knowledge or these skills quickly improve reading or impede progress? Is the child ready to learn this? In reviewing a proposed IEP for Joshua, a middle-school student with 7th-grade word recognition abilities but poor reading comprehension, Howard questioned the appropriateness of a reading goal that essentially said, "Joshua would learn to apply initial consonant sounds." He questioned it because children with even 4th-grade word recognition abilities can easily apply such sounds. Had Joshua been reading at a 1st-grade level and couldn't apply consonant sounds to decoding, this goal would probably have been relevant and important. Choosing or writing irrelevant goals wastes valuable, irreplaceable teaching time. Consequently, it sabotages hope.

[28]   Although many school personnel use the phrases *evaluation teams* and *eligibility teams*, when referring to them, the U. S. Department of Education uses the phrases *evaluation group* and *eligibility group*.

[29]   Under IDEA-2004, you can challenge the group's eligibility decision by taking the school to a formal due process hearing, a difficult, stressful legal entanglement with a doubtful outcome. In chapter 12, we offer an opinion about due process under "Beware of Pitfalls."

[30]   Rehabilitation Act of 1973, Pub. L. 93–112. Section 504's regulations can be downloaded from the U.S. Department of Education at http://www.ed.gov/policy/rights/reg/ocr/edlite-34cfr104.html.

[31]   The U. S. Department of Education has a model IEP that you can download from their website: http://www.ed.gov/policy/speced/guid/idea/idea2004.html. The IEP addresses many of IDEA-2004's key provisions.

[32]   34 CFR §104.33.

[33]   Very often, by politely asking or by politely making a reasonable argument, parents can get more than the minimum the law requires. Often, schools that care about children use the law as the minimum they can exceed (e.g., providing full- rather than half-day kindergartens); schools that care little use the law as both the minimum and the maximum. In this example, we doubt that Congress would argue against a school voluntarily using short-term objectives in a Section 504 Plan—

perhaps exceeding the minimum—if it served the needs of children and parents without harming others or making excessive demands. In other words, schools can voluntarily include short-term objectives in Section 504 plans despite the fact that they're not required.

34 These questions should be asked in a cooperative, information-seeking manner. If they're asked in angry, threatening ways, they may create defensiveness that solidifies resistance. And although many school personnel feel threatened by the No Child Left Behind Act (NCLB), in many States, schools "game" the system by not separately reporting the scores of small groups of minority students or students eligible for special education. In these instances, this last question about passing the NCLB tests may have little effect, especially if your child's reading disability is so severe that teachers think he'll fail, even with extensive help.

35 Wright, P., & Wright, P., 2006. *From Emotions to Advocacy: The Special Education Survival Guide* (2nd ed.). Hartfield, VA: Harbor House Law Press, p. 198.

36 34 CFR § 300.320, italics added.

37 We know that *relevant, objective, simple, specific* is a mouthful. But each word is important. The acronym ROSS may help you to remember the words.

38 34 CFR § 300.321.

39 34 CFR § 300.324.

40 34 CFR § 300.324, italics added.

41 34 CFR § 300.324.

42 Some authorities would disagree with our recommendation to send a certified letter; they argue that this makes the school defensive, which increases resistance. Sometimes they're right. But if the school is already resistant and non-cooperative, it's often critical to chronologically document events, especially if the issue may go to court. We recommend that you first send an e-mail, as it documents events and requests and is probably less threatening than a certified letter. If, in a week or so, the school doesn't respond satisfactorily, consider sending a certified letter (with the certification number on the letter), which communicates that you're serious about the issue and will persist. Whatever form of communication you use, be respectful. If you're angry, wait several days before sending your e-mail or letter; give yourself time to cool off; and then edit it for clarity and tone. If possible, have a friend read it to assure that your message is clear and your tone respectful.

43 34 CFR § 300.501.

44 Family Educational Rights and Privacy Act of 1974 (FERPA), 20 U.S.C. 1232g. You can download a copy from Cornell University's Legal Information Institute, www4.law.cornell.edu/uscode/20/1232g.htm.

45 If Sue learns one new word and Kelly correctly answers one more test item, each will have improved. But this is insignificant improvement that will put them further behind their peers.

46 34 CFR § 300.320, italics added.

47 Shapiro, E. S., 2004. *Academic Skills Problems: Direct Assessment and Intervention* (3rd ed.). New York: The Guilford Press, p. 32.

48 Monitoring improves instructional decision making, enables teachers to design more effective instruction, improves the consistency of instructional programs, and increases achievement. For further information, visit our website, www.reading2008.com and download Margolis, H., &

Alber-Morgan, S., 2007. Monitoring your child's IEP: A focus on reading. *Insights on Learning Disabilities, 4* (2), 1-26.

[49] Unfortunately, Section 504 does not state that progress needs to be monitored frequently. However, polite insistence often works, especially with school personnel with high ethical and professional standards. Such standards are far more common than many believe.

[50] Adapted from U.S. Department of Education, National Center for Education Statistics, 1995. *Listening to Children Read Aloud, 22.* Washington, DC: Author.

[51] McCormick, S., 2003. *Instructing Students Who Have Literacy Problems* (4th ed.). Upper Saddle River, NJ: Merrill, pp. 172-173.

[52] Portfolios, like all educational and psychological measures, are far from perfect. Different teachers will select different information to put in them and will interpret the information differently. This is not a shortcoming of teachers, but of portfolios. In technical terms, portfolios suffer from reliability difficulties. Nevertheless, they can help you to better understand your child's progress. Just make sure you view the information as suggestive, not definitive.

[53] Rasinski, T., & Padak, N., 2004. *Effective Reading Strategies: Teaching Children Who Find Reading Difficult* (3rd ed.). Upper Saddle River, NJ: Pearson Merrill Prentice Hall.

[54] Rupley, W. H., & Blair, T. R., 1989. *Reading Diagnosis and Remediation* (3rd ed.). Columbus, OH: Merrill, p. 144.

[55] Homework is a complicated subject. Moreover, homework can cause struggling readers grief. For a wealth of suggestions that you and your child's teachers can use, see Howard's articles on homework. You can read them on www.reading2008.com. They're available for download from the publishers or for free from your public library's electronic reference subscription service. After reading them, you may want to share one or two with your child's teachers.

[56] Hasbrouck, J., & Tindal, G. A., 2006. Oral reading fluency norms: A valuable assessment tool for reading teachers. *The Reading Teacher, 59(7),* 636–644, p. 636.

[57] Overton, T., 2006. *Assessment in Special Education: An Applied Approach* (5th ed.). Upper Saddle River, NJ: Pearson Merrill Prentice Hall, p. 151.

[58] If, after several weeks, you change the level of materials because the original level was too easy or too difficult, average the number of words read correctly over your child's first three or four samplings at the new level. This average is her new baseline; use it to start judging progress. In future samplings at this new level, increases in the number of words she correctly reads above her new baseline indicate progress; conversely, reading the same number or fewer words correctly indicates inadequate progress. The key is the trend. Ideally, you want to see the numbers going up, week after week after week. Of course, there's a limit to how many words anyone can read orally. Some rough target figures are provided by Douglas Carnine and his colleagues: last third of grade 1 materials = 60 words per minute (wpm), last third of grade 2 materials = 110 wpm; second half of grade 3 materials = 135 wpm; grade 4 and higher = 150 wpm (Carnine, D. W., Silbert, J., Kame'enui, E. J., & Tarver, S., 2004. *Direct Instruction Reading* (4th ed.). Upper Saddle River, NJ: Prentice-Hall, p. 193).

[59] Although tape recorders will work, digital recorders are far better: They're much smaller and lighter; many create files that you can play and store on a computer or CD and send as e-mail attachments. For $50 or less you can get one that holds 25 hours of recordings and works for 15 hours on a single AAA battery.

[60] Although there's a good argument for not telling your child the unknown words, two eminent authorities in reading, Michael McKenna of the University of Virginia and the late Steven Stahl of the University of Illinois, recommend that you tell her. Their directions say, "Try to read each word. If you come to a word you don't know, I'll tell it to you" (McKenna, M. C., & Stahl, S. A., 2003. *Assessment for Reading Instruction: Solving Problems in the Teaching of Literacy.* New York: The Guilford Press, p. 75).

[61] Lipson, M. Y., & Wixson, K. K., 2003. *Assessment and Instruction of Reading Disability: An Interactive Approach* (3rd ed.). Boston: Allyn & Bacon, p. 229.

[62] Cunningham, P., & Allington, R., 2007. *Classrooms That Work: They Can All Read and Write* (4th ed.). Boston: Pearson, Allyn & Bacon, p. 116.

[63] She may have problems with confidence, anxiety, hearing, general language, overall vocabulary, abstract words, central auditory processing, and attention and concentration. This is a small sampling of the possibilities. Thus, it's important to seek professional help.

[64] But remember, you're not a spy. You're not there to undermine anyone. You're there for ethical reasons: to help your child.

[65] "Round robin reading is often implemented as a result of the mistaken belief that it will increase the amount of time students spend reading. Despite this well-intentioned goal, round robin reading is ineffective at meeting this objective. In fact, research shows that it is a procedure that does not serve any students particularly well and it is especially ineffective—or even harmful—for those students who are experiencing the most difficulty with their literacy development" (Kuhn, M., & Schwanen-flugel, P., 2006. All oral reading practice is not equal or how can I integrate fluency into my class-room? *Literacy Teaching and Learning, 11 (1)*, 1-20, p. 3).

[66] Ysseldyke, J. E., & Christenson, S., 1993. *The Instructional Environment System II (TIES): A System to Identify a Student's Instructional Needs.* Longmont, CO: Sopris West. The likelihood increases that the observation will produce information that is relevant, useful, and verifiable if it systematically focuses on specific instructional factors like clarity of directions, classroom management strategies, informed feedback, frequency of reinforcement, and relevant practice; instruments like the TIES focus on such areas.

[67] 34 CFR § 300.502.

[68] Vellutino, F. R., Scanlon, D. M., Small, S., & Fanuele, D. P., 2006. Response to Intervention as a vehicle for distinguishing between children with and without reading disabilities: Evidence for the role of kindergarten and first-grade interventions. *Journal of Learning Disabilities, 39* (2), 157–169.

[69] Much communication comes through nonverbal messages contained in facial expressions, hand gestures, and body movements. Attending to words alone is often inadequate to understand someone's true message.

[70] Rupley & Blair, 1989, p. 144.

[71] Gresham, F. M., VanDerHeyden, A., & Witt, J. C., 2005. Response to Intervention in the identification of learning disabilities: Empirical support and future challenges. Unpublished manuscript.

[72] Fletcher, J. M., Lyon, G. R., Fuchs, L. S., & Barnes, M. A., 2007. *Learning Disabilities: from Identification to Intervention.* New York: Guilford Press, p. 73.

CHAPTER 8
SOLVING CONFLICTS

If your child's progress stalls, his behavior deteriorates, or he cries about homework, you have a problem that needs immediate attention. Usually, it means meeting with your child's teachers and any other school personnel whose expertise is needed to solve the problem, such as the school's reading specialist. If your child is eligible for special education under the *Individuals with Disabilities Education Improvement Act of 2004* (IDEA-2004), it also means asking that one or more members of your child's Individualized Education Program (IEP) Team attend.[1] The purpose is simple: To solve the problem.[2]

If you disagree with school personnel about the problem or solutions, you have a conflict. The issue then becomes how to solve it *in ways that work for your child, you, and school personnel.*

Yes—we did say *school personnel.* The reason is simple. To gain their commitment to implement solutions requires solutions that meet their needs. Without their commitment to skillfully implementing, monitoring, and revising solutions, success is unlikely.

Because your child, his class, his teachers, his program, and his school are unique, we can't prescribe specific solutions. But we can describe the General Problem Solving Model, a straightforward set of steps that diplomats, executives, and others use to solve problems and conflicts. It works well in groups. It can work for you, even if you can't use it in the idealized way described below.

THE GENERAL PROBLEM SOLVING MODEL

The General Problem Solving Model (Model) will help you work with school personnel to solve problems and conflicts. Before discussing how to use the Model in meetings with your child's teacher and other school personnel, we'll briefly define conflict.

Conflict does not mean fight. It does not mean animosity. It simply means that you and school personnel disagree about the nature and extent of your child's problem or how to solve it. Whatever the disagreement, you, your child, and school personnel have a problem, a problem that requires systematic problem solving.

The Model is a means for solving problems—systematically. It promotes logical thought. By structuring discussions to ensure that everyone understands the problem before discussing solutions, it minimizes anger, arguments, and power struggles. By systematically and objectively evaluating the value of proposed solutions and improving on them, it reduces resistance to trying solutions that others recommend. Table 8.1 provides an overview of the Model.[3]

Although straightforward, the Model makes demands on everyone's ability to listen, understand, suspend judgment, consider alternatives, and work collaboratively. Using it can take considerable time. If, however, the time invested solves the problem, the investment was worth every minute. In contrast, failure to invest the time needed will likely perpetuate and compound the problem, create more frustration and distress, and require more meetings and services.

Like all problem solving models, the Model is a map for action to help you get to where you want to go. Like a map, it presents options that you can adapt to the situation. If one road is blocked, it shows you others. If there's a shorter route, it shows you. For example, if everyone at the meeting understands the problem adequately and quickly agrees on well-justified solutions, streamline the Model to save time. Make sure, however, that the group develops and implements a good plan to monitor and evaluate its solutions.[4] Otherwise, a wonderful sounding solution may perpetuate failure, frustration, and despair.

If the problem is complex and you disagree with school personnel about solutions, try to use the Model in a structured, step-by-step manner. In the long run, this takes far less time and is far more productive than arguing about solutions or agreeing to ineffective ones.[5]

THREE GENERAL GUIDELINES

Problem solving works best when people know, like, and respect one another. From the first few weeks of school, work to establish good relationships with your child's teachers and other school personnel. If you do—if you habitually behave in trustworthy ways, treat them with respect, and listen carefully to understand them—they're more likely to contact you when problems arise. Again, it's simple: People tend to speak to those with whom they're familiar and comfortable.

To ensure that you're establishing good relationships and promoting open communication and a willingness to solve problems, we suggest that you examine your behavior in light of three general guidelines: act in trustworthy ways, treat school personnel with respect, and listen carefully to understand them. Because the guidelines overlap, when you're applying one, you're likely applying the others.

Guideline: Act in Trustworthy Ways. Trust takes time to develop. To build trust:

- Keep your word.
- Give complete, unhurried attention.
- Respond to legitimate requests for information.
- Respond in a timely fashion.
- Listen to understand rather than to challenge.
- Listen without interrupting.
- Share knowledge and viewpoints without dominating conversations or communicating superiority.
- Allow ample opportunity for people to share expertise and insight.
- Show impartiality when evaluating information, ideas, and opinions.
- Ask questions that convey understanding.
- Make accurate comments, supported by clearly recognized facts; avoid unsupported or exaggerated comments.
- Limit disagreements to program and instructional issues.
- Speak positively about people; don't criticize anyone.

TABLE 8.1: THE GENERAL PROBLEM SOLVING MODEL

At All Times
- Act in trustworthy ways.
- Treat school personnel with respect.
- Listen carefully to understand the views and needs of school personnel.

During Problem Solving Meetings
- Agree on a problem definition.
- Analyze the problem.
- Generate potential solutions.
- Evaluate and select solutions.
- Plan how to evaluate the effectiveness of the selected solutions.

After Problem Solving Meetings
- Send a summary letter.
- Collect data on the effectiveness of the solutions.
- Evaluate the effectiveness of the solutions and make needed adjustments.
- Request another meeting if progress is unsatisfactory.

Guideline: Treat School Personnel with Respect. By acting in trustworthy ways, you're treating people with respect. Perhaps more than anything else, people feel respected when they believe:

- You're trying to understand what they think and feel.
- You value their opinion, even if you disagree with it.
- You wouldn't harm them.

One way to show respect is to thank school personnel for their professionalism and their efforts. They'll likely interpret such statements as sincere if they're linked to facts. Here's an example: "Thanks for tutoring Eric last week. He can now divide words into syllables."

In contrast, if you're about to offer an undeserved compliment, don't. Remaining silent is better than looking insincere or manipulative.

Guideline: Listen Carefully to Understand School Personnel. Listening to understand others is hard work, especially if you have strong opinions. But it's worth the effort. Listening, more than speaking, makes problem solving work. It builds trust, conveys respect, and uncovers information indispensable to crafting solutions that meet your child's needs.

Listening encourages others to speak, which gives you a wealth of information. Often, school personnel's comments will inform and surprise you. You may learn that they view your child much differently than you do, believe they'll never get the support needed to help him, feel pressured to deny the need for remedial services, or lack the training needed to help. On the other hand, you may learn that they have tremendous knowledge about reading difficulties, are open to new ideas, agree with you, or want to recommend an even stronger, more intensive and ambitious program than you thought possible.

If school personnel disagree with you, and you've listened carefully, you'll probably have a more accurate understanding of their views, their values, their concerns, their logic, their motivations, and the pressures they feel. Knowing this will help you suggest solutions that meet two important sets of needs: your child's and theirs.

When you suggest solutions that meet everyone's needs, you'll likely get agreement with a critical ingredient: commitment.

To listen effectively:

- Face the speakers, look at them, make eye contact, and lean slightly toward them.
- Smile occasionally.
- Concentrate on the essence of their messages without contemplating responses.
- Nod slightly or make brief sounds like "uh-huh" to indicate you're following their messages.
- Make short, reflective, tentative remarks that summarize the essence of their messages and encourage them to further elaborate. If they sound frustrated, you might offer this tentative summary: "So, you're also frustrated. Am I correct?"
- Ask clarification questions to better understand confusing or incomplete statements. If you're unsure about their meaning, you might ask: "Do you mean …?"

These activities require moderation. For example, eye contact should be comfortable for you and the speakers—avoid staring; it's okay to blink. Nodding should be slight and intermittent, not incessant or exaggerated. Smiling should be relaxed and responsive, not plastic or frozen like the grin of the Cheshire Cat in *Alice in Wonderland*.

To convey understanding or to seek clarification, occasionally, at natural points, interject reflective, tentative summaries, such as "I think you're saying that Eric works better in small groups. Am I right?" Or ask open-ended questions, such as "What do you think?"

Together, these activities—acting in trustworthy ways, treating school personnel with genuine respect, and listening to understand—often resolve differences and secure the cooperation and commitment critical to the success of solutions.

MEETINGS

Many problem solving meetings start with a brief, superficial description of the child's problems, followed by a rush to adopt the first proposed solution, especially if it sounds plausible. This is a mistake. Discussion should first focus on understanding the nature and extent of the problem, and its external causes—modifiable, situational causes that can be eradicated or lessened, like the difficulty of reading materials or the length of seatwork assignments.[6] Only then should the group consider solutions.

Like many people, you and school personnel may be pressed for time. You may want to discuss solutions almost immediately. Don't. If you do, you may unwittingly support solutions that ignore the external causes of your child's difficulties. By failing to invest adequate time to fully understand these causes, the problems will likely intensify. The Model's steps guard against this, while increasing the likelihood of choosing effective solutions.[7]

Before using the Model's actual problem solving steps, discuss with school personnel what you'd like to accomplish at the meeting and the problem solving steps you'd like to use. What you're attempting to do—solve a problem *systematically*—may be foreign to them. They may rely on less systematic processes, processes that cause different school personnel to define the problem dissimilarly, attribute it to dissimilar causes, and discuss irrelevant issues; this wastes time, impedes progress, and allows the most vocal person to dominate, stymieing true understanding and problem solving.

In contrast, the Model asks everyone to focus on the same problem solving step, in the same way, at the same time. Thus, everyone would focus on defining the problem before suggesting solutions. This prevents or lessens confusion, wasted time, and animosity; it allows everyone to contribute to a more exact understanding of the problem. Ideally, it allows people to "own" the problem, analysis, and solution—after all, they helped the group to better understand the problem and craft a solution reflecting a well-reasoned analysis.

To help school personnel understand the Model, ask them if they want a description. If they do, give them Table 8.1 well before the meeting, along with a request that they use it or any other *systematic* problem solving model with which they're familiar. Offer to review the Model with them.

If they refuse to use or review the Model, or say "sure" but nonverbally scream "no," don't argue or make a fuss. Instead, plan to discreetly use the Model at meetings. Do this by asking questions and requesting information consistent with the Model's sequence.

One way to reduce resistance to systematic problem solving is to first meet and discuss the Model with an influential member of your child's instructional staff, one who'll attend the meetings.[8] This gives both of you an opportunity to fully explore the Model and for you to explain your reasons for suggesting it. It also gives you a chance to discuss your child's progress.[9]

Your discussion may reveal that school personnel have their own group problem solving model. If so, follow-up: Ask this person to show you how it works. Learn whatever you can about it. Give it a try. Because school personnel know it, it may prove superior. The general lesson is this: If school personnel have ways of solving problems—or teaching reading—that will likely succeed, try their way. Forget who offered the idea. Remember your purpose—to solve the problem.

If, however, school personnel don't use a group problem solving model, focus on learning and using the Model.

Before using it or any systematic problem-solving procedure, school personnel should decide on a facilitator or meeting leader. Generally speaking, it's best to honor their choice.

Here are the Model's steps.

THE MODEL: SEQUENCE OF STEPS

Agree on a Problem Definition. The meeting's facilitator would begin by asking participants to list, on a flipchart or a chalkboard, your child's current problems.[10] Throughout the session, she should put all relevant information and comments on the chart or chalkboard. By putting critical information in one place, for all to see, the facilitator focuses the discussion, structures the meeting, and saves time. Examining the same information, at the same time, helps everyone to quickly identify missing or poorly understood information and pinpoint difficulties.

Next, the facilitator asks the group to comment on the list, add or edit items, and clarify issues. This increases everyone's understanding of the problem and reduces conflict. To focus the discussion, you might ask school personnel to define *problem* as "What my child needs to do that he can't do, won't do, struggles to do, or doesn't do often enough or quickly enough." To help everyone accurately understand the problem, ask for examples of what it *is*, what it *is not*, and *when* it usually occurs. Table 8.2 shows how the facilitator might organize this information.

TABLE 8.2: FORMAT FOR ORGANIZING INFORMATION FOR EVERYONE TO SEE AND COMMENT ON

Definition of the problem: What Eric needs to do that he can't do, won't do, struggles to do, or doesn't do often enough or quickly enough.	An example of what the problem *is.*	An example of what the problem *is not.*	*When* does the problem usually occur?
Problem 1)			
Problem 2)			
Problem 3)			

By defining the problem in this way, the group has a good chance of producing practical, effective solutions. Here's a sample definition: "Ideally, what can be done to help Brian accurately recognize 99% of the words in a new 500 word selection from a 4th-grade book by the end of February?" In essence, this definition is a short-term objective that, if realistic, can probably be achieved in many ways. At this point, however, don't discuss means or solutions. Focusing on them can easily make the discussion too narrow, create win-lose power struggles, and prevent the group from adequately understanding the problem's external causes.

Once everyone agrees that the list is complete and the problems are well defined, the facilitator should ask the group to place each problem into one of three categories: Highly Important, Moderately Important, and Mildly Important. Because no one can handle too many problems at once, the Highly Important list should have three or fewer problems. For the next few weeks, these should be the group's focus.[11]

But be careful. When defining problems, analyzing them, offering solutions, and developing evaluation plans, the group should focus on one problem at a time. If the group tries to discuss and solve two or more at a time, it will likely produce what it must avoid: confusion.

Analyze the Problem. In this step, the group analyzes a Highly Important Problem to see if the available information supports its definition. If support is insufficient, the group revises it.

To analyze the problem, the group needs to determine:

- The problem's severity and frequency: How long does Eric sulk? How often does he refuse to read?
- The conditions under which it occurs: When does it happen? With what materials? With which teachers? With what type of activities?
- The consequences: What happens when Eric sulks? What do his teachers do when he won't read? How do his peers react?

Answers to straightforward, concrete questions like these can precisely pinpoint difficulties, making the problem manageable. Answers also lead to possible explanations. One possible explanation for Eric's sulking is that his 5th-grade books frustrate him. He's embarrassed when the aide sits next to him. Kids grimace when he stumbles over words.

At this point, explanations are speculative; school personnel need to gather data to assess their validity. Later they need to implement the most promising solutions and monitor and evaluate their effects.

Ideally, before the meeting, school personnel should gather and organize concrete information that clearly and convincingly illustrates your child's progress and problems. At the meeting they should show and discuss this information with you. Thus, they might share a portfolio of his work or the results of diagnostic lessons, structured observations, and informal testing, such as the percentage of words he read correctly from books at different grade levels.

To better understand their reasoning and your child's problem, we suggest that you listen carefully—without interrupting or asking questions. Consider everything they say. Write down your comments and questions. Once they're done, ask questions. Often, the simplest of questions—"You said _____ What does that mean?"—get answers critical to solving the problem. So don't let your lack of expertise or fear of embarrassment stop you from asking basic questions.

One common problem occurs when schools offer conclusions based on a single source, such as a standardized test or a test that's part of a reading program. Be skeptical about such conclusions as accurate assessment requires several sources of trustworthy information. If school personnel are relying on a single source of information, ask if its results accurately and fully reflect your child's reading in class. Ask yourself if these results match your impressions.

Once you adequately understand the opinions of school personnel, you may want to share your information and views. They're often as valuable as the school's. By sharing, you can help school personnel to better understand your child's difficulties. As an example, examine the information in Table 8.3. After meeting with Liam's IEP Team to discuss his "homework problem," his parents collected this information. It showed the Team that Liam was overwhelmed, not lazy. After viewing this information, everyone agreed that his typical homework assignment required him to succeed at his frustration reading level—an impossibility. Consequently, assignments were adjusted to foster success.

TABLE 8.3: HOME MONITORING FORM – LIAM

Date	Numbers of Assignments	Time Spent on Assignments (including breaks)	Re-quests for Help	Comments
11/20/08	4	2 hr 13 min	9	Ripped up papers several times
11/21/08	5	2 hr 33 min	11	Started crying. Said "I can't do it. I'm dumb."
11/22/08	4	3 hr 13 min	16	Got angry. Said he never gets time to play with his friends after school. (He's right.)
11/23/08	6	2 hr 53 min	8	Cried several times. Told me he was confused, didn't understand. Carelessly rushed through the work or stared into space. Got very tired.

Once the group believes its information is adequate, it should reexamine the problem definition. If it's inaccurate or too limited, the facilitator should ask the group to revise it. Without an accurate definition that can generate several potentially effective solutions, there's little chance of solving the problem.

If, however, the group lacks adequate information but needs to take immediate action, ask—or, if necessary, politely insist—that the agreed-upon solution be temporary: a maximum of three weeks. Make sure that during this period the group agrees to:

- Collect data to closely monitor the solution's effectiveness.
- Collect whatever information it needs to adequately understand the problem.
- Reconvene to discuss the information collected on the problem's possible causes and the solution's effectiveness.

If the temporary solution has not fully solved the problem, the group needs to generate ones that will likely succeed.

Generate Potential Solutions. This is the creative step. Here, you and school personnel should generate lots of potential solutions. The idea is to stimulate creativity. Ideally, as potential solutions are suggested, they're written on a flipchart or chalkboard for all to see. This encourages everyone to generate even more.

As counterintuitive as it seems, all suggested solutions—however radical or impractical—should be accepted, without evaluation. Why? Evaluation blocks creativity and idea sharing. It makes people defensive and engenders debates about the value of one or two possible solutions, eliminating opportunity to develop better ones. It freezes creativity. Thus, evaluation comes later. Right now, the aim is to get everyone, including you, to suggest lots of potential solutions.

Importantly, the most powerful solutions are often suggested late in the process. Once the group seems at a loss for new solutions, you might ask how previously suggested ones might be combined. This can re-energize the group and produce better ideas.

Evaluate and Select Solutions. Now that a list of potential solutions has been generated, the facilitator should ask the group to select the one with the greatest potential to solve the problem. The group could judge each solution's potential by answering these questions:

- What's required for the solution to work?
- What are its strengths and weaknesses?
- What does the scientific literature say about the solution, including its strategies or methods?
- What might prevent it from being carried out in a quality way?
- What additional problems is it likely to create?

And most important,

- If carried out correctly, is it likely to solve the problem, as stated in the problem definition?

Often, by answering these questions, groups generate better solutions.

But what if the facilitator doesn't raise these questions? You raise them. They're too important to ignore.

Throughout the steps of generating, evaluating, and selecting solutions, it's important to keep thinking about how to refine and combine potential solutions. If you're told they can't be combined, or one with considerable merit can't be selected, ask why. Compare the answers to the questions above. Similarly, if school personnel reject the only solution you think can succeed, ask one or all of these questions:

- What would make it acceptable?
- In deciding what's acceptable, what criteria does the literature recommend?
- How does the solution I support compare to the literature's criteria or to the critical questions we agreed to use for judging potential solutions?
  (These are the questions listed at the beginning of this section.)

Plan How to Evaluate the Effectiveness of the Agreed-Upon Solution(s). Even the best sounding, most carefully selected solution can fail. Thus, you need to work with school personnel to plan how to monitor and evaluate your child's progress. Otherwise, he might be stuck in a program that's failing him, aggravating his problems.

The plan should answer these questions:

- What type of data will be collected?[12]
- How frequently will data be collected?
- Who will collect the data?
- What criteria indicate sufficient progress?
- When will we meet to evaluate the data and determine if progress is adequate or the solution needs to be modified or replaced?

As part of the evaluation process, ask what information you can collect inconspicuously to shed light on your child's progress. Be careful, however, not to test him. Children tend to resent this, even if their parents are professionals. To children, parents should be parents, not professionals.

To ensure that school personnel adequately monitor your child's progress, schedule an evaluation meeting three to four weeks after implementing the solution. If it's working, it should be continued and perhaps refined and strengthened. If it's failing, it should be changed. To belabor the obvious—which is often ignored—failing solutions slash your child's chances for success.[13] For extensive information on monitoring progress, review chapter 7.

Send a Summary Letter. Because all human memory is flawed—we all forget, embellish, distort, and even create false memories—it's important that within hours of any meeting, you summarize, in writing, what was agreed to and what issues remain unresolved. Then put your summary in a simple, relatively brief, well-organized letter. If needed, request a meeting to resolve any remaining issues. Near the letter's end, ask that the school let you know, within ten days, if they think it's accurate.

To ensure the letter is effective, ask one or two friends to review it for politeness, accuracy, and clarity. If anything sounds angry or unfair, delete it. Only then should you send it to the meeting's facilitator, with copies to appropriate parties.

Collect Data on the Effectiveness of the Solution. For the most part, collecting data on the effectiveness of solutions is the responsibility of your child's teachers.[14] They should commit to systematically monitoring his progress on an ongoing basis. Failure to do so and to quickly respond to his difficulties may frustrate him and reinforce poor reading habits. As Marjorie Lipson and Karen Wixson asserted:

> Every instructional encounter ... is an opportunity for assessing and improving instruction. It is possible, and desirable, to continually monitor the effectiveness of the recommended instructional program and to make fine-tuning adjustments in the program as needed. Continuous monitoring of instructional progress is absolutely essential.... The full potential of this process can be realized only when it becomes part of daily practice.[15]

Evaluate the Effectiveness of the Solution and Make Needed Adjustments. Three to four weeks after implementing the solution, the group should examine the data to evaluate the solution's success. If the data fail to show sufficient progress, and school personnel have conscientiously carried out the solution, don't blame them. Developing effective solutions takes educated guesses, called hypotheses. Hypotheses are sometimes accurate, sometimes not. Sometimes success takes longer than expected. For these reasons, monitoring must be ongoing and meetings must be scheduled to assess progress.

If progress is poor, you should ask the group to identify the barriers to progress and ways to overcome them. If they can't, or you think their conclusions are faulty, take action. Request:

- *Temporary program adjustments.* These should be adjustments that school personnel think will accelerate progress and, if appropriate, are supported by research in reputable journals.[16]
- *Independent evaluations by specialists.* These evaluations should answer critical diagnostic questions. For example, a speech and language specialist might answer these questions: Does your child have the language abilities to readily comprehend 4th-grade reading materials? If not, what services does he need to achieve this level in reasonable time? A reading specialist might answer these: What lower-level skills, such as applying syllabication principles, does your child need to master to readily comprehend 4th-grade reading materials? What higher-level cognitive strategies, such as summarizing a story, does he need to master to readily comprehend 4th-grade reading materials? What services and curriculum does he need to achieve a 4th-grade independent reading level in reasonable

time? A behavioral specialist might answer these: What environmental and instructional changes are needed for your child to attend to independent reading tasks 95% of the time? What training and supports do his teachers need to effectively implement these changes?

- *Follow-up meetings.* These should involve you, relevant school personnel, and relevant specialists.[17] Discussion should first examine the specialists' findings and recommendations; the focus should then shift to planning a new, carefully coordinated, closely monitored program that the specialists and the group believe will meaningfully improve your child's abilities.
- *Continuous monitoring.* Of course, the school must carefully monitor whatever is agreed upon and implemented and must schedule meetings to evaluate progress. If the new program proves ineffective, you must again apply all the Model's steps and request whatever services your child needs.

But what do you do, after all this, if you find the problem is not services or plans or programs, but the teacher? Although uncomfortable, the solution is simple: You have to politely but firmly request a different teacher, one who knows how to teach reading to struggling readers. The teacher, as Timothy Blair and his colleagues noted, is the critical factor:

> Time and time again, research has demonstrated the importance of the teacher in effective reading instruction.... We know, for example, that teachers who include provisions for ongoing assessment, explicit instruction, opportunity to learn, attention to learning tasks, and accurate expectations are more effective teachers of reading than those who do not include provisions for these practices.[18]

And what do you do if the new program proves effective? Celebrate and thank everyone, especially the teachers. But keep monitoring it to ensure it remains effective.

THE MODEL: USING IT EFFECTIVELY
To use the Model effectively, you have to fully understand it, have patience, adapt it to your situation, and believe in its potential effectiveness.

Fully Understand It. This requires studying its steps, discussing them with other people, using it frequently in low-stakes, everyday situations, such as where to put a mailbox, and reflecting on how to use it more effectively. Doing this increases your familiarity and comfort with it, as well as your skills. Simply memorizing its steps, without analyzing why it succeeded or failed, will limit your effectiveness.

Have Patience. Patience comes from remembering that problem solving with other people can be a complex and emotionally draining experience that often doesn't work as neatly and as sequentially as we described. It also comes from understanding that not everyone will use the

Model and that some school personnel will think it's inappropriate for parents to make such suggestions—it's not. Finally, it comes from understanding that people generally do what they think is best to meet their needs. People who think the Model is antithetical to their needs— "It wastes time"—may reject systematic problem solving.

Adapt It To Your situation. Some situations will require that you combine or skip steps or keep silent about the Model. If a situation requires you to quickly revise the Model or not discuss it, silently think about its sequence of steps and their purposes. This will keep you on track, organize your efforts, and help you sidestep ineffective solutions.

Believe in Its Potential Effectiveness. If you don't, you'll quickly abandon the Model when difficulty arises. Believing in it fosters creativity and even doggedness in the face of difficulty. Belief flows from successful experiences. That's why we first recommended that you frequently use it in low-stakes, everyday situations and reflect on how to use it more effectively.

Often, just thinking about and discretely applying the Model's sequence of steps can solve problems despite insufficient opportunity to apply its steps in an idealized way. By knowing that groups need to problem solve in a structured, logical way, that understanding problems should precede selecting and implementing solutions, that solutions should be selected on their merits, and solutions require ongoing monitoring, you can inconspicuously stick to the Model while adapting it to your situation. Thus, when you can't use the Model in the neat and idealized way we described, you can use it as a conceptual road map.

THE SITUATION

No model for resolving conflicts and solving problems is perfect and using any model must consider the situation in which it's used. When working with school personnel, it's always important to consider the emotional nature of the situation and the language you use. In some situations, you also need to consider how to create legitimate power and assert it ethically.

Create Positive Emotions. Problem solving often occurs in an emotionally strained atmosphere in which people want to defend themselves and want their way, not yours. To defuse destructive emotions, build trust, cultivate respect, and promote rationality, we suggest that you do five things:

- Work to build trust.
- Treat people with genuine respect.
- Listen to fully understand their views, their reasons, and the pressures they're feeling.
- Find and discuss general areas of agreement, including values and views about education.
- Use the Model.

Together, these can reduce people's tendency to defend their past actions, dismiss the suggestions of others, and advocate for their solutions.

Occasionally, however, someone may get angry at you, treat you rudely, and even attack you verbally. It's usually best to assume that this is a good person under stress. In such situations, your job is to keep calm, protect yourself, minimize the effects of verbally abusive behavior, help the person regain her composure, and get everyone back to problem solving. To do so, you may want to use one or a combination of these strategies:

- *Invite the angry person to continue in a concrete fashion.* "Help me out. Why do you think my asking for tutoring is selfish?"
- *Employ reflective listening.* "Let me see if I understand. You think that tutoring for Jason will deprive other students of needed services."
- *Invite the criticism.* "Please tell me why you think tutoring is unnecessary. And perhaps you can describe something better."
- *Recast the attack on you as an attack on the problem.* "I agree that assessing the instructional environment may be time consuming and that it's hard to get Jason the instructional materials he needs. So then, how do we solve the problem so that his learning increases and he gets the reading materials he needs?"
- *Explore the angry person's ideas as legitimate options.* "I'd like to learn more about your idea. Can you show me the materials or the research you've been discussing?"
- *Invite the angry person to offer ideas.* "I understand that you think my request for one-to-one tutoring is unjustified. Perhaps you're right. Can you share your ideas to improve Jason's reading?"
- *Agree on at least one point.* "I agree. This has been a time consuming and frustrating situation for you and your colleagues. And yes, there are no easy answers."
- *Use a Yes-But.* "You make an important point—Jason is not ready for 3rd grade. But what does the literature say about the academic and emotional effects of holding him back, especially when he's worked so hard, has made some good progress, and is terrified about being retained? What does it say about promoting struggling readers and providing them with whatever supports they need? "
- *Listen empathically to the angry person and then request a break.* "So, basically you're frustrated and confused by Jason's lack of progress. It's taking you away from working with other students…. I'm getting a little tired, but want to continue. Can we take a ten minute break?"[19]

Choose Words Carefully. Whenever you use the Model or discuss your child with school or other professionals, it's critical to carefully choose the words you use to describe or *frame* your child's situation. Because words have many underlying meanings, they convey unconscious but powerful messages that affect the perceptions and reactions of others. Consider, for example, how different people react to the words *liberal* or *conservative, pro-choice* or *pro-life, psychiatrist* or *garbage collector.*

In discussing the Federal *rebates* for stimulating the 2008 economy, Nicholas Epley of the University of Chicago's Graduate School of Business argued that one word—*rebate*— might well undermine the program. Instead of *rebate*, he suggested bonus:

> Getting a rebate is more like being reimbursed for travel expenses than like getting a year-end bonus. Reimbursements send people on trips to the bank. Bonuses send people on trips to the Bahamas.... Describing the checks as rebates highlights that this is simply one's own money being returned. A bonus, however, is extra cash to be spent.

His assertions are based on numerous experiments, including his. His showed that people who received a $50 *bonus* spent far more of it than people who received a $50 *rebate*. He concluded that psychologically a bonus is "pure gain" or extra spending money whereas a rebate is "the return of a loss of one's own money."[20]

So, what does this have to do with your child? When discussing his educational needs and planning his program, avoid the term reading disabilities, a term that unconsciously implies a vast, mysterious, and intractable maze of physiological barriers that predestine poor progress. Instead, use words like *reading difficulties* or *reading problems*. Difficulties or problems can usually be overcome with effort, knowledgeable instruction, and problem solving. Instead of referring to your child as *learning disabled*, which implies a pervasive inability to learn, frame your description as a problem to be solved: "Eric has a learning problem. He hasn't learned to quickly recognize new words." This makes his problem temporary and manageable and solvable: "So, what teaching strategies will the school use to teach him to quickly recognize new words?"

In more legalistic situations, however, such as a formal meeting to decide eligibility for special education, it's better to use the term *reading disabilities*, as it better matches the purpose and vocabulary of IDEA-2004 and people's expectations. By changing the language you're not being deceptive or dishonest. You're simply tailoring it to the situation.

Create the Perception of Power. Sometimes, however, sincerity, good will, skilled listening, respectful treatment of others, and effective problem solving abilities just aren't enough. You need leverage, something that gives you the power to get things done. Although not a magic wand, the Federal special education laws can frequently give you this leverage if you understand them and know how to use them within a problem solving framework that continues to treat school personnel with respect.

An excellent book of tactical, practical suggestions for ethically using special education laws to increase your leverage and to prevail in a conflict, including litigation, is Peter and Pam Wright's *From Emotions to Advocacy* (2nd ed.).[21] Many of its suggestions can readily be used with the Model and can be effective even if your child is ineligible for special education. Here's a sampling:

- Create a paper trail by putting requests in writing, providing the school with relevant information, and keeping a contemporaneous log of calls, letters, meetings, and the like.

175

In the log, include who said what, the requests the school agreed to or denied, and the reasons it gave.

- Remember that good records are essential to effective advocacy. Keep copies of anything written, including letters, reports, and notes from you and the school.
- In person and in writing, treat people with respect; never say or write anything in anger as it will cast you as an "angry hothead" and damage your ability to advocate for your child's needs.
- Make requests, not demands. Demands create resistance.
- "Know what you want …. Make your requests in clear, simple language."[22]
- Record meetings, if allowed by your State's laws.
- Respond to the common denial, "The law does not allow us to do that," with a request, "Please show me where it says that."
- Use a worksheet to record your requests, the school's responses, the resolutions, the start dates, and the people responsible.
- Shortly after the end of any meeting, write your recollections. Send the school a polite thank you letter listing the agreements, the remaining issues, and an offer to meet to resolve them.

KEEP IN MIND

Although the suggestions in this chapter increase the odds of successfully resolving conflicts, they may not work.

If, however, your child is or might be eligible for special education under Federal laws, especially IDEA-2004, *and* you clearly understand how to use these laws, you may be able to get your child what he needs. Please notice that the previous sentence italicized the word *and*. It did so to emphasize that knowing the laws is not enough—you have to know how to use them. Thus, the next five chapters emphasize some of the more relevant aspects of these Federal laws, with suggestions for their ethical use.

ENDNOTES

[1] If only one member can attend, ideally it should be the one with the most interest in solving the problem, the most knowledge of how to solve it, and the most influence with Team members, teachers, and administrators. Thus, in addition to your child's teacher, it might be the school's applied behavior analysis specialist, learning consultant, reading specialist, or school psychologist.

[2] Although we use the word problem, children often have several problems that first look like a single problem. Sometimes, only a close analysis of the "problem" reveals that it's actually a combination of several smaller or contributing ones.

[3] An excellent book on how to structure meetings to solve problems is available in paperback: Doyle, M., & Straus, D., 1993. *How to Make Meetings Work: The New Interaction Method.* New York: Berkley Books. Although the book emphasizes the role of those in charge of meetings and has nothing to do with reading disabilities or special education, school personnel and parents

should benefit greatly from the authors' ideas.

4   Monitoring a child's program and evaluating its effectiveness are different. Monitoring is the ongoing collection of information to "gauge the extent to which an individual student is responding to instructional intervention" (Fletcher, J. M., Lyon, G. R., Fuchs, L. S., & Barnes, M. A., 2007. *Learning Disabilities: From Identification to Intervention.* New York: The Guilford Press, p. 71). Evaluating the effectiveness of a program is broader and uses the monitoring information, as well as other information, to gauge progress and *to make decisions* about changes to instruction and to programs. Changes to instruction might include using a different method; changes to programs might include increasing the hours of reading instruction.

5   Arguments about solutions are often caused by an inadequate understanding of the problem and a failure to offer an adequate plan to monitor and evaluate solutions and change or discard those that aren't working. These deficiencies can create positional bargaining, where each party tries to force the other to accept its solution. Win-lose power struggles like this often engender resistance, resentment, and retaliation. The logic of the Model, which starts with understanding, often minimizes or eliminates such struggles. The Model, however, is of little use when school personnel or parents demand their way and will not consider alternatives or problem solving, no matter the inadequacy of their proposed solution or the value of other possibilities.

6   Often, the current causes of a child's difficulties are external, such as teasing, hunger, frustration-level reading materials, or seatwork that requires him to sit for unreasonably long periods. Combined with long-standing internal difficulties that the child brings to the situation, such as high anxiety and poor ability to associate letters with sounds, external causes can trigger more intensive and complex problems.

7   Ideally, what's needed is an *elegant* solution, one that solves the problem permanently without creating additional ones. Unfortunately, in their pessimism and rush to solve problems, people often settle for *inelegant* solutions when *elegant* ones are possible. This perpetuates problems.

8   We intentionally used the plural *meetings* instead of *meeting.* For more complex problems, several meetings may be needed. Often, several meetings are needed for problems that are more complex and intensive because earlier they were ignored, or the solutions were poor, or they were implemented poorly, or a mix of these. For less complex and intensive problems, problems that were caught in their early stages, one meeting may suffice to develop a good understanding and a good solution.

9   Occasionally, this produces an unintended but beneficial side effect: an ally with a better understanding of the issues.

10   It's better to use a flipchart than a chalkboard as flipchart notes can be saved and used at future meetings. This provides a common memory and saves time.

11   Often, by solving the more critical problems, the less critical ones lose intensity or disappear.

12   The data should relate directly to the problem. For example, if your child identifies words accurately, but slowly, and he's in the fourth grade, it would be valuable to measure the number of words he correctly identifies per minute of oral reading. This is sometimes called Correct Words Per Minute. If his problem is not word recognition or fluency, but reading comprehension, it would be valuable to directly measure the percentage of questions he answers correctly about the materials he read.

[13] Recently, Timothy Blair and his colleagues captured the importance of ongoing monitoring: "Without the teacher's pervasive concern for knowing and responding to students' needs, reading instruction can be irrelevant and mindless drudgery.... Continuous progress monitoring and thoughtful reflection are integral parts of effective instruction.... Effective teachers use ongoing assessment to evaluate student outcomes regularly in relation to actual classroom reading instruction" (Blair, T. R., Rupley, W. H., & Nichols, W. D., 2007. The effective teacher of reading: Considering the 'what' and 'how' of instruction. *The Reading Teacher, 60* (5), 432-438, pp. 433-434).

[14] For children who are eligible for special education under IDEA-2004, responsibility for collecting some data may be assigned to other school personnel, such as case managers.

[15] Lipson, M. Y., & Wixson, K. K., 2003. *Assessment and Instruction of Reading and Writing Difficulty: An Interactive Approach* (3rd ed.). Boston: Allyn & Bacon, p. 68.

[16] If your child is eligible for special education under IDEA-2004, the school should do everything reasonable to ensure that the methods it uses are supported by research: IDEA-2004 states that the IEP must contain "a statement of the special education and related services and supplementary aids and services, *based on peer-reviewed research* to the extent practicable" (34 CFR § 300.320, italics added). To get further clarification and to ensure that people truly understand what they're proposing, with all its implications, you might ask how the strategies will be applied and how they differ noticeably from strategies that have proven ineffective with your child.

[17] The word relevant is particularly important. Occasionally, Howard has attended meetings in which the relevant teachers and specialists did not attend. Instead, the school sent whoever was available. In one instance, a school social worker was sent to solve a major problem with reading comprehension.

[18] Blair, Rupley, & Nichols, 2007, p. 437.

[19] For more information about these and other strategies, see Howard's article: Margolis, H., 1990. What to do when you're verbally attacked: The critical moment. *NASSP Bulletin, 74*, 523, 34-38. NASSP stands for the National Association of Secondary School Principals.

[20] Epley, N., 2008 January 31. Rebate psychology. *The New York Times*; retrieved 4/27/08, from http://www.nytimes.com/2008/01/31/opinion/31epley.html?_r=1&scp=1&sq=Rebate+psychology&st=nyt&oref=slogin.

[21] Wright, P. W. D., & Wright, P .D., 2006. *From Emotions to Advocacy: The Special Education Survival Guide.* Hartfield, VA: Harbor House Law Press.

[22] Wright & Wright, p, 262.

CHAPTER 9
SPECIAL EDUCATION EVALUATIONS

Once your child is referred for special education eligibility and you give informed consent for an evaluation, the school must quickly evaluate her.[1] This is more than a mere formality. The *Individuals with Disabilities Education Improvement Act of 2004* (IDEA-2004) has strict, complex requirements that you must understand to ensure they're followed. Many schools adhere strictly to the spirit and letter of these requirements; many don't.

These requirements are not trite technicalities—they're important educational practices for getting the information you need to help your child. Without such information, the likelihood of designing a program that produces meaningful progress is greatly diminished. Thus, the importance of an evaluation that adheres to IDEA-2004's requirements cannot be overstated.

This chapter discusses your veto power and six points that can affect the quality of your child's evaluation—its ability to help you and school personnel plan a reading program likely to produce important gains in reading.

THE VETO POWER OF PARENTS

Before a school can initially place a child in a part-time or full-time special education program or give her special education support in her regular classes, it must first get the parent's informed consent to evaluate her.[2] It must then formally evaluate her; reach agreement with the parent about her eligibility for special education; and, if eligible, meet with the parent to develop the child's Individualized Education Program (IEP) and get the parent's consent to provide her with special education services.

Many parents stop this process before it begins. They withhold consent to have their child evaluated for special education and related services. Their refusal is fueled by this question: If school personnel think the evaluation shows that my child is eligible for special education and I don't like the school's special education programs, is my child stuck with them?

The answer: "No." Here's what IDEA-2004's regulations say:

> If the parent of a child ... refuses to consent to ... the *initial* provision of special education and related services, the [school] ... may not use the ... due process procedures ... to obtain agreement or a ruling that the services may be provided to the child[3] .... If, at any time *subsequent* to the initial provision of special education and related services, the parent of a child revokes consent in writing for the continued provision of special education and related services, the [school] ... may not continue to provide special education and related services to the child, but must provide prior written notice. [Moreover, the school] ... may not use due process procedures ... to obtain agreement or a ruling that the services may be provided to the child.[4]

Without your informed consent *to begin* special education, the school cannot implement an *initial* IEP—it cannot provide your child with special education placement or services, including related services like counseling, and it cannot initiate court proceedings to force these issues. In other words, you have the power to veto her *initial* placement and program.

Even if you agree to special education placement and services, you can, at any time, change your mind and end them. You can revoke your consent. To do this, you must inform the school in writing; the school must then send you written notice that any special education placement and all special education services will end and then quickly end them. At this time, your child becomes a general education student.[5]

Furthermore, under new regulations, published on December 1, 2008, the school cannot challenge your veto in court. Your veto is absolute.[6] Here's how the U. S. Department of Education explains your rights:

> The IEP Team does not have the authority to consent to the provision of special education and related services to a child. That authority is given *exclusively* to the parent .... Allowing parents to revoke consent for the continued provision of special education and related services at any time is consistent with the IDEA's emphasis on the role of parents in protecting their child's rights and the Department's goal of enhancing parent involvement and choice in their child's education.[7]

So, should you withhold consent for an evaluation? If doing so is based on fear that the school will place your child in special education, regardless of your wishes, we see no reason to withhold consent. After all, the school cannot override your veto. Moreover, the evaluation may help everyone to better understand your child's reading disabilities and better plan instruction, whether or not she becomes a special education student.

Chapters 10, 11, and 12 offer more information about IEPs, special education, and what you might do if you believe your child should get special education services, but disagree with the program offered by the IEP Team.

IDEA-2004: SIX CRITICAL POINTS ABOUT EVALUATIONS
Point 1: Schools Must Evaluate All Areas Related to the Suspected Disability. *The child [must be] assessed in all areas related to the suspected disability, **including**, if appropriate, health, vision, hearing, social and emotional status, general intelligence, academic performance, communicative status, and motor abilities.*[8]

Comment. The evaluation to determine your child's eligibility for special education is also the basis for the program required to meet her educational needs. Therefore, you must make certain that the evaluation is designed to identify every educational need that may block or hinder her progress.

The decision about your child's eligibility must be made by a group of qualified professionals and by you:

> The determination of whether a child … is a child with a disability …
> must be made by the child's parents and a team of qualified professionals,
> which must include … the child's regular teacher; or … if the child does
> not have a regular teacher, a regular classroom teacher qualified to teach
> a child of his or her age [and] … at least one person qualified to conduct
> individual diagnostic examinations of children, such as a school psycholo-
> gist, speech-language pathologist, *or* remedial reading teacher.[9]

Because evaluation groups, like the one described above, typically lack a remedial reading teacher or reading specialist, they leave the evaluation of reading problems to learning consultants or educational specialists or school psychologists.[10] This is unfair to them and to struggling read-ers as often these group members have little education in reading disabilities. Even with the best of intentions, people with poor knowledge tend to design poor programs. To prevent this problem, formally, in writing, request a comprehensive evaluation from a certified reading specialist.

In addition to IDEA-2004's statement that a remedial reading teacher can be part of the evaluation group, you have another strong justification for requesting an evaluation by a read-ing specialist. Reading, general education, special education, school psychology, and speech and language are different fields, with different courses of study, different degrees, and differ-ent certifications. Reading specialists take many more courses in assessing and remediating reading disabilities than these other specialists. Thus, it should not be surprising that evalu-ations by reading specialists are often more comprehensive, in-depth, and insightful; their recommendations are often more instructionally relevant.

Although IDEA-2004 gives you the right to request an evaluation that assesses all areas related to your child's suspected disability, you may know little, if anything, about evaluations. This problem has two solutions:

- Write down your questions about what you want to learn from the evaluation and give them to the evaluation group. (For a list of questions, see Howard's article, *What Read-ing Program Does My Child Need?* on www.reading2008.com.) Then ask the members what instruments and procedures they'll use to answer your questions. Then ask them for literature, from independent sources, such as peer-reviewed professional journals or *The Mental Measurements Yearbook*, that evaluates the validity of their instruments and pro-cedures. Under Point 3 in this chapter, Schools Must Use Multiple Sources of Information, this is discussed in greater detail.
- Hire a reading specialist to help you develop your questions and assess the school's evalua-tion plan (and later, the results).

Hiring a reading specialist opens many doors as IDEA-2004 allows you to bring to meet-ings anyone who has "knowledge or special expertise regarding [your] … child."[11] As your consultant, the specialist becomes a member of the IEP Team. If school personnel don't real-ize this, you can refer them to this IDEA-2004 regulation:

> The determination of the knowledge or special expertise of any individual
> … must be made by the party (parents or public agency) who invited the
> individual *to be a member of the IEP Team.*[12]

An area of need for many struggling readers, an area that must be addressed for these readers to succeed, an area that evaluation groups often ignore, is motivation. Many groups act as if motivational problems are totally the reader's fault, that schools can do little to strengthen a struggling reader's motivation. Here's why they're wrong.

Motivation is not merely a product of a struggling reader's temperament and thoughts. Both are directly and powerfully influenced by what happens at home and in class. In part, a struggling reader's motivation is a product of the tasks her teacher presents, their difficulty, the teacher's relationship with her, the reinforcement and support he gives, the type of feedback he gives, and the structure and emotional climate of the class. In other words, teachers can do many things to strengthen a reader's motivation.

Simple principles and ideas for strengthening motivation have been discussed throughout this book, especially in chapters 2, 4, and 6. So, if you think motivational problems are inhibiting your child's progress, ask the evaluation group to systematically and scientifically evaluate the dynamics of your child's motivation as it directly relates to her suspected disability. If they offer resistance, share these thoughts:

- IDEA-2004 requires the evaluation group to assess your child "in all areas related to the suspected disability." The law does not exclude motivation.
- Since 2000, hundreds of peer-reviewed research and research-related articles, chapters, and books have been published on motivational problems and solutions.

For further information on motivation, visit our website, www.reading2008.com. But above all, if motivation is a problem, work to solve it. Don't ignore it. Struggling readers—unmotivated to improve their reading—will, at best, make trivial progress.

Point 2: Schools Must Use Valid, Non-discriminatory Evaluation Instruments and Strategies. *[Schools shall use assessment instruments] for the purposes for which the assessments or measures are valid and reliable…. [Schools shall use] assessment instruments and strategies that provide relevant information that directly assists persons in determining the educational needs of the child*[13] *…. Each public agency must ensure that … assessments and other evaluation materials used to assess a child under this part … are selected and administered so as not to be discriminatory on a racial or cultural basis [and] … are provided and administered in the child's native language or other mode of communication and in the form most likely to yield accurate information on what the child knows and can do academically, developmentally, and functionally, unless it is clearly not feasible to so provide or administer.*[14]

Comment. Before school personnel use tests, rating forms, or other assessment procedures to evaluate your child's reading and learning problems, ask them to share the published reviews of these measurement tools.[15] The reviews should demonstrate that these tests and other assessment procedures accurately and reliably:

- Measure what their publishers and school personnel claim they're measuring, and do so for children like your child.
- Measure children's abilities in non-discriminatory ways; they don't penalize children for language differences, cultural differences, and the like.
- Identify children's specific reading and related needs well enough to suggest what should be taught.

The reason for requesting the reviews is simple: If they suggest the tests and other assessment procedures the school plans to use will produce inaccurate, unreliable, partial, or invalid results, your child may be placed in a program that teaches her the wrong things, or is too easy, or is too hard.

Although many fine tests and assessment procedures are available to measure the different components of reading, such as vocabulary, word identification, word recognition, and comprehension, none is perfect. All have flaws. Moreover, different tests of reading measure reading differently, producing different results. If, for example, two tests measure reading comprehension differently, one may say your child's comprehension is at grade level; the other may say it's below. The poorer tests may be so fickle that your child earns vastly different scores at different times, though her actual reading achievement has not changed. Thus, you need to ensure that the tests and assessment procedures used will likely measure what they say they do, fully, accurately, and reliably.[16]

Because it's rare for parents to ask evaluators for published reviews of tests and assessment procedures, asking might stun them. Don't let this stop you and don't worry that you're asking for something extraordinary or something difficult to find. Reviews are usually easy to get.[17] Besides, evaluators have a professional responsibility to study the reviews of the tests and assessment procedures they're using. Unawareness of how to get the needed reviews, failure to have studied them, or resistance to sharing them with you signals danger—danger that the evaluator may lack essential knowledge, or care little about the appropriateness of the evaluation, or care little about making you a full partner in helping your child *beat the odds*.

Although it's critical that the tests and other assessment procedures receive good reviews— reviews saying they're accurate, reliable, and non-discriminatory—good reviews are insufficient. They're no better than the examiner's administration, scoring, and interpretation of the test. It's like a car and a driver. The safest car is no safer than its driver.

Like poor drivers who ignore or misinterpret road conditions and traffic signals, many professionals misinterpret basic data, data from well-reviewed tests and procedures. We've seen this happen many times, especially with grade equivalents. Often they erroneously treat grade equivalents as indicators of the level and types of materials children can successfully read.[18]

Because grade equivalents often present inflated pictures of abilities, and because school personnel often misinterpret or fail to interpret them, they're often used to deprive struggling readers of needed services. Howard has often heard school personnel argue that because a struggling reader's grade equivalent was on the borderline of average for "total reading" or "basic reading skills," extra reading help was not needed. He has also heard them deny services because the child's grade equivalent for reading resembled her IQ score. Such interpretations view grade equivalents as precise, reliable, and comprehensive indicators of a struggling reader's ability to read materials designed for particular grades: This is wrong.

Usually, grade equivalents are oversimplified summary scores that compare the number of test questions a struggling reader answered correctly to the number of questions children in the test's standardization group answered correctly. Additionally, the number of questions a struggling reader answered correctly—her raw score—often reflects how well she did on limited, splinter tasks that have little resemblance to daily reading tasks. Substitute one standardized test of reading achievement for another and her grade equivalent can change dramatically.

To determine if struggling readers are eligible for special education or should get extra help, some schools compare the grade equivalents or other standardized reading test scores of struggling readers to their IQ scores. From this they calculate discrepancy scores.[19] Perhaps cynically, perhaps mournfully, many reading and learning disability experts have called this achievement-IQ comparison the "wait and fail" or "wait to fail" model.[20] The good news is that blistering criticism from scholars and government officials has caused some schools to abandon discrepancy scores. The criticism has made clear that they cause far more harm than good. IDEA-2004 makes clear that schools do not have to use discrepancy scores to determine a child's eligibility for special education or extra or specialized reading help. The bad news is they can still use such scores. And some do. Similarly, they can still use grade equivalents to decide about a child's need for services or the level of instruction. And some do.

So, what can you do to ensure that the tests and assessment procedures your child's school wants to use are valid for assessing her reading abilities? What can you do to ensure that her evaluation is comprehensive and that the interpretation of the data is correct? Here are several suggestions:

- Ask for and study the published reviews of the tests and assessment procedures the school proposes to use.
- Ask the school to complement the standardized tests they use with one or two well-reviewed informal reading inventories, like the *Qualitative Reading Inventory*.[21]
- Study chapters 3 and 4, which discuss different kinds of reading difficulties.
- Study chapter 5, which discusses how to effectively use a reading evaluation and how to get help from an independent reading specialist.
- Read Howard's article, *What Reading Program Does My Child Need?* It lists many questions to ask. You can find it on www.reading2008.com.
- Make sure your child's IEP includes a plan for closely monitoring her progress. Chapter 7 discusses this.
- Read Howard's article, *Monitoring Your Child's IEP: A Focus on Reading*. You can find it on www.reading2008.com.

Point 3: Schools Must Use Multiple Sources of Information. *In conducting the evaluation, the [school] must ... **use a variety** of assessment tools and strategies to gather relevant functional, developmental, and academic information about the child.... [Schools should] not use any single measure or assessment as the **sole criterion** for determining whether a child is a child with a disability and for determining an appropriate educational program for the child.*[22]

Comment. Evaluations are expensive, time consuming, and fraught with error. All evaluation procedures, including tests and observations, assess only small samples of behavior.[23] The best of them cannot definitively or fully assess a child's functioning. Thus, to reduce error and more accurately estimate the functioning of struggling readers in all areas important to their education, IDEA-2004 requires that decisions about eligibility and programs be based on multiple measures, on multiple "assessment tools and strategies."

Although this sounds simple, it can get tricky. Does the school, for example, have to use multiple measures for each area of the suspected disability? Must it, for example, administer two reading measures to a child suspected of having a reading disability? Or can it administer only one measure per suspected area of disability, such as one test for reading, one for writing, and one for oral language?

To begin answering these questions, we'll first discuss the evaluation of intelligence. We'll discuss this in some detail as it's typically an important part of evaluations for specific learning disabilities, which includes dyslexia or reading disabilities. Second, we'll discuss the evaluation of reading, including some limits of testing, the struggling reader's instructional environment, and her motivation. Third, we'll discuss the need for current, relevant observations. Finally, we'll put the issue of multiple "assessment tools and strategies" into a perspective that might help you work with your child's school. As always, our opinions are not those of an attorney, but of an educator and a psychologist.[24]

Intelligence. Many use a single intelligence test to pinpoint a child's intelligence. They let the scores from this one test heavily influence their decision to provide or deny services. It's as if they believed the scores were absolutely accurate, comprehensive, and infallible. What they seem to ignore is that intelligence quotients or IQ scores, like all test scores, only partially represent what they claim to measure and provide only estimates of abilities. Like estimates from moving companies, some test estimates are far less accurate than others. The word estimate, by definition, means approximation, rough calculation, educated guess, error. So, beware of estimates, beware of IQ scores. Although they can be helpful, they're not infallible.

But what if the school uses the *Wechsler Intelligence Scale for Children-IV* (WISC-IV), arguably the most popular intelligence test for children, one that dominates many graduate courses in school psychology, one that's part of a respected family of intelligence tests that has been popular for decades? By itself, isn't the WISC-IV good enough to accurately, definitively, and permanently pinpoint a child's innate intelligence? The definitive answer: No!

All tests, including the better and more popular intelligence tests, have flaws. In their classic book, *Assessment in Special and Inclusive Education*, John Salvia, James Ysseldyke, and Sara Bolt, concluded that the WISC-IV has major flaws:

> Evidence for validity is limited.... [It's] of limited usefulness in making
> educational decisions.... [Many of its subtests] have limited reliability.[25]

As this suggests, the popularity of a test doesn't mean it fully and validly tests what it purports to test or that you can have great confidence in its scores.

Even if we assume the WISC-IV is far better than this review, consider how the reading habits of many struggling readers can depress their intelligence test scores. Because struggling readers tend to read little, or read materials of meager substance, they don't develop the vocabulary and knowledge that good readers do and that intelligence tests measure. This is called the Matthew Effect, named for the Bible story in which the rich get richer and the poor get poorer.

Moreover, because of repeated failures in school, many struggling readers feel intense anxiety about testing and feel hopeless in the face of intellectual challenges, like tasks on intelligence tests. Frequently they pay little attention to test items and quickly stop trying—they flood examiners with "I don't knows." Together with the Matthew Effect, struggling readers' feelings of anxiety and hopelessness often combine to depress their intelligence test scores, though their innate intelligence remains intact.

One way to counter such depressed scores is to request an intellectual evaluation that includes teacher impressions, work samples, oral language samples, diagnostic teaching, interviews of you and your child, and observations of her in and out of school, in casual and enjoyable situations as well as formal and stressful ones. Together, these strategies will help paint a more accurate, richer picture of your child's intellectual functioning, which may differ from her scores on a single intelligence test. Usually, the better your child's evaluation and the IEP Team's understanding of her intellectual functioning, the better they can meet her needs.

Notice that the previous paragraph didn't limit evaluation to testing. We went beyond testing. We spoke of teacher impressions, work samples, oral language samples, diagnostic teaching, interviews, and observations. And what intelligence tests measure is one author's unique definition of intelligence, one that can differ markedly from that of other authors.[26]

Given the many limitations of any one intelligence test, we strongly suggest that you ask your child's school to supplement intelligence test scores with information from non-standardized assessment procedures. This complies with IDEA-2004 and may well provide a more accurate and complete understanding of your child's *current* intellectual abilities.[27]

Reading. If the decoding subtest of a reading test samples only a small number of letter-sound relationships, if this is the only reading test or procedure the evaluator gives, and if the test reports the results as a grade equivalent—three common "ifs"—teachers won't know what phonic elements to teach. Moreover, testing only a few letter-sound relationships lets chance or luck appreciably influence the struggling reader's grade equivalent, meaning that little confidence should be placed in the score.

The same is true for reading comprehension. If the only test or procedure given measures comprehension by having the child give the missing word in short sentences, and she does fairly well, the evaluator cannot predict, with high certainty, her ability to comprehend far longer passages.

Clearly, in both cases, additional information is needed to get an accurate and full understanding of the struggling reader's knowledge and ability to apply it. Thus, the evaluator must supplement this one test with more comprehensive measures of decoding and comprehension. Failure to do so will result in a poor understanding of the struggling reader's needs and a poor reading program.

Another problem with limiting evaluations to a single test is that it's usually a standardized test. Such tests are usually static, like snapshots. They usually deal with small, stilted, contrived, narrowly-focused, one-dimensional slices of the moment, not the richness of the struggling reader's functioning in the areas of concern, such as fluency and reading comprehension. Thus, single tests, especially standardized ones, need to be supplemented by different kinds of measures that produce different kinds of information. Such information can alter the picture.

Consider a struggling reader who follows the evaluator's directions to identify a missing word on a test of oral language. Here, the reader presents one picture; she may present a far different picture when casually speaking to a friend.

Now consider a struggling reader who has learned only 100 sight words by mid-third grade. She presents one picture. But she presents a far different picture when diagnostic teaching with Method-A shows she can learn six new words per tutoring session, which translates into 30 words per week, or more than a thousand per year. Time and again, different situations and different types of information reveal important differences, paint markedly different pictures, offer more accurate and complete views of the reader's needs.

Another disturbing example of using a single test "for determining an appropriate program" is the dependence of some evaluators on standardized, individually-administered test batteries. These evaluators assume that a battery's many subtests equate to a variety of quality assessment tools. In one sense they're right, as a reading battery assesses many different aspects of reading. But often, a battery has many subtests that are superficial and limited in scope, letting chance play an important role in determining a struggling reader's scores. Here, for example, in The *Seventeenth Mental Measurements Yearbook*, is how Antonia D'Onofrio, a Professor of Education in Widener University's doctoral program, and Howard described several subtests of the *Gray Diagnostic Reading Battery-Second Edition*:

> Some subtests are insufficiently stable over time, signalizing the need for
> cautious interpretations.... The relatively lower correlations for the ...
> subtests suggest that examiners should be cautious in interpreting scores
> from these subtests, especially if they will be used in making decisions
> about individual children.[28]

One of the better and widely used standardized reading batteries is the *Woodcock-Johnson III Diagnostic Reading Battery* (WJ-III-DRB). Like the just-discussed *Gray Diagnostic Reading Battery-Second Edition*, it's inadequate to comprehensively describe the reading abilities of a struggling reader or to identify instructional levels. Although it does a fine job of comparing children to one another, it occasionally uses very narrow, limited tasks to do this, tasks that differ markedly from typical reading tasks. As Antonia D'Onofrio and Howard's review in the *Seventeenth Mental Measurements Yearbook* stated, the WJ-III-DRB should not be used alone:

> Together with tests that more closely approximate *typical reading activities*, a knowledgeable, informed examiner who engages in diagnostic teaching, who observes the examinees in different instructional situations, who is familiar with the local reading curricula and the skills and orientations of the instructors, and who arranges to have the examinees' reading progress carefully monitored, should be able to use the WJ-III-DRB to gather the information needed to help many examinees improve their reading abilities. To accomplish this, the WJ-III-DRB can be an excellent tool for examiners, but it should not be used alone.[29]

Why do we emphasize that even the better reading batteries are inadequate to fully measure reading? Because directly evaluating reading in limited and superficial ways produces limited and superficial understanding of struggling readers' problems, which produces limited, superficial, and ineffective programs.

Look at a struggling reader who's given the WJ-III-DRB's Passage Comprehension subtest. She does well on it because it uses exceedingly short paragraphs. She's not asked to comprehend long passages, like those in textbooks, because they're not on the test. But long passages are her problem: She struggles to understand them. This can create many absurdities.

Here's one absurdity: She may well be denied services as her score for comprehending short paragraphs touched the bottom of the average range. Here's another: By not assessing her comprehension of long passages, testing hasn't identified her problem as a problem. If she gets services, and they're based on her WJ-III-DRB test results, instruction will probably ignore her problem of comprehending long passages, perpetuating her struggle with reading.

Limiting reading evaluations to tests and procedures that directly measure reading—which is often the case—ignores many critical factors. Two of these commonly ignored, but critical factors are the struggling reader's motivation to read and her instructional environment.

Understanding how a struggling reader's instructional environment matches her needs is often a key to remedying her problems. As Marjorie Lipson and Karen Wixson concluded, evaluation must assess more than the reader's abilities:

> Traditional assessment looks only to the student as the source of reading and writing difficulties. Clearly, students' knowledge, skill, and motivation are crucial factors in reading and writing achievement. However, a growing body of research demonstrates that instructional context and methods can support learning or contribute to disability. Assessment that is intended to inform instruction requires careful descriptions of how different aspects of the instructional environment influence learning in general and how they match the needs of particular students.[30]

Another key to accelerating progress is understanding the struggling reader's motivation: What weakens her motivation to excel in reading? How can the instructional methods, materials, and environment be changed to strengthen her motivation? To answer these questions, her motivation must be systematically and knowledgeably evaluated, which few, if any, tests can do. Typically, this involves observing her in her instructional environment, interviewing her and her teachers and parents, completing questionnaires, and modifying her instructional environment and assessing its effects. This can take several hours and requires familiarity with the research on motivation.

Because evaluating motivation takes considerable time, requires specialized knowledge, and goes far beyond testing, it's often hastily evaluated or sidestepped. These are not minor mistakes; they're major. As Robert Sternberg, a leading expert on intelligence and motivation, so aptly noted:

> Motivation is perhaps the indispensable element needed for school success. Without it, the student never even tries to learn.[31]

Evaluators who fail to go beyond tests to fully assess the dynamics of a struggling reader's motivational problem will not get the information needed to identify what's fueling it and what can be done to overcome it and markedly accelerate her progress.

A major point to remember about this section is that any one test, no matter how good, cannot adequately measure the reading abilities of struggling readers and all the factors that schools must consider to help the reader *beat the odds*.

Observations. To determine if a child has a specific learning disability, the most common classification for struggling readers, or to reevaluate her, IDEA-2004 requires schools to:

- Ensure that the child is observed in the child's learning environment (including the regular classroom setting) to document the child's academic performance and behavior in the areas of difficulty.[32]
- [Provide] a statement of … the relevant behavior, if any, noted during the observation … and the relationship of that behavior to the child's academic functioning.[33]

These requirements are good, but not good enough. IDEA-2004 does not require that the observer be trained in objective observations, nor does it define such observations. Howard has questioned the value of many observations as they lacked relevant information and were highly subjective; they told more about the observer's predispositions than providing objective data about the child's behavior and academic performance. Many of these observations were written from memory, which is frequently flawed and unreliable.

To prevent inadequate observations, we suggest that you request a current, objective observation of your child. Such observations are critical, as they're just about the only way to assess her:

- Ability to apply her knowledge in her current classes.
- Motivation under different instructional conditions.

Furthermore, observing her in her current classes also allows the observer to determine if her current teachers' practices meet her needs. As Howard has often observed, struggling readers are poorly motivated to read because they're taught at their frustration, not instructional levels.[34] Because the current reading environment can powerfully affect a struggling reader's progress, understanding this environment is often a key to improving her reading. To continue quoting Marjorie Lipson and Karen Wixson:

> It is important to evaluate those aspects of the literate environment that *directly influence* the acquisition of reading and writing skills.... The literate environment can communicate to students both what is valued and what is acceptable. Inaccessible reading and/or writing centers and uninviting activities and spaces affect students' understanding of the value and purposes for reading and writing. They also influence students' voluntary reading and writing. Similarly, rigid seating arrangements do little to advance the cooperative or verbal interaction patterns that are necessary for many students' literacy development.[35]

Unfortunately, IDEA-2004 does not require the observation to be current. Evaluation groups can use previous ones.[36] Fortunately, if your child is being evaluated for special education eligibility or is eligible under IDEA-2004, you're part of the evaluation group and IEP Team. Therefore, to help you participate in an informed way, you can request a current observation.[37] So, we suggest that you request one.

We also suggest that you request that the observer use an observation system, like *The Instructional Environmental System-II* (TIES), which examines critical areas like lesson development, clarity of directions, classroom management, motivational strategies, and relevant practice.[38]

If the team won't use the TIES or a similar observation system, ask that the observation answer a set of written, instructionally-relevant questions, like these:[39]

- At what grade level and readability level were her independent reading assignments?
- When she was being taught to read, at what grade level and readability level were her materials?
- What support did she get when she had trouble with her work and how long did it take to get the support?
- On average, what percentage of each 5-minute observation period was she engaged in assigned activities? Did engaged time vary by activity, and if so, how?
- How much time did she spend reading connected text, such as paragraphs and stories?
- What are the likely effects of her behaviors and the specifics of the instructional environment, including methodology and instructional materials, on her reading achievement?

Who observes is as important as the questions posed. Without proper expertise in reading disabilities, the observer will likely miss important information. Take the example of Howard

190

and Gary. Although Howard has a doctorate in reading and Gary a doctorate in clinical psychology, if they had to analyze fMRI film, they wouldn't know what to look for or understand what they saw. Similarly, school psychologists, social workers, and other evaluation-group members who observe your child in reading will likely miss or misunderstand important information that's quickly seen and understood by a reading specialist. As an old saying goes, "You see only what you know."

So, what do you do if you disagree with the evaluation group's suggestion for an observer? After all, IDEA-2004 lets the team decide who will observe.

Do two things. First, remember that you're a member of the evaluation group, so you can recommend an observer. Then, politely recommend someone with the needed expertise. If necessary, identify the expertise.

Perspective. Must schools do all we suggested? Must they administer more than one test per area or supplement testing with other procedures? Perhaps not. But it's important for you to understand our concerns so you can knowledgeably critique the school's evaluations, and, if necessary, ask the school to supplement them with valid information from multiple procedures, including non-testing procedures, like systematic observations of your child in different situations.

It's also important to remember that the school's evaluation must be adequate to develop an IEP likely to produce meaningful rather than trivial progress. IDEA-2004 does not support practices, including evaluation practices, that knowingly fall short of this standard.

If your child's school insists on using a single test or assessment procedure to make decisions that affect her eligibility or program, request a comprehensive evaluation that can, as IDEA-2004 requires:

> Identify all of the child's special education and related services needs, *whether or not commonly linked* to the disability category in which the child has been classified.[40]

If this does not work, we suggest you study chapter 8, which discusses how to resolve conflicts. We also suggest that you carefully monitor your child's progress and quickly intervene if it's poor. Studying chapter 7 can help, as can Howard's article *Monitoring Your Child's IEP: A Focus on Reading.* It's available at www.reading2008.com.

Point 4: Schools May Use a Response to Intervention (RTI) Model. *The State ... must permit the use of a process based on the child's response to scientific, research-based intervention. [This is often called Response to Intervention, Response to Instruction, or RTI]*[41]*.... If the child has participated in [RTI, the school must document] ... the instructional strategies used and the student-centered data collected.*[42]

Comment. In simple terms, RTI models or programs evaluate students' abilities, provide students who do poorly on the evaluations with "scientifically-based" instruction to remediate their difficulties, monitor their progress, and offer more intensive instruction and services to students who continue to do poorly. Usually, RTI models start by evaluating all students in kindergarten.

But not all children go to schools that use RTI. Thus, our illustration will begin with Estella, a mythical second grader who just transferred from a school that did not use RTI. After discussing Estella, we'll discuss our concerns about RTI. Finally, we'll make several recommendations that might help you.

Within two days of Estella's enrollment in second grade, her teacher quickly noticed she struggled to read mid-first-grade materials. She and the school's reading specialist discussed Estella's problems with her parents. All agreed to try RTI. The reading specialist and teacher decided to use the XYZ reading program to instruct Estella in her general education class. She would join a group of five other children using this program, which the school considered scientifically based. Her general education teacher would teach the group, document the activities, collect progress data daily, and weekly assess the trend of the data. The school's reading specialist called this tier-1 instruction.[43]

All parties agreed that if Estella's progress was poor, the school would provide her with more intensive, more focused scientifically-based instruction that matched her needs. It was explained to her parents that more intensive and focused instruction, called tier-2 instruction, could take several forms, including daily, lengthier instruction in a group of three children, using the same or a different program, or daily pull-out tutoring by a reading specialist using the same or a different program. As her teachers made clear, the more they worked with Estella and examined the data documenting her progress, the better they would understand her needs and be able to suggest programs or methods that more precisely matched her needs.

Estella's teachers explained that *their* RTI approach was a highly individualized, problem solving approach that combined scientifically-based instructional principles with scientifically-based reading programs. The other major RTI approach, the standardized approach, limited itself to one or two standardized programs in the tier-1 general education class, in the more intensive instructional situation, called tier-2, and in the special education program, called tier-3. Although the standardized approach was less complicated and easier to use, they feared it might not meet the needs of some children.

Estella's teachers also explained that throughout the process, they would continue collecting data to document her progress. This would help determine if she had specific learning disabilities and, if so, the type and intensity of instruction needed.[44] At the end of eight weeks, if her progress—her rate of learning and her achievement level—was poor, the school would request parental permission to conduct a comprehensive evaluation for special education eligibility and would complete it well within the legal time frame. While the comprehensive evaluation was underway, Estella would continue to receive intensive instruction.

For identifying students with specific learning disabilities, like Estella's reading disabilities, IDEA-2004 has a strong preference for making RTI *part* of the evaluation. This preference is strongly supported by many experts on learning disabilities. Although we're far less optimistic than most experts about the *practicality* of RTI, especially when it's adopted by thousands of schools, we hope their optimism proves right.

One of our concerns is that RTI is not a well-tested model, but a set of emerging models and conceptualizations that must be converted into precise, operational models and tested nationwide to assess their effectiveness and efficiency with all kinds of children, in all kinds of schools, with teachers of wide-ranging competence.[45] Districts and schools within districts may use the term RTI to mean different things. Some may have a well-designed model that is carefully spelled out in writing, carefully supervised, and carefully evaluated and refined. Others may have a vague, confusing paragraph or two referring to a model that few teachers in the district or school understand.

Below are several additional concerns. Because you may run into them, and they may undermine—fully or partially—the trustworthiness of the data produced by RTI and the appropriateness of decisions about your child, you should be aware of them:

- No commercial reading program has a large, impressive, compelling, independent body of direct scientific support.[46] For many publishers, however, this is not a major problem. Their advertisements can link their programs to *related* research. Phonics programs, for example, can claim they're scientifically based because they teach phonics, which the Federally-funded National Reading Panel recognized as a building block of reading instruction. Like medications, however, some commercial phonics programs may be far less effective than others.
- Teachers, including excellent ones, seldom use programs exactly as they're designed, unless they're forced to use scripts, scripts that can ignore the needs of children, demoralize teachers, and provoke their resentment.[47] Often, teachers do not carefully follow scripts.
- The labor, expertise, and materials needed to assure the faithful implementation of reading programs used in RTI instruction, as specified in the programs' manuals, may exceed the teachers' and school's resources.[48]
- Many teachers lack adequate education in and support for applying the RTI-related methods they'll be required to use. In December 2008, Edweek, a national education newspaper, reported that a large portion of teachers knew little about RTI and had received little or no RTI training.[49]
- Teachers who are required to modify their instruction and evaluation routines for one or several children may face numerous time-management problems, giving them less time to work with individual children. Although this problem can be lessened if a school's RTI process forgoes highly-individualized programs and uses a standardized program or method, standardization may undermine the individualization needed to benefit the child being evaluated.[50]
- IDEA-2004 specifies neither the time required to determine the effectiveness of RTI-related instruction nor the criteria for determining success. For good reasons, it leaves these decisions to the evaluation group. This, however, can create major problems if the team is influenced by poor budgets, poor resources, poor knowledge, or administrative pressures.
- Many general education and special education teachers may resist two essential

components of RTI: frequently monitoring the effectiveness of instruction and diligently following the directions for the monitoring procedures. Some may lack sufficient knowledge, some may feel threatened, and some may feel overwhelmed with the relentless increase of mandated responsibilities.

- *No Child Left Behind* (NCLB) testing, scripted programs, and a desire to make monitoring quick and easy may result in quick, easy, and superficial monitoring that inadequately assesses progress and creates a narrow, unbalanced reading curriculum.[51]
- Teacher turnover is high in some schools and may well get higher, given budgetary problems, teacher layoffs, and high retirement rates. Thus, many general and special education classes are taught by new or relatively new teachers and teachers reassigned to new grades and subjects. Even with mentoring, in-service training, graduate courses, and coaching from reading specialists, these teachers may be ill equipped to effectively implement RTI. Simply put, RTI requires a great deal of on-site, hands-on education and support for teachers and high teacher morale. In many schools, both are missing.[52]
- With the relentless pressure of NCLB and State testing, many teachers and administrators may look at RTI as one more unnecessary administrative burden. Furthermore, because many schools judge teachers on their students' standardized test scores, many teachers do not want to teach children with or suspected of having learning disabilities.[53] These teachers may fear that RTI requirements will divert them from teaching to the standardized test, especially if the struggling readers' instructional needs are far more basic than those of their other students.
- General education teachers, special education teachers, and reading specialists may not have adequate time to work together. They may have mismatched schedules and too many competing obligations. Although collaboration among these groups is critical to RTI's success, administrators may not have made it a priority.
- IDEA-2004 does not require that RTI pull-out instruction be coordinated with on-going reading instruction in the struggling reader's general education classes. As many reading authorities have noted, coordination is critical for success:

> Pull-out programs are unlikely to be effective unless there is coordination between the classroom and the clinic [e.g., pull-out reading center]. Teachers must provide opportunities for classroom practice and application of the skills and techniques developed in the clinic. Similarly, clinicians can no longer ignore the content and context of classroom instruction, believing that remediation of some specific disability will transfer to other settings.[54]

Given our concerns, should you reject or oppose RTI? No. Many of our concerns may prove less dire than we think. Much depends on your district's RTI model and your school's resources and instructional culture. Moreover, you may not have a choice; as it can legally do, your district may have made RTI *part of its eligibility evaluation.* However, RTI may help your child. Think of it as extensive diagnostic teaching that provides critical information about your child's learning under different instructional conditions. In other words, how much does she benefit from this kind of reading instruction, in this setting, with this support?

Note that the last paragraph italicized the phrase, *part of its eligibility evaluation*. Under IDEA-2004, schools cannot use RTI as their entire evaluation for determining if struggling readers have learning disabilities. Schools must "use a variety of assessment tools and strategies to gather relevant functional, developmental, and academic information about the child."[55] Thus, your child's eligibility for special education services, like tutoring, does not depend solely on RTI data. RTI can be part but not all of an evaluation.

Our advice is to first discuss the details of your district's RTI process with the evaluation group, which generally includes your child's teacher. Pay particular attention to the details, as RTI procedures can vary greatly among districts and even among schools in a district. After analyzing the model and its details, if you believe any of our concerns are relevant, discuss and resolve them with the team. Then carefully monitor the RTI process so you know if the school is implementing it knowledgeably and skillfully for at least several weeks. Also, examine the data the school is required to collect about your child's responsiveness to RTI-related instruction. Finally, remember that RTI is only part of the eligibility process and that you can request a full evaluation—anytime. You can request it before RTI begins, during RTI, or after RTI.[56]

Point 5: Schools Should Distinguish between Academic Achievement and Performance. *'Academic achievement' generally refers to a child's performance in academic areas (e.g., reading or language arts, math, science, and history). We believe the definition could vary depending on a child's circumstance or situation, and therefore, we do not believe a definition of 'academic achievement' should be included in these regulations.[57].... [Frequently, children exhibit] a pattern of strengths and weaknesses in performance, achievement, or both, relative to age ... [and] State-approved grade level standards.[58]*

Comment. Unfortunately, IDEA-2004's regulations fail to adequately define *performance* and *achievement*, though at times, it's clear they differ. Look, for example, at how the regulations above list each separately and then use the word *both*: "A pattern of strengths and weaknesses in performance, achievement, or both."

IDEA-2004 is correct in distinguishing between the two as the difference is important and often striking. Here's how Cathy Spinelli, Professor and Director of the Special Education Program at St. Joseph's University in Philadelphia and an authority on assessing children, defines performance:

> Performance assessments are based on the *application* of knowledge and the use of meaningful, complex, relevant skills *to produce products.* They are a method of measuring progress by having students demonstrate, produce, perform, create, construct, build, plan, solve, apply, illustrate, explain, convince, or persuade, as opposed to regurgitating answers on a test form.[59]

It's also unfortunate that many schools ignore the differences between achievement and performance. This can hurt your child, immeasurably. Here's why. Schools that ignore the differences often determine eligibility for services and measure achievement and progress solely on scores from standardized achievement tests. Such tests can help—but they're not sufficient. Often they overestimate a child's abilities:

> Most standardized tests tend to provide a measure of a student's highest level of performance, or frustrational level, rather than of instructional or independent levels.[60]

Many professionals and parents mistakenly believe that achievement tests make clear what children can do. They don't. They don't tell anyone how successfully your child can combine achievement test knowledge with other knowledge or how she can apply it in unstructured situations, such as writing an essay that needs to draw on different kinds of reading materials.

To illustrate the difference between achievement testing and performance, answer this question: Would you knowingly fly with a pilot who earned an "A" on the standardized achievement test for landing the TreeHugger-785, but when landing it usually careened off the runway and snapped the propeller? We suspect that your answer sounds like ours: "Fly with him? Never. Great achievement test score, lousy performance. He'll kill someone."

So it is with some children. They may do well on standardized tests of reading achievement that asks them to read short passages and supply missing words, but do terribly in class because they can't comprehend and summarize long passages.

Howard has frequently dealt with this achievement-performance problem. Lisa, a composite of many struggling readers, was in the 6th grade. On several standardized reading tests she achieved grade equivalents around 6.0, which her IEP Team interpreted as mastery of 6th-grade reading. But subsequently her teachers found that she could not comprehend 5th-grade books. Often, when reading these books, her attention wandered, she fidgeted, she daydreamed, she ignored her assignments, she complained, "The books are too hard." When Howard gave her 4th-grade passages to read, passages that were much longer than those on the school's standardized tests, she became frustrated; she read the words quickly, with good accuracy, but had trouble understanding the passages.

For Lisa, the difference between achievement and performance was caused by the type of items on the achievement test and how the scores were calculated. A struggling reader's grade equivalent or standardized score simply compares the number of items she answered correctly to the number correctly answered by students in different grades, not to what she can actually do on tasks that are typically assigned.

Lisa suffered unnecessarily because her IEP Team didn't understand that standardized tests are, in many ways, economic substitutes for working with children to learn what they have mastered and what they need to learn. In addition to standardized achievement testing— which can be valuable—schools can and should measure performance. Sometimes, achievement test scores and performance on typical school tasks are strikingly out of sync.

So, what can you do? Always ask the school to complement achievement tests with perfor-mance tasks, like your child's ability to *independently* read the actual books the school assigns at different grades, to *independently* write answers to end-of-chapter questions, or to *indepen-dently* summarize a section of a chapter.[61] Such information—how well your child performs typical school tasks—is far more critical to developing IEP goals and to daily instruction than achievement test scores.[62]

Point 6: Schools Must Respect the Parents' Role in Evaluations. *The [school] must make reasonable efforts to obtain the informed consent from the parent for an initial evaluation ... [and] ... any reevaluation.[63]... As part of an initial evaluation [or] ... reevaluation, the IEP Team [which includes the parents] and other qualified professionals, as appropriate, must ... review existing evaluation data on the child, including ... evaluations and information provided by the parents ... [and] on the basis of that review, and input from the child's parents, identify what additional data, if any, are needed to determine ... whether the child is a child with a disability ... and the educational needs of the child.... [The school] must notify the child's parents of ... the right of the parents to request an assessment to determine whether the child continues to be a child with a disability, and to determine the child's educational needs[64].... In interpreting evaluation data ... [the school] must ... draw upon information from a variety of sources, including ... parent input ... [and] ensure that information obtained ... is documented and carefully considered.[65]*

Comment. IDEA-2004 is clear: Parents have an important role in evaluations. Evaluations are not the sole domain of schools.

IDEA-2004 does this by specifying your rights. Your child's school must, for example, give you details about the proposed evaluations of your child and seek your informed consent; the school cannot evaluate her on a whim. Moreover, when planning the evaluation, it must consider your requests for additional information.

Because the contents of your child's IEP should directly flow from her evaluations, because IDEA-2004's regulations say that when developing the IEP, the IEP Team "must consider ... the concerns of the parents for enhancing the education of their child,"[66] and because you need specific information from your child's evaluations to help write her IEP, school personnel cannot arbitrarily dismiss your request for specific information as unimportant and your opinions and information as uninformed.

But what if you have concerns about the evaluation? What if your concerns are vague, even to you? What if you don't know what information is needed? What if you think the evaluation group is ignoring critical needs?

Our answer: Look at the questions raised throughout this book. You can find a rich list of questions near the end of chapter 3, under "A Comprehensive Reading Evaluation." They deal with critical reading needs and roadblocks. In addition to reading, they deal with your child's motivation, confidence, and ability to work independently. Like pure reading competence, these abilities can determine your child's success or failure. If you suspect that your child struggles in any of these areas, request that they be evaluated. Do so by asking specific questions, like those we listed.

Also, look at the questions about your child's teacher and classroom situation. The reason is simple: The quality of teaching and the nature of your child's class can dramatically affect her success or failure. You can find many of these questions in chapter 2, under "Instructional Problems," in chapter 7, under "Observe Your Child in Class," and in chapter 10, under "Your District's Programs."

If you agree to an evaluation, IDEA-2004 encourages you to provide information to help guide it. Moreover, the evaluation group must carefully consider your information. The reason is practical: You know your child in ways the school never will. Accordingly, your insights about her needs, habits, likes and dislikes can sharpen the evaluation's focus. By actively participating, you can give the evaluation group the information it needs to design an evaluation likely to identify all your child's educational needs, to more accurately interpret its results, and to develop an IEP that effectively addresses all her needs.

Perhaps because IDEA-2004's regulations are so legalistic, many parents forget this next statement, a statement that transcends the law's individual provisions and embodies its spirit: Parents are *important* members of their child's evaluation group, eligibility group, and IEP Team. They have a right to participate in *meaningful* ways and to influence decisions.

Our advice: Know your rights. Ask questions. Make requests. Participate.

KEEP IN MIND

Keep in mind that even the best evaluation is only a starting point. It does not guarantee that your child will get a reading program that produces meaningful progress. Critical to increasing the odds that her program will succeed is your understanding of the IEP process, IEP Teams, IEP components, and often ignored principles for developing and monitoring IEPs. Also critical is your knowledge of alternatives to IDEA-2004 and pitfalls to avoid. You can find valuable information about these topics in the next three chapters:

- Chapter 10: The Program Planning Process and the IEP Team
- Chapter 11: The IEP
- Chapter 12: Principles, Options, and Pitfalls

ENDNOTES

---

[1] The school "proposing to conduct an initial evaluation to determine if a child qualifies as a child with a disability ... must ... obtain informed consent ... from the parent ... before conducting the evaluation.... Parental consent for initial evaluation must not be construed as consent for initial provision of special education and related services.... The [school] must make reasonable efforts to obtain the informed consent from the parent for an initial evaluation" (34 CFR §300.300).

IDEA-2004's discussion of its regulations clarifies the term *informed consent*: "The definition of consent requires a parent to be *fully informed* of all information relevant to the activity for which consent is sought. The definition also requires a parent to agree *in writing* to an activity for which consent is sought. Therefore, whenever consent is used in these regulations, it means that the consent is both informed and in writing" (34 CFR Discussion, p. 46551, italics added).

The Discussions in IDEA-2004's rules and regulations are the interpretations of the U. S. Department of Education. Usually, the courts have great respect for the agency's interpretations of rules and regulations. Discussions, however, do not have the force of law.

[2] 34 CFR 300.300.

[3] 34 CFR 300.300, Amended December 21, 2008, italics added.

[4] 34 CFR 300.300, Amended December 21, 2008; 34 CFR Discussion, Amended December 1, 2008, p. 73011.

[5] 34 CFR 300.300, Amended December 21, 2008.

[6] 34 CFR Discussion, Amended December 1, 2008, p. 73009, italics added.

[7] 34 CFR Discussion, Amended December 1, 2008, p. 73009.

[8] 34 CFR § 300.304, bold added.

[9] 34 CFR § 300.308, italics added.

[10] Some States, like New Jersey, distinguish between reading specialist and reading teacher. In New Jersey, for example, certification as a reading specialist requires far more reading education than certification as a reading teacher. Other States, like New York, have only one certification in reading.

[11] 34 CFR § 300.321.

[12] 34 CFR § 300.321, italics added.

[13] 34 CFR § 300.303.

[14] 34 CFR § 300.304.

[15] We refer to assessment instruments and strategies as measurement tools, as that's what they are. They're tools to measure current knowledge, skill, and ability. They're nothing more. We hope this removes their mystique. And like all tools, they're never better than the people who use them. In this case, they're never better than the people who administer them and interpret the results.

[16] No test score is perfectly accurate or reliable. Every score contains what test experts call error. Thus, if a child has not changed on what "Test A" measures, a second administration, a week later, will generally produce a similar score. A child who earns a standard score of 86 on the first administration of a highly reliable test might earn a standard score of 84 on the second administration, a week later. Knowledgeable evaluators know there's no difference between the two scores. The two point difference was probably due to chance or error. If the test is highly unreliable, however, and your child's ability on what the test measures has not changed much, the scores might be vastly different. If she earned an 86 on the first administration, a week later she might earn a 73 on the second administration. This vast 13 point error makes it impossible to determine your child's "true" score, which can be very costly to your child.

[17] Most large libraries, for example, subscribe to Buros *Mental Measurements Yearbook*, which, over the decades, has compiled thousands of reviews from leading scholars and is constantly updated. If your school library or local library does not subscribe, school personnel can download reviews for specific tests and instruments from the Buros Institute at the University of Nebraska: buros.unl.edu/buros/jsp/search.jsp.

[18] More than a quarter century ago, the world's largest association of reading professionals, the International Reading Association, condemned grade equivalents: "The misuse of grade equivalents has lead to such mistaken assumptions as: (1) a grade equivalent of 5.0 on a reading test means that the test-taker will be able to read fifth-grade material, and (2) a grade equivalent of 10.0 by a fourth-grade student means that student reads like a tenth grader even though the test may include only sixth-grade material as its top level of difficulty …. [The Association] strongly advocates that those who administer standardized reading tests abandon the practice of using grade equivalents to report performance" (Resolution passed by the Delegates Assembly of the International Reading Association, April 1981. Reprinted in Baumann, J. F., 1988. *Reading Assessment: An Instructional Decision-making Perspective.* Columbus, OH: Merrill, p. 41).

[19] Grade equivalents should not be used to make statistical comparisons between IQ and achievement scores. If an "IQ-achievement" discrepancy score is calculated—which we advocate against—other scores, like standard scores, should be used. They have essential mathematical properties that grade equivalents lack.

[20] Fuchs, L. S., & Mellard, D. F., 2007. Helping educators discuss responsiveness to intervention with parents and students. National Research Center on Learning Disabilities (available for download from http://www.nrcld.org/resource_kit/general/Q&AEducators2007.pdf).

In discussing the IQ-achievement discrepancy model, Fuchs and Mellard, like many, call it the "wait to fail" model. Their article provides an excellent overview of the Response to Intervention (RTI) model, an alternative to "wait to fail." As part of an evaluation for learning disabilities, IDEA-2004 allows schools to replace "wait to fail" with RTI. Although RTI has potential merit, schools, State departments of education, universities, and the U.S. Office of Education will have to do a great deal of work to make it practical and successful. An examination of documents at www.nrcld.org suggests that the U. S. Office of Education is making a good start.

[21] Leslie, L., & Caldwell, J., 2005. *Qualitative Reading Inventory-4.* Boston: Allyn & Bacon.

[22] 34 CFR § 300.304, bold added.

[23] You may have noticed that we used the words *evaluation* and *assess.* Although many professionals and parents use the words *evaluation* and *assessment* interchangeably, their meanings can differ.

"The primary purpose of assessments," notes Cathleen G. Spinelli, "is to obtain information to facilitate effective decision making" (2006, *Classroom Assessment for Students in Special and General Education* (2nd ed.). Upper Saddle River, NJ: Merrill Prentice Hall, p. 4). Evaluation extends assessment by interpreting data and making decisions. "Evaluation," notes Gerald Tindal and Douglas Marston, "utilizes criteria for making a judgment, decision, or selection. It consists of analyzing a problem or situation to determine factors that one should consider in making a judgment or decision and weighing each of these factors…. It involves anticipating the consequences of an act and then judging whether those consequences are acceptable" (1990, *Classroom-based Assessment: Evaluating Instructional Outcomes.* Columbus, OH: Merrill Publishing, p. 35).

This distinction between assessment and evaluation is more than meaningless academic dribble. Too often, professionals accept assessment data at face value without thinking about the meaning of the results and probable explanations. As Brian R. Bryant, J. Lee Wiederholt, and Diane P. Bryant so justifiably assert, "Too often examiners forget the dictum that 'tests don't diagnose, people do' and base their diagnoses exclusively on test results, a hazardous enterprise at best. Test results are merely observations, not diagnoses. They specify a performance level at a given time under a particular situation, but they do not tell the examiner why a person performs as he or she did" (2004. Manual for the *Gray Diagnostic Reading Tests-Second Edition*. Austin, TX: Pro-Ed, p. 34). This latter, critical process—analysis and interpretation—is evaluation.

Despite these differences, listen carefully for how school personnel use *assessment* and *evaluation*. Many use these words interchangeably to mean listing test results without doing the analysis and thought needed to make informed, valid interpretations.

[24] Throughout this book, we interpret the laws from an educational and psychological perspective, not a legal one. To function in special education, we, as an educator and a psychologist, have had to interpret and apply the applicable laws. In a sense, the applicable laws define special education.

[25] Salvia, J., Ysseldyke, J. E., & Bolt, S., 2007. *Assessment in Special Education* (10th ed.). Boston: Houghton-Mifflin Company, pp. 307-308.

[26] "For centuries, philosophers, psychologists, educators, and laypeople have debated the meaning of intelligence. Numerous definitions of the term intelligence have been proposed, with each definition serving as a stimulus for counterdefinitions and counterproposals.... Debate and controversy have flourished about [what intelligence tests] ... measure.... No one, however, has seen a specific thing called 'intelligence'.... All tests, including intelligence tests, assess samples of behavior.... In most cases, the kinds of behavior sampled reflect a test author's conception of intelligence. The behavior samples are combined in different ways by different authors, usually on the basis of the ways in which they view the concept of intelligence.... Intelligence tests differ markedly" (Salvia, Ysseldyke, & Bolt, 2007, pp. 281, 282, 331).

[27] Although the word *current* is implied in the sentence, we made it explicit because many people erroneously believe that intelligence is static—it can't change. It can.

[28] Margolis, H., & D'Onofrio, A., 2007. Review of the Gray Diagnostic Reading Tests-Second Edition. *Mental Measurements Yearbook* (17th ed.) (pp. 356-360). Lincoln, NB: Buros Institute of Mental Measurements, University of Nebraska, pp. 357, 359.

[29] Margolis, H., & D'Onofrio, A., 2007. Review of the Woodcock Johnson III Diagnostic Reading Battery. *Mental Measurements Yearbook* (17th ed.) (pp. 866-872). Lincoln, NB: Buros Institute of Mental Measurements, University of Nebraska, p. 871, italics added.

[30] Lipson, M. Y., & Wixson, K. K., 2003. *Assessment and Instruction of Reading Disability: An Interactive Approach* (3rd ed.). Boston: Allyn & Bacon, p. 116.

[31] Sternberg, R. I., 1998. Abilities are forms of developing expertise. *Educational Researcher, 27* (3), 11-20, p. 17.

[32] 34 CFR § 300.310.

[33] 34 CFR § 300.311.

[34] Unfortunately, this is an old and frequent problem. "One of the most serious problems in elementary school classrooms today is the very large percentage of children who are kept reading at their frustration level. If the book is too difficult, if too many new concepts appear and are not repeated several times, and if the decoding process of unlocking new words has not been learned, boys and girls spend much time in school trying to gain information that is beyond their grasp.... Learning does not

progress when children work at the frustration level" (Zintz, M. V., & Maggart, Z. R., 1984. *The Reading Process: The Teacher and the Learner.* Dubuque, IA: Wm. C. Brown, p. 92).

[35] Lipson & Wixson, 2003, pp. 153, 155, italics added.

[36] "[The evaluation group] ... must decide to— (1) Use information from an observation in routine classroom instruction and monitoring of the child's performance that was done *before* the child was referred for an evaluation; *or* (2) Have at least one member of the [evaluation group] ... conduct an observation of the child's academic performance in the regular classroom *after* the child has been referred for an evaluation" (34 CFR § 300.310, italics added).

[37] "As part of an initial evaluation (if appropriate) and as part of any reevaluation... the IEP Team [which includes the child's parents] ... must ... review existing evaluation data on the child ... and ... on the basis of that review, and input from the child's parents, identify *what additional data, if any, are needed* to determine ... whether the child is a child with a disability ... and the educational needs of the child" (34 CFR § 300.305, italics added).

[38] Ysseldyke, J. E., & Christenson, S., 1993. *The Instructional Environment System II (TIES): A System to Identify a Student's Instructional Needs.* Longmont, CO: Sopris West.

[39] Giving the evaluation group a set of written questions is important for several reasons. It clarifies your thinking and results in more focused questions. It provides specific guidance to the team and the observer. It structures the follow-up discussion. It becomes part of the record. And finally, it communicates, in a precise and reasonable way, that you're knowledgeable and serious about making your child's program succeed. This helps to establish your credibility.

[40] 34 CFR § 300.304, italics added.

[41] 34 CFR § 300.307.

[42] 34 CFR § 300.311.

[43] Some schools might call this tier-2 as the method used differed from that used with most of the class's other children.

[44] RTI differs among districts. As Douglas and Lynn Fuchs, two outstanding special education researchers, have noted, RTI can begin with yearly, systematic screening to identify students at risk for learning disabilities. First, an at-risk subgroup of students is identified; to do this, districts can use various methods and criteria. Then, the at-risk children's "responsiveness to general education instruction is monitored.... At-risk children unresponsive to classroom instruction are given more intensive instruction at a second tier, or level, either in or outside the classroom." After screening, districts will use different models of RTI: "Different RTI versions have two to four tiers of instruction.... The nature of the academic intervention changes at each tier, becoming more intensive as a student moves across the tiers. Increasing intensity is achieved by (a) using more teacher-centered, systematic, and explicit (e.g., scripted) instruction; (b) conducting it more frequently; (c) adding to its duration; (d) creating smaller and more homogenous student groupings; or (e) relying on instructors with greater expertise" (Fuchs, D., & Fuchs, L., 2006. Introduction to Response to Intervention: What, why, and how valid is it? *Reading Research Quarterly, 41* (1), 93-99, pp. 93, 94).

[45] "Although RTI [response to intervention, response to instruction] represents a promising way of addressing many issues associated with SLD [specific learning disabilities] identification, unanswered implementation questions remain.... We must consider how well schools could implement

an assessment process that incorporates significant changes in staff roles and responsibilities while lengthening the duration of disability determination assessment.... Current research literature provides scant scientific evidence for how RTI applies in curricular areas other than early reading and beyond primary or elementary school-age children" (Johnson, E., Mellard, D.F., Fuchs, D., & McKnight, M.A., 2006. *Responsiveness to Intervention (RTI): How to Do It.* Lawrence, KS: National Research Center on Learning Disabilities, p. i.4; retrieved 2/21/08, from htwww.nrcld.org/rti_manual/pages/RTIManualIntroduction.pdf).

[46] One example of the inadequate research supporting many reading programs is provided by Dr. Elfrieda Hiebert, recipient of the International Reading Association's Citation of Merit. After examining many current reading programs, she concluded "Existing beginning reading programs leave many questions unanswered. Components appear to have been added and adjusted in response to the mandates of policymakers and perceptions of the wishes of consumers rather than on the basis of ... what children need to learn to become successful readers and how they acquire this information" (Hiebert, E. H., Martin, L. A., & Menon, S., 2005. Are there alternatives in reading textbooks? An examination of three beginning reading programs. *Reading & Writing Quarterly: Overcoming Learning Difficulties, 21* (1), 7-32, p. 30).... "Relative to the amount of the expenditure on texts [such as basal-reading programs], the amount of research on appropriate texts for beginning and struggling readers has been inconsequential. This *sparse research base* is surprising in light of claims by policymakers and publishers that the current basal-reading programs have been validated empirically.... The massive swings in text features for beginning readers over the past 20 years ... have had little research examination (although an extensive amount of rhetoric).... This seesawing of policies has resulted in texts with features that are *contrary* to long-standing findings ... that beginning readers are challenged by multisyllabic words and ... that developing readers require at least a modicum of repetition with some words to develop automatic word recognition" (Hiebert, E. H., 2009. The (mis) match between texts and students who depend on schools to become literate. In E. H. Hiebert & M. Sailors (Eds.), *Finding the Right Texts: What Works for Beginning and Struggling Readers* (pp. 1-20). New York: The Guilford Press, pp. 1-2).

[47] "There is evidence from multiple studies of what scripted programs may do to the spirits of teachers and learners. Many claim that forced teaching of these models creates dispirited teachers who exercise subtle and open acts of resistance, feel hopeless, frustrated, and drained, and consider their professional decision making to be undermined. In one look at the data we present, the instruction in a few of the scripted classrooms seemed to put some children to sleep, cause tension in some classrooms, and was startlingly unresponsive to students' emotional and academic needs" (McIntyre, E., Rightmyer, E. C., & Petrosko, J. P., 2008. Scripted and non-scripted reading instructional models: Effects on the phonics and reading achievement of first-grade struggling readers. *Reading & Writing Quarterly: Overcoming Learning Difficulties, 24* (4), 377-407, 383, references removed).

[48] The National Association of State Directors of Special Education recently concluded, "Perhaps the most serious threat to attaining the effects that are possible with use of Response to Intervention (RtI) is the degree to which implementation correctly occurs. There is a long history of poor implementation integrity in school systems for intervention, and this is likely to be a persistent challenge to RtI.... Several scholars have suggested that implementation integrity of RtI will be the major

obstacle to overcome because data will be needed to show that the interventions were implemented as designed" (Griffiths, A., Parson, L. B., Burns, M. K., VanDerHeyden, A., & Tilly, W. D., 2007. *Response to Intervention: Research for Practice*. Alexandra, VA: National Association of State Directors of Special Education, Inc., p. 153).

[49] Samuels, C. A., 2008 December 5. Response to Intervention on NEA's Agenda. Edweek; retrieved 12/10/08, from http://www.edweek.org/ew/articles/2008/12/10/15rti.h28.html?tmp=1916812017.

[50] Michael Yell and Erik Drasgow of the University of South Carolina noted that IDEA-2004 requires "that assessments must be matched carefully and precisely to referral concerns and to a student's behavior and learning needs.... [They] must be individually tailored to each student" (2007. Assessment for eligibility under IDEIA and the 2006 regulations. *Assessment for Effective Intervention*, *32* (4), 202-213, p. 203; the online version can be found at: http://aei.sagepub.com/cgi/content/abstract/32/4/). It's unclear if standardized RTI interventions always meet this requirement. Thus, in some instances it may be possible that standardizing on a core program may run counter to IDEA-2004's requirements. As always, the devil is in the details.

[51] "Ideally, instruction would dictate the content and form of assessment, but it is clear that ... the desire for quick and easy information has [often] resulted in a narrowing of the reading curriculum. If progress is monitored on only one or two dimensions of reading [e.g., phonics], then these one or two things will become the most important focus for instruction, at the expense of the other equally important components [e.g., comprehension]" (Lipson, M. Y., & Wixson, K. K., 2008. New IRA commission will address issues. *Reading Today, 26* (1), 1, 5, p. 5).

[52] The day we edited this section on RTI, the *New York Times* reported that New York State's governor proposed major budget cuts that would create havoc in many schools: "School districts across New York State said on Wednesday that the governor's proposed midyear reductions in state aid would be painful to absorb, leading in some cases to staff reductions, larger class sizes, and fewer sports and extracurricular programs" (Hu, W., 2008 November 13. Schools See Pain Ahead if the State Cuts Aid. *The New York Times*; retrieved 11/13/08, from http://www.nytimes.com/2008/11/13/nyregion/13schools.html?ref=education). Unfortunately, many other States are proposing similar budget cuts. Such cuts can severely undermine RTI and the services children need to overcome reading disabilities.

[53] Some districts have proposed using students' test scores to make tenure and salary decisions. In 2008, the New York State legislature stopped New York City from using test scores to help make tenure decisions. The City's attempt infuriated many of its teachers (Medina, J., 2008 March 18. Bill Would Bar Linking Class Test Scores to Tenure. *The New York Times*; retrieved 4/6/08, from http://www.nytimes.com/2008/03/18/nyregion/18teacher.html?_r=1&scp=4&sq=teacher+%2B+testing&st=nyt&oref=slogin).

Also, in 2008, the Schools Chancellor for Washington, D.C. imposed an evaluation system on teachers that was based "primarily on student test scores and other achievement benchmarks." The head of the teachers' union denounced the Chancellor's action, charging that she was trying to "terminate" teachers (Turque, B., 2008 October 3. Rhee bypasses talks, Imposes dismissal plan. *The Washington Post*; retrieved 10/5/08, from http://www.washingtonpost.com/wp-dyn/content/article/2008/10/02/AR2008100201672.html?hpid=moreheadlines). As you can imagine, the Chancellor's action angered many teachers.

54   Lipson, M. Y., & Wixson, K. K., 1997. *Assessment and Instruction of Reading Disability: An Interactive Approach* (2nd ed.). New York: Longman, p. 58.

55   34 CFR § 300.304. The inappropriateness of using *only* RTI was made clear by the Federally-funded National Research Center on Learning Disabilities (NRCLD). It noted that "RTI can be used as ... one part of the evaluation for the determination of SLD [specific learning disabilities].... Although RTI addresses some significant shortcomings in current approaches to SLD identification ... RTI should be considered to be one important element within the larger context of the SLD determination process. RTI as one component of SLD determination is insufficient as a sole criterion for accurately determining SLD" (Johnson, Mellard, Fuchs, & McKnight, 2006, p. i.2).

56   34 CFR Discussion, p. 46658; 34 CFR § 300.311.

57   34 CFR Discussion, p. 46662.

58   34 CFR § 300.311.

59   Spinelli, 2006, p. 92, italics added.

60   Manzo, A. V., & Manzo, U. C., 1993. *Literacy Disorders: Holistic Diagnosis and Remediation*. Ft. Worth, TX: Harcourt Brace Jovanovich, p. 68.

61   By asking for performance measures, you're not asking for anything unusual. In fact, most textbooks on educational assessment devote considerable space to them. In her excellent book on assessment, Cathleen G. Spinelli notes that "performance assessment of reading abilities measures specific skill components and evaluates *demonstrations* of reading abilities. During performance assessment students read a passage or story for a purpose, use one or more cognitive skills as they construct meaning from the text, and write about or perform a task about what they read, usually in response to a prompt or task" (2006, p. 274, italics added).

62   You may also want to ask the school to compare your child's achievement test scores to tasks she may need to perform outside of school, like reading menus, comprehending software manuals, and writing letters.

63   34 CFR § 300.300.

64   34 CFR § 300.305.

65   34 CFR § 300.306.

66   34 CFR § 300.324.

CHAPTER 10
PROGRAM PLANNING AND THE IEP TEAM

Special education helps some children, but not others.

If your child's reading will likely improve because of the programs, protections, and services available only through special education, consider it. If this isn't the case, and your child doesn't have other learning disabilities, avoid it.

YOUR DISTRICT'S PROGRAMS

To determine if special education can help your child, you need to learn what your district's special education programs offer. To get a realistic understanding, speak to parents in your district whose children, because of reading disabilities, get special education services. Ask to see the district's written plan for special education and any documents evaluating the effectiveness of its reading and special education programs.[1] Ask to observe your district's programs.

Observe general education classes in which special education or reading teachers provide extra reading instruction; these services may be called in-class support, push-in support, or in-class resource programs. Observe pull-out resource programs and self-contained classes for students with reading problems, often called learning disabilities classes. Speak to the staff, look at the students. Ask yourself:

- Are classes well organized?
- Do the teachers use time productively?
- Do the teachers model and explain what they're teaching?
- Do the teachers encourage reading, writing, and oral expression throughout the day?
- Are the children good role models?
- Do the children treat each other with respect?
- Do the children get interesting work?
- Do the children enjoy the work?
- Do the children often work in small, interactive groups?
- If children have difficulty, do they get tutoring or personalized instruction in small groups?
- Are the children intellectually challenged or bored or frustrated?
- Are all children productively included in all school activities?
- Do the children often have fun?

Ideally, each answer is "yes." Now, answer these questions:

- In which program or placement will my child most likely be happy: a general education class with in-class reading support, a pull-out program for reading, a special class, a combination of these, or something else?[2]
- Which program or placement will most likely improve my child's reading?

Finally, try to observe specific teachers—it's what teachers do, more than anything else, that makes special education special. Children benefit most from highly knowledgeable, skilled teachers who carefully and systematically:

- Teach children the knowledge, concepts, and learning strategies they must master to succeed in school and the community.
- Plan lessons to help children achieve specific goals.
- Apply valid instructional principles and strategies to meet children's learning goals.
- Divide complex concepts and activities into manageable chunks, and then, as each is mastered, teach children to combine them.
- Present children with intellectually challenging lessons that motivate rather than frustrate them.
- Use reading materials that match children's instructional and independent reading levels.
- Use reading materials that children find interesting, useful, or important.
- Teach children in small, interactive groups.
- Structure lessons and assignments to produce moderate challenges and high levels of success.
- Schedule frequent practice sessions to help children quickly and accurately apply important knowledge, skills, and learning strategies.
- Monitor children's progress and quickly revise instruction to eliminate difficulties.
- Give children frequent task-related feedback that explicitly tells them what they did that produced success, and, if necessary, shows them how to improve their work.
- Engage children in activities that promote their social and emotional development.
- Integrate children in general education classes, in ways that advance their development, academically, socially, and emotionally.

To succeed, teachers need very small classes with the right interpersonal and academic mix of students. Teachers also need lots of time and opportunity to:

- Give children extra help.
- Prepare and monitor lessons.
- Coordinate children's programs with general education teachers, other special education teachers, and the reading specialist.
- Plan joint lessons and team teach with other teachers.
- Work with parents.
- Observe other teachers teaching.
- Extend and refine their professional skills.

Sadly, this picture seldom reflects reality. Other than having fewer students, each with educational difficulties—difficulties that typically require extensive attention—you'll often find little that's special about special education. Many special education classes emphasize unambitious or overly ambitious goals,[3] drill sheets, unproven instructional strategies, watered-down general education curricula, activities that constantly frustrate children, and narrow and unimportant reading activities. Such practices stymie progress.

Whatever the setting, struggling readers require teachers who are conscientious and extremely knowledgeable about reading disabilities. Such teachers need to provide reading instruction that's focused, explicit, diagnostic, and responsive to struggling readers' immediate needs and difficulties. In special education, it's often difficult to find such teachers and instruction. In many cases, struggling readers make little or no progress in reading because their reading programs are planned by teachers and other school personnel, such as learning consultants and school psychologists, with little or no coursework in reading disabilities.[4] In New Jersey, for example, certification as a special education teacher requires little coursework in reading disabilities despite the fact that they often provide the bulk of reading instruction to struggling readers.[5]

By now, you're probably discouraged, given that teachers, highly knowledgeable and skilled in reading disabilities, are often unavailable. Fortunately, there's also good news.

First, many special education teachers and support staff, such as learning consultants, work diligently and creatively to help children, despite less than ideal backgrounds and teaching conditions. Some seek additional education in reading disabilities.

Second, reading instruction can be improved if highly knowledgeable reading specialists provide ongoing consultation to teachers. Consequently, many States and districts are beginning to hire reading specialists, often referred to as reading or literacy coaches, to help teachers improve instruction.

Third, research has produced a great deal of readily available knowledge about how to teach reading effectively.

Fourth, if you understand and skillfully apply the key provisions of *the Individuals with Disabilities Education Improvement Act of 2004* (IDEA-2004) and *Section 504 of the Rehabilitation Act of 1973* (Section 504), you can often improve the quality of your child's reading program and encourage or compel your child's school to provide the services and accommodations he needs and is entitled to.

For designing your child's program, carrying it out, instructing him, monitoring progress, and guaranteeing services, one legally-mandated component of IDEA-2004 is invaluable: the Individualized Education Program, usually referred to as the IEP. Although we will soon discuss the IEP planning process and the IEP Team in more detail, we urge you to remember what one Federal Circuit Court said about the IEP:

> The IEP is more than a mere exercise in public relations. It forms the basis for a handicapped child's entitlement for an individualized and appropriate education. Thus, the importance of the development of the IEP to meet the individualized needs of a handicapped child cannot be underestimated.[6]

Although not panaceas, IDEA-2004 and Section 504 can help make special education special in the finest sense. Understanding several key provisions of these laws can provide you with the leverage you need to dramatically increase your child's odds of becoming a competent, motivated reader. Regrettably, if you don't understand and don't know how to use these laws, he may not get the program he needs.

IDEA-2004 AND SECTION 504

All school districts must comply with IDEA-2004 and Section 504, which give you and your child many rights and protections. Under IDEA-2004, for example, schools must:

- Comply with your request to initially determine if your child has a disability and to identify his educational needs.[7]
- Get your consent to evaluate your child.[8] If you consent to an initial evaluation, it must be "full and individual."[9]
- Use assessment strategies and materials that are reliable and valid for the purposes used.[10]
- Evaluate your child in all areas of suspected disability.[11]
- Use multiple sources of information to determine eligibility for special education, including an observation of your child in his regular classroom.[12]
- Invite you to help determine your child's eligibility for special education.[13]
- Get your consent to begin special education and related services.[14]

If your child is found eligible for special education under IDEA-2004 *and* you agree that the school should provide services, the school must abide by IDEA-2004's many requirements. For example, it must:

- Work with you to write an Individualized Education Program (IEP) that states, among other things, your child's levels of academic achievement; a set of measurable annual goals that his program will help him achieve; the placement that for him is least restrictive; the related services he will get, such as speech and language therapy; how the school will measure his progress toward meeting his goals and when the school will provide you with periodic progress reports; the supports school personnel will get to help your child achieve his annual goals.[15]
- Work with you to develop an IEP that considers your child's strengths, the results of his most recent evaluation, and his academic, developmental, and functional needs.[16]
- Treat you as a full-fledged member of your child's IEP Team, the Team that plans his IEP.[17]
- Schedule IEP meetings with you at mutually agreed upon times and places.[18]
- Give you periodic reports on your child's progress toward meeting his IEP goals.[19]
- Meet with you *at least* annually to assess your child's progress, and, if appropriate, revise his IEP.[20]
- Comply with your request for one reevaluation a year, although more are permissible if you and the school agree.[21]
- Allow you to raise questions and concerns and make recommendations at evaluation, IEP, and reevaluation meetings.[22]

The rights, protections, and requirements described in IDEA-2004 are not mere formalities: They're obligations that schools must follow. For example, schools must do more than develop IEPs with the specific components described in IDEA-2004—they must implement them exactly as written. Notice, for example, that IDEA-2004's regulations use the phrase *in effect*:

> At the beginning of each school year, each [school] … must have *in effect*, for each child with a disability … an IEP.[23]

Also notice that it uses the phrases *as soon as possible* and *in accordance*:

> Each [school] must ensure that … *as soon as possible* following development of the IEP, special education and related services are made available to the child *in accordance* with the child's IEP.[24]

And the U. S. Department of Education's (USDOE) discussion of IEPs states:

> The [school] will be bound by the IEP that is developed at an IEP Team meeting.[25]

If your child's school is not providing him with a service listed in his IEP—such as the 45 minutes of extra reading instruction it lists as a related service—you can invoke the law's power by formally requesting your State to investigate or by requesting a formal due process hearing. As with much of IDEA-2004, the rules and regulations governing due process hearings are precise and extensive.

In contrast to IDEA-2004, Section 504's regulations for children in school are far less precise and extensive. For many reasons, which we discuss in chapter 12, Section 504 is generally less powerful and less responsive to struggling readers' needs than IDEA-2004. Nevertheless, if your child is ineligible for services under IDEA-2004, Section 504 might help you get them.

As with all laws, you must study IDEA-2004 and Section 504's statues, regulations, and the government's published discussions of them. These tell everyone, including schools, judges, hearing officers, and State departments of education, how to use and interpret IDEA-2004 and Section 504. Often, the laws and their regulations have provisions and language of enormous help in understanding your rights and the obligations of schools. Moreover, the more you study them, the more your questions and comments will convey knowledge—knowledge that conveys power. Often, this alone can get needed services.

The remainder of this chapter discusses the IEP program planning process, the IEP Team, and your right to challenge the decisions of the school and the IEP Team. It does this by presenting and discussing excerpts from IDEA-2004. If difficulties arise about your child's IEP, you might share these excerpts and our comments with school personnel. In many cases, the excerpts will add authority to your concerns, recommendations, and requests. They may well cause school personnel to change their minds.

THE IEP PROGRAM PLANNING PROCESS

Point 1: IEP Meetings. *The IEP Team ... reviews the child's IEP periodically, but not less than annually, to determine whether the annual goals for the child are being achieved; and ... revises the IEP, as appropriate, to address ... any lack of expected progress toward the annual goals ... and in the general education curriculum, if appropriate*[26]*.... The parent can request an additional IEP Team meeting at any time.*[27]

Comment. Your child's first IEP provides the standard for subsequent IEPs: So make sure each component is exemplary. To help you, the next chapter discusses many of the IEP components in detail and provides explicit guidance for developing each, including the Present Levels of Academic Achievement and Functional Performance, measureable annual goals and short-term objectives, related services, involvement and progress in the general education curriculum, and placement in the least restrictive environment.

Ideally, at IEP meetings, evaluations and progress are fully discussed and programs are carefully designed. Regrettably, school personnel often rush through these meetings, seeking signatures. Typically, such IEPs are terrible. If the school proposes an IEP that's inadequate to meet your child needs, don't sign it. Instead, express your concerns and ask for a follow-up meeting. Ask for additional meetings until the IEP is satisfactory.

If, during the year, you suspect that your child's progress is poor, request both specific information about his progress (see our monitoring recommendations in chapter 7) and a new IEP meeting, even if the current IEP is only six-weeks old. Although the following is obvious, it's often ignored: Keeping children in reading programs in which they struggle hurts them.

Under IDEA-2004, once you've agreed to an IEP for the school year, and you request that it be revised, the entire IEP Team need not meet with you to revise it. Instead, you can agree to meet with one or two IEP Team members. If you do this, we recommend two things. First, make sure that the Team members have the expertise needed to suggest effective changes and are committed to meeting your child's needs. Second, make sure that your child's teachers and related service providers understand the changes, agree with them, know how to implement them, have the resources to do so, and carefully monitor their effects.

Throughout this section, we referred to IEPs as annual documents. You may, however, be offered the option of a multi-year IEP, which IDEA-2004 may allow some States to offer.[28] Our opinion about multi-year IEPs is simple and unwavering: They're a terrible idea—reject them.

If you lack confidence in your understanding of IEP issues and the IEP process and think that you can't adequately represent your child's needs at IEP meetings, we strongly recommend that you consult with an independent reading specialist who can fully understand your child's needs, is skilled in group dynamics and problem solving, thoroughly understands IDEA-2004 and the IEP process, and knows how to monitor reading. By asking the specialist to examine your child's progress and attend his IEP meetings, you may dramatically increase your child's odds of getting the program he needs.

THE IEP TEAM

Point 2: The IEP Team. [The IEP Team is] *responsible for developing, reviewing, or revising* *an IEP for a child with a disability²⁹....The IEP Team ... includes the parents; ... not less than one regular education teacher of the child (if the child is, or may be, participating in the regular education environment); not less than one special education teacher of the child; ... a representative of the [school] who is qualified to provide, or supervise the provision of, specially designed instruction to meet the unique needs of children with disabilities;... an individual who can interpret instructional implications of evaluation results;... [and] at the discretion of the parent or [school], other individuals who have special expertise ... including related service personnel;... [and] whenever appropriate, the child³⁰ ....It is important ... that the [school] representative have the authority to commit agency resources and be able to ensure that whatever services are described in the IEP will actually be provided.... The [school] will be bound by the IEP that is developed at an IEP Team meeting.³¹*

Comment. Like many parents, you might find such a group intimidating. To eliminate or reduce intimidation, remember three things: The law requires the IEP Team to help your child, which may involve giving services to you. The law gives you and your child many rights. And perhaps most important, many IEP Team members are wonderful, knowledgeable people who want to help. If they run well-organized meetings, have the expertise needed to solve your child's problems, know how to listen, know when to speak, and know how to problem solve, their expertise can help enormously.

Here's something else that might eliminate or reduce intimidation. Although you probably don't have the professional expertise of the other IEP Team members, you have expertise in two areas: You know your child in ways they cannot, and you know yourself, your family, and your family's strengths. Moreover, you know that you're committed to learning all you can about reading disabilities and the special education laws. Such commitment and knowledge can accomplish a great deal. To help you with this, the next chapter will discuss the components of IEPs. By understanding them, you can help the Team write an IEP that's precise, focused, and relevant enough to increase your child's chances of becoming a competent, motivated reader.

Before attending an IEP meeting, ask the Team to invite the related service personnel needed to write and implement an IEP that meets all your child's needs—academic, social, emotional, physical, recreational, and vocational. IDEA-2004's regulations allow this; they say you can invite "other individuals who have special expertise ... including related service personnel." Thus, you should consider asking the Team's coordinator to invite some or all of these professionals: your child's speech and language specialist, reading specialist, guidance counselor, occupational therapist, and physical therapist. Their participation can improve understanding of your child's needs and streamline instructional coordination.

You can also bring your own expert to an IEP meeting. Bringing your own reading specialist may improve the IEP and reduce your anxiety. As IDEA-2004's regulations note, your expert becomes a member of the IEP Team: "The Act ... allows other individuals who have knowledge or special expertise ... to be included as members of a child's IEP Team *at the discretion of the parent* or the agency."³²

Before requesting the Team coordinator to invite specific people, consider that more people means the need for more time. Plus, too many participants can undermine effectiveness. So, do two things. First, if you think it's important to invite more than the core IEP Team, limit your request for invitations to the people you think are needed to develop and implement a quality IEP. Second, ask the coordinator to schedule enough time for everyone to fully participate.

IDEA-2004 allows schools to ask you to excuse school personnel from IEP meetings. To excuse IEP Team members, related service personnel (e.g., the speech and language specialist), or teachers requires your written permission.[33] If the school asks, withhold your answer until you answer these questions for yourself:

- Will their participation provide critical information and insights that their written reports do not?
- Will their participation help to create a better program?
- Will their participation improve the implementation of the IEP?

If you answer "yes" to any of these, withhold permission.

In general, everyone who can improve the IEP should attend the meeting. So, be cautious about granting written permission to excuse people, even if they provide written reports or there are no plans to discuss their expertise. Never agree to excusing teachers. And if your child's teachers for next year or semester are known, ask that they be invited. After all, they have to implement the IEP.

Another IEP Team member who should never be excused from IEP meetings is the school's representative. The USDOE's formal discussion of IDEA-2004's regulations makes clear the representative's importance. Pay careful attention to the italicized words:

> It is important ... that the [school's] representative have the *authority to commit* agency resources and be able to *ensure* that whatever services are described in the IEP will actually be provided.... The [school] will be *bound* by the IEP that is developed at an IEP Team meeting.[34]

Thus, at IEP meetings, you need to make sure that the school's representative signs the attendance sheet as such, even if she also functions in other ways, such as the Team's school psychologist. This is important because representatives do not always sign in as such. Moreover, the official presence and agreement of the representative obligates the school to implement the IEP. So, make sure that the school sends a qualified representative to the IEP meeting. Also make sure that all Team decisions are written into the IEP and that you leave the meeting with a copy of the latest IEP, even if it's incomplete and crammed with scribbled notes. This is consistent with IDEA-2004's spirit:

> The [school] must give the parent a copy of the child's IEP at no cost to the parent[35].... Upon request, a parent must be provided with a revised copy of the IEP with the amendments incorporated.[36]

Keep in mind that the IEP Team is charged with developing a program for your child that requires more than involvement in the general education curriculum; it must develop an IEP that will likely lead to meaningful *progress* for every identified educational need. Unfortunately, many IEP Teams focus on involvement in the general education curriculum and ignore progress. If so, respectfully but firmly insist that the Team write an IEP that is likely to produce meaningful progress for every identified educational need, including academic, social, and emotional needs.

If the Team produces an IEP similar to ones that failed, insist—politely but firmly—on major changes likely to produce substantial progress. For example, if small-group reading instruction has produced trivial progress, you might request that a reading specialist provide one-to-one tutoring daily. Don't worry about the cost or availability of a specialist—that's the school's responsibility. Your responsibility, as a member of the IEP Team, is to "act in the best interest of the child."[37] Your responsibility as a parent is to get your child whatever he needs to succeed in reading.

Because States can require more IEP Team members than IDEA-2004, review your State's code to see if additional people must attend meetings. Although State codes are dry reading, they're remarkably informative.

Point 3: Active Parent Participation. *The parents of a child with a disability must be afforded an opportunity to participate in meetings with respect to ... the identification, evaluation, and educational placement of the child; and ...the provision of FAPE [free appropriate public education] to the child*[38].... *Parents have the right to bring questions, concerns, and preliminary recommendations to the IEP Team meeting as part of a full discussion of the child's needs and the services to be provided to meet those needs*[39].... *As part of an initial evaluation ... and as part of any reevaluation ... the IEP Team [which includes the parents] must – (1)Review existing evaluation data on the child including evaluations and information provided by the parents ... [and] (2) On the basis of that review, and input from the child's parents, identify what additional data, if any, are needed*[40].... *In developing each child's IEP, the IEP Team must consider ... the concerns of the parents for enhancing the education of their child.*[41]

Comment. As this and the previous excerpt show, you are a full-fledged member of the IEP Team, a member with specific rights. But rights without knowledge mean little. Thus, you should consider these suggestions.

First, read about your child's difficulties and how to help him *beat the odds*, as you're doing right now. After studying our book, study the relevant parts of IDEA-2004; also, study other books on reading disabilities. Both the rules and regulations for IDEA-2004 and a list of helpful books on reading disabilities are posted on our website: www.reading2008.com.

Second, join national organizations that specialize in educating parents of children with learning disabilities and influencing government policy. Ask them questions. Attend their conferences. Study their websites and newsletters. Three of the more helpful organizations are the Learning Disabilities Association of America, Learning Disabilities Worldwide, and the National Center for Learning Disabilities.

Third, register with a non-profit child advocacy organization. Many such organizations are staffed by professionals and volunteers. Because they generally have far fewer professionals than they need, they usually make extensive use of trained volunteers who can meet with you to discuss your child's difficulties and accompany you to special education meetings. They, like a knowledgeable friend, can offer emotional support and help you problem solve, resolve conflicts, and ensure that the school follows your State's special education laws and procedures.

Despite good intentions, however, the staff and volunteers of advocacy organizations often have a major weakness: They lack the strong background in reading disabilities needed to develop an IEP that offers your child an excellent chance of making meaningful progress in reading. Nevertheless, advocacy organizations can often teach parents a great deal about State laws, procedures, and resources, and can help parents achieve their goals at meetings.

Fourth, if you have major concerns about an upcoming meeting, and your child is eligible for special education under IDEA-2004, meet individually with an IEP Team member to informally discuss your concerns and problem solve. To focus the meeting, give her a list of your questions and concerns. At the meeting, never—yes, the word was *never*—say anything negative about anyone in the school. Select someone who is trustworthy, respects confidentiality, has relevant expertise, and is motivated to help your child.

Finally, consider hiring an expert in reading disabilities to assist you at IEP and related meetings. Meet the expert beforehand to develop and discuss relevant, measurable goals, the expert's role, the school's responsibilities, and your role.

Point 4: Teacher Access and Responsibilities. *Each [school] must ensure that ... the child's IEP is accessible to each regular education teacher, special education teacher, related services provider, and any other service provider who is responsible for its implementation; and ... each ... is informed of ... his or her specific responsibilities related to implementing the child's IEP; and ... the specific accommodations, modifications, and supports that must be provided for the child.*[42]

Comment. All too often, in the name of confidentiality, school districts have denied regular and special education teachers access to their students' IEPs or have failed to inform them of their responsibilities in implementing the IEPs of specific students. This makes little sense, as IEPs are developed to guide instruction and direct the evaluation of progress in general and special education. This regulation makes clear that schools must not deny teachers access to their students' IEPs and must ensure that teachers understand their responsibilities in implementing the individualized provisions of each student's IEP. And because IEPs will differ— hence the "I" for Individualized in IEP—so will teacher responsibilities.

But simply informing teachers and related personnel about their responsibilities is often inadequate. For example, your child's IEP may require that reading instruction emphasize the Language Experience Approach. If his general education or special education teachers have not had extensive instruction and extensive practice in using this approach, they may need to read about it; discuss it with a reading specialist; observe the reading specialist demonstrate it, several times, in their classes; and use it several times while the reading specialist observes and then offers feedback.

Even this support, however, may be inadequate for teachers to learn a new method well enough to effectively implement and modify it to meet the struggling reader's needs. Developing such knowledge and skill is often far more time consuming, complex, and difficult than outsiders think. It can easily take a year. Moreover, if several students have IEPs requiring different reading methods, teachers will likely become overwhelmed. We would. This is one reason it's usually better for parents to focus on developing goals and objectives and monitoring progress than demanding the IEP require specific reading methods.

To ensure that you and your child's teachers fully understand the IEP, meet with them to discuss the items you view as particularly important. Also, ask how they'll monitor progress for each goal (and objective for IEPs that require them) and how and when they'll report progress to you. Although IEPs must contain this information, discussing it with teachers highlights its importance and allows you to communicate your expectations and ask how you might help. It also gives you insight about their knowledge of your child, their understanding and commitment to the IEP, their flexibility, their personalities and values, and their willingness to work with you. Such discussions can identify unexpected problems and give you and the teachers a chance to solve them, before your child is hurt.

If you suspect that your child's teachers don't understand the IEP, or lack the knowledge or skill or resources to implement it, ask questions like these:

- To ensure that my child readily achieves all his IEP goals (and objectives), what supports or resources do you need?
- What can I do to help you get the supports or resources you need?
- Since three teachers are involved in implementing the IEP, how often will the three of you meet to coordinate lessons and assess progress?
- When would it be good for us to meet to discuss my child's progress? Is two weeks reasonable, or is three better?

When scheduling the IEP meeting, request that those teachers who will implement the IEP attend the meeting. This is important for three reasons. First, it helps your child's new teachers understand his needs and learn what works and doesn't work with him. Often, written words don't adequately convey such information. Second, it gives the new teachers a chance to craft the IEP to meet your child's needs without disrupting their routines and ways of teaching. This increases the odds of success. Third, participation strengthens commitment.

THE RIGHT TO CHALLENGE DECISIONS

Point 5: Parents can Challenge a School or an IEP Team's Decisions. *A parent always has the right to file a due process complaint and request a due process hearing on any matter concerning the identification, evaluation, or educational placement of his or her child, or the provision of FAPE [Free Appropriate Public Education].*[43]

Comment. If you disagree with the school about having your child evaluated, the nature of the evaluation, eligibility, classification, or the IEP, including its goals, services, and placement, you can challenge the school's decisions by discussing the issues with them and problem solving, or by filing a due process complaint and then engaging in the conflict-resolution processes that flow from the complaint: a resolution meeting with district personnel, State mediation, or an impartial due process hearing.

We recommend that you view a hearing as the last resort, to use only if discussions, problem solving, resolution meetings, and mediation fail. Whereas these last four options can help you build alliances and secure cooperation, hearings often sharpen divisions, fuel animosity, and encourage resistance.

Many parents request hearings to challenge IEP Team decisions about placement. Some parents want their child in special education classes, not general education classes, for all or some of his instruction. Others demand that he spend his entire school day in general education classes supplemented by in-class services. They demand what's called "full inclusion." This critical, emotionally-loaded issue can influence your decision to challenge the IEP Team. Your view about full- or part-time special education placement or inclusion can help or harm your child. It can cost you untold anguish and thousands of dollars. So, which placement is best?

Scientifically, the answer is mixed: Both inclusion and pull-out programs help some struggling readers, but hurt others. Fortunately, Naomi Zigmond, one the most astute and practical scholars in special education, offers guidelines that can help you and the IEP Team's other members make better decisions about placement. Instead of asking, *Is inclusion or pull-out better?* she asks a more illuminating question, *Better for what?* Here are two of her answers:

> The general education classroom provides students with disabilities with access to students who do not have disabilities; access to the curricula and textbooks to which most other students are exposed…. If the goal is to have students learn … subject information [such as social studies] or how to interact with nondisabled peers, the general education setting is the best place.[44]

> Pull-out settings allow for smaller teacher-student ratios and flexibility in the selection of texts, choice of curricular objectives, pacing of instruction, scheduling of examinations, and assignment of grades. Special education pull-out settings allow students to learn different content in different ways and on a different schedule. A pull-out special education setting may be most appropriate if students need (a) intensive instruction in basic academic skills well beyond the grade level at which nondisabled peers are learning how to read or do basic mathematics, (b) explicit instruction in controlling behavior or interacting with peers and adults, or (c) to learn anything that is not customarily taught to everyone else.[45]

In broad terms, Zigmond is saying that if you want your child to learn what's typically taught in the general education class, and if he can succeed without extensive modifications and adaptations, this is the preferred placement. If, however, he requires extensive modifications and adaptations—such as a specialized curriculum and specialized instructional strategies—he's unlikely to get these in general education classes; he'll likely do better in a special setting. If his reading abilities are so far below his peers, if reading the general education books will be a titanic struggle that will overwhelm him, and if instruction will not emphasize the strategies and materials he needs to markedly improve his reading abilities, placement in general education is probably a poor choice.

Of course, Zigmond's guidelines are abstractions. As such, they should be tempered by assessing each placement's teachers (their knowledge, skills, flexibility, optimism, ability to modify instruction), curriculum, students, organization, structure, and emotional climate. By doing this, rationally and systematically, you and the other members of the IEP Team will likely agree on which placement offers the best prospects of success, at the moment. We say "at the moment" because all placements and programs are hypotheses that need to be tested by the kind of careful monitoring discussed in chapter 7.

KEEP IN MIND

Whenever you're involved with IDEA-2004, keep in mind its definition of special education. It provides perspective for understanding IDEA-2004's complexities and can guide you through difficult situations. It mandates that school personnel and special education programs treat your child as an individual, not a number:

> Special education means specially designed instruction ... to meet the *unique* needs of a child with a disability.... Specially designed instruction means *adapting*, as appropriate to the needs of an eligible child ... the content, methodology, or delivery of instruction.[46]

The next chapter will help you make the IEP a plan of action that meets your child's unique needs.

ENDNOTES

1   Don't be surprised if your district hasn't evaluated the effectiveness of its programs, or has done so in superficial ways, like limiting program evaluations to yearly standardized testing. Few districts have directors of research or directors of evaluation. Few districts use research designs to seriously examine the effectiveness of their programs. Lack of quality program evaluations perpetuates ineffective programs and practices and encourages the purchasing of new programs that offer more of the same. To understate this problem, it's unfortunate.

2   Many parents and educators believe that all children with special needs prefer inclusion. They're wrong. Although many children do, many don't. In summarizing much of the research, here's what Sharon Vaughn and Janette Klingner found: "The majority of students with learning disabilities

preferred to receive specialized instruction outside of the general education classroom for part of the school day.... Students stated that they liked the resource room because the work is easier and fun and they get the help they need to do their work" (Vaughn, S., & Klingner, J., 1998. Students' perceptions of inclusion and resource room settings. *Journal of Special Education, 32*, 79-88, p. 79).

[3] A good goal is one that's important to the child's future. It's achievable if the child makes a moderate effort. Conversely, one that's important but causes incessant struggle is too difficult and should be modified or momentarily abandoned; one that requires little if any effort is too easy and should be replaced by one that's both important and modestly-to-moderately challenging. Think of it this way: Is it more fun to play tennis against someone you always crush, someone who always crushes you, or someone who plays at or slightly above or below your level? The extremes—you crush or get crushed—produce boredom and frustration. "At or slightly above or below" produces challenge: If you make a moderate effort, you may well win. Generally, you'll enjoy yourself.

[4] Many professionals responsible for developing and implementing reading programs for struggling readers have little background in reading. For example, in a national survey of school psychologists, Marian C. Fish and Howard found that a large percentage of school psychologists stated that despite inadequate training in reading, they frequently made recommendations for reading (Fish, M. C., & Margolis, H., 1988. Training and practice of school psychologists in reading assessment and intervention. *Journal of School Psychology, 26*, 399-404). A recent follow-up study supported Fish and Margolis' findings (Nelson, J. M., & Machek, G. R., 2007. A survey of training, practice, and competence in reading assessment and intervention. *School Psychology Review, 36* (2), 311-327). Similarly, Mary W. Strong and Elaine Traynelis-Yurek found that "special education teachers … are under prepared concerning the diagnosis and treatment of reading problems of their students." Moreover, many failed to regularly consult with reading specialists about their students' reading problems (Abstract for the 16th World Congress on Learning Disabilities, Learning Disabilities Worldwide, November, 2007).

[5] The majority of students with learning disabilities have reading problems; their reading problems are often the primary or only reason they're classified as having a learning disability. As LD OnLine notes, "Approximately 80 percent of students with learning disabilities have been described as reading disabled" (http://www.ldonline.org/indepth/reading).

[6] Greer v. Rome City School District, U. S. 11th Circuit Court, 1991. This case refers to one of IDEA-2004's predecessors, PL 94-142. When reading the decisions of a U.S. Circuit Court of Appeals, it's important to realize that its decisions bind only Federal courts *in* the States for which the Circuit Court has jurisdiction. The decisions of an individual Circuit Court of Appeals often influence Federal courts for other States, but *do not bind them*. For example, the U. S. 6th Circuit Court of Appeals may adopt or reject the logic and decisions of the U. S. 3rd Circuit Court. Perry Zirkel, University Professor of Education and Law at Lehigh University, noted that in 2004 the 6th Circuit Court "adopted the Third Circuit's 'meaningful benefit' substantive standard for FAPE [free appropriate public education]" (Courtside: Deal right? *Phi Delta Kappan, 86* (10), 799-800, p. 800). It did not have to. Thus, when reading quotations and decisions from Circuit Courts other than the Circuit Court for your State, remember that they may influence the Federal courts in your State, but they do *not* bind them. Only decisions of the U. S. Supreme Court bind all Federal courts.

7   34 CFR § 300.301. When we refer to the Federal regulations for IDEA-2004, the reference is 34 CFR, which stands for Title 34 of the Code of Federal Regulations; it's followed by the symbol § which stands for section, followed by the section. As we've previously said, the regulations are so important that we urge you to study them in their entirety. You can download a copy from our website: www.reading2008.com.

8   If you do not consent, the school does not have to pursue the matter. Moreover, consent for an evaluation is not consent for special education placement or services. For more information, see 34 CFR § 300.300.

9   34 CFR § 300.300.

10   34 CFR § 300.304.

11   34 CFR § 300.304.

12   34 CFR § 300.304, 34 CFR § 300.310.

13   34 CFR § 300.306.

14   34 CFR § 300.300. If you do not consent to the initial provision of services, the school cannot take you to court to force the issue.

15   34 CFR § 300.320.

16   34 CFR § 300.324.

17   34 CFR § 300.321.

18   34 CFR § 300.322.

19   34 CFR § 300.320.

20   34 CFR § 300.324.

21   34 CFR § 300.303.

22   34 CFR Discussion, p. 46678; 34 CFR § 300.305.

23   34 CFR § 300.323.

24   34 CFR § 300.323.

25   34 CFR Discussion, p. 46670.

26   34 CFR § 300.324.

27   34 CFR Discussion, p. 46676.

28   Individuals with Disabilities Education Improvement Act of 2004, § 1414.

29   34 CFR § 300.23.

30   34 CFR § 300.321.

31   34 CFR Discussion, p. 46670.

32   34 CFR Discussion, p. 46669; italics added.

33   34 CFR § 300.321.

34   34 CFR Discussion, p. 46670; italics added.

35   34 CFR § 300.322.

36   34 CFR § 300.324.

37   34 CFR Discussion, p. 46676.

38   34 CFR § 300.501.

39   34 CFR Discussion, p. 46678.

40   34 CFR § 300.305.

[41]   34 CFR § 300.324.

[42]   34 CFR § 300.323.

[43]   34 CFR Discussion, p. 46601.

[44]   Zigmond, N., 2003. Where should students with disabilities receive special education services? Is one place better than another? *Journal of Special Education, 37*, 193-199, p. 197.

[45]   Zigmond, 2003, p. 197.

[46]   34 CFR § 300.39, emphasis added.

CHAPTER 11
THE IEP

The *Individuals with Disabilities Education Improvement Act of 2004* (IDEA-2004) requires that every child in special education have an Individualized Education Program (IEP). If your child's in special education, it's the core of her program. It's the critical document—it can dramatically affect her reading, her self-confidence, and so much more.

The IEP is a summary of your child's accomplishments and educational needs. It's your contract with the school: It specifies where your child will be placed, services the school will provide, where they'll be provided, how often, how much time per session, the starting date, the ending date. It's her instructional game plan: It tells everyone what her teachers will teach her and what she's expected to accomplish.[1] It's an accommodation plan: It specifies what accommodations, such as extra time or frequent breaks, the school will provide so State and districtwide testing accurately assesses her achievements. It's an architectural plan: It shows how the IEP's components relate to one another. In sum, the IEP is a logical blueprint for action and support: It begins with a description of what your child can do, what she's achieved, and what she needs to learn. It then specifies what achievement is reasonable to expect and what the school will do, what services it will provide, to help her realize and demonstrate this achievement.

This chapter focuses on the components of IEPs that are particularly important to struggling readers. It does not discuss every component. For example, it does not discuss transition planning; behavioral intervention plans; special factors, such as hearing difficulties; multiyear IEPs, which we abhor; excusal of Team members from IEP meetings; the rights that transfer from parents to their children with learning disabilities at the child's age of majority; or the rights of children with learning disabilities who attend parochial schools. Free, excellent information on these and other IEP components is available from the National Dissemination Center for Children with Disabilities (NICHCY).[2]

When reading about the components, ask yourself if they're logically sequenced. We'll briefly discuss the sequence at the end of this chapter.

COMPONENTS

Component 1: Present Levels of Academic Achievement and Functional Performance. *[IDEA-2004 requires that the IEP include] a statement of the child's present levels of academic achievement and functional performance, including ... how the child's disability affects [her] involvement and progress in the general education curriculum.*[3]

Comment. The Present Levels of Academic Achievement and Functional Performance, which we'll call Present Levels, is the IEP's foundation. It's the basis and justification for your child's IEP goals and, in some situations, her short-term objectives. Together, the Present Levels and the goals and objectives influence virtually every aspect of her program: placement, related services, supplementary aids and services, modifications of curriculum, and accommodations. Thus, to ensure appropriate goals and objectives, you must ensure that the

Present Levels is accurate and complete. To achieve this, we recommend that for each area of difficulty, it states:

- The level at which your child can succeed, with the teacher's help and without feeling frustrated. This is your child's instructional level.
- The level at which she can succeed, without help. This is her independent level.
- The level at which she makes many errors and becomes frustrated, even with the teacher's help. This is her frustration level.
- The kinds of activities she can do quickly and accurately.
- The kinds of activities she struggles with.
- How well she performs on tasks that represent the State's standards for her grade.
- The teaching strategies that have been successful and unsuccessful with her.
- What she needs to learn over the next year.

In addition to reading difficulties, the Present Levels should address any other problems that interfere with your child's success, including academic, social, and emotional difficulties. Consider, for example, the emotional needs of a fourth-grade special education student in a general education class who feels "stupid" and "humiliated" about her reading difficulties. To avoid the anxiety and embarrassment she associates with reading, she habitually disrupts her class. This hinders her progress in reading and interferes with other students' learning, which, under IDEA-2004, might eventually justify placement in a self-contained special education class. By crafting a new IEP that accurately describes this problem—What happens? Where and when? How often? With what level reading materials? On what kind of reading tasks?—the Present Levels provides justification for goals, services, and instructional practices to improve the situation and eliminate the problem. These can include shorter assignments, less writing, easier reading materials, twice-weekly counseling, a functional behavioral assessment, twice-weekly in-class consultation to the teacher by a behavioral expert, positive behavioral supports, and a special education co-teacher for all academics. This in-class support is justified by a very important statement in IDEA-2004's regulations:

> Each [school] must ensure that … to the maximum extent appropriate, children with disabilities … are educated with children who are nondisabled; and … special classes, separate schooling, or other removal of children with disabilities from the regular educational environment occurs *only* if the nature or severity of the disability is such that education in regular classes *with* the use of supplementary aids and services cannot be achieved satisfactorily.[4]

Practically speaking, however, IEPs need a complete, accurate, and explicit Present Levels section to justify the services needed to keep children in their regular education classes and to ensure they prosper.

If your child's Present Levels ignores critical needs, it will likely result in an IEP that lacks goals in critical areas, resulting in programs that lack critical services and supports.

If your child's Present Levels is inaccurate, it may hurt her. It may, for example, place her in books that are far too difficult. This can easily block progress, cause despondency, intensify emotional distress, provoke tantrums, and erode motivation for reading—regrettably, the negative consequences of an inaccurate Present Levels can multiply.

For the Present Levels to be accurate, it must be explicit. If it makes vague statements, the IEP's goals will be vague. The vague statement, "Fay has reading comprehension and language problems," will produce vague goals, like "Fay will improve her reading comprehension and language." Vague statements and goals like these make it impossible to monitor progress reliably, accurately, and meaningfully. Without such monitoring, many children languish and struggle in programs that intensify their difficulties and dramatically reduce their chance of success.[5]

In addition to focusing on difficulties, the Present Levels needs to state what your child does well and what motivates or interests her. This communicates that she's much more than a list of problems—she's a person with competencies, interests, and feelings. It identifies areas or skills not requiring instruction, avoiding the all-too-common pitfall of teaching children what they've previously mastered. Finally, it tells teachers what they should emphasize to motivate her and to make school enjoyable. Instructionally, this information is critical in designing lessons and providing incentives to energize her efforts.

One problem common to Present Levels is the use of grade equivalents. As we discussed in chapters 5 and 9, they look accurate and scientific ("On the XYZ Test of Reading Abilities, Shayna achieved a grade equivalent of 5.3"), but often they're misleading; they *do not* tell anyone what children can read.[6] Thus, we strongly recommended that you ask the IEP Team to use information from informal reading inventories, called IRIs, and actual books to estimate your child's independent, instructional, and frustration reading levels.[7] Usually, a good reading evaluation provides such information.

Another problem with many Present Levels is that they ignore one of IDEA-2004's purposes:

> To ensure that all children with disabilities have available to them a free appropriate public education ... designed to ... prepare them for further education, employment, and independent living.[8]

Thus, when you're helping your child's IEP Team to write the Present Levels, make sure it forms the basis—with reading and other subjects—for establishing goals, and, in some instances, objectives, that successfully prepare your child for "further education, employment, and independent living." Clearly, this may require her IEP to consider more than academics.

Component 2: Measurable Annual Goals (and, in some cases, Benchmarks or Short-term Objectives). *[The IEP] must include ... a statement of measurable annual* *goals, including academic and functional goals designed to ... meet the child's needs that result from the child's disability to enable the child to be involved in and make progress in the general education curriculum; and ... meet each of the child's other educational needs that result from the child's disability .... For children with disabilities who take alternate assessments [the IEP must also contain] ... a description of benchmarks or short-term objectives.*[9]

Comment. Without relevant, precise, measurable goals that direct teachers to focus on the struggling reader's most critical reading needs, including those prescribed by the State's standards for her grade, instruction has little chance of succeeding. In other words, if IEPs lack relevant, precise, measurable goals, teachers often emphasize everything in the curriculum. A little emphasis here, a little there, a little everywhere, means no emphasis, which causes untold problems. Why? For children with reading disabilities, reading instruction must emphasize what's most important *for them* to master, including that measured by State and districtwide tests.[10] To master what's most important and difficult for them to learn, they need far more instruction, practice, and time than average readers. This means that emphasis must be precise, focused, and concentrated.

If, for example, your child's word identification, word recognition, and fluency abilities are solid fourth grade, but her reading comprehension fluctuates around mid-second grade, 10 minutes of daily instruction in reading comprehension, 20 minutes in phonemic awareness, and 30 minutes in word identification is a poor, destructive allocation of instructional time. Because her word identification is strong, she may need only 10 minutes daily of such instruction to advance her skills. Because her word identification is a solid fourth grade, even 2 minutes of daily instruction in phonemic awareness wastes time as students with her word recognition abilities have long ago mastered phonemic awareness. Instruction in her critical need—reading comprehension—should increase to 50 minutes daily and might well include developing background for the stories she's about to read as well as instruction in vocabulary, listening comprehension, summarizing, asking questions, and relating sentences and paragraphs to one another. If, however, the IEP uses imprecise, immeasurable goals, such as "Fay will improve her reading," teachers will probably treat all areas of reading as equally important, giving too much instructional time to what's strong and not enough to what's weak. Thus, IEPs need to have precise, measurable goals that direct instruction to the critical areas in which the child performs poorly.[11]

Without precise, measurable goals it is virtually impossible to accurately and reliably gauge progress. And without gauging progress—accurately and reliably—your child might languish for months, even years, in programs and classes that frustrate her and block progress. This is one reason we devoted chapter 7 to monitoring your child's progress and to explaining what constitutes measurable goals and objectives.

Even more precise and measureable than annual goals are short-term objectives and benchmarks. Regrettably, IDEA-2004 has eliminated them for all but a few children. They are required only for students with the most severe cognitive difficulties, which usually excludes struggling readers. Nevertheless, some States, like New Jersey, continue to require that all

IEPs have short-term objectives. Even if you live in a State without this requirement, we strongly advise that you request them. As an old saying goes, "If you don't ask, you don't get."

Unfortunately, we have never seen examples of what the U.S. Department of Education (USDOE) considers exemplary goals and objectives. Nevertheless, the professional literature often discusses measurable goals and objectives. We incorporated much of the literature's recommendations for goals and objectives in chapter 7 and provided several examples. We urge you to study the examples and work with your IEP Team to write similar ones for reading, writing, listening, and other educational needs.

Other educational needs often fall beyond academics. Here, in part, is what IDEA-2004's regulations require for such needs:

> A statement of measurable annual goals, including academic and *functional goals* designed to ... meet each of the child's *other educational needs* that result from the child's disability.[12]

Given the effects of reading difficulties, emotional and social problems may qualify as other educational needs:

> The child who experiences difficulty in learning to read usually becomes frustrated and conspicuous in class. [She] becomes convinced that she ... is inferior and loses confidence in her ... ability to learn. The child is hurt and often learns to dislike reading. Her lack of success and her feelings of inadequacy may contribute to emotional and social maladjustment. She ... may become aggressive, put on a bold front, and become cruel and destructive. On the other hand, [she] may become timid, passive, and withdrawn.[13]

In addition to eroding a child's mental health, emotional and social problems can impede her learning and that of her peers; they can prevent her from benefiting from special education. Thus, IEPs should include measureable goals that address these difficulties and list whatever related services she needs to achieve her goals, such as counseling, and whatever supports her teachers need to help her achieve her goals, such as in-class team teaching with a reading specialist and weekly consultation from a specialist in applied behavior analysis. Why? It's the law.[14]

Because social and emotional needs are so important and so often ignored, we will return to them later in this chapter, under General Curriculum—Involvement and Progress.

Component 3: Related Services. *[Related services refers to] transportation and such developmental, corrective, and other supportive services as are required to assist a child with a disability to benefit from special education, and **includes** speech language pathology and audiology services, interpreting services, psychological services, physical and occupational* *therapy, recreation, **including** therapeutic recreation, early identification and assessment of disabilities ... counseling services ... medical services for diagnostic or evaluation purposes ... school health services and school nurse services, social work services in schools, and parent counseling and training.*[15]

Comment. Notice that the regulations use the words *includes* and *including*; this means that other services can be provided. Thus, related services might include music therapy, movement therapy, or mentoring. The term refers to whatever educational services your child needs to benefit from special education, including school health services that do not require the attendance of a physician. If your child's chances of succeeding in special education, of achieving the goals in her IEP, are markedly reduced without a non-physician service, it probably qualifies as a related service. If a service ends, and your child's progress declines significantly, the service probably qualifies as a related service, even if it's uncommon, like music therapy.

Beyond the definition—services "required to assist a child with a disability *to benefit* from special education"—two factors help to define a related service. The first is justification: Without compelling justification that your child needs the specific service to benefit from special education, the school doesn't have to provide the service. Justification is especially important for services the school may view as unusual, such as art therapy, or unwarranted, such as counseling. Thus, you may need a report from a professional, such as a psychologist, to justify your request.

The second factor refers to medical services. If you're requesting a medical service that a physician must provide, such as psychiatric counseling, the school need not provide it, regardless of your justification. However, if a non-physician can provide a similar service, such as counseling from a school psychologist that your child needs to learn to read and write, it's probably a related service. If, to have the energy to participate in reading and writing instruction, she needs a nurse to administer asthma medication twice daily, nursing is a related service. As the USDOE's discussion of IDEA-2004 shows, related services can be extensive:

> The [school] ... is responsible for providing services necessary to maintain the health and safety of a child while the child is in school, with breathing, nutrition, and other bodily functions (e.g., nursing services, suctioning a tracheotomy, urinary catheterization) if these services can be provided by someone who has been trained to provide the service and are not the type of services that can only be provided by a licensed physician.[16]

If the school challenges your request for what they deem a medical service, you may have to consult experts to discuss the particulars of your child's needs and the school's responsibility.

When identifying related services, it's sometimes smart to agree with the IEP Team and sometimes it's not. If you want an expensive service for which the IEP Team can substitute a less expensive one that offers similar benefits, go with the Team's suggestion—it's not the specific service or ideological argument that's important, but the benefit. On the other hand, if the Team tries to deny your child a needed service because it's expensive, unusual, or not read-ily available, we recommend that you provide the Team with strong justification from a highly qualified professional. If this does not suffice, you might ask the Team relevant questions and listen to fully understand their answers.

Questions include, "What's your rationale? On what data did you base your conclusion? What's the consensus of research in the professional literature? What's your rationale for rejecting the recommendations in the report I provided?" You might also make simple, rel-evant requests, such as "Please give me copies of the research and literature on which you based your opinion."

If your manner is respectful, and you demonstrate that you're open-minded, interested in understanding the Team's rationale, and focused on obtaining only services for which there's justification, your odds of prevailing increase. Be careful, however, not to create the impres-sion that you're pressuring or attacking them. Many Teams will counter-attack: They'll dig in and justify why they're right and you're wrong. In battle, everyone loses.

Component 4: General Curriculum—Involvement and Progress. *[Each IEP] must include ... a statement of ... how the child's disability affects the child's involvement and prog-ress in the general education curriculum ... a statement of measurable annual goals, includ-ing academic and functional goals designed ... to enable the child to be involved in and make progress in the general education curriculum ... a statement of the special education and related services and supplementary aids and services ... to be provided ... to enable the child ... to advance appropriately toward attaining the annual goals ... [and] to be involved in and make progress in the general education curriculum ... and to participate in extracurricular and other nonacademic activities.*[17]

Comment. These regulations, plus previous case law, mean that the school must provide your child with whatever non-physician supports she needs to make and show meaningful progress in her special education and general education classes.[18] IEPs likely to produce regression, stagnation, or trivial progress are inappropriate. Your child's IEP must offer her a program that has both:

- A reasonable chance of producing meaningful gains in the school's general education cur-riculum, the curriculum for children without disabilities.[19]
- A reasonable chance of meeting her needs that arise from her disability but which the general education curriculum minimizes or ignores, such as overcoming any emotional difficulties caused by her reading disability.[20]

If she's *included* in general education classes—as are most struggling readers—and fails to get the services, modifications, and accommodations she needs, she'll likely regress. At best, progress will be distressingly slow.[21] This is dumping. It's a far cry from two of IDEA-2004's purposes:

To ensure that all children with disabilities have available to them a free appropriate public education that emphasizes special education and related services designed *to meet their unique needs and prepare them for further education, employment, and independent living* ... and ... to assess and *ensure the effectiveness* of efforts to educate children with disabilities.[22]

Whatever class your child is in—general education, resource room, self-contained special education—her teachers and others who instruct her, such as the reading specialist, will likely need to adjust her work to promote success without stigmatizing her or damaging her self-concept. If, for example, she has fluency difficulties and her general education class has only 15 minutes to read an assignment, her teacher may slip her a note, asking her to read only the first half. If she has word-recognition difficulties and the reading material for her general education class is too difficult for her, her teacher may give her easier reading materials on the topic. To prevent stigma, the materials may be in a book that's covered like the other students' books. Alternatively, the teacher may, before class begins, tape easy-to-read summary paragraphs in her book, the book read by her classmates.

But what if your child has severe reading difficulties that are exacerbated by despondency and little ability to handle frustration? Does the school have to address these non-academic issues? Although every case is different and the justification for services can vary, the USDOE's discussion of IDEA-2004 offers insight:

> [Schools] must ensure that consideration has been given to *the full range* of supplementary aids and services that could be provided to the child in the regular educational environment to accommodate the unique needs of the child with a disability.[23] .... In situations where a child's educational needs are *inseparable* from the child's emotional needs and an individual determination is made that the child requires the therapeutic and habilitation services of a residential program in order to *'benefit from special education,'* these therapeutic and habilitation services may be 'related services' under [IDEA-2004]. In such a case, the SEA [State Educational Agency] is responsible for ensuring that the entire cost of that child's placement, including the therapeutic care as well as room and board, is without cost to the parents.[24]

Although a residential program is rarely needed to remediate reading difficulties, this excerpt from IDEA-2004's discussion of a residential program is important: It illustrates that your child is entitled to whatever non-physician services she needs to benefit from special education, even if they're unusual, expensive, or non-academic. Of course, the justification must be compelling.

More often, however, services need not be unusual or extremely expensive. The related service your child needs may be as common and as simple as preteaching, a service that enables some children "to advance appropriately toward attaining [their] annual goals [and] ... make progress in the general education curriculum."[25] In preteaching, a struggling reader might study a topic with her reading specialist two days before her general education class studies it. By using her 6th-grade social studies textbook to teach reading and by instructing her on its concepts and words—before they're taught in her general education class—her reading specialist can increase her odds of success in her general education class and strengthen her reading abilities.

Fortunately, IDEA-2004's regulations are not limited to academic situations: They discuss participation in extracurricular and other nonacademic activities. This means that your child should have the same opportunity as average or above-average readers "to participate in extracurricular and other nonacademic activities." IDEA-2004's Discussion provides an illustrative comment that's important to remember:

> Each [school] must ensure that children with disabilities have the supplementary aids and services determined necessary by the child's IEP Team for the child to participate in nonacademic and extracurricular services and activities to the maximum extent appropriate to the needs of that child.[26]

But why is this important? What do nonacademic and extracurricular services and activities have to do with reading disabilities? Such activities can be highly motivating. They can expose children to a variety of powerful language experiences. They can reinforce children's reading abilities and help them see that reading is important. They can make school fun. They can make struggling readers feel as if they're an important part of school—that they belong, that they have friends, that they're part of a caring and supportive community.

Some school personnel act as if after-school programs are unimportant, frivolous, a waste of time. You may have to help them understand how important and effective such programs can be. To do this, you might want to share the research with them. Here's what an extensive review of research found:

> Youth who participate in after-school programs improve significantly in three major areas: feelings and attitudes, indicators of behavioral adjustment, and school performance. More specifically, after-school programs succeeded in improving youths' feelings of self-confidence and self-esteem, school bonding (positive feelings and attitudes toward school), positive social behaviors, school grades and achievement test scores. They also reduced problem behaviors (e.g., aggression, noncompliance and conduct problems) and drug use. In sum, after-school programs produced multiple benefits that pertain to youths' personal, social and academic life.[27]

So, given the requirements of IDEA-2004 and the findings of the research, if your child wants to join the chess or theatre club and reading is an obstacle, ask the school to help her overcome the obstacle so she can participate fully. Simple solutions might include assigning someone to help her read the materials, reading the materials to her, or putting the materials on a digital voice recorder. Of course, solutions should minimize or prevent stigma.

Counseling is another non-academic service that can be critically important to the success of struggling readers in remedial, special, and general education. If your child is lonely, depressed, anxious, upset, angry, aggressive, distracted, or troubled in any way, she may not benefit from extra reading help unless she gets counseling. Fortunately, IDEA-2004 notes the importance of counseling as a related service:

> Related services means ... service[s] ... required to assist a child with a disability to benefit from special education, and includes ... counseling services.[28]

Furthermore, professional ethics require school professionals to support the provision of whatever educational services a child might need.

This raises the question: Can counseling be effective? The answer: Yes. Look, for example, at the effects of cognitive-behavioral programs on depression and anxiety, which often plague children with learning disabilities. Using a highly structured cognitive-behavioral program over 22 sessions, researchers helped a large group of 9- to 14-year old girls rid themselves of depressive symptoms.[29] Similarly, researchers found that cognitive-behavioral strategies "can successfully treat anxiety disorders and symptoms in school settings."[30] There's little doubt that reading instruction will be far more effective when struggling readers are freed of depressive and anxiety disorders.

Component 5: Placement in the Least Restrictive Environment (LRE). [IDEA-2004's] *overriding rule ... is that placement decisions for all children with disabilities must be made on an individual basis.*[31]*.... Placement decisions ... must be appropriate for the needs of the child*[32]*.... [IDEA-2004 has a] strong preference for educating children with disabilities in regular classes with appropriate aids and supports.... States must [ensure] ... that, to the maximum extent appropriate, children with disabilities ... are educated with children who are nondisabled, and that special classes, separate schooling, or other removal of children with disabilities from the regular educational environment occurs only if the nature or severity of the disability is such that education in regular classes with the use of supplementary aids and services cannot be achieved satisfactorily.*[33]

Comment. If your child can effectively learn to read and can achieve her other educational goals in regular or general education classes, then that is the least restrictive environment (LRE) *for her.* To succeed in regular classes, she may need counseling, or adaptive equipment, or extra in-class instruction from a reading specialist, or reduced amounts of homework, or easier homework assignments, or text-to-speech and speech-to-text software, or non-stigmatizing books matched to her reading levels, or personalized reading lessons at her instructional and independent reading levels, or some combination of these.

If your child needs some or all of these, the school must provide her with those and any other aids and supports and related services she needs to succeed in her regular classes.[34] After all, the USDOE's discussion of IDEA-2004's regulations does not say the IEP Team should consider "only a *few* supplementary aids and services." Instead, it says "the *full* range":

> Before a child with a disability can be placed outside of the regular educational environment, *the full range* of supplementary aids and services that could be provided to facilitate the child's placement in the regular classroom setting must be considered. Following that consideration, if a determination is made that a particular child with a disability cannot be educated satisfactorily in the regular educational environment, even with the provision of appropriate supplementary aids and services, that child could be placed in a setting other than the regular classroom.[35]

Please keep in mind that the opening quotation uses the phrase *strong preference*: "[IDEA-2004 has a] *strong preference* for educating children with disabilities in regular classes." A preference is not a mandate. If, with what the IEP Team considers appropriate aids and supports and related services, your child is unlikely to make meaningful progress in reading in a regular class, it is not her *LRE*. If she needs a specialized environment to make meaningful progress in reading, a specialized environment as similar as possible to a regular education environment becomes *her LRE*.[36]

A specialized environment can be one hour daily of individual tutoring in a reading center; or specialized, small-group instruction in reading, writing, and mathematics, four periods daily, in a resource center; or, if she needs a highly intensive, highly integrated all-day reading and writing program, full-time placement in a special class or a school that specializes in overcoming reading disabilities.[37] Decisions about the nature of the specialized environment must be based on the child's unique needs, not on what's available or what's given to other children with reading difficulties. "No ifs, ands, or buts."

Some school personnel, however, argue that for social reasons, *all* students with mild disabilities, such as reading disabilities, must remain in regular classes. They're wrong. If your child must overcome reading difficulties, and placement in a regular class, with supplementary aids and services, is unlikely to achieve this, such placement is *not* her *LRE*.[38] In fact, it's too restrictive because it denies her an opportunity for learning what's essential for success in life. If she does not learn what's essential, her adult options and life will be far more restricted.[39]

So, if for social reasons, school personnel insist on placing your child in regular classes that have little chance of markedly improving her reading, share these quotes with them. They come from the USDOE's discussion of IDEA-2004 and its regulations:

- The Act [IDEA-2004] does not require that every child with a disability be placed in the regular classroom regardless of individual abilities and needs…. Regular class placement may not be appropriate for every child with a disability…. [IDEA-2004 requires] a range of placement options ... to meet the unique educational needs of children with disabilities. This requirement ... reinforces the importance of the individualized inquiry, not a 'one size fits all' approach, in determining what placement is the LRE for each child with a disability.[40]

- Special education and related services are based on the identified needs of the child and *not on the disability category* in which the child is classified.[41].... Each child's educational placement must be determined on an individual case-by-case basis depending on each child's *unique educational needs* and circumstances, rather than by the child's category of disability, and must be based on the child's IEP.[42]
- If a ... child with a disability cannot be educated satisfactorily in the regular educational environment, even with the provision of appropriate supplementary aids and services, that child could be placed in a setting other than the regular classroom.[43]
- [Schools must provide] a continuum of alternative placements ... to meet the needs of children with disabilities for special education and related services.... The continuum ... must ... include ... instruction in regular classes, special classes, special schools, home instruction, and instruction in hospitals and institutions.[44]

If school personnel continue to insist that your child, like all children with reading disabilities, must remain in a regular class, you might show them these quotations from Federal court decisions:

- The least restrictive environment guarantee ... cannot be applied to cure an otherwise inappropriate placement.[45]
- The child's right to derive meaningful benefit outweighs any LRE considerations.[46]

You may also want to share the conclusions of Michael Yell and Antonis Katsiyannis, two eminent scholars of special education law:

> [In Hartmann v. Loudoun County Board of Education, the 4th Circuit Court] established a test to assist districts in determining whether placement in the general education classroom is necessary. The criteria are as follows: (a) inclusion is not required if a student with disabilities will not receive educational benefit from the placement in the general education classroom, (b) inclusion is not required where any marginal benefit from mainstreaming would be significantly outweighed by benefits that could feasibly be obtained only in a separate instructional setting.[47]

This and the previous quotations indicate that any placement in which a child is unlikely to achieve her IEP goals—like making one and one-half years progress in word identification, word recognition, and reading comprehension—is inadequate.[48] For this child, it is not her LRE.

LREs must be determined on an individual basis. A program and placement that's appropriate for Jean, a nine-year old with a reading disability, may be inappropriate for Linda, also a nine-year old with a reading disability. The nature of their reading disabilities and their responsiveness to instructional methods and strategies may differ. Jean may need a far more intensive program than Linda. To determine your child's LRE, ask, at minimum, these questions:

- With the supports offered, is my child likely to make meaningful progress in reading and achieve her IEP's goals in a regular class?
- In what environment, as similar as possible to a regular environment or class, is my child most likely to achieve her reading and other IEP goals?
- In what environment is she likely to make larger gains in reading?
- How will placement in the proposed environments affect her socially and emotionally?

Over time, the answers may change.

Component 6: Reporting of Progress Toward Annual Goals. *[Each IEP] must include ... a description of ... how the child's progress toward meeting the annual goals ... will be measured ... and ... when periodic reports on the progress the child is making toward meeting the annual goals ... will be provided.*[49]

Comment. We included this again because it's so important that you monitor your child's program. Much of the information you need is in chapter 7.

Component 7: Extended School Year (ESY). *Extended school year [ESY] services must be provided only if a child's IEP Team determines, on an individual basis ... that the services are necessary for the provision of FAPE [free appropriate public education] to the child.... A [school] ... may not ... limit extended school year services to particular categories of disability; or ... unilaterally limit the type, amount, or duration of those services*[50] *.... States may use recoupment and retention as their sole criteria but they are not limited to these standards.*[51]

Comment. Many children with reading disabilities need an extended school year (ESY), usually a summer program that emphasizes reading and writing, or they'll forget what they learned and will need an excessively long time to relearn it. Such forgetting will cause them to fall further behind their average-achieving peers. As two literacy researchers, Maryann Mraz and Timothy V. Rasinski, noted:

> Summer reading loss seems to have its greatest impact on low-achieving students and at-risk students—those who can least afford to fall further behind.[52]

Other struggling readers require an ESY to achieve the goals and objectives in their IEPs.

Still others may require an ESY as they approach a breakthrough in reading that would otherwise be thwarted—perhaps forever. Still others need an ESY for different reasons.

Despite the need of many struggling readers for ESY programs, the decision to offer an ESY program is not automatic and eligibility criteria vary from State to State. What doesn't vary under IDEA-2004 is that eligibility must be based on the child's needs.

Usually, to determine a child's eligibility for an ESY, schools use the criterion of recoupment and retention. This generally refers to the length of time it takes a struggling reader to recover the reading abilities she lost (or is expected to lose) over a school break, like a winter or summer break. If your child loses far more than the average student,[53] if regaining what she lost takes her far more time and instruction than it takes the average student, and if this happens summer after summer, she won't make sufficient progress. She'll likely have greater problems in her general education classes; emotionally, the cumulative losses may depress her and destroy her motivation for reading; she'll always need special education and related supports. Thus, she may well be eligible for an ESY as her loss and recoupment problems undermine past progress and will frustrate future progress.

Consider this hypothetical example that ignores the fact that many average-achieving middle-class students make reading gains over the summer months. Assume that average-achieving readers fall behind one month every summer and it takes them two weeks to regain their loss. Also assume that your child falls behind three months every summer and it takes her three months to regain her loss. (This is not far-fetched as struggling readers usually need more time to master reading skills, concepts, and strategies.) Compared to her average-achieving peers, she'll have fallen further behind and will need many more months of re-learning. Time spent re-learning will not close the gap. Moreover, her regression and recoupment problems are probably cumulative: A loss of three months an academic year and the need for three months of additional instruction means that over four years she'll lose 12 months, which is more than a full academic year. In contrast, her average-achieving peers will need only two months to regain what they lost. By losing a full school year, which is 10 months, your child is unlikely to make much progress in reading. Thus, she's unlikely to achieve two of IDEA-2004's main goals: to make good progress in the general education curriculum[54] and to develop the abilities needed for further education, employment, and independent living.[55]

Denying services your child needs, like an ESY, flies in the face of one of IDEA-2004's main purposes:

> To ensure that all children with disabilities have ... a free appropriate public education ... designed to meet their unique needs and prepare them for further education, employment, and independent living.[56]

It must be obvious that we referred to this purpose more than four times—it's that important. If your child needs an ESY (or any other service that a non-physician can provide), if the need is documented, and if her school refuses to provide it, the school is failing to meet her "unique needs" and failing to fully prepare her for "further education, employment, and independent living." If anything, the school is dramatically increasing her chances of frustration and failure.

To understand the extent of a struggling reader's gains or losses over the summer and how long it will take her to regain what she lost, schools must take relevant, precise, and reliable measurements of the child's progress before the summer break, immediately after it, and over subsequent months. Such measurements must focus on the child's areas of difficulty, such as word identification, and be little influenced by re-administering the tests or by other contaminating factors, such as the child's guessing. Rarely do parents have sufficient expertise to take such measurements; rarely do outside experts have sufficient opportunity. Usually, only the school has both the expertise and opportunity; thus, schools need to take the necessary measurements.[57] Without measurements, schools are forced to guess about regression and recoupment—dramatically increasing the odds of egregious error, error that can harm the child. Unfortunately, our experience is that schools rarely collect such information. In such situations, they should err on the side of caution: Make a decision which if wrong is least likely to harm the child. Usually, this supports an ESY.

How do you know that caution supports an ESY? In addition to the experiences of untold thousands of teachers and parents, research has shown that struggling readers lose a great deal over the summer and must struggle to regain it. Look again at Maryann Mraz and Timothy Rasinski's conclusion. Now look at what Richard Allington and Patricia Cunningham have concluded:

> Struggling readers most often lose ground over the summer. Thus, even when the school is doing a good job, these children often cannot match their more advantaged peers' rate of literacy development year after year because the lack of summer reading experiences leads to an overall loss of some of the gains made in school.[58]

Here's another factor to throw into the decision-making mix. If your family and neighborhood are poor, the need for a quality ESY is even greater. Doris Entwisle, Karl Alexander, and Linda Steffel Olson, three researchers from Johns Hopkins University, found that during summer break, "relatively affluent children continued to gain ... whereas poor children stopped gaining or even lost ground."[59] When interpreting this research, keep in mind that these affluent children, as a group, were not struggling readers. So, what can we say about the combination of struggling readers and poverty? It's a greater risk for dangerous regression.

So far we have emphasized regression and recoupment. This, however, is not the only criterion: The USDOE's discussion of IDEA-2004's regulations allows for other criteria:

> States may use recoupment and retention as their sole criteria.... [However,] they are not limited to these standards and have considerable flexibility in determining eligibility for ESY services and establishing State standards.[60]

Thus, it's critical to ask your State department of education for copies of those parts of its special education statutes, codes, and policies that describe ESY eligibility.

Even if your child is legally eligible for an ESY, school personnel may not offer one as they have an unwritten policy of limiting recommendations to students with moderate-to-profound cognitive or physical disabilities. If the school denies your child an ESY because her problems are primarily reading and writing, here's some good news. IDEA-2004 states that a school "may not ... limit extended school year services to particular categories of disability."[61]

So, if your child needs an ESY, request one, orally and in writing. If the IEP Team rejects your request, they must give you a written statement of their reasons and the information on which it was based. Specifically, its statement must include:

> A description of the action refused [such as the ESY].... An explanation of why the [school] ... refuses to take the action.... A description of each evaluation procedure, assessment, record, or report the [school] used as a basis for the ... refused action.... A description of other options that the IEP Team considered and the reasons why those options were rejected.... A description of other factors that are relevant to the [school's] ... refusal.[62]

This implies that the school must have valid reasons—such as information they collected describing your child's gains or losses over previous summers and the time it took her to regain what she lost. As we previously noted, schools rarely collect such information.

To avoid disagreements about the need for an ESY, you might give the Team information on its importance. For example, you might show them the article by Maryann Mraz and Timothy Rasinski,[63] the book by Richard Allington and Patricia Cunningham,[64] your State's ESY policies, and the parts of your State's special education code that provide reasons for an ESY. Two excellent websites for case law on ESY, some of which you might download and share with the IEP Team, are www.wrightslaw.com and www.special-ed-law.com. You may also want to show them this section of *Reading Disabilities: Beating the Odds*.

Like every other aspect of a child's special education program, the school must individualize the ESY to meet her needs: academic, social, emotional, physical, organizational, motivational, and so on. This means that the ESY portion of the IEP must be tailored to her needs, including the length of the school day, the instructional strategies, the related services. In some instances, 90 minutes of one-to-one tutoring daily from a reading specialist can meet all of a struggling reader's ESY needs; in other instances, the reader may need a four-hour school day with small-group instruction for reading, writing, and oral language development, interspersed with baseball, volleyball, and music to make summer feel like summer. As IDEA-2004's regulations state, the decisions must be determined "on an individual basis" and offer the child an "appropriate" education.

Appropriate may well mean that your child's ESY program must be designed to sustain or develop a high level of motivation to read. Thus, basketball, photography, and arts and crafts might be incorporated into her reading lessons. This, Richard Allington has argued, can be critical:

> [Struggling readers] often see summer school as a personal penalty for something over which they had little control. Unfortunately, in too many cases they seem to be right.... Summer-school programs for such students need to be both engaging and powerfully instructional. In fact, it is difficult to achieve the latter without the former.[65]

No doubt about it—ESY is a complex topic and there's much more to learn. We spent a lot of time discussing it and could have easily spent more. Why spend so much time? The reason is simple: If your child has a reading disability, she likely needs a quality ESY. Not having one may well jeopardize her future.

Component 8: State and Districtwide Testing. *The State must ensure that all children with disabilities are included in all general State and districtwide assessment programs ... with appropriate accommodations ... if necessary, and as indicated in each child's respective IEP.[66] ... [The IEP] must include ... a statement of any individual appropriate accommodations that are necessary to measure the academic achievement and functional performance of the child on State and districtwide assessments.[67]*

Comment. Under the Federal *No Child Left Behind Act* (NCLB), schools are required to administer State and districtwide reading tests to virtually all children in grades three to eight and once in high school between grades ten and twelve. All children, but those with the most severe intellectual or physical disabilities, must take them. Thus, starting in third grade, your child will probably have to take your State's reading tests. Starting in kindergarten, district policy may require her to take additional tests.

The vast majority of State and districtwide tests are standardized tests, in the sense that they're "paper-and-pencil" tests that are administered and marked in standardized, objective ways.[68] If your child takes such tests, remember that *IDEA-2004 may require testing accommodations*:

> The IEP [must] include a statement of any individual appropriate accommodations that are necessary to measure the academic and functional performance of the child on State and districtwide assessments.[69]

The word *accommodations* refers to how test items are presented to your child, how she must respond, and the environment in which she takes the test. Any of these factors—presentation, response, environment—can result in inaccurate test scores, scores that misrepresent your child's knowledge, skill, achievement, and functioning levels. This, in turn, can lead to an inappropriate IEP and to your child being held back. Thus, you must ensure that her IEP includes whatever accommodations she needs to produce accurate scores.

Typical accommodations include scribes, extended time, frequent breaks, individual administration of tests, the repetition and discussion of directions, and special rooms in which to take tests. As such, accommodations do not change what's measured, but how and where. Because States must approve accommodations for State testing, their websites usually publish a list of approved accommodations.

Recently, the U. S. 7th Circuit Court of Appeals for Illinois, Indiana, and Wisconsin added a nasty twist to IDEA-2004's protections for testing and accommodations. In 2008 the Court ruled that NCLB must be followed, even if it contradicts IDEA-2004. Although most ramifications of this ruling have yet to be explored, and it does not bind but may influence courts outside these three States, one sentence may have frightening implications for *all* the nation's struggling readers: "A Federal court cannot forbid application of legislation enacted in 2001 [NCLB] just because it may undermine legislation enacted between 1970 and 1990 [IDEA-2004]."[70] As Michelle C. Laubin, a special education attorney from Connecticut, wrote, "It may come as a surprise to many educators, parents, and advocates of children with disabilities that the 'individualized' accommodations required by IDEA can be pushed aside in favor of the mass-testing requirements of NCLB."[71]

Regrettably, if your child takes a State or districtwide test and fails, she may be retained in grade, denied graduation, or placed in a particular class or program—all on the basis of one test. Yes—she may be held back, denied graduation, or put in classes with many struggling or unmotivated learners who feel defeated. Such decisions differ from State to State, and sometimes, from district to district.[72]

Using State or districtwide standardized tests to make high-stakes decisions about retention and graduation is troublesome for many reasons.

- Tests alone are inadequate for the task. Even the better ones sample only a small portion of what's been taught, often test what hasn't been taught,[73] and often misrepresent the progress and achievement of struggling readers. Moreover, the quality of many high-stakes tests is poor.[74]
- Retention usually harms rather than helps children. Instead of the academic acceleration claimed by politicians, retention typically demoralizes children, fails to reverse their academic difficulties, and substantially increases the odds that they'll drop out of high school.[75] In essence, it punishes students for their reading disabilities.
- Preventing older students from graduating because they failed a high-stakes test may well dampen the motivation of younger students with reading disabilities; they may think, "Why try? No matter how hard I work, I'll fail the test. I'll never graduate."

Naomi Zigmond captured much of this unfairness when she asked a simple but powerful question:

> Of what benefit is it to a senior with learning disabilities—finally performing on an 8th grade reading level after years of hard work and relentless special education instruction—to fail the proficiency standards in reading required to graduate from high school?[76]

To protect your child, ask that her IEP include a statement like this: "The results of State or districtwide testing will not be used to make or influence decisions about Shayna's program or placement, and will not be used to make decisions about retention or graduation." If the Team refuses, again make this request, but now in writing. Because the request is now in writing, IDEA-2004 requires the Team to give you a written rationale for their decision and the data on which it was based.

Some may argue this is wrong. After all, the Discussion section of IDEA-2004's regulations say that "a child's performance on State or districtwide assessments logically would be included in the IEP Team's *consideration* of the child's academic needs.... In ... an initial evaluation or reevaluation ... the IEP Team [must] ... *review* existing evaluation data, including data from ... local ... and State assessments."[77]

Consideration and review, however, does not mean that the Team should *rely* on data from State or districtwide tests to make or influence decisions. One argument against relying on such data is that tests designed for group administration are of doubtful validity for making decisions about individual children or diagnosing their academic needs. Another argument is that any test, even an excellent, individually-administered test, is only one source of information, which should limit the confidence placed in it. Moreover, their scores are not definitive and irrefutable:

> Reliance on measurement [test] data alone can ... prove to be detrimental to decision making. Although such data are objective, we must remember that they are only estimates of a student's behavior. Test data are *never* 100% accurate![78]

Chapter 9 extensively discusses the need and legal requirement for multiple sources of information.

If the Team insists on using the results of a State or districtwide test to make or influence important decisions about your child, you might offer this from IDEA-2004's regulations about evaluation procedures:

> In conducting the evaluation, the [school] must ... use a variety of assessment instruments and strategies to gather relevant functional, developmental, and academic information about the child .... Each [school] must ensure that ... assessments and other evaluation materials used to assess a child ... are used for the purposes for which the assessments or measures are valid and reliable.[79]

Given NCLB's regulations and policies and those of many States and districts, these arguments, though scientifically sound, may fail. Nevertheless, to protect your child from the political, unethical, and uninformed nature of many testing policies, they're worth trying.[80]

Related to our views of testing and test policies are two warnings and several recommendations about high-stakes testing and its consequences.

The first warning is that States have different standards, regulations, and policies. For example, 22 States require students to pass a high school exit exam to graduate; but even here, policies differ. Some States offer alternative routes for students who fail. "With few exceptions," the Center on Education Policy notes, "States have moved toward greater flexibility in their exit exam policies."[81] This may help you. It means that you must learn about your State's policies and keep up with the changes. Nationally, things are in flux.

The second warning is that many schools, especially those in lower-middle to poor economic areas, feel extremely pressured to look good—to avoid newspaper stories that call them "failing schools." To solve this dilemma, some schools retain students in the hope they'll make major academic gains. Few, if any, do.

Some high schools use retention, including multiple and undeserved retentions, to pressure struggling readers to dropout. This is a harmful, unethical, shameful practice.[82]

Yes—high-stakes reading and language arts testing is bizarre and confusing, replete with regulatory and political pitfalls and scientific contradictions. Although the vast majority of schools are staffed by good, ethical, hard-working people, some schools are overwhelmed by political pressures, poor policies, and human frailties. Some schools, with the best of intentions, have policies whose unintended consequences harm struggling readers. Arguably, that's why newspaper stories abound with testing absurdities and dishonesty.[83]

So, beware of test policies that are venal, short-sighted, and harmful. Be careful—distinguish between what's said and done. Be alert—look at results. Be informed—learn all you can.

To learn about testing standards, regulations, and policies that may affect your child, you must investigate what your State is saying and doing. Study the relevant information on its department of education's website, then speak to one of the department's testing or special education officials about the meaning and implementation of its regulations, policies, and procedures, and then do the same with your district.

Monitor the changing requirements of NCLB. As we're writing this chapter, Congress is arguing about how to change it. Any changes will change your State and school district's regulations, policies, and procedures for testing. Because NCLB is in flux, you might visit, call, or write your legislators—Federal and State—to let them know what you support and oppose. By influencing Congress and your State legislature, you influence your district, which influences your child's chances for promotion and graduation.

Component 9: Alternative Assessment. *If the IEP Team determines that the child must take an alternate assessment instead of a particular regular State or districtwide assessment of student achievement, [the IEP must state] why ... the child cannot participate in the regular assessment [and state why] ... the particular alternate assessment selected is appropriate for the child.*[84]

Comment. Despite the Federal push to have all struggling readers take State and districtwide reading and language arts tests, in rare instances children may not have to take these tests. Instead, in some States a very small number of special education students may take an *alter-*

nate assessment, which, in theory, is personalized to match the child's curriculum. Instead of paper-and-pencil tasks, it may consist of teacher observations, rating scales, work samples, and other assessment information.

To comply with NCLB regulations, the Team can substitute an alternate reading assessment *only if*:

- Your child's cognitive and learning problems are so severe that what she's been taught is far more basic than what's measured by the reading and language arts test. Here's an example: Your child's 14-years old, the test she's scheduled to take assesses eighth-grade reading comprehension, but she's just learning to recognize letters.
- Your child cannot behave appropriately when tested. For example, she may have an extremely serious attention deficit hyperactivity disorder (ADHD) that prevents her from attending or sitting for more than four minutes at a time and will likely invalidate her scores as the test requires her to sit for 45 minutes. Her ADHD is chronic and documented. It was a reason for her IDEA-2004 eligibility.
- With accommodations, the test results will not be valid.[85]

For struggling readers, substituting alternate assessments for State and districtwide standardized tests seems sensible. After all, assessment should measure what's been stressed during instruction, not what hasn't; it should accurately measure the knowledge, skill, and functioning levels of struggling readers, not the negative influences of excessive hyperactivity, anxiety, or behavioral problems. Beware, however, of a major downside, one that can have devastating effects on struggling readers: By taking alternate assessments, they may be ineligible to earn a regular high school diploma.[86]

Also be mindful that few, if any, struggling readers are eligible for *alternate assessments*. At the moment, the criteria are too stringent, too limiting. We think such stringent criteria are poor policy; among our colleagues, we're probably in a minority.

KEEP IN MIND

Keep in mind the order of the first five components:
1. Present Levels of Academic Achievement and Functional Performance
2. Measurable Annual Goals (and in some cases, short-term objectives)
3. Related Services
4. General Curriculum—Involvement and Progress
5. Placement in the Least Restrictive Environment (LRE)

By encouraging the IEP Team to follow this order when meeting to plan your child's IEP, you're helping its members consider information logically. This reduces the likelihood of unnecessary conflicts and errors in judgment. One variation from this order is justified: Discussing your child's ability to function in general education *before* discussing goals (and in some situations, objectives).

In contrast, the Present Levels of Academic Achievement and Functional Performance section and the Goals (and objectives) should always be agreed upon *before* discussing placement or related services. Prematurely discussing placement and related services can quickly lead to power struggles as there's no justification for decisions.[87]

Logically, placement and related services should flow from the Present Levels and Goals, as they provide the necessary understanding and justification. To determine placement and services, the IEP Team must know what your child can and cannot do, her instructional and functional levels, what she needs to learn, what goals are reasonable, and what supports and services she needs to achieve her goals.

Also keep in mind that it's not enough to understand the IEP process, the nature and responsibilities of IEP Teams, and the components of the IEP. To get your child an effective reading program, you need to know much more about Federal special education laws. You need to know about several of IDEA-2004's critical but often ignored principles, about options for struggling readers ineligible for special education under IDEA-2004, and about pitfalls that can undermine your child's success and stress you and your family—financially and emotionally. These are discussed in the next chapter.

ENDNOTES

[1] Although the IEP establishes goals, your child's school and teachers are not responsible for meeting them, only for implementing what's in the IEP. Thus, it's critical that you make sure her IEP provides whatever she needs to achieve her goals and that they're realistic, but ambitious. We define realistic in terms of effort: With moderate effort your child can achieve her IEP goals by the end of the school year.

[2] www.nichcy.org or, 800-695-0285. Although the acronym does not match the Center's name, the acronym is correct: NICHCY.

[3] 34 CFR § 300.320.

[4] 34 CFR § 300.114, italics added.

[5] Here's one of many problems with this vague set of statements about Fay's language: It doesn't tell you Fay's level when the IEP was written. Since it doesn't state Fay's starting or baseline level, you can't measure or judge her progress because you don't know where she started. If she ended the year at a fourth-grade instructional level, but started at a third-grade level, she made moderate progress; if she started at a fourth-grade instructional level and ended at a fourth-grade level, she made no progress. You can't measure progress if you don't know the starting point.

[6] Look, for example, at the warning of Robert Wilson and Craig Cleland: "Matt scored a 6.2 reading score on this group, norm-referenced achievement test, and he's only in third grade! He must be able to read sixth-grade-level materials. Is this judgment warranted? Absolutely not! .... It is entirely possible that the third-grade test that he took did not even contain any sixth-grade-level reading material on it" (Wilson, R. M., & Cleland, C. J., 1989. *Diagnostic and Remedial Reading for Classroom and Clinic* (6th ed.). Columbus, OH: Merrill, p. 49).

[7] Note that we said *estimate*. No test is perfect, including the best of informal reading inventories (IRI). Like all tests, IRIs provide estimates that must be supplemented by the examiner's obser-

vations and other relevant information.

8   34 CFR §300.1.

9   34 CFR § 300.320.

10   Ideally, what's measured on State and districtwide tests reflects the school's curriculum. But often, this is not so. Tests and curricula are often out of alignment. Thus, to avoid the negative consequences of your child failing a State or districtwide test—consequences that can include grade retention—it's important to have goals that ensure the school is teaching your child what's tested. Although State standards are a guide, they too are often misaligned with State and districtwide tests. For a full discussion of this problem, see Glidden, H., & Hightower, A. M., 2007. Mismatch: When state standards and tests don't mesh, schools are left grinding their gears. *American Educator*; retrieved 2/3/08, from http://www.aft.org/pubs-reports/american_educator/issues/spring07.

11   This, however, does not mean that students should not be instructed in the general education curriculum. They should. IDEA-2004 clearly prefers instructing students in this curriculum. However, for struggling readers, the IEP's reading goals should emphasize only that which should be emphasized during reading and related instruction so the struggling reader gets an adequate amount of instructional time devoted to overcoming her specific reading difficulties.If struggling readers get little instruction in what's important, they make little progress. As Gregory Harper and his colleagues noted more than a decade ago, "Academic achievement is related directly to the amount of time students spend actually thinking about and working with *important* instructional content. Student involvement, in turn, is influenced by ... allocated time—amount of time scheduled for a *particular* subject, topic, or skill; [and] engaged time—amount of time students are actively engaged with [the] academic content" (Harper, G. F., Maheady, L., & Mallette, B., 1994. The power of peer-mediated instruction. In J. S. Thousand, R. A. Villa, & A. Nevin (Eds.), *Creativity and Collaborative Learning*. Baltimore, MD: Paul H. Brookes Publishing, pp. 229-241, p. 231, italics added).

12   34 CFR § 300.320, italics added.

13   McGinnis, D. J., & Smith, D. E., 1982. *Analyzing and Treating Reading Problems*. New York: Macmillan Publishing, p. 162. Although the original quotation refers to a male, our substitution of female pronouns retains its meaning: Whether male or female, the consequences are often disastrous.

14   The IEP "must include ... a statement of the special education and related services and supplementary aids and services ... to be provided to the child, or on behalf of the child, and a statement of the program modifications or supports for school personnel that will be provided *to enable the child ... to advance appropriately toward attaining the annual goals* ... to be involved in and make progress in the general education curriculum ... and to participate in extracurricular and other nonacademic activities (34 CFR § 300.320, italics added).

15   34 CFR § 300.34, bold added.

16   34 CFR Discussion, p. 46571.

17   34 CFR § 300.320.

18   The importance of meaningful progress is shown in the following quotation from the U.S. 4th Circuit Court of Appeals: "Although the amount of appropriate advancement will necessarily vary depending on the abilities of individual students ... the district court did not err in finding that a goal

of four months' progress over a period of more than one year was rather modest for a student such as Shannon and was unlikely to permit her to advance from grade to grade with passing marks. Thus, it was proper for the district court to conclude that the ... program *failed to satisfy the Act's requirement of more than minimal or trivial progress*" (italics added; this decision and the subsequent Supreme Court ruling can be found at www.special-ed-law.com; with some variation in the titles, the 4th Circuit's and the Supreme Court's decisions are entitled Shannon Carter v. Florence County School District Four. When reading this quotation, note that the Court of Appeals declared that IDEA required more than minimal progress).

[19] We purposely put the word school's before the phrase *general education curriculum*. We did this to stress that in different schools the general education curriculum may differ.

[20] The U.S. Department of Education's (USDOE) discussion of IDEA-2004 states that "There are ... many opportunities for the IEP Team to consider the affect of emotional issues on a child's learning. For example, ... the IEP Team [is required] to consider the strengths of the child; the concerns of the parents for enhancing the education of their child; the results of the initial evaluation or most recent evaluation of the child; and the academic, developmental, and functional needs of the child, all of which could be affected by emotional issues and would, therefore, need to be considered by the IEP Team" (34 CFR Discussion, p. 46581).

[21] Inclusion is a poorly defined term that usually means a child is enrolled in and spends the bulk, if not all, of her day in general education classes. Consistent with this, most struggling readers spend the majority of their day in general education classes. Many of them fail to get the type of instruction and the supports they need to make meaningful progress. This is *dumping*. As such, it causes severe harm.

[22] 34 CFR § 300.1, italics added.

[23] 34 CFR Discussion, p. 46589, italics added.

[24] 34 CFR Discussion, p. 46581, italics added.

[25] 34 CFR § 300.320.

[26] 34 CFR Discussion, p. 46589.

[27] Durlak, J. A., & Weissberg, R. P., 2007. *The Impact of After-School Programs that Promote Personal and Social Skills*. Chicago, IL: Collaborative for Academic, Social, and Emotional Learning (CASEL), p. 7.

[28] 34 CFR § 300.34.

[29] Stark, K. D., Herren, J., & Fisher, M., 2009. Cognitive-behavioral interventions for depression during childhood. In M. J. Mayer, R. Van Acker, J. E. Lochman, & F. M. Gresham (Eds.), *Cognitive-behavioral Interventions for Emotional and Behavior Disorders* (pp. 266-292). New York: The Guilford Press.

[30] Weisman, A. S., Antinoro, D., & Chu, B. C., 2009. Cognitive-behavioral therapy for anxious youth in school settings. In M. J. Mayer, R. Van Acker, J. E. Lochman, & F. M. Gresham (Eds.), *Cognitive-behavioral Interventions for Emotional and Behavior Disorders* (pp. 173-203). New York: The Guilford Press, p. 191.

[31] 34 CFR Discussion, p. 46587.

[32] 34 CFR Discussion, p. 46589.

[33] 34 CFR Discussion, p. 46580, bold added.

[34] This includes school health services that do not require administration by a physician.

[35] 34 CFR Discussion, p. 46588, italics added.

[36] "As similar as possible" refers to factors like the proportion of students with and without disabilities in the class, the structure, organization, and curriculum of the class, the teacher's instructional strategies, and the nature of student interactions with peers. In other words, to what extent does the specialized environment resemble that of the regular class? To what extent does the student with special needs have opportunities to interact positively with non-disabled peers and to master the general education curriculum? As you might have gathered, defining the least restrictive environment (LRE) can be a difficult task, fraught with subjectivity and relativism. With regard to LRE, relativism means that for one child "Environment A" is too restrictive; for another child of the same age, with the same general disability (e.g., learning disabilities), it's not.

[37] Some authorities would consider pull-out services for tutoring and resource centers to be related services. With respect to reading, what's most important for your child is not the designation of the service, but the content, the quality, the effectiveness, the other students involved, and the minimization of stigma.

[38] In discussing the Least Restrictive Environment for a child in special education, the Federal government wrote: "The Act [IDEA-2004] does not require that every child with a disability be placed in the regular classroom regardless of individual abilities and needs. This recognition that regular class placement may not be appropriate for every child with a disability is reflected in the requirement that LEAs make available a range of placement options, known as a continuum of alternative placements, to meet the unique educational needs of children with disabilities. This requirement for the continuum reinforces the importance of the individualized inquiry, not a 'one size fits all' approach, in determining what placement is the LRE for each child with a disability" (34 CFR Discussion, p. 46587).

[39] To get a flavor for how restricted life becomes for children and adults with poor reading abilities, read these three comments. The first is from the American Federation of Teachers, the second from a national panel of scholars who summarized much of the research on preventing reading difficulties, and the third from an outstanding textbook on reading difficulties.

"This we can say with certainty: If a child in a modern society like ours does not learn to read, he doesn't make it in life. If he doesn't learn to read well enough to comprehend what he is reading, if he doesn't learn to read effortlessly enough to render reading pleasurable, if he doesn't learn to read fluently enough to read broadly and reflectively across all the content areas, his chances for a fulfilling life, by whatever measure—academic success, financial success, the ability to find interesting work, personal autonomy, self-esteem—are practically nil" (Editorial, 1995. Learning to read: Schooling's first mission. *American Educator*, 19 (2), 3-6, p. 3).

"Reading is essential to success in our society. The ability to read is highly valued and important for social and economic advancement.... Current difficulties in reading largely originate from rising demands for literacy, not from declining absolute levels of literacy. In a technological society, the demands for higher literacy are ever increasing, creating more grievous consequences for those who fall short" (Snow, C. E., Burns, M. S., & Griffin, P. (Eds.), 1998. *Preventing Reading Difficulties in Young Children*. Washington, D.C.: National Academies Press, p. 1).

"Every poor reader is at risk for psychological disturbance, almost always as a result of … and frequently as a further contribution to the poor reading" (Eisenberg, L., 1975; quoted in Lipson, M. Y., & Wixson, K. K., 2003. *Assessment and Instruction of Reading and Writing Difficulty: An Interactive Approach.* Boston: Allyn & Bacon, p. 46).

Because effectively teaching children to read is a moral as well as a professional and political issue, we urge you to share these quotations with school personnel who are hesitant to offer your child whatever services she needs to become a highly motivated, proficient reader. You might be amazed at the number of people, including teachers and administrators, who do not understand the long-term, devastating consequences of reading disabilities.

[40]   34 CFR Discussion, p. 46587.

[41]   34 CFR Discussion, p. 46549.

[42]   34 CFR Discussion, p. 46586, italics added.

[43]   34 CFR Discussion, p. 46588.

[44]   34 CFR § 300.115.

[45]   This statement is widely quoted. One case in which it appears is *Town of Burlington v. Department of Education*, U. S. 1st Circuit Court, 1984. Another is *Egg Harbor Township Board of Education v. S.O.*, U. S. District Court for New Jersey, 1992. If you need copies of these or other cases in this book, you might ask your county or local college librarian to help you or you might download them from www.special-ed-law.com or from www.wrightslaw.com.

As we previously noted, when reading the decisions of a U.S. Circuit Court of Appeals, it's important to realize that its decisions bind only Federal courts *in* the States for which the Circuit Court has jurisdiction. The decisions of an individual Circuit Court of Appeals often influence Federal courts for other States, but *do not bind them.* Only decisions of the U. S. Supreme Court bind all Federal courts.

[46]   This quotation is from an insightful article on special education law and transition (McAfee, J. K., & Greenawalt, C., 2001. IDEA, the Courts, and the Law of Transition. *Preventing School Failure, 45* (3), 102-107; retrieved 4/1/08, from http://web.ebscohost.com). Although the quotation refers to a Federal case that is not about reading (Urban vs. Jefferson County, 1994, 1996), the quotation's central concept applies to reading: Learning counts. After all, what good is placing a child in a class in which she doesn't learn? Long term, lack of learning will create far fewer opportunities and many restrictions. Thus, restrictiveness deals not only with the present, and who surrounds a child, but with the future and the opportunities created by learning as well as the restrictiveness created by not learning.

[47]   Yell, M., & Katsiyannis, A., 2004. Placing students with disabilities in inclusive settings: Legal guidelines and preferred practices. *Preventing School Failure, 49* (1), 28-35, p. 32. Although this article deals with IDEA-1997, its discussion debunks many of the harmful myths that still guide placement and services.

[48]   With proper services, some struggling readers can make far more than one year's growth in one year's time. When it's possible and won't stress the struggling reader, it's important to try. Deborah Simmons and Edward Kameenui offer an excellent rationale: "Children with disabilities constantly face the tyranny of time in trying to catch up with their peers who continue to advance in their literacy development. Simply keeping pace with their peers amounts to losing more and more ground for

students who are behind…. The opportunities for [struggling readers] to advance or catch up diminish greatly over time" (Simmons, D. C., & Kameenui, E. J., 1996. A focus on curriculum design: When children fail. *Focus on Exceptional Children, 28* (7), 1-16, p. 3; retrieved 4/12/05, from http:// search.epnet.com).

49 34 CFR § 300.320.

50 34 CFR § 300.106.

51 34 CFR Discussion, p. 46582.

52 Mraz, M., & Rasinski, T. V., 2007. Summer reading loss. *The Reading Teacher, 60*, 784-789, p. 785.

53 Many average students actually make modest gains over the summer months. See Mraz & Rasinski, 2007.

54 34 CFR § 300.320.

55 IDEA-2004, Sec. 601.

56 IDEA-2004, Sec. 601. Should your child's IEP Team refuse to provide a needed service for which there's strong justification, you may want to show them this quote. You may also want to ask, "Without this service, how are you effectively meeting her unique needs and preparing her for further education, employment, and independent living?" If they say they are and they give a vague rationale, ask, "What short-term benchmarks will you use to demonstrate that you're effectively meeting her needs, that she's making progress sufficient to prepare her for further education, employment, and independent living?"

57 Criterion-referenced Measurement (CBM) usually provides excellent data for making such decisions. Chapter 7 discusses CBM. Our website, www.reading2008.com, offers additional information.

58 Allington, R. L., & Cunningham, P. M., 2007. *Schools that Work: Where All Children Read and Write.* Boston: Allyn & Bacon, p. 143.

59 Entwisle, D. R., Alexander, K. L., & Olson, L. S., 2001. Keep the faucet flowing: Summer learning and home environment. *American Educator, 25* (3), 10-15, 47, p. 12. Alone, lack of family resources or a poor neighborhood is insufficient rationale for an ESY. Thus, it's important to get the criteria used by your State's department of education.

60 34 CFR Discussion, p. 46582. Although the factors that IEP Teams must consider vary by State, they're broad. In New Jersey, for example, the IEP Team "must consider all relevant factors, such as the degree of the child's impairment; the degree of regression suffered by the child during interruptions in educational programming and the recovery time from this regression; the ability of the child's parents to provide the educational structure at home during school vacation or on weekends; the child's rate of progress; the child's behavioral and physical problems; the availability of alternative resources; the ability of the child to interact with non-disabled children; the areas of the child's curriculum which require continuous attention; the child's vocational needs; and whether the requested service is extraordinary to the child's condition, as opposed to a necessary part of a program for those with the child's condition" (Education Law Center, undated. *The Right to Special Education in New Jersey: A Guide for Advocates*, p. 36. Available for download from www.edlawcenter.org).

61 34 CFR § 300.106.

[62] 34 CFR § 300.503.

[63] Mraz & Rasinski, 2007.

[64] Allington & Cunningham, 2007.

[65] Allington, R. L., 2001. *What Really Matters for Struggling Readers: Designing Research-Based Programs.* New York: Addison-Wesley, p. 133.

[66] 34 CFR Discussion, p. 46718.

[67] 34 CFR § 300.320.

[68] Many people confuse the words *standardized* and *objective* with *fair* and *accurate.* Often, standardized tests that are objectively scored are neither fair nor accurate. For a sampling of the vast literature on this topic, you may want to look at any of the Mental Measurements Yearbooks, published by the University of Nebraska, which are available at most large libraries. You can also study their test reviews on line: buros.unl.edu/buros/jsp/search.jsp.

[69] 34 CFR Discussion, p. 46666.

[70] Board of Education of Ottawa Township High School District 140 v. Spellings, U. S. 7th Circuit Court, 2008.

[71] Laubin, M. C., 2008. *NCLB Testing Requirements May Trump IDEA*; retrieved 2/19/08, from http://www.connecticuteducationlawblog.com.

[72] "Some states have policies that attach high stakes, such as grade retention or awarding of high school diplomas, to test performance. Such 'stakes' are not a requirement of NCLB" (Cortiella, C., 2005. *No Child Left Behind: Understanding assessment options for IDEA-eligible students*; retrieved 3/8/08, from www.ncld.org, p. 8).

[73] Glidden, H., & Hightower, A. M., 2007. Mismatch: When state standards and tests don't mesh, schools are left grinding their gears. *American Educator*; retrieved 2/3/08, from http://www.aft.org/pubs-reports/american_educator/issues/spring07.

[74] Bracey, G. W., 2006. *Reading Educational Research: How to Avoid Getting Statistically Snookered.* Portsmouth, NH: Heinemann. This excellent book exposes many of the dangers, inadequacies, and shenanigans of high-stakes testing. One of its illuminating quotes about what many educators consider the gold standard of achievement testing—the National Assessment of Educational Progress (NAEP)—is from the National Academy of Sciences: "NAEP's current achievement level setting procedures remain fundamentally flawed.... The procedures have produced unreasonable results" (p. 149). If the NAEP—a gold standard of standardized testing—is so lacking, would your State's high-stakes tests be better?

[75] If you ever face the prospect of having your child retained, we recommended that you read and share these two journal articles with school personnel: (a) Jimerson, S., 2001. Meta-analysis of grade retention research: Implications for practice in the 21st century. *School Psychology Review, 30*, 420-437; (b) Jimerson, S., & Kaufman, A. M., 2003. Reading, writing, and retention: A primer on grade retention research. *The Reading Teacher, 56*, 622–635. Both articles contain critical information that school personnel may find new and disturbing. Here's a critical example: "Grade retention has been identified as the single most powerful predictor of dropping out" (Jimerson & Kaufman, 2003, p. 626).

[76] Zigmond, N. 2001. Special education at a crossroads. *Preventing School Failure, 45* (2), 70-74, quote found in paragraph 7 of section One Size Fits All; retrieved 4/20/08, from http://web.ebscohost.com.

77 34 CFR Discussion, p. 46683, italics added.

78 Kubiszyn, T., & Borich, G., 1987. *Educational Testing and Measurement* (2nd ed.). Glenview, IL: Scott Foresman and Company, p. 11, italics added.

79 34 CFR § 300.304.

80 An argument against our position is that the testing of students with reading and learning disabilities creates accountability for schools, forcing them to teach rather than ignore such students. Law and policy, however, can accomplish this goal by assessing and reporting the performance of groups of students and not punishing or retaining individual students who fail to meet predetermined standards.

81 The figure of 22 States and this quotation are found in *State high school exit exams: A challenging year* (August 2006). This, and related documents, may be downloaded from the Center on Education Policy's (CEP) website, www.cep-dc.org.

82 Recently, scholars from Rice University and the University of Texas at Austin reported that the separation of NCLB test scores by race, disability, and similar factors "puts our most vulnerable youth … at risk of being *pushed out of their schools* so the school ratings can show 'measurable improvement.' High-stakes, test-based accountability leads not to equitable educational possibilities for youth, but to avoidable losses of these students from our schools" (McNeil, L. M., Coppola, E., Radigan, J., & Vasquez Heilig, J., 2008. Avoidable losses: High-stakes accountability and the dropout crisis. *Education Policy Analysis Archives, 16* (3), 1-48, p. 2, italics added; retrieved 2/18/08, from http://epaa.asu.edu/epaa/v16n3/

83 For a scholarly, yet blistering review of high-stakes testing, along with numerous examples of the problems, you may want to download *The Inevitable Corruption of Indicators and Educators Through High-Stakes Testing* (Nichols, S. L., & Berliner, D. C., 2005. Tempe, AZ: College of Education, Arizona State University, Education Policy Studies Laboratory; retrieved 3/7/08, from http://www.asu.edu/educ/epsl/EPRU/documents/EPSL-0503-101-EPRU.doc).

84 34 CFR § 300.320.

85 Although the IEP Team is responsible for determining a child's eligibility for taking an alternate assessment, the Team must follow Federal and State laws and regulations. New Jersey's Administrative Code has a relatively clear definition for eligibility that reflects the NCLB requirements: "Students with disabilities shall participate in [an alternate assessment] where the nature of the student's disability is so severe that the student is not receiving instruction *in any* of the knowledge and skills measured by the general Statewide assessment and the student cannot complete *any* of the types of questions on the assessment in the content area(s) even with accommodations and modifications" (N.J.A.C. 6A:14-4.10(a)2, italics added). Few struggling readers would meet these criteria.

86 The USDOE's discussion of IDEA-2004's regulations describes students eligible for alternate assessments and the reason they're eligible. Eligible children are those "with the most significant cognitive disabilities who are not expected to meet grade-level standards even with the best instruction." Their "alternate achievement standard sets an expectation of performance that differs in complexity from a grade-level achievement standard" (34 CFR Discussion, p. 46558).

87 Occasionally, schools insist that parents agree to placement and services before agreeing to their child's Present Levels and Goals; this may violate IDEA-2004.

CHAPTER 12
PRINCIPLES, OPTIONS, AND PITFALLS

This chapter discusses how several underlying principles of the *Individuals with Disabilities Education Improvement Act of 2004* (IDEA-2004) affect struggling readers' programs and their ability to succeed on high-stakes tests. It does so by discussing quotations from IDEA-2004 that are particularly relevant to struggling readers. These quotations and our commentary help explain important, but often misunderstood and ignored concepts: individualization, opportunity for achieving academic standards, preference for instructional methods supported by research, and supports for children and teachers. Understanding these principles will increase your odds of getting your child a program that helps him progress in all areas of educational need, including reading.

This chapter also answers the question, "How can I get services for my child if he's ineligible under IDEA-2004?" Consequently, we discuss *Section 504 of the Rehabilitation Act of 1973* (Section 504), IDEA-2004's "early intervening services" for children not receiving special education services, the *No Child Left Behind Act's* (NCLB) Basic Skills Instruction, and the NCLB's requirement that schools make adequate yearly progress.[1] We discuss these later in the chapter, after discussing several of IDEA-2004's critical but often ignored principles.

Finally, this chapter discusses numerous pitfalls that parents often ignore, pitfalls that can cause grief and perhaps lasting harm.

As always, our comments are not legal advice; they are the views of an educator and a psychologist who, for decades, have interpreted these laws, as they define and govern special education.[2]

CRITICAL BUT OFTEN IGNORED PRINCIPLES
Principle 1: Decisions Must be Individualized to Meet Your Child's Unique Needs.
[A major purpose of IDEA-2004 is] *to ensure that all children with disabilities have available to them a free appropriate public education [FAPE] that emphasizes special education and related services **designed to meet their unique needs**.*[3] *... Special education means specially designed instruction ... to meet the unique needs of a child with a disability.... **Specially designed instruction** means adapting, as appropriate to the needs of an eligible child ... the content, methodology, or delivery of instruction—to address the unique needs of the child that result from the child's disability; and ... to ensure access of the child to the general curriculum, so that the child can meet the educational standards.*[4]

Comment. This means that the school must focus on meeting your child's unique needs. Cookie-cutter programs are inappropriate. That's why Arthur Shapiro, Professor Emeritus of Special Education from Kean University of New Jersey, often says, "IEP means Individualized Education Program, not Identical Education Program." This view was highlighted in a well-known Federal case, Deal v. Hamilton County:

> The School System seemed to suggest ... that it is entitled to invest in a program ... and then capitalize on that investment by using [it] ... exclusively.

But this is precisely what it is not permitted to do, at least without fully considering the individual needs of each child.... In other words, the school district may not ... decide that because it has spent a lot of money on a [reading] program, that program is always going to be appropriate for educating children with a specific disability, regardless of any evidence to the contrary of the individualized needs of a particular child.[5]

Given the requirement that special education programs must meet your child's unique needs and help him to make meaningful progress in the general education curriculum, the school cannot place him in just any program for children with reading difficulties. If, for example, his word identification is strong and his reading comprehension is weak, it would be inappropriate to place him in an instructional program that stresses word identification, not comprehension.

Similarly, if he's despondent about his reading difficulties and his despondency severely impedes his learning to read and his progress in the general education curriculum, his IEP must offer goals and ways of eliminating or minimizing his despondency. If the school refuses to provide goals and ways that have a reasonable chance of succeeding, it's failing to meet his unique needs; it's failing to meet its responsibilities.

In essence, your child's program—as described in his IEP—must be designed to meet his unique needs, including his academic, social, emotional, communication, recreational, and physical needs.

To address your child's unique needs, his program must provide special education and the "related services and supplementary aids and services" he needs to have a reasonable chance of achieving each goal in his IEP and of meeting the standards of the general education curriculum.[6] If one of his IEP goals calls for one-year's growth in reading comprehension, and to achieve this he needs one-to-one tutoring by a reading specialist, the school must provide it. If what the school offers is unlikely to produce one-year's growth, the school is failing to meet its obligation—its program is inappropriate.[7]

If you're facing a situation in which the school will not offer the special education and the aids and services your child needs to meet his IEP's goals *and* to achieve the standards of the general education curriculum, you may want to show school personnel these quotations from IDEA-2004's regulations and two Federal Appeals Court decisions:

[The IEP requires] a statement of the special education and related services and supplementary aids and services ... to be provided to the child, or on behalf of the child, and a statement of the program modifications or supports for school personnel that will be provided to *enable the child to advance appropriately toward attaining the annual goals*; to be involved in and *make progress in the general education curriculum* ... [and] to participate in extracurricular and other nonacademic activities.[8]

Before a child with a disability can be placed outside of the regular educational environment, *the full range* of supplementary aids and services that could be provided to facilitate the child's placement in the regular classroom setting must be considered.[9]

[Schools must review] the child's IEP ... not less than annually to determine whether the annual goals for the child *are being achieved* ... [and revise] the IEP, as appropriate, to address ... any *lack of expected progress toward the annual goals.*[10]

The ... [IDEA-2004] calls for more than a trivial educational benefit .... The teaching of Diamond [a case previously heard by the 3rd Circuit Court of Appeals[11]] is that when the Supreme Court said 'some benefit' ... it did not mean 'some' as opposed to 'none.' Rather, 'some' connotes an amount of benefit greater than mere trivial advancement.[12]

Third Circuit [Court of Appeals] cases have affirmed that IEPs must be tailored to provide meaningful benefit. For example, in *Ridgewood*, the court held that a mere finding that an IEP had provided 'more than a trivial educational benefit' was insufficient to establish that the IDEA's standards had been met.... The court found that because the benefit provided 'must be gauged in relation to a child's potential'... the determination of 'meaningful benefit' requires 'a student-by-student analysis that carefully considers the student's individual abilities'.... The *Kingwood* court, in turn, emphasized that the educational benefit must be *'meaningful,'* and acknowledged that a district court must 'analyze the type and amount of learning' of which a student is capable in order to determine how much of an educational benefit must be provided.[13]

To reduce the need for services, some schools offer unambitious IEP goals that will, perhaps unintentionally, keep children in special education as the school's goals fall far short of what children can likely achieve with adequate, quality services. As you can see from the following Circuit Court of Appeals decision, a decision that was upheld by the U.S. Supreme Court, this violates the concept of meaningful benefit:

Although the amount of appropriate advancement will necessarily vary depending on the abilities of individual students ... the district court did not err in finding that a goal of four months' progress over a period of more than one year was rather modest for a student such as Shannon and was unlikely to permit her to advance from grade to grade with passing marks. Thus, it was proper for the district court to conclude that the ... program failed to satisfy the Act's requirement of more than minimal or trivial progress.[14]

You might have noticed that several of the previous quotations spoke about potential: "a student such as Shannon," "in relation to a child's potential." In practical terms, assessing potential requires professionals and parents to accurately predict what a child *can* learn. Unfortunately, the Federal courts discuss "potential" as if educators and psychologists can definitively measure it, can accurately predict what a child can learn. Educators and psychologists can't. Often, however, they can accurately estimate a child's likely rate of short-term progress in narrow areas.

For example, if a 14-year-old child's word recognition abilities are mid-second grade, he's had many fine reading teachers, and he's worked hard to achieve this level, it's unlikely that in the next six months his word recognition level will soar to 6th grade, though it might reach 3rd. If he's in an excellent program, with excellent instruction, and he's learned about 60 sight words a month over the last four months, he'll likely learn about 180 sight words over the next three months (60 x 3 = 180). If reading instruction increases from 45 to 60 minutes daily, an increase of 33%, he might even learn 80 words per month. Why a 33% increase? It's a logical guess, a hypothesis that increasing instructional time by 33% will produce a 33% increase in sight words. Chances are good, but not perfect, that on-average, he'll now learn about 80 words per month.[15]

Compared to short-term prediction, our ability to accurately and definitively predict long-term potential or achievement is poorer. Take, for example, Howard. His high school grade-point average and SAT scores were good, not great. His first semester's average at Brooklyn College, a highly competitive school with free tuition, was barely passing. At the end of his first semester, his advisor pressured him to quit and learn a trade before he inevitably flunked out. Short term, his advisor's prediction was nearly right; long term, it was wrong. Howard's second semester average also flirted with failure, but was marginally passing. Nevertheless, he persevered, seeking strategies that would make him successful. Long term, he graduated with honors, earned a doctorate, published more than a hundred articles and columns, edited journals, became a full professor, and directed two graduate programs in the same system that pressured him to quit.

The lesson: Despite the Federal court's insistence on identifying a child's potential, our long-term estimates and predictions of achievement are often wrong.[16] Moreover, to estimate short-term potential and foster meaningful achievement, the child must be in the right program, must have the right degree of challenge, must value what's taught, must try to do well, must use the right learning and study strategies, and must be taught by knowledgeable, skilled teachers who believe in his abilities to succeed. In Howard's case, all these factors fell into place.[17]

So, how can parents and schools resolve this court-mandated problem of identifying potential?[18] Stick to relatively narrow areas, such as phonemic awareness, word identification, word recognition, fluency, and reading comprehension. Measure rates of progress under current conditions and use these rates to estimate the short-term progress likely to result from quality instruction and sufficient, appropriate resources, such as one hour of daily instruction from a reading specialist in an interactive group of three students. Stick to goals that predict what your child will likely achieve in a year or less, with quality instruction and sufficient, appropriate resources. And monitor progress and monitor progress and monitor progress and monitor progress. (Sorry for the repetition, but we're obsessive about the message: Monitor progress continuously.) This will make it possible to quickly identify and remove obstacles or revise predictions. Chapter 7 provides guidance for monitoring progress.

Principle 2: Schools Must Ensure Opportunities for Your Child to Achieve his State's High Academic Standards. *State rules, regulations, and policies ... must support and facilitate ... school-level system improvement designed to enable children with disabilities* **to meet the challenging State student academic achievement standards.**[19] *... [IDEA-2004] focuses on high academic standards and clear performance goals for children with disabilities that are consistent with the standards and expectations for all children.*[20]

Comment. Congress was explicit: Schools must have high aspirations for students with educational disabilities. They must do what's needed to enable such students to "make progress in the general education curriculum."[21] Accordingly, schools must ensure that such students have adequate opportunities to meet the academic standards required of students without educational disabilities. To do this, IDEA-2004 requires schools to offer IEPs that provide the goals, special education, supplementary aides and services, and related services that students with disabilities need to achieve high academic standards.

For your child's school to meet his unique needs and to give him ample opportunity to achieve his State's high academic standards, his IEP may have to provide one-to-one tutoring from a reading specialist, an extended school year for reading, in-class support from a reading specialist, specialized instruction from a speech and language therapist, monthly meetings to review and coordinate instruction, or a combination of these and other services. Providing the instruction and services needed for children with disabilities to meet their State's high academic standards is consistent with Congress's aims:

> The education of children with disabilities can be made more effective by—having high expectations for such children and ensuring their access to the general education curriculum in the regular classroom, to the maximum extent possible, in order to—meet *developmental goals* and, to the maximum extent possible, the *challenging expectations* that have been *established for all children*; and be prepared to lead *productive and independent adult lives*, to the maximum extent possible.[22]

Be careful, however, not to pressure your child unrealistically. Many intelligent, motivated, hard-working children, given quality instruction and multiple opportunities to achieve, will fall short of statewide standards. As Naomi Zigmond asserted:

> Students with learning ... disorders do not fail to learn to read because we have set low expectations for them; they fail to learn to read because

they have a disability that interferes with their capacity to benefit from instruction that is sufficient to produce learning in children without this disability.[23]

So how do you and the other members of your child's IEP Team develop the high standards—the criteria or achievement levels—for his IEP goals? Ideally, you and other members of your child's Team should assess what he recently accomplished when, for several weeks, he received high quality, highly relevant, highly focused, moderately challenging, carefully-monitored instruction that emphasized instructional strategies supported by peer-reviewed research.

Although this last sentence was a mouthful, each element is important; each must be in place to accurately estimate what he can learn with *similar* curricula. Take, for example, his rate of progress in learning how to apply short-vowel sounds. It should help predict his rate of progress in learning to apply long-vowel sounds, but not multiplication. Similarly, his rate of progress in reading fluency should help to accurately predict future progress in fluency, but not organizational abilities.

All of this loops back to the Present Levels information and the goals for your child's IEP. The Present Levels must be relevant, accurate, and comprehensive. It should clearly state "how [your] child's disability affects [his] involvement and progress in the general education curriculum."[24] To further understand the "how," it should go beyond listing his instructional levels; ideally, it should list the barriers to progress he encounters in general education classes and in mastering the curriculum. It should also identify what has helped him or is likely to help him overcome these barriers.

Consistent with the information in the Present Levels, the goals in your child's IEP should focus on what he has to learn and do to make meaningful progress in the general education curriculum. This is far more complex than it sounds. For example, to stimulate success, his IEP goals must focus on what's of major importance for him to learn and do in his general education classes and ignore what's minor. They should use realistic criteria, criteria that he can achieve in a semester or school year if his effort is reasonable and sustained rather than herculean.

Related to these recommendations about goals are two common pitfalls. One is requiring your child to achieve grade level in the general education curriculum in only a year, when his achievement is years below. This will create frustration and failure. The other is requiring him to make a sustained, herculean effort. He'll burnout. So do what you can to avoid these pitfalls while developing general education goals that are ambitious, relevant, and realistic.

Principle 3: To the Extent Practicable, Schools Must Use Instructional Methods Supported by Research. *[Each child's] IEP ... must include ... a statement of the special education and related services and supplementary aids and services, **based on peer-reviewed research to the extent practicable**, to be provided to the child, or on behalf of the child.[25]... School districts and school personnel must, therefore, select and use methods that research* *has shown to be effective, to the extent that methods based on peer-reviewed research **are** available.... Nothing in [IDEA-2004 suggests] that the failure ... to provide services based on peer-reviewed research would automatically result in a denial of FAPE [Free Appropriate Public Education].*[26]

Comment. Ideally, high quality instruction should use programs, methods, and strategies supported by peer-reviewed research in academic journals; usually, such journals hide the authors' names from reviewers and vice versa, increasing the likelihood of impartial reviews.[27]

Clearly, Congress wanted schools to use programs, methods, and strategies supported by peer-reviewed research and avoid those lacking such support. Many parents believe that school personnel review such research before they match interventions to children's needs. In our experience, few do, many don't. Many professionals know little about the relevant research.

Let's take the case of a very old and popular method for teaching reading to struggling readers, a method that many parents demand for their children, that some teachers swear by, that others swear at: the Orton-Gillingham method.[28]

Based on their recent review of the research, Kristen D. Ritchey of the University of Delaware and Jennifer L. Goeke of Montclair State University concluded that it was currently impossible to tell if Orton-Gillingham was effective:

> Given the small number of studies, the lack of methodological rigor of the existing studies, and the inconclusive findings of the effectiveness of Orton-Gillingham (OG) programs, additional research is needed before the scientific basis can be established.... The major conclusion ... is that the research is currently inadequate, both in number of studies and in the quality of the research methodology, to support that OG interventions are scientifically based.... It may be premature to reconsider the implementation and use of OG reading instruction programs for children with reading disabilities.[29]

Like Orton-Gillingham, it's unfortunate that no compelling body of research supports the effectiveness of most commercial reading programs.[30] Thus, Richard Allington's comments should not be surprising:

> Currently, the [Federal research] website ... lists only two findings as meeting the 'gold standard' for empirical evidence: Reducing class size and providing expert one-to-one tutoring for struggling readers. These are the only areas where findings are supported by the results from multiple independent experimental studies.... Research will not be of much help in identifying effective core or supplemental reading programs. There is no

set of independent studies that meets the Federal gold standard that supports the use of any specific core or supplemental reading program.[31]

But what if school personnel say that despite your child's poor progress, they'll continue to use the same reading program with him because it's supported by research? First, you may want to ask for copies of the peer-reviewed research they're referring to. You might learn that it doesn't exist, or they're referring to a publisher's brochure, not research, or the research did not prove effective for all children or children like your child.

If you suspect that the IEP Team doesn't accurately understand IDEA-2004's position on peer-reviewed research, you might share these thoughts with them: Although schools are encouraged to use methods supported by peer-reviewed research, IDEA 2004 does not require them to do so.[32] If your child is making poor progress in a program that has elements supported by research and has a good teacher who has made whatever well-justified modifications to the program that might work for your child, the school should use a different program. *For him*, it's inappropriate.

If you suspect that the IEP Team views research in absolute terms—a program supported by research is good for all students, you might discuss these points with them: Because research deals with children in general, your child's progress must be monitored—continuously. What's good for most people in a group may harm some. Just look at penicillin: A savior to most people, an anaphylactic killer to some. That's why the *I* in *IEP* stands for *individualized*. That's why it's critical to continuously monitor progress and quickly modify or change programs to improve outcomes. That's also why IDEA-2004 requires IEP Teams to review and modify IEPs (and by implication, instruction) at least once annually and more often if progress is poor.

If you share these thoughts with IEP Team members, be sure to speak respectfully and listen carefully for agreement, disagreement, and their reasoning. Then, if there's disagreement, invite the Team to problem solve. You might ask, "So, how do you think we can resolve our differences? Any ideas?"

As you might conclude, no method or strategy works with all children. Thus, we recommend that you follow a logical progression that first discusses programs, methods, or strategies that have relatively good support from direct or indirect research.[33] If none of these interventions is appropriate, you may need to discuss interventions that have far less research support, but have the unbridled support of your child's teachers.[34] After all, teachers' support and commitment to a program, plus their knowledge and skill about reading instruction, dramatically influence the success of any child's reading program: "Study after study points to teacher expertise as the critical variable in effective literacy instruction."[35]

Many politicians, newspaper editors, and school administrators will disagree with our last suggestion. What we're suggesting is not the neat, tidy, and well-orchestrated picture they want. To them, our suggestion may look messy, even chaotic. But here are four important facts they may not know. Fact: No packaged reading program can meet all the reading needs of struggling readers. Fact: Teachers use programs differently than their authors intended. Fact: Many of the best teachers need opportunities to create, to make instructional decisions that match their expertise. Fact: Good teachers mix-and-match programs and their components to quickly address students' difficulties and successes.

Thus, good teaching is not neat and simple, like picking software off a shelf or ordering a coffee. It's more like painting a mural. It requires continuous appraising and responding, examining and experimenting, reflecting and revising. As Timothy Blair, William Rupley, and William Dee Nicholas so aptly asserted:

> Without the teacher's pervasive concern for *knowing and responding* to students' needs, reading instruction can be irrelevant and mindless drudgery for all concerned.... The use of continuous progress monitoring and thoughtful reflection are integral parts of effective instruction.... Effective teachers use assessment to select instructional strategies appropriate to the desired students' learning outcomes.... Ongoing assessment ... enables teachers to identify instructional procedures that increase success.[36]

So, given IDEA-2004's preference for programs supported by peer-reviewed research, Allington's comments about programs and teachers, our comments about "good teachers," and Blair, Rupley, and Nicholas' assertions about monitoring, what should you do?

Advocate for starting with programs that match the goals of your child's IEP and have components supported by peer-reviewed research, even if it's only related research.

Advocate for programs that teachers have a commitment to, are knowledgeable about, and skilled in using.

Advocate for the supports that teachers need to correctly implement your child's IEP and reading program.

Advocate for whatever training teachers want or need to correctly implement your child's IEP and reading program.

Advocate for continuous monitoring of your child's progress and for teachers to modify in-class instruction to reflect the results of monitoring.

Advocate for the supports that teachers need to continuously and easily monitor your child's progress.

Advocate for the time needed by teachers to meet with and make suggestions to the IEP Team.

One thing you should not do is incessantly insist that the IEP specify the reading programs, methods, or strategies that teachers will use. Is it okay to request that the IEP specify these? Yes. But a request differs radically from incessant insistence. Although some parents and advocates may infer that IDEA-2004's regulations require IEPs to specify the methods to be used, the U. S. Department of Education's (USDOE) discussion and interpretation of IDEA-2004 undermines this view. It permits but does not require specification:[37]

> Nothing in [IDEA-2004] ... requires an IEP to include specific instructional methodologies.... The Department's longstanding position on

including instructional methodologies in a child's IEP is that it is an IEP Team's decision. Therefore, if an IEP Team determines that specific instructional methods are necessary for the child to receive FAPE, the instructional methods may be addressed in the IEP.[38]

Another reason to avoid incessant insistence on particular reading approaches is that insistence often backfires. Here are several reasons. Few if any approaches have a compelling body of research supporting their superiority, which is one reason courts tend to let schools determine methodology. Teachers and other IEP Team members may resent attempts to force them to use a particular approach. They may lack the needed skills to implement and monitor the approach and may not like it, which can dampen their enthusiasm for using it, which can severely reduce its effectiveness. It may take teachers years to fully master the approach; in the meantime, your child is being instructed by someone who's just learning what to do and may not know how to adjust the approach to meet his needs.

So, if progress remains poor, what do you do? Request that the school evaluate your child's needs and investigate external factors that may be causing or adding to his difficulties. These include classroom management, instructional practices, feedback practices, reading materials, time allotted to reading, and opportunities for him to apply what's taught. Once the impediments are identified, ask for an IEP meeting to revise the IEP so it's likely to offer instruction and services that overcome or bypass the impediments and accelerate progress. And make sure that the new or amended IEP has a solid monitoring plan that's carefully implemented.

While doing *all* of this, keep in mind that a critical factor in producing success—perhaps *the* critical factor—is the teacher: Her knowledge, skill, commitment, and willingness to adapt curriculum and methodology to your child's needs.[39]

Principle 4: Schools Must Provide Adequate Supports To and For Your Child. *[The IEP must] include ... a statement of the special education and related services and supplementary aids and services ... to be provided **to the child, or on behalf of the child** ... to advance appropriately toward attaining the annual goals ... to be involved in and make progress in the general education curriculum ... to participate in extracurricular and other nonacademic activities.[40]... Children with disabilities must be provided special education and related services and needed supplementary aids and services to enable them to be involved in and make progress in the general curriculum.[41]*

Comment. IDEA-2004 requires the school to provide your child whatever educational accommodations, modifications, related services, and supplementary aids and services he needs to achieve his IEP goals, to make meaningful progress in the general education curriculum and to succeed on his State and districtwide tests. Thus, a school violates IDEA-2004 if it places him in regular classes without the supports he needs to succeed. Because supports are not the same for everyone, but unique to each child's needs, you and the IEP Team may disagree about what's needed:

As with all special education and related services, it is up to each child's IEP Team to determine the special education and related services that are needed to meet each child's unique needs in order for the child to receive FAPE [free appropriate public education].[42]

If you disagree with the other members of the IEP Team, remember that many Federal courts have been very clear: IEPs must be designed to produce far more than trivial progress; taking the child's potential into account, IEPs must provide the services needed to produce meaningful progress. With this in mind, ask yourself these questions:

- Does my child's IEP meet his unique needs?
- Will the progress he's making or is likely to make with the services provided in the proposed IEP adequately prepare him for "further education, employment, and independent living"?[43]
- At his current rate of progress, will he make, in reasonable time, enough progress to read at grade level, or, if his estimated potential is less, to read in line with his potential?

If any one of your answers is "no," *and* you have good reason to believe that with reasonable supports and services your child can achieve much more, his IEP is failing to meet the purposes of IDEA-2004.[44] The next step is to reexamine his IEP's Present Levels of Academic Achievement and Functional Performance (Present Levels) and discuss it with his IEP Team.

With the IEP Team, make sure that your child's Present Levels *accurately documents all his educational levels and needs*—academic, social, emotional, communication, recreational, vocational, and physical—and that for each need, the IEP lists measurable, realistically ambitious goals, with, if possible, short-term objectives.

Once the Present Levels is comprehensive and accurate, and the IEP's goals realistically address all areas of educational need, it's time to discuss the help your child needs, including special education, related services, supplementary aids and services, extended school year, instructional modifications and accommodations.[45] You may want to ask questions like this: "To achieve his IEP's goals, to succeed in the general education curriculum, and to pass the State and districtwide tests, does he need one-to-one tutoring daily from a reading specialist, specialized materials, modified assignments, computers with special software, help with homework, all these, or other help?"[46]

If you make requests for services to the IEP Team and it rejects them, send the Team an e-mail or certified letter with your requests. This requires the Team to notify you, in writing, about its decision, its reasons, and the data it used to reach its decision.

Knowing IDEA-2004's specific regulations about notices—regulations with which the school must comply—can increase your power to influence the school and the decision of an administrative hearing, especially if the IEP Team failed to provide you with "a description of each evaluation procedure, assessment, record, or report the [school] used as a basis for the … refused action…. [and a] description of other options that the IEP Team considered and the reasons why those options were rejected."[47]

If your request is again rejected, we suggest that you send the IEP Team an e-mail or certified letter, with questions like these:

- Given my child's history of reading disabilities, and his slow rate of progress, what are your reasons for thinking he will make meaningful progress in achieving his *IEP goals* without the services I requested? (List them.)
- How and by when will you know if my child's progress is sufficient to meet *all* the goals in his IEP?
- Given my child's history of reading disabilities, and his slow rate of progress, what are your reasons for thinking he will make meaningful progress in his *general education* classes without the services I requested? (List them.)
- Given my child's history of reading disabilities, and his slow rate of progress, how will you monitor his progress in the general education curriculum so we know, every few weeks, if progress is meaningful? How and when will you report his progress to me?
- If, by the *end of this marking period*, my child does not make meaningful, substantial progress in mastering the content of his general education classes and meaningful, substantial progress in achieving all his IEP goals, will you provide him with the services I requested in my letter of (give the date and list the services)? If not, please provide your rationale.

Keep in mind that one frequent response to parents—"We don't provide such services to students with learning disabilities [reading disabilities]"—is wrong. IDEA-2004 is explicit: The types and extent of services and supports needed by a child cannot be determined by his special education classification or general category of disability; instead, services and supports must be based on his unique constellation of needs and abilities. Again, IDEA-2004's definition of special education:

> *Special education* means *specially* designed instruction ... to meet the *unique* needs of a child.... Specially *designed instruction* means *adapting*, as appropriate to the needs of an eligible child ... the content, methodology, or delivery of instruction ... to address the unique needs of the child ... [and to] ensure access of the child to the general curriculum, so that the child can meet the educational standards.[48]

If you're faced with a refusal of services and supports based on your child's classification, such as specific learning disabilities, rather than on his unique needs, you might ask questions that reflect IDEA-2004's definition of special education:

- Exactly how does the program you propose meet my child's "unique needs"?
- Exactly what about your proposed program makes it "specially designed instruction" that clearly meets my child's unique needs?
- How is the denial of services, based on my child's classification, consistent with the

USDOE's interpretation of IDEA-2004? Wait for an answer; then share the USDOE's interpretation: "Special education and related services are based on the identified needs of the child and not on the disability category in which the child is classified."[49]

OPTIONS FOR CHILDREN INELIGIBLE UNDER IDEA-2004

Simply put, schools should not be allowed to abandon children. Many schools will do whatever they can to help children. But clearly, many does not mean all.

If your child's school is unwilling to help him overcome his reading problems, you may have to do more than develop good interpersonal relationships. You may have to formally request services under Section 504.

Section 504 of the Rehabilitation Act of 1973. Under IDEA-2004, you and your child have many rights, with protections and procedures that are, for the most part, spelled out explicitly in IDEA-2004's statute, in its regulations, and in the U. S. Department of Education's discussions of its regulations.[50] Under Section 504 your child may also have rights, but Section 504 does not spell these out with IDEA-2004's explicitness. In a practical sense, Section 504 is far less powerful. So, why discuss it?

If your child is ineligible for special education and extra help under IDEA-2004, there's a slight chance he may be eligible under Section 504.[51] He may be eligible because of its purpose: to prevent discrimination, to prevent exclusion. Specifically, Congress wanted to prevent students with actual or presumed disabilities from being "excluded from the participation in, be denied the benefits of, or be subjected to discrimination."[52]

He may also be eligible under Section 504 because its definition of disabilities is broader than IDEA-2004's and is functional:

> [A student is considered to have a disability if he] has a physical or mental impairment that substantially limits one or more major life activities, has a record of such impairment, or is regarded as having such an impairment.

If your child has been found ineligible for services under IDEA-2004, and you believe he needs accommodations, or extra help, or more specialized help, requesting a Section 504 evaluation makes sense. At a minimum, it should ask two basic questions:

- Does your child have a reading disability that, under Section 504, is a mental impairment?[53]
- If so, does it substantially limit his learning or another of Section 504's major life activities?[54]

When reviewing the answers to these questions, remember that:

- Children who read far below that of average students of their age or grade may have a disability that many experts would diagnose as dyslexia, a "mental impairment" covered by Section 504.[55]

- Children whose reading disability is so severe that it substantially and adversely affects their learning or another of Section 504's major life activities *may* be eligible for special education or other services under Section 504.

Section 504 states that if your child has a disability—of sufficient intensity to substantially impair functioning in a major life activity, like learning—schools must not deprive him of the opportunity to achieve the educational benefits available to nondisabled children; they must provide him with a Free Appropriate Public Education (FAPE) "designed to meet [his] individual needs to the same extent that the needs of nondisabled students are met."[56] His FAPE may involve only regular *or* only special education.[57] If, to meet his needs "to the same extent as the needs of students without disabilities are met,"[58] he needs only tutoring twice weekly from a reading specialist, this is his FAPE. A FAPE for other children may not require tutoring. It might require less: only books with larger print and more time for taking tests. Or it might require more: speech and language therapy in a small group for one hour weekly and one hour of extra reading instruction daily in a group of three students.[59]

Although Section 504 talks about meeting "individual educational needs," the words have a different meaning than IDEA-2004's. It's tricky. Because Section 504 is not a special education law designed to produce meaningful educational gains, but a discrimination law, it emphasizes opportunity to benefit, not actual benefit. Because this may sound illogical, we'll repeat it: Section 504 emphasizes opportunity to benefit, not actual benefit. This is more logical if you remember Section 504's limited purpose: "To protect the student from exclusion, not to entitle the student to services."[60]

This differs from IDEA-2004's concern with meaningful benefit. As Peter and Pamela Wright warn about Section 504:

> The school must provide your child with access to an education, to and through the schoolhouse door. The school may have to make modifications to the school and provide other accommodations so your child has access to an education.... [However,] Section 504 does not include any guarantee that a child will receive an education that provides educational benefit.[61]

To ensure that Section 504-eligible children have equal opportunity to benefit from their education in the least restrictive environment (LRE), schools must make a reasonable attempt to meet each child's needs in the environment that is least restrictive *for* the particular child. The LRE for most Section 504-eligible children is their regular classroom, with perhaps some pull-out services. Their in-class supports might include special education consultation to their regular teacher, in-class instruction from a reading specialist, or instructional and testing accommodations. Their pull-out services might be an hour of counseling per week or three hours of extra reading instruction.

While Section 504's services and accommodations may sound good, and often help children with disabilities, especially when school personnel are well intentioned, highly knowledgeable, and highly skilled, the law is fraught with difficulties.

One difficulty is Section 504's failure to operationally define a person with a disability with more precision than having an "impairment that substantially limits one or more major life activities." Such ambiguity can create considerable subjectivity, subjectivity that can cause ongoing, bitter disagreements between parents and schools. Phrases like "substantially limits" and "major life activities" are open to widely different interpretations by parents, school personnel, the courts, and the Office for Civil Rights of the Department of Education (OCR).[62] Recently, diverging interpretations of the definition have made it more difficult to get services. In 2008, Rachel Holler and Perry Zirkel reported that courts have "established relatively restrictive standards for interpreting this definition, particularly its third essential element [substantial limitation]."[63]

Given the difficulty of getting services, parents seeking Section 504 eligibility for their child's reading disability will have to show that it substantially impairs his ability to learn or to succeed in other of Section 504's major life activities. They will have to show that for his age or grade he reads far below that of average children. In some schools, this severity of impairment, combined with a history of quality instruction, would make him eligible for IDEA-2004 services; in other schools it wouldn't. It may be absurd and may not comply with law, but practically speaking, the criteria for IDEA-2004 and Section 504 eligibility and the availability of services may depend on the child's zip code and the views of the particular school personnel in his particular evaluation and eligibility group. Reviewing the same information, different personnel may reach different conclusions.

A second difficulty is the lack of Federal funding for Section 504 services. This can negatively affect a school's willingness to provide services.[64] If your child is eligible under Section 504, and, in your opinion, the school will not provide him with a FAPE, you can request an impartial hearing from the school district or the State, or file a complaint with the regional OCR. A problem with OCR investigations is their narrow focus. They focus on whether the school has complied with Section 504's procedural requirements, not whether the child's educational program and accommodations are educationally appropriate.[65] In other words, procedure trumps appropriateness and benefit.

A third difficulty is that Section 504 does not offer the many protections that IDEA-2004 considers essential, such as independent educational evaluations and a clear obligation for schools to provide prior written notices. Under IDEA-2004, parents are members of the evaluation and eligibility groups and the program development team; as such, they help to make important decisions. Section 504 does not offer equivalent rights.

Finally, school personnel are often unfamiliar with the Section 504's case law and its requirements.[66] Yet, Section 504 requires school district personnel to "establish [the] standards and procedures for the evaluation and placement of persons who, because of handicap, need or are believed to need special education or related services."[67] In other words, school personnel unfamiliar with Section 504 may develop the procedures and standards that inadvertently help or hinder a struggling reader's chance to get needed services.

Similar to IDEA-2004, for Section 504-eligible students, schools must develop a plan to implement services or accommodations. These plans are commonly referred to as Section 504 Plans or Individualized Accommodation Plans. Again, this sounds better than it is: These plans do not have to meet the exacting standards of IEPs.

If your child is Section 504-eligible, request that his Section 504 team prepare an IEP for him, an option recommended by the U. S. Department of Education.[68] This benefits everyone. It protects the school by documenting the plan and provides teachers and parents with a road-map for instruction. Some schools do this for all Section 504-eligible students. Some don't. Some won't.

Although not nearly as precise or as exacting or as helpful as IDEA-2004, Section 504 can occasionally help struggling readers. To use it effectively, it's important that, as with IDEA-2004, you go beyond our book to familiarize yourself with its many details.[69] It's also impor-tant that you practice what was discussed in chapters 7 and 8: Understand the views of school personnel, listen empathically, and work systematically to resolve conflicts in mutually satis-fying ways. Despite the legal limits of Section 504 and the restrictiveness of recent court deci-sions, combining Section 504 with relationship building and problem solving can occasionally get children the services and accommodations they need.

Three More Options. Here are parts of three more Federal laws you might use to get your child the services he needs.

IDEA-2004's Early Intervening Services. Under IDEA-2004, schools may direct a portion of their IDEA-2004 money to prevent reading problems. To receive services, children need not be eligible for special education. Usually, schools use this money to provide "early interven-ing services" to children in kindergarten through grade three. Schools can, however, use this money to help struggling readers in high school.[70] For your child to get "intervening services," we suggest that you ask the school how it's spending the money. If it's spent on a program that can help your child, ask that he be included. If school personnel don't know how it's being spent (a common situation), ask the business office.

NCLB's Basic Skills Instruction. Under Title I of NCLB, the Federal government gives school districts money based on the number of low-income children they serve. How schools spend this money differs by district. One district may use the money to reduce class size in a particular building. Another may offer Basic Skills Instruction in reading and mathematics to struggling learners in particular grades, regardless of the learners' family income. What surprises many parents is that some richer districts get Title I money, as they too have students from low-income families. As with IDEA-2004's Early Intervening Services, ask the school how it's spending its Title I money. If it's spent on a program that can help your child, ask that he be included.

NCLB's Requirement for Annual Yearly Progress. Under NCLB, a school must demon-strate that its students have made adequate yearly progress in reading and language arts in grades three to eight and once after grade nine. In addition to progress for the school as a whole, the school must demonstrate annual progress for specific groups, such as students with disabilities. If the school as a whole, or one of the designated groups does not make adequate yearly progress, the school is labeled as needing improvement and may be sanctioned if future test scores are inadequate.

After two consecutive years of needing improvement, a school may have to provide transfers to public schools in the same district that have achieved their targeted progress; after three consecutive years of less than adequate progress, the school may have to offer supplemental services, such as tutoring. Neither option is as good as it sounds.

First, unlike IDEA services, NCLB transfers and supplemental services, such as tutoring, depend on the school's finances, especially Federal funding, which is often inadequate. Second, if one school in a district needs improvement, others probably do. Unfortunately, if a school needing improvement is near an exceptionally "good" school, too many transfers may destroy the "good" school's quality. Finally, the quality of tutoring may vary tremendously, as tutoring is provided by a hodgepodge of private companies and non-profit organizations. Reports about NCLB tutoring paint a picture of rushed, inadequate, disorganized efforts that produce little, if any, academic gain.

Perhaps the most important leverage NCLB provides to parents is fear, the fear of school officials that newspapers will publically condemn their school as "failing." Thus, some schools feel pressured to remediate reading problems, especially mild to moderate ones that might quickly show improvement. Although NCLB does not give you specific rights unless the school is formally classified as needing improvement, the fear that NCLB evokes in schools may provide you with psychological and political leverage. To use this leverage, be polite, be respectful, be honest, but if the school denies your child needed services, be assertive: Remind school personnel that your child's poor test scores can hurt everyone, including them—use the NCLB as legitimate leverage to get services your child needs. After all, the purpose of NCLB is to:

> Ensure that all children have a fair, equal, and significant opportunity to obtain a high quality education and reach, at a minimum, proficiency on challenging State academic achievement standards and State academic assessments.[71]

We recommend that in addition to IDEA-2004 and Section 504, you investigate these resources. Although far from perfect, they may help your child.

PITFALLS

Beware of pitfalls. No matter how much you learn, pitfalls abound.

Beware of programs that claim quick fixes or almost perfect success; they're full of pitfalls. More often than not, their claims are—to be charitable—grossly exaggerated. Even programs that have helped other struggling readers may not help your child.

Beware of believing that an outstanding IEP or Section 504 Plan will solve your child's difficulties. IEPs and 504 Plans need monitoring, even if implemented by outstanding teachers.

With an excellent IEP, it's reasonable to expect meaningful progress; in some cases more than a year's growth in a year's time. Reality, however, often falls short of expectations, which is why we've stressed monitoring.

Beware of demanding so much from your child that he gets "stressed-out" and begins to hate reading and school. Despite the political rhetoric about "high standards," success requires moderate challenge that asks children to stretch without breaking. Demanding more—demanding that children reach beyond their reach—harms them. Its primary product? Failure.

Beware of becoming too legalistic. Many schools want to help your child and will do all that they can to help. Use the laws to get your child what he needs when the school won't or can't provide what he needs. Don't use the laws as sledgehammers that you swing wildly and forcefully because you can. The laws can provide leverage and protections—understand them, but don't abuse them. In the final analysis, your child's education depends on the professionalism and good will of teachers, administrators, and related service personnel. Remember that relationships, respect, and sincerity can powerfully influence others. In contrast, threats, sarcasm, and constant criticism often provoke resentment, resistance, and retaliation.

Beware of starting legal actions, like an impartial due process hearing before a hearing officer or an administrative law judge, or taking actions in State or Federal court. In addition to their high financial and emotional costs, there's a good chance you might lose, despite having a valid case. Just note, for example, what the National Center on Assessing the General Curriculum has written about IDEA-2004's predecessor, IDEA-1997:

> Courts and hearing officers seem to have a *minimal standard* for sufficiency that is relatively easy for districts to satisfy with respect to [the general education curriculum: access, involvement, and progress].... The interpretation given by the courts and hearing officers means that districts must show that they have met their obligations concerning these statements, but *only on a minimal level.*[72]

Also note what the Wall Street Journal recently reported:

> [Parents and advocates] say administrative reviews in many parts of the U.S. overwhelmingly back school districts in disputes over paying for special-education services.... In most states that keep count [of administrative hearings], districts usually win. In New Jersey, districts prevailed in 27 of 28 hearings in 2005-2006. In California, parents only won 11 of 119 hearings in that year.[73]

These two reports may mean that the courts will side with your child's school if it refuses to provide him with the services and supports he needs to succeed. The courts may see these as luxuries, not essentials.

Because hearing officers and judges often have low standards for what the law requires, families often lose special education cases in which schools fail to provide children with an adequate education. For two reasons, this should not be surprising. One reason advanced by Perry Zirkel, University Professor of Education and Law at Lehigh University, is that "reasonable and impartial decision makers can interpret cases, particularly those with the individualized orientation and procedural/substantive complexity of the IDEA, very differently."[74] We agree. But we think the next reason is even stronger: On average, hearing officers and judges have an inadequate understanding of education, special education, and reading disabilities. It's not their fault, as this is rarely the focus of their education or experience. A better system is needed.[75]

So, should you consider initiating an impartial due process hearing, and if necessary, an appeal to State or Federal courts? We don't know. Every case and family situation is different.

If you cannot resolve critical issues through problem solving, resolution meetings with school personnel, or mediation, and if your child is regressing or making marginal progress, you should consider initiating an impartial due process hearing, and its preceding step, mediation. But initiate a hearing only if you have a very strong and well-organized case, if you have the documents and experts needed to prevail, if you have the financial resources and strength to continue for months or years, and if you have an attorney who has an enviable track record in special education litigation.

Although many advocates will heavily criticize us for the next statement, the hard reality is that it's sometimes better to move than to fight for your child's rights. While you're fighting, your child may lose more ground, your entire family may become distressed, and you may deplete the money you could have used to get your child tutoring or to move.[76] And after all this sacrifice, there's a good chance you'll lose, no matter the law or the decisions of other Circuit Courts. So, beware: Take litigation seriously—very seriously.

Beware of focusing so much on overcoming your child's reading disabilities that you, your child, and other family members feel emotionally battered and distraught. Make sure to plan "fun" activities for your family, activities that strengthen relationships, and activities that strengthen your child's belief in his abilities, including non-academic ones.

KEEP IN MIND

Keep in mind that many parents fail to get needed services for their children because they're afraid of not knowing enough, sounding stupid, or having their requests rejected. They may be right—but so what? With many schools, if you don't ask, you don't get.

In all likelihood, you don't know as much as school personnel do about teaching and school psychology and special education and reading disabilities. These are complicated disciplines. But you're reading this book, and we hope many others on reading disabilities and special education. By doing so, you should learn a great deal about what your child needs, what quality special education and reading instruction should look like, and your rights and your child's rights.

If you think you lack the needed knowledge and negotiating skills, we hope you'll seek help to negotiate the maze of regulations, requirements, and services. If possible, get help from an expert in reading and special education.

If you think you'll sound stupid, remember that occasionally everyone sounds stupid—including Howard and Gary. That everyone gets rejected—including Howard and Gary. It's just part of life. So, if your requests are rejected, and your child needs the services that were rejected, your job is to do whatever is ethical to get those or comparable services. The reason is simple: Rarely do poor readers succeed in life—academically, economically, socially, or emotionally.

The next and final chapter, *Beating the Odds*, will help you put much of what you've learned into practice. By helping you to organize your information, use it, and support your child outside of school, it will help you to help your child *beat the odds*.

ENDNOTES

---

1 The *No Child Left Behind Act of 2001* (NCLB) is the new name for the Elementary and Secondary Education Act (ESEA). The part of NCLB that's directly aimed at helping at-risk or failing students is Title I.

2 For example, Howard Margolis was a Special Education Hearing Officer for the State of New Jersey; he also ruled on special education administrative appeals for the State of Delaware.

3 34 CFR § 300.1, bold added.

4 34 CFR § 300.39, bold added.

5 Deal v. Hamilton County Board of Education, U. S. 6th Circuit Court, 2004.

6 34 CFR § 300.320; 34 CFR § 300.39.

7 The services needed to achieve goals are often in dispute. Thus, the initial IEP may not include all the services you think are needed. This is one reason it's critical to review the monitoring strategies in chapter 7 and to make sure your child's progress is frequently and adequately monitored. If monitoring shows that he's not making appreciable progress toward meeting his goals, you're justified in asking for services that will likely accelerate learning. This would require revising the IEP to specify the needed services.

8 34 CFR § 300.320, italics added.

9 34 CFR Discussion, p. 46588, italics added.

10 34 CFR § 300.324, italics added.

11 Diamond was originally decided by Howard Margolis when he was a Special Education Hearing Officer for New Jersey. His decision was upheld and expanded by the U. S. District Court for New Jersey and the U. S. 3rd Circuit Court.

12 Polk v. Central Susquehanna Intermediate Unit 16, U. S. 3rd Circuit Court, 1988. As previously noted, Howard Margolis was the Hearing Officer who wrote the original decision in the Diamond case.

13 Deal v. Hamilton County Board of Education, U. S. 6th Circuit Court, 2004.

14 Shannon Carter v. Florence County School District Four, U. S. 4th Circuit Court, 1991.

15 Many factors can affect the outcome. For example, a child's memory might limit mastery to 70 words per month.

16 Science predicts far better for groups of people than for individuals. For example, insurance companies can tell you that X% of men will get diabetes in their late 50s, but cannot, with certainty, tell you which men.

[17] Here's what Howard wrote about one of his freshman-year teachers: "English Composition [was] the toughest course I have ever taken. Dr. Starkey, my instructor, was demanding, fair, and motivating. My average in her class improved from an F to a B. Despite all the 'As' I subsequently earned in my college career, the 'B' in Dr. Starkey's course was the 'best' grade I ever earned. It gave me confidence, because I earned it. My college counselor had been urging me to withdraw from Brooklyn College as I lacked the potential to graduate. I was now armed with Dr. Starkey's 'B' and my dogged persistence. I was on my way" (Margolis, H., 1996. A long, hard, surprising road. In G. G. Brannigan (Ed.). *The Enlightened Educator: Research Adventures in the Schools.* New York: McGraw Hill, pp. 44-60, p. 46).

[18] In Deal v. Hamilton County Board of Education, the U. S. 6th Circuit Court summarized the concept of potential and emphasized that an unduly low estimate was unacceptable: In *Ridgewood*, the court held that a mere finding that an IEP had provided 'more than a trivial educational benefit' was insufficient to establish that the IDEA's standards had been met.... The court found that because the benefit provided 'must be gauged in relation to a child's potential' ... the determination of 'meaningful benefit' requires 'a student-by-student analysis that carefully considers the student's individual abilities' .... The *Kingwood* court, in turn, emphasized that the educational benefit must be 'meaningful,' and acknowledged that a district court must 'analyze the type and amount of learning' of which a student is capable in order to determine how much of an educational benefit must be provided.... Only by considering an individual child's capabilities and potentialities may a court determine whether an educational benefit provided to that child allows for meaningful advancement. In conducting this inquiry, courts should heed the congressional admonishment not to set unduly low expectations for disabled children."

[19] 34 CFR § 300.199, bold added.

[20] 34 CFR Discussion, p. 46552, bold added.

[21] "Each child's IEP must include annual goals to enable the child to be involved in and make progress in the general education curriculum, and a statement of the special education and related services and supplementary aids and services to enable the child to be involved and make progress in the general education curriculum" (34 CFR Discussion, p. 46552).

[22] Individuals with Disabilities Education Improvement Act of 2004, P. L. 108-446, 20 U.S.C. § 1400 et seq., italics added.

[23] Zigmond, N., 2001. Special education at a crossroads. *Preventing School Failure, 45* (2), 70-74; retrieved 4/20/08, from http://web.ebscohost.com. This article may be more relevant today than when first published. It describes how special education is abandoning the individual child and jumping on the bandwagon of unproven methods, how it and Congress are establishing unrealistic standards, and blaming teachers and children with disabilities for not achieving what may well be unrealistic.

[24] 34 CFR § 300.320.

[25] 34 CFR § 300.320, bold added.

[26] 34 CFR Discussion, p. 46665, bold added.

[27] IDEA-2004 does provide a specific definition of "peer-reviewed" research.

[28] The Orton-Gillingham method has many variations, such as Alphabetic Phonics, the Herman

Method, Recipe for Reading, The Slingerland Approach, and the Wilson Reading System.

[29] Ritchey, K. D., & Goeke, J. L., 2006. Orton-Gillingham and Orton-Gillingham-Based reading instruction: A review of the literature. *The Journal of Special Education, 40* (3), 171-183, p. 182. Unfortunately, school personnel are often unaware of the literature. If your child's school insists on using Orton-Gillingham or similar programs, because teachers have received training in it, you might want to show them this journal article. But above all, make sure your child's progress is monitored frequently, carefully, and validly.

[30] In contrast to the dearth of research on complex, commercial reading programs, a great deal of research has focused on teaching narrower but important aspects of reading, such as comprehension strategies. Strategies to teach these narrower aspects of reading are often incorporated into larger, more complex, commercial reading programs. Beware, however, of overgeneralization: Incorporating several such strategies with a respectful research base into a large, complex, commercial reading program is insufficient to support the validity of the entire program. A related factor is fidelity: To what extent, with what knowledge and skill, do teachers typically implement different aspects of complex, commercial reading programs?

[31] Allington, R. L., December 2005/January 2006. What counts as evidence in evidence-based education? *Reading Today, 23* (3), p. 16. This is an important, straightforward, sobering editorial, devoid of the hype that typically accompanies publishers' advertisements and brochures.

[32] 34 CFR Discussion, p. 46665, states "there is nothing in [IDEA-2004] to suggest that the failure of a [school] to provide services based on peer-reviewed research would automatically result in a denial of FAPE [free appropriate public education]. The final decision about the special education and related services, and supplementary aids and services … must be made by the child's IEP Team based on the child's individual needs."

[33] Direct research is research that evaluates a specific program or some of its parts. An example is research that evaluates the effectiveness of the phonemic training part of the ABCD reading program. Indirect research would be that which evaluates the effectiveness of a different phonemic training program. With regard to the quality of a program, direct research is usually more impressive.

Even if there's direct research support for a program or some of its parts, beware of four possibilities. The direct research may not be independent; the researchers may have a financial stake in the outcome. Your child's teachers may not implement the program with the knowledge, skill, and enthusiasm of the teachers in the research. The groups which received ABCD phonemic training may have gotten more instruction than the groups that did not get ABCD phonemic training. Finally, direct research may support one part of a program but not others.

[34] Several excellent books describe and evaluate reading programs, methods, and strategies. One of our favorites, which we've mentioned before, is Tierney, R. J., & Readence, J. E., 2005. *Reading Strategies and Practices: A Compendium* (6th ed.). Boston: Pearson, Allyn & Bacon, pp. 245-248. Earlier, less expensive editions might also be helpful.

[35] Allington, December 2005/January 2006, p. 16.

[36] Blair, T. R., Rupley, W. H., & Nichols, W. D., 2007. The effective teacher of reading: Considering the "what" and "how" of instruction. *The Reading Teacher, 60* (5), 432-438, p. 434, italics added. This article provides an excellent summary of the factors required for reading instruction to succeed.

[37] Because State special education codes can exceed IDEA-2004's requirements, you should check your state's code to see if it requires the IEP to specify instructional methodologies.

[38] 34 CFR Discussion, p. 46665.

[39] This can create a serious problem: What should you do if a teacher is committed to a program that has yet to garner adequate research support? Our belief, which has yet to be adequately tested, is to follow the teacher's lead. Our reason: A teacher who is committed and enthusiastic about a program and has mastered its concepts and procedures is likely to do a far better job of helping a struggling reader learn to read than a teacher who resents a program being forced on her, or who has a ho-hum attitude about a program and is uninterested in mastering its concepts and procedures. No matter the program, however, your child's progress must be frequently and carefully monitored so, if needed, changes can be made—quickly.

[40] 34 CFR § 300.320, bold added.

[41] 34 CFR Discussion, p. 46587.

[42] 34 CFR Discussion, p. 46568.

[43] 34 CFR § 300.1.

[44] IDEA-2004 does not require that children achieve their *potential* or get the "best" program. It, however, does require that children have an "*appropriate*" program likely to produce meaningful progress in the general education curriculum and in achieving their IEP goals. Meaningful progress is not absolute; instead, it's viewed in terms of each child's *potential*. *Potential* is a complicated, error-prone, dangerous word that is open to disparate, contradictory interpretations. So is *appropriate*, a word that has caused untold disputes.

[45] *Modifications* usually refer to changes to the curriculum, whereas *accommodations* refer to how materials are presented and how students are asked to express their knowledge or skill. Making a student responsible for three curriculum topics rather than six is a modification; allowing him to answer a test orally rather than in writing is an accommodation. An accommodation does not change the curriculum he must master, but only how it's presented or how he's asked to respond.

[46] A mistake that many schools and parents make is assuming that instruction in special education settings, such as self-contained classes or resource centers, will, by itself, meet the child's educational needs. What's critical is the nature of the instruction, including the curriculum and methods the teachers use as well as the social and emotional nature of the settings. Placement itself— without instructional changes personalized to meet children's needs—perpetuates failure.

[47] 34 CFR § 300.503.

[48] 34 CFR § 300.39.

[49] 34 CFR Discussion, p. 46549.

[50] IDEA-2004's rules and regulations and the U.S. Department of Education's (USDOE) discussion of their meaning are found in the Federal Register, Vol. 71, No. 156 , Monday, August 14, 2006, Rules and Regulations, Department of Education, 34 CFR Parts 300 and 301. These rules and regulations can be downloaded as a pdf file from http://idea ed.gov.

[51] The University of Iowa's College of Law has an excellent Section 504 training website that emphasizes sections of the law relevant to students in public schools. The site also has a question-and-answer section. Its web address is www.uiowa.edu/infotech/504Training.htm.

[52] The formal citation is Section *504 of the Rehabilitation Act of 1973*, as amended, 29 U. S. C. 794. Perhaps an easier place to find this quotation and related information is this government publication: U. S. Department of Education, 2007. *Free Appropriate Public Education for Students with Disabilities: Requirements Under Section 504 of the Rehabilitation Act of 1973*. Jessup, MD.: Author, p. 1; retrieved 4/2/08, from http://edpubs.ed.gov.

[53] Although we abhor the negative and often disparaging stereotypes and meanings associated with the phrase "mental impairment," it's the language of the law. Keeping these drawbacks in mind, we suggest you use the phrase to show familiarity with Section 504. We also suggest that you not take offence at school personnel who use it; in some situations, they have no choice.

[54] Tom Smith, Professor of Special Education at the University of Arkansas, compiled a list of major life activities from Section 504 and court cases. They are walking, talking, seeing, hearing, speaking, breathing, learning, working, performing manual tasks, sitting, reaching, stooping, and procreating. (Smith, T. E., 2002. Section 504: What teachers need to know. *Intervention in School and Clinic, 37* (5), 259-266, p. 261.)

[55] Recently, two researchers, Rachael Holler and Perry Zirkel, surveyed schools to assess the percentage of students eligible under Section 504, but not IDEA-2004. They found that 19% of their sample of "504-only students" had dyslexia. The implication is that these students were 504-eligible because they had dyslexia. (Holler, R. A., & Zirkel, P. A., 2008. Section 504 and public schools: A national survey concerning 'Section 504-Only' students. *NASSP Bulletin, 92* (1), 19-43.)

[56] U. S. Department of Education, 2007, p. 4. This provides an excellent though non-critical introduction to Section 504.

[57] In contrast to Section 504, IDEA-2004 requires that children need special education to get related services. IDEA-2004 defines related services as "supportive services ... required to assist a child with a disability to *benefit from* special education (34 CFR § 300.34; italics added).

[58] Office for Civil Rights, Chicago Region. (n.d.). *Frequently Asked Questions about Section 504 and the Education of Children with Disabilities*; retrieved 4/14/08, from http://www.ed.gov/about/offices/list/ocr/504faq.html.

[59] Tom Smith notes that under Section 504, "meeting the needs of students with disabilities ... can include a variety of services, such as education in general education classes, education in general education classes with supplementary aids, or special education and related services outside the general education setting.... In most situations, simple, inexpensive, commonsense accommodations and modifications are sufficient" (Smith, 2002, p. 262).

[60] Holler & Zirkel, 2008, p. 20.

[61] Wright, P., & Wright, P., 2005. *IDEA 2004: Parts A & B*. Hartfield, VA: Harbor House Law Press, p. 132. This book provides a brief though valuable discussion of Section 504.

[62] Kevin Brady of North Carolina State University notes that "the determination of whether a particular disability 'substantially limits' a major life activity according to Section 504 is largely a subjective one with no explicit criteria" (Brady, K. P., 2004. Section 504 student eligibility for students with reading disabilities: A primer for advocates. *Reading & Writing Quarterly: Overcoming Learning Difficulties, 20* (4), 305-329, p. 316). Similarly, Tom Smith notes that Section 504 relies primarily on the subjective opinion of school personnel: "Unlike IDEA, eligibility determination under Section

504 is not based on a categorical approach to disabilities, but rather on whether there is a substantial limitation to a major life activity resulting from a physical or mental impairment. This is a subjective professional judgment. Although some guidelines for facilitating this determination are available, the ultimate decision falls to the professionals" (2002, p. 263). Thus, much depends on the education, training, and motivation of school personnel.

[63]   Holler & Zirkel, 2008, p, 23.

[64]   S. James Rosenfeld, Esq. notes that "Section 504 requires that schools not discriminate, and in some cases undertake actions that require additional expenditures, but provides no additional financial support. For this reason, schools often drag their feet in providing needed services to children under Section 504, and are less hesitant to openly discuss the limitations of funding" (*Section 504 and IDEA: Basic Similarities and Differences*, n.d.; retrieved 4/13/08, from www.wrightslaw.com).

[65]   See the University of Iowa's College of Law's questions and answers about Section 504 (www.uiowa. edu/infotech/504Training.htm). Another excellent reference that you can download is S. James Rosenfeld, Esq.'s *Section 504 and IDEA: Basic Similarities and Differences* (www.wrightslaw.com).

[66]   Holler & Zirkel, 2008.

[67]   *Section 504 of the Rehabilitation Act Regulations*, 34 CFR § 104.35, Evaluation and placement, 2000; retrieved 4/14/08, from http://www.ed.gov/policy/rights/reg/ocr/edlite-34cfr104.html#S35.

[68]   U. S. Department of Education, 2007.

[69]   Yell, M. L., 2006. *The Law and Special Education* (2nd ed.). Upper Saddle River, NJ: Merrill Prentice Hall. Yell provides a clear explanation of special education law, with an excellent chapter on Section 504.

[70]   34 CFR § 300.226.

[71]   No Child Left Behind Act, P.L. 107-110, Sec. 1001. Statement of Purpose.

[72]   Karger, J., 2004. *Post IDEA '97 Case Law and Administrative Decisions: Access to the General Curriculum*. Wakefield, MA: National Center on Accessing the General Curriculum, p. 10; retrieved 4/20/08, from http://www.cast.org/publications/ncac/ncac_idea97html.

[73]   Golden, D., 2007 July 24. Staying the Course: Schools Beat Back Demands for Special-Ed Services. *The Wall Street Journal*; retrieved 7/26/07, from http://online.wsj.com/article/SB118524665215575918.html?mod=dist_smartbrief.

[74]   Zirkel, P. A., 2005. Deal Right? *Phi Delta Kappan, 86* (10), 799-800, p. 800.

[75]   One idea is for hearing officers and judges to receive ongoing education in these complex and often subtle areas, and, if necessary, consult with impartial experts, randomly chosen from a group of prequalified experts, to explain the relevant literature but not to discuss the case at hand.

[76]   Unfortunately, to prevail in an impartial due process hearing or in higher level courts, IDEA-2004, like its predecessors, usually requires parents to spend lots of money (e.g., $30,000) for attorneys and experts. Experts often charge $200 per hour and attorneys much more. To win a case, especially a hard fought one, many experts may have to spend untold hours on the issues. Under IDEA-2004, if parents prevail, they cannot recoup their costs for experts. Thus, in many ways, IDEA-2004 is a law for the affluent.

CHAPTER 13
BEATING THE ODDS

Although struggling readers may have substantially different reading problems, for their parents the process of *beating the odds* is the same. To illustrate, let's look at three struggling readers.

Alexis is a first grader who's had extensive instruction in phonics, but is struggling unsuccessfully to decode words. Kierstin is a fourth grader who's been a good reader, but is now having severe comprehension problems. She doesn't understand her social studies and science books. And Michael is a seventh grader who accurately recognizes words, but reads at an excruciatingly slow rate. When he submits an assignment—an increasingly rare event—it's messy and wrong. Despite these readers' differences, their parents have the same role. They need to:

- Get the evaluations essential to fully understand what's blocking progress.
- Keep learning about reading disabilities and special education.
- Work with school personnel to develop a program likely to markedly accelerate progress.
- Carefully monitor their child's progress so they can quickly ask the school to modify or replace an ineffective program.
- Provide whatever support and encouragement their child needs, especially outside of school.

ACTIONS

Get the Evaluations Needed to Fully Understand What's Blocking Progress. As soon as you suspect that your child might have reading difficulties—even if you're unsure—formally ask the school to evaluate her to determine the degree of difficulty in *all* areas that might affect progress. Besides reading (e.g., word identification, word recognition, comprehension, fluency), it may be important to examine how well she:

- Writes compositions.
- Understands and uses grade-level vocabulary.
- Understands and uses oral language.
- Attends and concentrates.
- Functions in work and social groups.
- Works independently.
- Applies study skills.

Although the school may use norm-referenced tests to evaluate her, it should also ensure that each evaluation is functional. A functional evaluation should give you and your child's teachers a clear idea of what to teach her, what level materials to use, what methods or strategies to use, how to monitor progress, and how to use her current skills and interests to strengthen or maintain her confidence and interest in reading.

A thorough evaluation may have revealed the following information about Alexis, Kierstin, and Michael.

Alexis. Alexis's decoding problems are caused by difficulties with phonemic awareness; she has difficulty isolating, recognizing, and manipulating small, single sounds within words. Her teachers can probably help her minimize or eliminate this problem by systematically integrating phonemic awareness training into phonics instruction.

Her decoding problems are also caused by fear of failure—she refuses to try anything new. Most likely, her fear can be minimized by small-group counseling twice weekly, small-group instruction for phonemic awareness and decoding, tasks of moderate challenge likely to produce considerable success, and task-specific, growth-oriented feedback from her teachers, such as "You used the strategy I've been teaching you. You sounded out the first and last letters, read to the end of the sentence, and then asked yourself, 'What word makes sense?' Then you indentified the word. Your decision to use the strategy was a good one. Great job."

Kierstin. Kierstin's comprehension problems are caused by a vocabulary that's insufficient for comprehending her social studies and science books and by difficulty understanding long, complex sentences. To dramatically improve her vocabulary and her sentence comprehension, she needs a program that provides daily language instruction in a small interactive group and a case manager who carefully coordinates and monitors all aspects of her vocabulary and language instruction. Her program should also provide her teachers and parents with training on how to improve her vocabulary and overall language development.

For Kierstin to immediately understand her social studies and science books, and to do well in these classes, she needs to read and discuss—in advance—summaries of the book sections her class will soon read. The summaries should use simple sentences and short compound sentences and should help her define, illustrate, and use any upcoming vocabulary she might find difficult.

Michael. Michael is overwhelmed by the amount of work he's given. What takes the average 7th grader 30 minutes to read takes him more than 60. By the time he's near the end of an assignment, he's forgotten the beginning. He's given up, as trying doesn't help. Physically and emotionally, he's tired—he can't finish his work before midnight.

To improve his fluency, Michael needs extra daily instruction in chunking, Repeated Reading, and previewing text.[1] To compensate for his slow rate of reading, he needs shorter assignments, instruction in using text-to-speech software,[2] instruction in systematically using memory strategies, and textbooks that highlight the more important sentences in each section.

Michael's teachers should also help him develop the strong belief that correctly using the right strategy and making a good effort typically yields success. This belief is as important to his success as anything else. In other words, instruction needs to stress both belief and strategy.

Once everyone knows what's blocking progress, they can focus on removing the barriers, solving the problems, and accelerating progress. But whatever they recommend, it should reflect the findings of relevant, high-quality evaluations.

Keep Learning about Reading Disabilities and Special Education. Unfortunately, the recommendations of school personnel are often inadequate. Often, their recommendations:

- Are superficial.
- Are boilerplate paragraphs unrelated to the struggling reader's problems.
- Have already failed.
- Are ones the reader's teachers don't understand, don't like, or don't have the knowledge and skills to implement or monitor.
- Are ones their administrators are pushing or demanding.

Thus, it's critical that you learn all you can about their recommendations. Let's look at those for Alexis and Michael.

For children like Alexis, who struggle to recognize words, especially unfamiliar ones that must be decoded, a typical recommendation is an Orton-Gillingham (OG) based approach to phonics instruction. After all, many parents, teachers, and "experts" argue, "It works." And they're right. But to be accurate, one word must be added: "It works—*sometimes.*" Unfortunately, it often fails.

This last statement—it often fails—will trouble the many professionals and parents who fervently embrace OG as "the answer." But our experience and the research fail to support it or its variations, such as the Wilson Reading System, as "the answer" for *every* struggling reader.[3] Nor is there compelling scientific support for the beliefs that failure means the child isn't trying or that intensifying OG instruction will help.

But what if the evaluator, Alexis's teacher, and other school personnel insist that she needs OG instruction and assert that it's supported by dozens of research studies with children just like her? As Alexis's parents are not enrolled in a graduate program in reading disabilities, and may lack access to the relevant research, they might heed an old, clear-cut piece of advice to counter the assertion that "research shows...." The advice: Ask the person making the assertion for the five most compelling research studies supporting the program's use and effectiveness with children just like Alexis. For most commercial programs, five compelling studies don't exist.

But this simple advice can backfire, especially if Alexis's parents don't have a better recommendation and her teacher and other school personnel are enthusiastic about OG's ability to improve her decoding abilities. Unless her parents have a compelling reason to reject OG or any other program that her teacher is enthusiastic about, we recommend that they suggest a six-week trial. A trial, however, is only a good idea if instructional conditions are good:

- The teacher knows a great deal about implementing OG.
- Alexis gets sufficient instructional time.
- Alexis is taught in small, interactive groups.
- Instruction is coordinated throughout the day.
- Alexis's progress is carefully monitored.
- A meeting to evaluate progress and perhaps change her program is scheduled around the 20th day of instruction.

If OG instruction is successful, it should continue and be continually monitored. If it's unsuccessful, and the school insists it continue unabated, it's time for Alexis's parents to ask for the five most compelling studies. Not finding adequate research may encourage the school to systematically investigate the reasons for Alexis's difficulties and seek other methods. If, however, the school does find compelling research on the method they used, Alexis's parents should ask the school to systematically seek answers to its ineffectiveness with Alexis. Even with research supporting the effectiveness of particular programs, such as Reading Recovery, students failed. In such cases, it's the school's responsibility to find out why and remediate the difficulties.

Michael presents a different picture. He accurately recognizes words, but slowly, laboriously. Often, to help children like Michael increase their reading fluency, evaluators and teachers fail to recommend validated practices like Repeated Reading.[4] A common reason is that they're not certified reading specialists with graduate degrees—they don't know about Repeated Reading and its sound research base.

Here's where parents' knowledge, or that of an expert they hire, is critical. If Michael's mother read a book or two about reading disabilities, she probably read one or two chapters on fluency that listed several valid ways of improving it, including Repeated Reading. She might then suggest, "What about trying Repeated Reading? Although fluency instruction is often less successful with older readers with chronic fluency problems, it's worth a try. The other fluency ideas you proposed—previewing, shorter assignments, and highlighted pages—are great, and we should try them, but they're work-arounds. We also need to teach Michael to become fluent. If you give him a tutor, the tutor could use Repeated Reading. It's perfect for tutors."

Our discussion of OG and Repeated Reading illustrate our strong belief: Only if you know a great deal about reading disabilities and special education can you know what's likely to work, what's likely to fail, and what your child is entitled to. By reflexively agreeing with professionals, because they have the titles, specialized vocabularies, and test results, you may block your child's development.

Yes, schools have many excellent professionals who are often right. But they also have some inadequately educated people with professional titles who read little about their field and give little thought to properly individualizing children's programs. Thus, you need to know a lot about reading disabilities and special education. Without a lot of knowledge, whatever you agree to is a gamble, a gamble that may cost your child a great deal. With knowledge, you increase the odds of making better decisions. So, learn as much as you can—it will help your child *beat the odds*.

Work with School Personnel to Develop a Program Likely to Markedly Accelerate Progress. Although most of our chapters offer guidance for developing a program, chapters 4 and 5 emphasize program development. They encourage you to ask questions about your child's reading evaluation, about its recommendations, how the school intends to implement her program, and how it intends to monitor progress.

To prepare for program planning meetings with school personnel, we suggest that you prepare a one-page outline that lists what your child needs to learn; related information that's important but might be ignored; her independent, instructional, and frustration levels; what strengthens and weakens her motivation; your concerns; and your requests. Distribute this to everyone at the meeting.

My Child_____ My Name_____ Date _____

What My Child Needs to Learn

Relevant Information to Consider

My Child's Independent, Instructional, and Frustration Levels

What Strengthens and Weakens My Child's Motivation

My Concerns

My Requests

A completed outline has several advantages. It establishes you as a knowledgeable, organized, and determined parent. It helps everyone understand your thinking and helps to focus the meeting on your concerns. It also helps ensure that any recommendations reflect your child's needs while avoiding mismatches between the curriculum, its level of difficulty, and her current abilities.

We also suggest that—*in writing, for yourself*—you answer nuts-and-bolts questions like those in Table 13.1.

TABLE 13.1: SAMPLE QUESTIONS TO ANSWER BEFORE MEETING WITH SCHOOL PERSONNEL

QUESTION	ANSWER AND SOURCE	NEW INFORMATION
• What does my child do well? • What does she need to learn? • What motivates her? • What does she dislike? • What is her instructional level for oral reading? • What is her instructional level for silent reading?		*continues...*

QUESTION	ANSWER AND SOURCE	NEW INFORMATION
• What goals can she achieve with moderate effort? • How much daily instruction in reading does she need to reach these goals? • What size instructional group does she need? Or does she need 1-1 tutoring? • What specific methods and strategies have been recommended? • What specific methods and strategies have failed? • What specific methods and strategies should be tried? • How should her progress be monitored? • How frequently should her progress be monitored? • What accommodations and modifications should be made for classwork and homework? • What accommodations should be made for testing? • How often should I meet with school staff to monitor progress?		

When writing answers in the middle column, document their sources —an article (e.g., Margolis & McCabe, 2006, Improving self-efficacy, p. 219), your child's school records (e.g., Report Card, 9/22/08, comment 2), private reports (e.g., Reading Evaluation, Dr. Margolis, 1/25/09). Use the third column for information you get at the meeting.

Why should you *write* your answers to critical questions? Our answer has three words: organizing, thinking, influencing.

Writing and organizing information helps to clarify thinking, focus more precisely, separate the less important information from the more important, remember the important information, quickly and accurately answer questions, quickly identify flawed ideas and program recommendations, and quickly identify gaps in proposed programs. It also helps to project an image of informed competence at meetings and increase your confidence. Thus, writing and organizing information increases your chances of influencing decisions in informed, relevant, and responsible ways. In contrast, fumbling for information at meetings, not knowing the critical information, such as what level materials should be used for instruction, may cause confusion for you; it may make you oblivious to flawed recommendations, increasing the odds of an inadequate program.

You should use our questions, or similar ones, to make requests and engage school personnel in conversation. For example, "Trying to teach Lori the sounds of individual letters has backfired. In 6 months of instruction, her teacher said she's learned only 5 sounds. The reading specialist's report said the same. The specialist's report also said that Lori had much more success using Fernald's Visual-Auditory-Kinesthetic-Tactile (VAKT) method. How can you implement this?"

If they see problems with VAKT, you might say, "I agree that you may have problems implementing VAKT. So let's figure out how to overcome them."

If you sense dogged resistance, you might ask, "What other method can you suggest that differs greatly from teaching individual sounds to Lori and having her blend them? And if possible, can you show me some of the more important research supporting its use with struggling readers like Lori?" After agreeing on the method, you might ask, "Can we also discuss how and how often Lori's progress should be monitored?"[5]

After agreeing on monitoring, you might request, "So I can better support Lori at home, can you please e-mail me the monitoring report a day or two after you collect the information?" Note that the process is systematic and sequential; asking for too much at once can evoke resistance.

Because many important questions require answers from school personnel, we also recommend that you *write* a list of critical nuts-and-bolts questions that only they can answer. At appropriate times, ask them. Write down their answers. Your questions might include ones like these:

- What will you do to ensure that my child is highly motivated to read?
- What exactly will reading instruction emphasize?
- What will you do to ensure that she does not struggle with what you're teaching?
- How will you ensure that each day she gets an adequate amount of reading instruction?
- How will you ensure that each day she gets an opportunity to read lots of interesting materials?
- How will her classwork be adapted so it doesn't stigmatize, frustrate, or overwhelm her?
- How will her homework be adapted so it doesn't stigmatize, frustrate, or overwhelm her?
- How will you coordinate each part of her program so she doesn't get confused or overwhelmed?
- What ideas do you have for monitoring and reporting progress?

- What ideas do you have for keeping me informed about her progress?
- What ideas do you have for quickly modifying or changing her program if progress is poor?

One key to your success at program planning meetings is having four or fewer sheets of critical information and questions laid out so you can see everything at once. You can always keep back-up reports and related information in a binder.

By organizing information in simple ways, like our question-and-answer format—with plenty of white space for answers—you can quickly identify needed information and ask important questions: "I agree that instruction should help Lori identify second-grade sight words quickly and accurately. That's exactly what the reading specialist's report recommended. I also think we ought to plan for instruction that brings her vocabulary and reading comprehension up to age and grade level. Both the reading specialist's and the speech and language specialist's reports said she was bright, but for her reading comprehension to improve, she needs daily instruction in vocabulary and listening comprehension. Shall we first develop vocabulary and listening comprehension goals and then plan on how the school can help Lori achieve them?"

Throughout this book, you probably noticed that we have far more faith in knowledgeable, skilled teachers with the time and resources to adequately teach reading than we have in commercial reading programs. We're not against them. It's just that they're like bricks people use to build a house. Bricks can add greatly to the warmth, stability, and durability of a house, but a house needs much more. And bricks require bricklayers who know what they're doing. So, if the school recommends a commercial reading program, we recommend that you think of it as a small, incomplete portion of your child's program, *not* her total program. Think of it as one of the many tools a knowledgeable, skilled teacher can use.

Here are three reasons for thinking of commercial programs as part—not all—of your child's reading program:

- Peer-reviewed journals have not provided a compelling body of research showing that most commercial reading programs are highly effective for most struggling readers when they're used by average teachers who lack abundant, ongoing training and in-class support.
- Evidence may exist that Program A adheres to principles that help students in particular grades strengthen their decoding abilities; however, it may not adhere to principles that effectively improve reading comprehension. Similarly, evidence may exist that Program B adheres to principles that strengthen the listening comprehension of particular kinds of students; however, it may not adhere to principles that effectively strengthen decoding. Bottom line: Little evidence exists that most commercial programs are, by themselves, highly effective in helping diverse groups of struggling readers improve all aspects of reading.[6] For information on the effectiveness of packaged or commercial programs, visit the Federal government's new website, www.whatworks.gov. Although we have concerns

with much on the website, it's a good place to start. At the very least, it may help to dispel some myths embraced by many school personnel and promoted by many publishers.[7]

- Most teachers don't and most teachers shouldn't use commercial programs in a rigid, by-the-manual fashion or as their total program. Commercial programs can be part of a comprehensive reading program, but should not be the whole program. Many fail to provide adequate amounts of daily reading. Most have weaknesses. And none, not even software programs, know your child: They don't know what she likes and dislikes, they don't know anything about her confidence and aspirations, they don't know her language abilities, they don't know how long she can attend, they don't know if she can or wants to self-monitor her work, they don't know if she needs small-group instruction or one-to-one tutoring, they don't know if today she's upset about a friend or excited about reading the next chapter in a mystery. And they can't—with sensitivity and sophistication—adapt to her changing needs, especially her social and emotional ones; only teachers can.

You also may have noticed that we never suggested that you dictate instructional methodology to schools, even if what they're advocating is wrong. People resist dictatorial demands. Teachers may not know how to or want to implement your preferred methodology. Moreover, courts generally leave decisions about methodology to schools.[8] Thus, it's important that you develop good relationships with school personnel, demonstrate knowledge, and monitor your child's progress. Together, these may help you to influence your child's instruction.

But what do you do if you disagree with the school's recommendations? Before meeting with the school, study chapter 8. If possible, first discuss issues on which agreement is likely; this builds momentum for agreeing on sticky issues.

But, if you can't reach agreement on all issues, seek agreement to implement those agreed on and schedule a meeting to again discuss remaining issues.[9] Before this meeting, examine your child's school records for information that illuminates the remaining issues, study the literature on the issues, discuss the issues with experts, consider hiring an expert to accompany you, and, if possible, meet with individual school personnel to better understand their views. Individual meetings can reduce the likelihood of grandstanding and increase the likelihood of open, frank, honest discussions. At these meetings, prepare to change your mind if the recommendations of school personnel make sense and agree with the professional literature.

Also, prioritize. Focus on what's most important. If you're at an impasse on important issues, look for different solutions that satisfy everyone's needs, especially your child's. If necessary, on relatively unimportant issues, give in.

But no matter how issues are resolved, keep monitoring, monitoring, monitoring.

Carefully Monitor Your Child's Progress so you can Quickly Ask the School to Modify or Replace an Ineffective Program. Here's a sad fact: The greatest experts in reading cannot guarantee that a particular program will succeed with your child, no matter the facts and logic supporting it.

Here's a hypothetical scenario that may be extreme, but contains nuggets of valuable truth: Ms.

McCormick is an excellent teacher, but with Reading Program A her students' reading achievement is slightly below par; with Reading Program Z, which differs in approach but has the same objectives, achievement is excellent. For Ms. Bennett, it's just the opposite. Why? The effectiveness of programs can easily be affected by teachers' beliefs, preferences, philosophies, and skills.

Other factors also influence a reading program's effectiveness: the organization of the class, the emphasis of instruction, the time devoted to teaching reading, the teacher's motivational strategies, the intellectual excitement of the curriculum, the difficulty of materials and assignments, the struggling reader's self-efficacy for reading, the availability of interesting books at her proper instructional and independent levels, the type of feedback and emotional support she gets from teachers and classmates, the time she spends reading interesting materials. The list can continue for several paragraphs.

The bottom line is that professionals cannot predict what program will succeed—even a highly personalized one. It must be tried. Though a program that reflects the findings of a high-quality reading evaluation is far more likely to succeed than one based primarily on guesswork, no one can guarantee success. So what should you do? Again, three words: monitor, monitor, monitor. Study chapter 7, which is devoted to monitoring. Also, download and study *Monitoring Your Child's IEP: A Focus on Reading* by Howard Margolis and Sheila Alber-Morgan. It's available at our website, www.reading2008.com and at www.ldworldwide.org.

Provide Whatever Support and Encouragement Your Child Needs, Especially Outside of School. Perhaps the greatest gift you can give your child is your support—what you *do* and *say*, especially in times of stress. By providing your child with ongoing support and encouragement that reflect positive values and much of what researchers know about the psychology of happiness, feedback, and parenting, your child can better weather the frustration, despondency, and turmoil that reading disabilities often cause.

In chapter 6 we offer guidance about what you and others can do and say at home and in the community. Here, we add to that by briefly discussing important ideas from three complementary books. One is about happiness, one mindset, one parenting.

Although practical, these books are not cookbooks. Instead, they provide insightful frameworks for thinking about your particular situation. Moreover, they're not "pop psychology." They're written by eminent researchers and scholars from three of America's top universities. As such, they offer a wealth of guidance for dealing with the daily stresses and concerns of parents (including Howard and Gary), and for helping just about anyone become a more insightful, more supporting, more encouraging, more motivating, and more effective parent. By understanding these books, by thinking about how to apply their basic concepts, what you do and say will likely influence your child, both positively and profoundly.

Happiness. In *Authentic Happiness*,[10] Martin E. P. Seligman of the University of Pennsylvania argues persuasively that people are much happier, and much more productive and resilient, if they engage in activities that maximize their use of signature strengths, strengths that are deeply characteristic of them. For you and your child, these might include curiosity, perseverance, honesty, kindness, creativity, nurturance, leadership, and love of learning. The good news is that unlike inborn characteristics, such as height, many signature strengths can be learned and strengthened. Unfortunately, for struggling readers, schools often put them in situations where success depends on their weaknesses, such as reading frustration-level materials, not their strengths. So, outside of school, what can you do?

To help your child compensate for such frustrating experiences, look and listen. Look and listen for what she does well, or wants to do well, or wants to learn. If she likes building model airplanes, forget that it's associated with boys. Instead, build them with her, read her the directions, help her paint and display them. Since friends are so important to children's development, invite her friends to join her. Take her, and perhaps her friends, to model airplane shows. While doing this, help her strengthen other abilities in which she can take pride, like curiosity, perseverance, honesty, kindness, and love of learning.

Mindset. When she does well, what should you say to her? Should you tell her she's smart, she's talented? No! As Carol Dweck of Stanford University, author of *Mindset*,[11] argues, this will set her up for failure. Instead, focus on the process, on what she can control: effort, persistence, decision making. "Maryann, you really stuck to it. You spent more than 2 hours carefully painting your model plane. Wow. Your effort and careful attention to detail paid off. Your plane's superb."

Dweck persuasively argues that the comments of parents, teachers, and coaches help children develop fixed or growth mindsets. Children with fixed mindsets believe that intelligence is innate, that if they succeed or fail, it's because their intelligence is fixed, immutable, unchangeable. Therefore, they avoid difficult or challenging tasks—their goal is not to learn, not to overcome problems, but to look good, to look smart. When failing an activity, their mindset kicks in: they can't rely on their intelligence—it's fixed, inadequate. Failure proves them "dumb." Why keep trying? To protect their image, to show to the world they're smart, they'll often quit the activity or lie about their accomplishments.

In contrast, children with growth mindsets care little about initial difficulty or initial failure. They see these as opportunities to learn, to grow. They think all people sometimes fail—it's part of learning. Intelligence, they think, is like a muscle: The more it's exercised, the stronger it gets. Challenge, difficulty, even failure, can be *fun*. After all, it allows them to explore new ideas, learn new concepts.

So, how can you encourage a growth mindset? As our model plane example shows, Dweck's formula is surprisingly simple. Don't tell your child she's smart; instead, describe her effort, her persistence, her choice of strategies. Describe the process—the actions she can take, what she can control.

If she's doing poorly on something, tell or show her how to improve: "Maryann, to make the plane good enough to display, you need to sand the paint drips off the tail. Let me show you how and then you can do it." This establishes challenging but realistic standards and communicates a critical message: With *moderate* effort, you can do better. I believe in you.

Thus, to support and encourage struggling readers, we recommend that their parents help them develop *moderately* challenging goals and standards, ones that capitalize on their signature strengths, ones that capitalize on their interests, ones they can achieve and feel satisfied about achieving if they make a moderate, sustained, and reasonable effort.

Of course, what's moderate, sustained, and reasonable is subjective—it varies with the child and the task. So, when your child is trying to achieve a standard or goal, assess her responses: Does she look extremely tense? Is she trying to avoid or escape the task? Is she passive, fidgety, or angry? Or does she communicate, "If I try, I can do it. This is not failure, it's a challenge, it's fun."

Also ask yourself, if she tries, is success likely? If not, can you show her how to apply the strategy needed to succeed? If you don't show her, and she keeps making herculean efforts, but uses the wrong strategy, failure and frustration are likely.

Parenting. By encouraging your child to develop her signature strengths, by showing her how to overcome difficulties, by helping her create moderately challenging, interesting goals, and by focusing on her ability to learn rather than on "fixed," innate abilities, you're following Maurice Elias, Steven Tobias, and Brian Friedlander's "Twenty-four-Karat Golden Rule: Do unto your children as you would have other people do unto your children." *In Emotionally Intelligent Parenting,*[12] Elias, of Rutgers University, and his colleagues go even further. Applying the principles of emotional intelligence to parenting, they show you how to think about parenting so you can increase your family's fun and enjoyment, improve relationships, and help your children develop healthy, positive emotional lives.

More than a bunch of abstractions about parenting, *Emotionally Intelligent Parenting* is concrete and practical. It shows you how to think about parenting, listen to your child, understand her views, set realistic goals for you and her, and model important behaviors. It provides guidelines and examples for what to do and say.

In nitty-gritty detail, it describes how to avoid or solve common problems, such as getting your child to do chores without the age-old problem of arguing. One of their simple but practical suggestions is to have her pick music to play for certain chores.

To their credit, the authors have embedded their many suggestions for doing and saying within a clearly-written framework of emotional intelligence, a framework that should help you to generate your own ways of saying and doing and to solve unexpected problems.

CAUTION, REALITY, AND OPTIMISM

In *Reading Disabilities: Beating the Odds*, we've given many examples of asking the school for tutors, small-group instruction, reading specialists, and so on. These are expensive services. In some districts, primarily rich ones, such requests are often honored, especially if the parents provide strong evidence, a good rationale, and are both persistent and respectful.

In contrast, some districts, especially poor and lower middle class ones, will fight parents every step of the way, regardless of their child's needs. Although the reasons are many, two stand out: awful budgets and fear of setting precedents. As Howard has often heard, money's tight, teacher layoffs are likely, and what's done for one child will cause other parents to make similar demands.

So what do you do? Develop your knowledge of reading disabilities, nurture good relationships with school personnel, ask the right questions, use your problem solving skills, persist, and adhere to the belief that if you don't ask, and sometimes if you don't insist, your child doesn't get.

But will you always get everything your child needs? Will you always prevail? Will using the information in this book always work? No. But by using the information, by studying it and the many resources in the endnotes, you'll dramatically increase the odds of getting what your child needs.

One question that plagues many parents who have successfully advocated for their children is this: Is it fair that my child is getting what other children need but can't get? That's the wrong question. Your first obligation is getting your child what she needs. But your efforts don't have to end with her. You can advocate for better budgets, for better policies, for enlightened school boards. In other words, if you want, you can advocate for both your child and other children. But the audiences differ.

When you're advocating for your child, you're usually discussing issues with a small group of school personnel, who may not be interested in budgets and policies. Often, they don't even know the names and backgrounds of their school board members. When you're advocating for all children, your audiences are newspaper editors, groups of parents, boards of education, departments of education, legislators, and occasionally, governors. The good news is that all the reading and studying you did for helping your child *beat the odds* will be of enormous help in advocating for all children. So, we recommend that you put your child's needs first, but remember the other children. If you're so inclined, and you help make things better for all children, you make things better for your child.

FINAL WORDS

Being a parent of a struggling reader is tough. You might use stronger words: maddening, exasperating, infuriating, enraging, terrifying, daunting, frightening. The list can go on indefinitely. It may make you angry at your child, your spouse, your other kids, yourself, the school. Again, the list can go on.

In practical terms, however, having a child with reading disabilities is just part of your life. It's a far bigger and troubling part of your child's life. But you've recognized this—that's why you're reading this book. By studying its chapters, you've expressed a critical value: Your child is dear to you, so dear that you're going to learn and do whatever is needed to help her succeed—academically, emotionally, socially. By following the advice in this book, you're going to act ethically and knowledgeably. You're going to persist—by reading, studying, attending conferences, nurturing constructive relationships with school personnel, problem solving, and monitoring, monitoring, monitoring.

Now that you're at the end of this book, a question and an answer. Was *Reading Disabilities: Beating the Odds* the final, absolute word? No.

There's always more to learn, always new discoveries, always other books with valuable information and viewpoints.

So, we encourage you to do five things: One, study this book, but consider it a start. Underline parts, write notes, question our suggestions, look for what we've missed, and discuss parts of it with friends, experts, and parents of struggling readers.

Two, seek answers to questions you think we missed or dealt with superficially. If you need more information on how to help your teenager who struggles with reading or your child for whom English is a second language or your child whose eligible for special education but attends a parochial school, meet with experts, read other books, take courses, go to lectures, review the information on our website, www.reading2008.com.

Three, commit yourself to monitoring your child's progress, meeting regularly with school personnel, refining your knowledge of your child's school, and continuing to love her even if her struggles frustrate you. In all likelihood, they frustrate her more.

Four, remember you're just one person, and no one person can do it all. Try to build a support system to help you. Ask friends to accompany you to meetings. Ask librarians to tell you about new books on reading disabilities. Join national and local organizations dedicated to helping children overcome their reading difficulties.

Five, keep everything in perspective, especially responsibility. You're not responsible for your child's reading disabilities or her progress. You're only responsible for doing the right things, not for the outcomes. Simply put, no one controls the universe.

And, because "luck" is often a product of what we do and say, of our knowledge, planning, and perseverance, we wish you and your child "Good Luck." It's this luck—the luck you create—that will help your child *beat the odds.*

ENDNOTES

---

[1] Chunking teaches children to read in meaningful phrases. Repeated Reading asks children to reread the same material until they achieve a targeted rate of reading; progress is charted to gauge improvement and provide reinforcement. Previewing asks children to identify the topic, activate their background knowledge, turn headings and subheadings into questions, identify difficult words, and set their purposes for reading. As such, it can make reading easier and more purposeful, and thus faster.

[2] TextAloud and Flamereader are excellent, inexpensive text-to-speech programs. You can download a trial copy of each from www.download.com. Both programs read text aloud from Internet and document files (e.g., Word, Word Perfect) on computer screens. Both can save text in mp3 files for play on inexpensive mp3 players. By scanning written materials into text files, schools can use these programs to create mp3 files.

[3] Here again is what Kristen Ritchey and Jennifer Goeke concluded: "[The] research literature provides both evidence that supports, as well as evidence that fails to support, the effectiveness of OG instruction" (Ritchey, K. D., & Goeke, J. L., 2006. Orton-Gillingham and Orton-Gillingham-Based reading instruction: A review of the literature. *The Journal of Special Education, 40* (3), 171-183, p. 182). Similarly, here is what Florida State University's Florida Center for Reading Research concluded about the Orton-Gillingham Approach: "Although the Orton-Gillingham Approach contains many of the characteristics of effective intervention programs that have been identified in scientifically based research on reading, there are no studies available at present to provide an estimate of its impact on the reading growth of young children" (Florida Center for Reading Research, n.d. *Orton-Gillingham Approach*; retrieved 4/20/08, from http://www.fcrr.org/

FCRRreports/PDF/Orton_Gillingham_Approach.pdf).

These findings are consistent with findings from 1976: The Orton-Gillingham type approach "produced no better reading achievement ... than a more flexible, eclectic method" (McCormick, S., 2003. *Instructing Students Who Have Literacy Problems* (3rd ed.). Upper Saddle River, NJ: Pearson Merrill Prentice Hall, p. 441). To be fair to teachers, parents, and struggling readers, proponents of the approach should fund independent, objective research that vigorously and systematically evaluates the effectiveness of the approach.

[4] The National Reading Panel concluded that "Repeated Reading ... [has] clearly been shown to improve fluency and overall reading achievement" (National Institute of Child Health and Human Development, 2000. *Report of the National Reading Panel: Teaching Children to Read: An Evidence Based Assessment of the Scientific Research Literature on Reading and Its Implications for Reading Instruction.* Washington, DC: U.S. Government Printing Office, NIH Publication No. 00-4769, p. 3-28).

[5] Many parents of children eligible for special education have phoned Howard, asking him to represent them as a reading expert in a due process hearing because the school refused to implement a particular reading program, which they thought their child needed. Howard refused to represent them for these reasons: (a) what the school offered seemed reasonable; with knowledgeable, skilled, motivated teachers, the school's program had a good chance of working; (b) overall, the research has not supported the program the parents wanted, making it likely that the courts would reject the parents' position; (c) courts have usually deferred to the school's choice of methodology. Here, for example, is Tessie Rose and Perry Zirkel's tally of Orton-Gillingham legal decisions: "Districts won completely in 75% of the decisions, with parents succeeding completely or partially in only 23% of cases" (Rose, T. E., & Zirkel, P., 2007. Orton-Gillingham methodology for students with reading disabilities: 30 years of case law. *Journal of Special Education, 41* (3), 171-185; retrieved 4/28/08, from http://www.accessmylibrary.com).

Howard, however, usually offered to review the records, observe the child in school, evaluate the child's instructional environment, evaluate the child if necessary, and meet with the parents and school personnel to design a program that fit the school's culture, had ambitious, measurable goals that the child would likely achieve with moderate effort, and that could easily be monitored. Usually, parents rejected this offer. In all likelihood, they made the mistake of believing that the method used was more important than quality teachers, extra instructional time, and careful coordination of all reading instruction.

[6] What Richard Allington said in 1997 holds true today: "What I find most amazing is the number of products for which there are research claims in which there is no published research evidence in any journal, but instead series of what are called site reports, evaluation studies, unpublished dissertations, unpublished monographs. There's a reason they're unpublished" (Transcript from *Critical Balances: Early Instruction for Lifelong Reading, Reading Online,* 1997; retrieved 5/1/08, from http://www.readingonline.org/critical/houston/alling.htm).

[7] One myth is that Fast ForWord© software programs cure dyslexia. Although we cannot comment on the claim that having children practice extensively with these programs reorganizes their brains to better process information, we can comment on the peer-reviewed journal research examining

Fast ForWord's ability to cure dyslexia: It's not impressive.

[8] Although courts have generally left decisions about methodology to schools, courts may infrequently deviate from this if the methodology proposed by the school (a) has been used with your child for a reasonable period, by knowledgeable and skilled teachers , but has failed to produce sufficient progress; or (b) has little chance of working.

If you challenge a school's proposed methodology in court, you must present compelling evidence that your proposed methodology is likely to produce meaningful gains, and the school's is not. With respect to research about reading methods, this argument is fraught with difficulties. Usually, it's better to focus on developing meaningful and measurable goals and objectives for your child and to assiduously monitor her progress.

[9] If your child is eligible for special education under IDEA-2004, and you and the school disagree about parts of the IEP, the school must implement the agreed-to parts.

[10] Seligman, M. E. P., 2004. *Authentic Happiness: Using the New Positive Psychology to Realize Your Potential for Lasting Fulfillment.* New York: Free Press.

[11] Dweck, C., 2006. *Mindset: The New Psychology of Success.* New York: Random House.

[12] Elias, M. J., Tobias, S., & Friedlander, B., 1999. *Emotionally Intelligent Parenting: How to Raise a Self-Disciplined, Responsible, Socially Skilled Child.* New York: Three Rivers Press.

AUTHOR INDEX

A

Abrams, J.C., 3, 8
Alber-Morgan, S., 158, 159, 285
Alberto, P.A., 14, 25, 101, 102
Alexander, K.L., 236, 248
Allington, R.L., 46, 59, 60, 93. 102, 107, 123, 148, 160, 236, 237, 248, 249, 257, 258, 272, 290
Antinoro, D., 245
Aronson, E., 154, 155

B

Barnes, M.A., 153, 154, 160, 177
Berliner, D.C., 250
Blachman, B.A., 7, 8
Blair, T.R., 144, 153, 159, 160, 172, 178, 259, 272
Bolt, S., 185, 186, 201
Booher-Jennings, J., 88, 101, 155
Borich, G., 250
Boulware-Gooden, R., 60
Bowman, L.J., 155
Bracey, G., 127, 155, 249
Brady, K.P., 274, 275
Bryant, B.R., 200, 201
Bryant, D.P., 200, 201
Burns, M.K., 203, 204
Burns, M.S., 246, 247

C

Caldwell, J.S., 24, 25, 65, 81, 92, 102, 200
Carlson, J.F., 56
Carnine, D., 71, 83, 102, 128, 156, 159
Catts, H.W., 29, 55
Chafouleas, S., 39, 58

Chard, D.J., 55
Choutka, C.M., 16, 25
Christenson, S., 160, 202
Christophersen, E., 26
Chu, B.C., 245
Cleland, C.J., 243
Cooper, H., 83
Cooter, R.B., 81
Coppola, E., 250
Cortiella, C., 249
Crawford, A.N., 24, 25
Cunningham, P.M., 59, 81, 82, 148, 160, 236, 237, 238, 248, 249

D

Daly, E.J. III, 39, 58, 125, 154
Dickson, S.V., 55
D'Onofrio, A., 187, 188, 201
Doyle, M., 176, 177
Drasgow, E., 204
Duffy, G.G., 59, 60, 83, 102
Durlak, J.A., 245
Dweck, C.S., 124, 286, 287, 291

E

Edwards, L.L., 16, 25
Ehri, L.C., 29, 30, 55
Eisenberg, L., 246, 247
Ekwall, E.E., 63, 80
Elias, M.J., 287, 291
Elliott, S.N., 125, 154
Ellis, E.S., 70, 82
Entwisle, D.R., 236, 248
Epley, N., 174, 175, 178
Etscheidt, S.K., 154

F

Fanuele, D.P., 152, 160
Fish, M.C., 219
Fisher, M., 245
Fletcher, J.M., 153, 154, 160, 177
Friedlander, B., 287, 291
Fuchs, D., 202, 203, 205
Fuchs, L., 153, 154, 160, 177, 200, 202

G

Geisinger, K.F., 56
Gillet, J.W., 24, 25
Glidden, H., 244, 249
Goeke, J.L., 257, 272, 289, 290
Golden, D., 275
Graves, B.B., 25, 58, 80, 81
Graves, M.F., 25, 58, 80, 81
Greenawalt, C., 247
Greene, L.J., 72, 83
Gresham, F.M., 125, 153, 154, 160
Griffin, P., 246, 247
Griffiths, A., 203, 204

H

Harper, G.F., 244
Harris, T.L., 25, 56, 57, 83
Hasbrouck, J., 68, 82, 146, 159
Heilman, A.W., 81, 82
Herren, J., 245
Hevesi, D., 61
Hiebert, E.H., 203
Higgins, B., 155
Hightower, A.M., 244, 249
Hodges, R.E., 25, 56, 57, 83
Hogan, T.P., 29, 55
Holler, R.A., 265, 274, 275
Hu, W., 204

J

Jacobsen, R., 155
Jacobson, L.A., 16, 25
Jennings, H.J., 65, 81
Jimerson, S.R., 101, 249
Jitendra, A.K., 16, 25
Johnson, E., 202, 203, 205
Johnston, P.H., 123
Juel, C., 25, 58, 80, 81

K

Kame'enui, E.J., 26, 71, 83, 102, 128, 156, 159, 247, 248
Karger, J., 275
Katsiyannis, A., 233, 247
Kaufman, A.M., 101, 249
Klingner, J., 218, 219
Kramer, J.J., 125, 154
Kubiszyn, T., 250
Kuhn, M., 160

L

Lakoff, G., 124
Laubin, M.C., 239, 249
Lembke, E.S., 98, 103, 104, 147, 156
Lerner, J.W., 65, 81
Leslie, L., 24, 25, 92, 102, 200
Lipson, M.Y., 81, 101, 103, 147, 160, 171, 178, 188, 190, 201, 202, 204, 205
Lyon, G.R., 7, 84, 153, 154, 160, 177

M

Machek, G.R., 219
Maggart, Z.R., 201, 202
Maheady, L., 244
Mallette, B., 244
Manzo, A.V., 205

TOPIC INDEX